The Body

A Reader

Edited and introduced by

Mariam Fraser and Monica Greco

Routledge
Taylor & Francis Group

LONDON AND NEW YORK

First published 2005
by Routledge
2 Park Square, Milton Park, Abingdon, Oxon OX14 4RN

Simultaneously published in the USA and Canada
by Routledge
270 Madison Ave, New York, NY 10016

Reprinted 2007 (twice)

Routledge is an imprint of the Taylor & Francis Group, an informa business

© 2005 Selection and editorial matter, Mariam Fraser and
Monica Greco; the chapters, the contributors

British Library Cataloguing in Publication Data
A catalogue record for this book is available from the British Library

Library of Congress Cataloging in Publication Data
A catalog record for this book has been requested

ISBN 978–0–415–34007–6 (hbk)
ISBN 978–0–415–34008–3 (pbk)

The Body

A Reader

The body has become an increasingly significant concept over recent years and this Reader offers a stimulating overview of the main topics, perspectives and theories which surround the issue. This broad consideration of the body presents an engagement with a range of social concerns, from processes of racialization to the vagaries of fashion and performance art. Individual sections cover issues such as:

- The body and social (dis)order
- Bodies and identities
- Bodily norms
- Bodies in health and disease
- Bodies and technologies
- Body ethics.

Containing an extensive critical introduction, as well as a series of introductions summarizing each section, this Reader offers students a practical guide and a thorough grounding in the fascinating topic of the body.

Mariam Fraser and **Monica Greco** are lecturers in the Sociology Department at Goldsmiths College, University of London.

Routledge Student Readers

Series Editor: Chris Jenks, Professor of Sociology,
Goldsmiths College, University of London.

Already in this series:

Theories of Race and Racism: A Reader
Edited by Les Back and John Solomos

Gender: A Sociological Reader
Edited by Stevi Jackson and Sue Scott

The Sociology of Health and Illness: A Reader
Edited by Mike Bury and Jonathan Gabe

Social Research Methods: A Reader
Edited by Clive Seale

The Information Society Reader
Edited by Frank Webster

We dedicate this book to the becoming of generation

For Farideh and Robin
For Ezra and his sister Anna

Contents

PART FOUR
Normal bodies (or not)

PART FIVE
Bodies in health and disease

PART SIX
Bodies and technologies

Notes on contributors

Mikhail Bakhtin (1895–1975) is best known for his analysis of the dialogic or polyphonic nature of linguistic production. His books include *Problems of Dostoevsky's Poetics* (1929), *Rabelais and His World* (1965) and *Dialogic Imagination* (1975).

Jean Baudrillard is a foremost theorist of culture and consumption. His books include *Consumer Society* (1976), *For a Critique of the Political Economy of the Sign* (1981), *Fatal Strategies* (1990), *Transparency of Evil* (1993) and *Power Inferno* (2002).

Zygmunt Bauman is Professor Emeritus in Sociology at the University of Leeds and Professor Emeritus at the University of Warsaw. He has published a number of books in social theory, including *Legislators and Interpretors* (1987), *Modernity and the Holocaust* (1989), *Modernity and Ambivalence* (1991) and *Postmodern Ethics* (1993).

Pierre Bourdieu (1930–2002) was a leading French sociologist. His most important book is probably *Distinction: A Social Critique of the Judgement of Taste* (1984). Other books include *Sociologie de L'Algerie* (published in America as *The Algerians*) (1962), *Rules of Art: Genesis and Structure of the Literary Field* (1992), *On Television* (1996) and *Acts of Resistance: Against the Tyranny of the Market* (1999).

Peter Brown is Phillip Beulah Rollins Professor of History at Princeton, and one of the most prolific and authoritative scholars of late antiquity. His books include *Augustine of Hippo: A Biography* (1967/2000), *The Cult of the Saints: Its Rise and Function in Latin Christianity* (1981), *Society and The Holy in Late Antiquity* (1982), *The Rise of Western Christendom: Triumph and Diversity, 200–1000 A.D.* (1996) and *Poverty and Leadership in the later Roman Empire* (2002).

Judith Butler is Maxine Elliot Professor in the Department of Rhetoric and Comparative Literature at the University of California, Berkeley. She is the author of numerous articles on philosophy, feminism, and queer theory. Her books include *Gender Trouble: Feminism and the Subversion of Identity* (1993), *Bodies that Matter: On the Discursive Limits of 'Sex'* (1993), *The Psychic Life of Power: Theories of Subjection* (1997) and *Excitable Speech* (1997). She is currently conducting a critique of ethical violence in relation to modernist philosophical and literary texts.

Georges Canguilhem (1904–95) was Professor of History and Philosophy of Science at the Sorbonne, and successor to Gaston Bachelard as director of the Institut d'Histoire des Sciences et des Techniques at the University of Paris. Trained as a physician, Canguilhem specialised in the history and philosophy of medicine and the life sciences. His most famous work is *The Normal and the Pathological* (1989). Other publications in English include: *Ideology and Rationality in the History of the Life Sciences* (1988) and *A Vital Rationalist: Selected Writings by Georges Canguilhem* (1994).

Barbara Creed is Associate Professor in the School of Art History, Cinema, Classics and Archaeology at the University of Melbourne. She has published widely in the spheres of contemporary film, surrealism, feminist and psychoanalytic theory. Her books include *The Monstrous-Feminine* (1993) and *Media Matrix: Sexing the New Reality* (2003). She is also co-editor of *Body Trade: Captivity, Cannibalism and Colonialism in the Pacific* (2001) and *The Sexual Subject: A Screen Reader in Sexuality* (1992).

Douglas Crimp is Fanny Knapp Allen Professor of Art History/Visual and Cultural Studies at the University of Rochester. His books include *Melancholia and Moralism: Essays on AIDS and Queer Politics* (2002) and *On the Museum's Ruins* (1993).

Lennard J. Davis is Professor in the English Department at Binghamton University, New York. Recent books include *Enforcing Normalcy: Disability, Deafness and the Body* (1995), *The Disability Studies Reader* (1997) and *My Sense of Silence: Memoirs of a Childhood with Deafness* (2000).

Gilles Deleuze (1925–95) was one of the important French post-war philosophers. He is well known for his collaborative work with Félix Guattari, such as *Anti-Oedipus* (1972), *A Thousand Plateaus* (1980) and *What is Philosophy?* (1991). Other books include *Expression in Philosophy: Spinoza* (1968), *Difference and Repetition* (1968) and *The Logic of Sense* (1969). Deleuze has also published books on film, painting, and literature.

Nicky Diamond is Senior Lecturer and Director of PhD Studies in Psychotherapy at Regent's College (validated City University). She is also a Psychoanalytic Psychotherapist with the British Association of Psychotherapists (BCP reg) in private practice. She has written numerous articles on the body as well as relational psychoanalysis. Her recent book, *Attachment and Intersubjectivity*, is co-authored with Mario Marrone (2003). She is currently writing a book entitled *Between Skins*.

Mary Douglas is an anthropologist, who has written numerous books on human culture including *Purity and Danger* (1966), *Natural Symbols* (1970), *How Institutions Think* (1986), *Thought Styles* (1996), and *Leviticus as Literature* (1999). Her appointments have included Oxford University and University College London, University of London in Great Britain, and in the US they have included Northwestern University, Princeton University, and the Russell Sage Foundation, where she was Director for Research on Culture.

Norbert Elias (1897–1990) was a German-Jewish sociologist. He coined the expressions 'process sociology' and 'figurational sociology' to describe his approach, which now influences work by many other scholars. His main work, *The Civilizing Process*, was first published in German in 1939 (latest English edition 1994) but remained largely unknown and unread among the German- and English-speaking publics for nearly thirty years, due to Elias' precarious academic existence as a refugee from Nazi Germany. His other works include: *The Established and the Outsiders* (1965), *What is Sociology?* (1978), *The Court Society* (1983), *The Loneliness of the Dying* (1985), *Involvement and Detachment* (1987), *The Symbol Theory* (1991), *The Society of Individuals* (1991) and *Time: An Essay* (1992).

Michel Foucault (1926–84) was one of the most influential thinkers in the contemporary world, and was Professor of History of Systems of Thought at the Collège de France. His books include *Madness and Civilization* (1961), *The Order of Things* (1970), *The Archaeology of Knowledge* (1972), *The Birth of the Clinic* (1973), *Discipline and Punish* (1975) and *The History of Sexuality* Volume I (1981), Volume II (1987) and Volume III (1990).

Arthur Frank is Professor of Sociology at the University of Calgary, Canada. He has written extensively on the illness experience and medical ethics, and on the sociology of the body. His books include *At the Will of the Body: Reflections on Illness* (1992), *The Wounded Storyteller: Body, Illness and Ethics* (1995) and *The Renewal of Generosity: Illness, Hospitality and Dialogue* (2004).

Peter Freund is Professor of Sociology at Montclair State University in New Jersey. He is the author of numerous articles linking the sociology of the body to that of the emotions and of health and illness. His books include *The Civilized Body: Social Domination, Control and Health* (1982) and *Health, Illness and the Social Body: A Critical Sociology* (2002, 4th ed., with M. B. McGuire and L. S. Podhurst).

Chris Gilleard is Director of Psychology for South West London and St. George's Mental Health Services NHS Trust. He has published in the areas of ageing and mental health.

Paul Gilroy is Professor of African–American Studies and Sociology at Yale University. He was previously Professor of Sociology and Cultural Studies at Goldsmiths College, University of London. A key theorist and writer on questions of race and culture, his books include *There Ain't No Black in the Union Jack* (1987), *The Black Atlantic* (1993) and *Between Camps: Nations, Culture and the Allure of Race* (2000).

Erving Goffman (1922–82) was a sociologist and 'ethnographer of the self', whose work focused on the structure of face-to-face interaction. His books include *The Presentation of Self in Everyday Life* (1959), *Asylums: Essays on the Social Situation of Mental Patients and Other Inmates* (1961), *Stigma: Notes on the Management of Spoiled Identity* (1963), *Interaction Ritual: Essays on Face-to-face Behaviour* (1967), *Relations in Public: Micro-studies of the Public Order* (1971), *Frame Analysis: Essays on the Organization of Experience* (1974) and *Gender Advertisements* (1979).

Stephen J. Gould is Professor of Geology and Zoology at Harvard University. An influential evolutionary biologist, he has published across a range of different media. His books include *Ever Since Darwin: Reflections in Natural History* (1980), *The Panda's Thumb: More Reflections in Nature History* (1983), *The Mismeasure of Man* (1983), *Time's Arrow, Time's Cycle* (Penguin 1988) and *Wonderful Life* (1991).

Elizabeth Grosz has published widely in the areas of contemporary French philosophy, feminist theory and architectural theory. Her books include *Volatile Bodies: Towards a Corporeal Feminism* (1994), *Space, Time, Perversion: Essays on the Politics of Bodies* (1995) and *Architecture from the Outside: Essays on Virtual and Real Space* (2001). She is currently teaching in the Department of Women's Studies at Rutgers University.

Donna J. Haraway is a Professor in the History of Consciousness Department at the University of California at Santa Cruz, where she teaches feminist theory, science studies, and women's studies. She is the author of many influential books, including *Primate Visions: Gender, Race, and Nature in the World of Modern Science* (1989), *Simians, Cyborgs, and Women: The Reinvention of Nature* (1991) and *Modest_Witness@Second_Millennium. FemaleMan_Meets_OncoMouse™* (1997). Her most recent book is *The Companion Species Manifesto: Dogs, People and Significant Otherness (2003).*

Paul Higgs is Senior Lecturer in Sociology at the Department of Psychiatry and Behavioural Sciences at University College London. He is currently finishing the follow-up to *Cultures of Ageing: Self, Citizen and the Body* (2000), with a book entitled *Contexts of Ageing: Class, Community and Cohort*. He is also the author of *The NHS and Ideological Conflict* (1993) and, with Graham Scambler, of *Modernity, Medicine and Health* (1998).

Hans Jonas (1903–93) was a German-Jewish philosopher whose last appointment was at the New School for Social Research in New York. He has written on a wide range of topics including early gnosticism, the philosophy of biology, ethics, social philosophy, cosmology and Jewish theology. His most significant work is *The Imperative of Responsibility* (1984). Other books include *The Gnostic Religion: The Message of the Alien God and the Beginnings of Christianity* (1972), *Mortality and Morality: A Search for the Good after Auschwitz* (1996) and *The Phenomenon of Life* (with Lawrence Vogel, 2000).

Arthur Kleinman is Professor of Social Anthropology at Harvard University, as well as the Maude and Lillian Presley Professor of Medical Anthropology and Professor of Psychiatry at Harvard Medical School. He has written extensively on international mental health, cross-cultural perspectives on depression, the experience of chronic illness, and on the anthropology of social suffering. He has researched and written particularly on Chinese society. His books include *Patients and Healers in the Context of Culture* (1981), *Social Origins of Distress and Disease: Depression, Neurasthenia and Pain in Modern China* (1986), *The Illness Narratives: Suffering, Healing, and the Human Condition* (1989), *Rethinking Psychiatry* (1991) and *Writing at the Margin: Discourse Between Anthropology and Medicine* (1997).

Thomas Laqueur is Professor of History at University of California, Berkeley. He has written extensively on aspects of the history of the body and of sexuality. His books include *Religion and Respectability: Sunday Schools and Working Class Culture 1780–1850* (1976) and *Making Sex: Body and Gender from the Greeks to Freud* (1990).

Margaret Lock is Professor of Anthropology at McGill University in Montreal, Canada. She has written extensively on the anthropology of the body in health and illness from a comparative perspective (focusing on Japan and North America). She is currently investigating how molecular and population genetics are being theorized, researched, and implemented in clinical practice, within the broader objective of monitoring the emergence of forms of biocapitalism based on 'future promise'. She is probably best known for

Encounters with Aging: Mythologies of Menopause in Japan and North America (1993) and for *Twice Dead: Organ Transplants and the Reinvention of Death* (2002).

Celia Lury is a Professor of Sociology at Goldsmiths College, University of London. Her research interests include the sociology of culture and consumption, the sociology of gender and women's studies, and the sociology of technology. Her books include *Consumer Culture* (1996), *Prosthetic Culture: Photography, Memory and Identity* (1998) and *Branding: The Logos of the Cultural Economy* (2004).

Anne McClintock is Simone de Beauvoir Professor in English and Women's Studies at the University of Wisconsin-Madison. She has written numerous articles on gender, race and sexuality. Her monographs and books include *Simone de Beauvoir* (1990), *Olive Shreiner* (1991) and *Imperial Leather: Race, Gender, and Sexuality in the Colonial Contest* (1995). She is also co-editor of *Dangerous Liaisons: Gender, Nation and Postcolonial Perspectives* (1997). She is currently working on a chronicle of gender and the sex industry.

Emily Martin is Professor of Anthropology at the Institute for the History of the Production of Knowledge, University of New York. She is the author of *Flexible Bodies* (1995) and *The Woman in the Body: A Cultural Analysis of Reproduction* (2001).

Marcel Mauss (1872–1950) was a sociologist and anthropologist, nephew and pupil of Emile Durkheim. With Durkheim he produced *L'Année Sociologique*. He was influential in turning the attention of philosophers, sociologists and psychologists to the value of ethnology, and in making links between anthropology and psychology. His best known works are *Sacrifice: Its Nature and Function* (1899) and especially *The Gift* (1925).

Maurice Merleau-Ponty (1908–61) was elected to the chair of philosophy at the Collège de France, the youngest ever appointed to the position, which he held until his death. An influential French philosopher, his major works include *The Visibile and the Invisible* (1968), *The Phenomenology of Perception* (1945) and *The Structure of Behaviour* (1942).

Michael Moon is Professor in the Department of English at Johns Hopkins University. His books include *Disseminating Whitman: Revision and Corporeality in Leaves of Grass* (1991) and *A Small Boy and Others: Imitation and Initiation in American Culture from Henry James to Andy Warhol* (1998).

Carlos Novas obtained his PhD from Goldsmiths College before becoming post-doctoral research fellow at the Centre for the Study of Bioscience, Biomedicine, Biotechnology and Society (BIOS) at the London School of Economics.

Orlan is a French performance artist who has exhibited worldwide with the support of the French Ministry of Culture and Ministry of Foreign Affairs. She has recently completed a 10-year long project entitled *The Reincarnation of Saint Orlan* that involved her undergoing plastic surgical operations designed to transform her into a compendium of quotations from the history of art, with references to Venus, Diana, Europa, Psyche and Mona Lisa. Her website at www.orlan.net includes writings by Orlan on carnal art and related topics as well as listings of her projects and exhibitions.

Nikolas Rose is Professor of Sociology and director of the Centre for the Study of Bioscience, Biomedicine, Biotechnology and Society (BIOS) at the London School of

Economics. He has written extensively on a wide range of subjects, including in particular the social and political history of the human sciences, on the genealogy of subjectivity, and on changing rationalities and techniques of political power. His current research concerns the social, cultural, ethical and legal implications of genetic psychiatry and behavioural bioscience. His books include *The Psychological Complex* (1989), *Inventing Our Selves* (1996), *Governing the Soul* (1999, 2nd ed.) and *Powers of Freedom: Reframing Political Thought* (1999).

Roberta Sassatelli is a lecturer in Politics and Sociology at the University of East Anglia. She has published articles in a range of edited collections and journals, including *Body and Society*, *Acta Sociologica*, and *Sociological Research Online*. Her forthcoming book is entitled *Figuring Cultural Theory*.

Elaine Scarry is Professor in the Department of English at Harvard University. She is best known for *The Body in Pain: The Making and Unmaking of the World* (1985). Other books include *Resisting Representation* (1994), *Dreaming by the Book* (1999) and *On Beauty and Being Just* (1999).

Nancy Scheper-Hughes is Professor of Medical Anthropology at the University of California (Berkeley), where she directs the doctoral programme in Critical Studies in Medicine, Science and the Body. She has developed a 'militant' anthropology that focuses on the violence of everyday life and that has been broadly applied to medicine, psychiatry and to the practice of anthropology itself. She is co-founder and director of Organ Watch, a medical human rights project, and advises the World Health Organisation on issues relating to organ transplants in a global context. Her books include *Death Without Weeping: The Violence of Everyday Life in Brazil* (1993), *Saints, Scholars and Schizophrenics: Mental Illness in Rural Ireland* (2001), *Commodifying Bodies* (co-edited with L. Waquant, 2002) and *Violence in War and Peace: An Anthology* (co-edited with P. Bourgeois, 2003).

Eve Kosofsky Sedgwick is one of the leading queer theorists in America. She is Distinguished Professor at The Graduate Centre for The City University of New York. Her books include *Between Men: English Literature and Male Homosocial Desire* (1985), *Epistemology of the Closet* (1991), *Tendencies* (1993) and *Novel Gazing: Queer Readings in Fiction* (1998).

Allan Sekula is a photographer, writer, and critic. He is based in the School of Art Faculty at the California Institute of Arts. His published books include *Fish Story* (1995), *Geography Lesson: Canadian Notes* (1997) and *Dismal Science: Photoworks 1972–1995* (1999).

Beverley Skeggs is Professor of Sociology at the University of Manchester. She has published widely across a range of subjects, including class, gender, sexuality, violence, and feminist theory. Her books include *Formations of Class and Gender* (1997), and *Class, Self and Culture* (2003). She is co-editor of, among other books, *Issues in Sociology: The Media* (1992), *Feminist Cultural Theory: Production and Process* (1995), *Transformations: Thinking Through Feminism* (2000) and *Sexuality and the Politics of Violence* (2003).

Claudia Springer is a Professor at Rhode Island College. She teaches in the Film Studies Programme, the English Department, and the Media Studies Programme. She has published numerous articles on science fiction in popular culture, and is the author of *Electronic Eros: Bodies and Desire in the Postindustrial Age* (1996). She is currently writing a book on rebel iconography entitled *James Dean Transfigured: Reading the Rebel Icon*.

Allucquère Rosanne Stone has been a filmmaker, rock'n'roll engineer, neurologist, social scientist, cultural theorist and performer. She has published numerous articles and a book entitled *The War of Desire and Techology at the Close of the Mechanical Age* (1996). She is associate Professor at and Founding Director of the Advanced Communication Technologies Laboratories (ACTLab) and the Convergent Media programme of the University of Texas at Austin, Senior Artist at the Banff Centre for the Arts and Fellow of the Humanities Research Institute, University of California, Irvine.

Marilyn Strathern is Professor in the Department of Social Anthropology at the University of Cambridge. She has published on both Melanesia and the UK. Research in Papua New Guinea involved gender relations, feminist scholarship, dispute settlement and legal anthropology and most recently intellectual property. In the UK her writings on 'English' culture and society have focused on English kinship and the new reproductive technologies, and on the audit culture, as well as the area of bioethics. Books include *The Gender of the Gift: Problems with Women and Problems With Society in Melanesia* (1988), *After Nature: English Kinship in the Late Twentieth Century* (1992), *Reproducing the Future: Essays on Anthropology, Kinship, and the New Reproductive Technologies* (1992) and *Property, Substance and Effect: Anthropological Essays on Persons and Things* (1999).

Catherine Waldby teaches Medical Sociology at the University of New South Wales, Sydney and is Adjunct Professor in Sociology and Communications at Brunel University, London. She has published widely in the areas of sexuality and medicine, biotechnology, and the philosophy of the body. Her books include *AIDS and the Body Politic: Biomedicine and Sexual Difference* (1996) and *The Visible Human Project: Informatic Bodies and Posthuman Medicine* (2000).

Preface

THIS BOOK HAS HAD a long genesis and we have accumulated many debts along the way.

First and foremost, we would like to thank all the authors who gave their permissions to have selections from their previously published articles or books reproduced here.

We are grateful to those who generously allowed us to look at their course outlines and reading lists of various kinds: Malcolm Ashmore, Chetan Bhatt, Kirsten Campbell, Sarah Kember, Roberta Sassatelli, and Helen Thomas. There is an awesome wealth of learning here, much of which we have not been able to include in this book. The comments of the anonymous academic referees used by Routledge to look at drafts of the Reader were also extremely useful.

Our thanks go to friends and colleagues for advice and encouragement along the way. Among them, Andrew Barry, Les Back, Neil Brown, Rebecca Coleman, Stephen Cross, Arthur Frank, Mike Gane, Michael Halewood, Stephanie Lawler, Celia Lury, Angela McRobbie, Mike Michael, and Marsha Rosengarten.

Like most book projects, this one has placed at times extraordinary demands on our partners and families and would not have been possible without their love and support. This came in many forms, from the most material to the most ethereal, from the serious to the hilarious. Heartfelt thanks go to Steven Warburton and Paul Stenner.

Finally, thanks to Mari Shullaw for getting us started on this project, and to Lizzie Catford for bringing it to a close.

Mariam Fraser
Monica Greco
Goldsmiths College, 2004

Introduction

■   Mariam Fraser and Monica Greco

No one ever says, Here am I, and I have brought my body with me.
(Alfred North Whitehead (1938),
Modes of Thought, page 156)

THIS READER OPENS, WE hope, with a most bodily sensation: laughter. In this simple line, Alfred Whitehead humorously captures something of the incongruity of conceiving of the 'I' and the 'body' in terms of two separate entities. The body, here, is akin to something like baggage, something that could potentially be left behind, or which might get lost. The body is something that we would have to remember not to forget. If we laugh, it is on account, to quote Michel Foucault, of 'the stark impossibility of thinking *that*' (2002: xvi).

And yet many analyses of the body begin by underscoring that it is precisely *that* – the 'absence' of the body – which has implicitly informed much of sociology and perhaps other related disciplines too (although not socio-cultural anthropology, for whom the study of the body has been a significant topic). For while the body and the organism have offered *metaphors* for the social world, they have not traditionally been considered relevant as subjects for sociological analysis in their own right (Shilling 1993; Turner 1984/1996). Since 1984 however, when Bryan Turner's agenda-setting work appeared in its first edition, the call for renewed attention to the body has been heeded by a veritable explosion of interest, evident not only in the exponential growth of publications concerned specifically with the body (Featherstone *et al.* 1991; Frank 1990; Freund 1988; O'Neill 1985; Shilling 1993; Synnott 1993), but also in a proliferation of undergraduate courses, and the founding of a new journal, *The Body and Society* (the first issue came out in March 1995). The body now constitutes the theoretical and empirical focus of a relatively novel subdiscipline, the 'sociology of the body', and is also a concern for a wide range of sociological specialisms including the sociology of health and illness, of the emotions, of sport, as well as social studies of science and technology. The 1980s, in short, mark a threshold in terms of the conditions of possibility for this book. Explicitly named as a theoretical and methodological 'problem' for social science, the body has become a crucial site for rethinking the scope and the limits of the social scientific imagination.

A number of important social changes may help to account for the relatively recent turn to the body in social theory. Bryan Turner has addressed these as the rise of a 'somatic society', by which he means 'a society within which our major political and moral problems are expressed through the conduit of the human body' (1996: 6). The first and probably broadest change is the transition to a postindustrial and postfordist economy, associated with a rise in the opportunities for leisure and in the relative importance of consumption. As well as restructuring the material conditions of labour, this transition has eroded the 'puritanical orthodoxy' that constituted the traditional moral backbone of bourgeois industrial capitalism. In so doing, it has provided new legitimation to pleasure and playfulness, and generally to desire associated with bodily hedonism. A corresponding change has been identified by Anthony Giddens (1991a) as the 'transformation of intimacy', where the body appears as the vehicle of new emotional intensities in interpersonal interaction. To these broad transformations we must add an important shift in the demographic structure of Western societies in late modernity (the ageing of populations), which in turn is related to an epidemiological shift towards a prevalence of chronic rather than acute disease and illness, and corresponding changes in the structure of therapeutic relationships. In the postmodern context, as Arthur Frank has argued (1995), a growing number of people inhabit a *no man's land* between health and disease, where it is possible to live longer and reasonably well, but where at the same time it may not be possible to be cured of conditions with life-threatening potential. Disease and illness can no longer be spatially and temporally segregated from the contexts of normal social interaction; on the contrary, they are integrated into patterns of work and leisure, and are an increasingly visible presence in the discursive domains of politics, art and entertainment. While living with illness thus makes the body salient as a problematic aspect of everyday life, the medical emphasis on prevention means that the body – even in the most technical aspects of its internal workings – is no longer the exclusive province of specialist interest and curiosity. Equally important in this regard, of course, are the changes associated with developments in medical biotechnologies. The introduction of genetic diagnostics, organ and xeno-transplantation, cyborgs, 'new generation' psychopharmacology – to name just a few examples – raises major *practical* questions that cannot be divorced from philosophical ones, as to the nature and limits of the human body and its relationship to personhood and identity.

Last but not least, the body has come to the foreground as a sociological concern through the political impact of 'liberation' movements, in close association with their intellectual and theoretical underpinnings. Feminism and feminist theories, the black and gay civil rights movements (together with developments in the sociology of race and ethnicity and new perspectives on sexuality and sexual identity), the disability rights movements, among others, have undoubtedly all played their part. Many of these interventions are engaged in a critique of positivism and are often closely associated with postcolonial, postmodern, and/or poststructuralist theories. In the wake of these movements, sociology has been led to regard the body as highly relevant to any theorisation of socially situated subjectivity, and simultaneously to problematise any notion that 'the body' can be thought of as a single and coherent conceptual entity. Indeed, it is commonplace now not to refer to *the* body but to *bodies* in the plural, to recognise that there is no body as such which is given and fixed for all time, and to recognise also that experiences rooted in different forms of embodiment may be radically incommensurable.

In preparing this Reader, we have felt a double responsibility. On the one hand, a responsibility towards acknowledging the diversity and range that is implied in the reference to *bodies* in the plural. We have therefore consciously selected texts for their ability to illustrate a variety of approaches and perspectives, at times mutually contrasting, at times reaching similar conclusions by very different routes. On the other hand, however, we have felt a responsibility towards acknowledging that the multiplication of bodies itself reflects a *particular* way of construing the requirements of theory – a particular solution, that is, to the problem of theorising the body – which as such is not inherently desirable or unproblematic. As Thomas Osborne has put it,

> we do have good grounds for thinking there is such a thing as the body, so that saying unequivocally that the body does not exist – that there are only bodies in the plural, or organs, or incorporations – is almost if not quite as misguided as saying that the body is everything.
>
> (1996: 189)

A better approach to the question of body/bodies, Osborne continues, may thus not be to seek

> a representation of what the body is (of providing a theory of the body, or of asserting its irreducibility) but [to log] the ways in which the body is a problem; and a problem in the positive sense – not just as an 'obstacle', but as a vehicle for thought and action.
>
> (1996: 192)

We have embraced this objective in the preparation of this volume. Rather than as a series of discrete *answers* to the questions raised by the body, or as a set of definitive positions *on* the body itself, we present this selection of texts in the spirit of a 'toolbox': a coherent whole as such, but one that implies no definitive content, nor self-enclosed discreteness. On the contrary, tools are explicitly oriented towards problems and tasks as these present themselves, in their potentially infinite variety; tools may have to be used together, or new ones may have to be invented in response to novel situations. The image of a toolbox is thus an explicit invitation to focus on the variety of problems the body poses, and the demands it places in its encounter with (the task of) theory. It is also an invitation to reflect on what different theoretical formulations *do*, what specific tasks they accomplish, rather than deciding on how 'right' or accurate they may be as accounts of what the body *is* (or different bodies *are*).

In the interest of making the texts more accessible to the reader, we have grouped them under eight broadly identifiable headings or themes, corresponding to different (albeit related) areas of debate. Similarly, we have provided a discussion of some of the important dimensions of those debates in this general Introduction. The very diversity of the contributions we have chosen in terms of their individual style and/or level of abstraction, whilst being a positive quality in itself, may make it difficult for the non-specialist reader to see how they are mutually relevant. We have addressed this problem by including shorter Introductions at the beginning of each part, where we summarise the main arguments in the chosen extracts within a single space, such that the connections become more apparent. In general, we have intended the Introduction at the start of the volume not to reproduce the arguments of our chosen authors but to be broadly complementary to them, in the sense that we have used it to clarify key background concepts and/or to address some of the materials we were otherwise unable to include.

Of our eight sections, Part One introduces a number of fundamental approaches to the body. It includes texts by philosophers that engage in different ways with the notion of the body as something we *have* (the body as object), as something we *are* (the body as subject), and as something we *become* (the body as process and performativity). We describe these approaches as 'fundamental' because many of the arguments presented in the sections that follow are implicitly or explicitly informed by one, or a combination, of these perspectives. Part Two follows by taking up the issue of the boundaries and relations between the individual body and the body of the collectivity, or 'society'. The texts included here are considered classic among social theoretical approaches to the body and they are thus equally 'fundamental' within the narrower context of social scientific research. They concern themselves with the implication of the body in social relations of power and in the problem of social order and disorder, especially with reference to the control of bodily capacities and functions. The texts in Parts One and Two are distinguished from most of the others in this volume insofar as they attempt to tackle the body 'head on' and, as we have seen, in that they provide the (sometimes implicit) theoretical background for a lot of more empirically or topic-focused research. Although the texts in Part Three address broad sociological categories such as sexuality, gender, age, 'race', and class, they also speak to the intimate relations between bodies and identities. This issue has been and continues to be of central interest to a wide variety of scholars. The objective in this part is not to display an exhaustive range of identities however, but rather to introduce the reader to some of the diverse ways in which identities and bodies can be connected to or disconnected from each other, and to explore some of the implications of those dis/connections. Parts Three and Four have several points of overlap, not least insofar as they both address themselves to the construction of legitimate and illegitimate (or even abject) bodies. In Part Four however, the focus lies on the concept of 'normal bodies', or on the definition of those bodies and bodily characteristics that serve as the norm against which other bodies are to be evaluated or judged. The texts included here (with the exception of one) present research on historical and contemporary examples of the construction of bodily norms through a range of practices and technologies, in contexts that extend from scientific debate to the recording of crime or to urban planning. Part Five moves on from bodies considered in the context of the normal/abnormal dichotomy to bodies considered in the context of an obliquely related domain, that of health and illness. The salience of the body is probably more obvious here than in relation to other spheres of experience, not only because it is bodies that fall ill and recover, but also because it is in the context of medicine that dominant forms of expert knowledge about bodies have been developed. And yet, as the texts we have collected illustrate, not much can be taken for granted about the values that health, disease and medicine represent for bodies; indeed the event and/or experience of disease can almost be regarded as a spontaneous laboratory where, through the body, new and surprising perspectives on social relations are developed.

Technologies is a much debated and contested term. Historically, it has served to draw attention both to the limits of human bodily boundaries, and to the extension of the human body. In Part Six, we have brought together a group of texts which explore the implications of what are often called 'new' technologies. Many of these texts have a strong empirical focus, or focus on a very specific context, such as the 'micro-contexts' of genetics, the immune system, or the neurotransmitter system. While the authors in this section broadly agree that such technologies have given rise to new perspectives on the body in contemporary culture, they have very different takes on whether, and to what extent, these technologies confirm or contest many of the underlying themes that appear throughout the Reader, such as the borderlines between nature and culture, body and mind, and the relations between bodies and identities. In Part Seven we address the body in consumer culture. Like the 'sociology of the body', consumer culture represents another relatively new subdiscipline within the social sciences. Here, we have gathered together a range of texts which explore how the logic of consumption impacts on the body, as well as some of the demands that are placed on bodies that are caught up in the web of practices, discourses, regimes, and values that are loosely associated with consumer culture. In this context too, the body can be understood as a site through which power relations are consolidated and/or contested. Finally, in Part Eight we bring together a set of very heterogeneous texts, each of which illustrates in a different way how the body may be salient to questions of an ethical character. What all the texts have in common is a shared concern with how bodies are implicated in the exercise of freedom and responsibility, and/or how responsibility is in turn implicit, or folded into, the becoming of bodies.

We cannot stress enough that, despite being presented here as separate categories, these different areas of debate are profoundly interlinked and in practice cannot always be clearly demarcated from each other. The rise of consumer culture, for instance, has arguably informed much Anglo-American identity politics today. It also shapes the kinds of expectations and demands that are directed towards contemporary medicine (as well as the welfare state). The changes in developments in medicine and technology raise questions regarding what counts as 'normal', as well as what constitutes health or illness. Rather than reify these spheres therefore, we understand them as interpenetrating sites in which particular issues concerning the body often get raised. Conversely, various manifestations of the body will have an impact on how these domains are articulated. It is worth noting once again that this volume is not intended to be an audit of texts on the body. We have not been able to include pieces which address the body and work for example (Adkins and Lury 2000; Cockburn 1981), or the body and movement (Braun 1992; Foster 1995; Thomas 2003). There are other themes too, that we could have integrated more thoroughly by addressing them as subjects in their own right (such as the body and art, the body and psychoanalysis, or the body and space). In the face of a dazzling array of scholarship and research, we have had to make difficult, and in some respects, arbitrary decisions about what should or should not be included. We have deliberately selected texts to reflect a wide range of perspectives, which we believe are further enriched by being read in combination. We hope the reader will find much to engage with here, whether or not they agree with our choices. With these points in mind, the following discussion seeks to offer a broad overview of some of the key themes that have emerged out of a set of complex and wide-ranging debates.

What is a body?

As we have seen, the inaugurating motif of the sociology of the body has been the denunciation of its absence from the research agendas of traditional social science. How has that absence been explained? In large part, it has been accounted for with reference to the legacy of Rene Descartes (1596–1650), who radicalised the distinction between the mind and the body (the mental and the material, soul and nature) and who privileged the former over the latter. Corporeal events might have an impact on processes of thinking, but the final product – thought 'itself', with its concomitant relations of meaning – was to be valued precisely insofar as it was *dis*embodied (cf. Descartes 1985; 1991). The reference to Cartesian dualism is certainly a ubiquitous feature of accounts of the body in contemporary social science, and is here duly recorded as such. It should, however, be treated with caution. Gordon Baker and Katherine Morris, for example, address it as the 'Cartesian legend' and expose its largely fictional character in relation to Descartes' own texts (Baker and Morris 1996). It is on the basis of this legend, they claim, that 'Descartes is today commonly seen as the *malin génie* in almost every conceivable field: not just philosophy of mind but animal rights, feminism, medicine, and environmental ethics' (1996: 2); for the same reason, modern Anglo-American philosophers (and social scientists, we add) 'have a large investment in the *truth* of the Cartesian Legend (even if they are equally committed to the falsity of Cartesian Dualism)' (1996: 3).

Whatever the historical and textual accuracy (or otherwise) of attributing this version of dualism to Descartes, it clearly constitutes a powerful set of ideas regarding the nature of bodies, the nature of knowledge, and the relationships between the two terms. It is characteristic of approaches to the body in the social sciences and humanities to take these ideas as a negative starting point. Steven Shapin, for example, objects to academic colleagues in philosophy and in the history of ideas who claim that they are interested in disembodied knowledge: 'to tell the truth, I have never seen a "disembodied idea," nor, I suspect, have those who say they study such things. What I and they have seen is embodied people *portraying* their disembodiment and that of the knowledge they produce' (1998: 23). To illustrate this point, Shapin explores some of the stories of asceticism, moderation, and abstinence associated with the bodies of 'truth-lovers' from antiquity through to twentieth-century modernity. His intentions are not to take these stories at face value (despite rumours about Newton's abstemiousness, manuscript evidence shows that he had plenty of meat – including goose, turkeys, rabbits and chicken – delivered on a weekly basis), but rather to consider their testimony to the co-constitution 'of knowledgeable bodies and to the status of bodies of knowledge' (1998: 44).

As a number of theorists from diverse perspectives have pointed out, that constitution – of the relations between bodies and knowledges – is shot through with power relations in multiple ways and at multiple levels. Donna Haraway offers a striking example of this when she notes that although women could watch Robert Boyle's demonstrations of the workings of the airpump, they could not *witness* them. Even though they might have been present at these experimental events, their names were not documented in the records of the Royal Society. This was because, she writes,

> [t]he kind of visibility − of the body − that women retained glides into being perceived as 'subjective,' that is, reporting only on the self, biased, opaque, not objective. Gentlemen's epistemological agency involved a special kind of transparency. Colored, sexed, and laboring persons still have to do a lot of work to become similarly transparent to count as objective, modest witnesses to the world rather than to their 'bias' or 'special interest.' To be the object of vision, rather than the 'modest,' self-invisible source of vision, is to be evacuated of agency.

> (1997: 32)

The frequent feminisation and racialisation of any notion of the body *at all* indicates that the 'Cartesian' dualism, which provides a reference point for much contemporary sociology of the body, is indeed hardly neutral.

In a general sense, therefore, the body-object is *other* to the subject of knowledge. But how does this account for the absence of bodies from the concerns of sociology specifically? It is worth remembering that there is a close historical connection between the emergence of the social sciences and that of modern medicine (Burchell, Gordon and Miller 1991; Foucault 1980; Hacking 1990), in the light of which the exclusion of the body from the sociological imagination may initially seem very surprising. This exclusion, however, may precisely be explained as a function of the attempt to establish sociology as an institutionally autonomous discipline, by distancing its concerns from those of both medicine and biology. As Bryan Turner has argued, 'the epistemological foundations of modern sociology are rooted in a rejection of nineteenth-century positivism, especially biologism which held that human behaviour could be explained causally in terms of human biology' (1996: 60; cf. Parsons 1968 [1937]). Insofar as sociology was concerned with reality as collectively constructed through the mediation of consciousness and culture, 'any attempt to direct sociology towards a theory of the body must appear as a heretical betrayal, since such a movement suggests simultaneously biologism and methodological individualism' (Turner 1996: 62).

The equation of corporeality with biology and the correlated assumption that natural science has a more direct access to the 'truth' of the body are still commonplace today, although they may be contested even by natural scientists. The neurobiologist Steven Rose, for example, objects to the way that 'we even use the name given to the science, *biology*, to replace its field of study − life itself and the processes which sustain it; the science has usurped its subject. So "biological" becomes the antonym not for "sociological" but for "social"' (Rose 1998: 5). It is for this reason that Rose seeks to 'restrict the use of the word biology to its proper limits, the *study* of those processes and systems' (Rose 1998: 20*n*). Of course, the equation of corporeality with biology is also among the beliefs that contemporary social theorists have sought to challenge by diagnosing the absence of the body from sociological thinking as an anomaly to be corrected. In doing so however, it is not always clear whether they see their own accounts of the body as providing a *complement* or an *alternative* to biological ones. The first possibility would imply an acceptance of the fundamental validity of biological accounts and a willingness to coexist alongside them, despite stressing their incompleteness. The second possibility, by contrast, implies that sociological accounts seek (and would expect) to affect both how research in natural science is conducted, and how that research is received among the public more widely. The polemically critical tone of many interventions would suggest that at least some social scientists do see themselves as providing such an alternative. With the exception of the work of feminist scholars, however, this aim is rarely explicitly stated or evaluated in its implications (on feminist approaches to science see for example Fox Keller 1992; Haraway 1991; Harding 1986; Jordanova 1989; Merchant 1990).

It should also be stressed that the polemic as to who (or what approach) legitimately 'owns' the body as an object of inquiry does not only concern differences and tensions *between* disciplines, but also differences and tensions *within* them. In other words, dualism – and the possibility of considering the body as an object or a subject, from the perspective of matter or of language – cuts transversally across disciplines and can produce at least some degree of interdisciplinary coherence (matched by infradisciplinary conflict) along method-ological lines. The tension between discursive/constructionist and positivist approaches in sociology, for example, is parallel (although by no means identical) to the tension between phenomenological/hermeneutic and experimental approaches in psychology, or between mechanistic and 'vitalist' traditions in biology itself.

We do not intend to suggest, however, that the displacement of biological explanations in much social scientific work is solely due to border skirmishes. Consider, for example, fem-inist theorists in the West who have, for good reason, sought to shift attention away from, and to critique any privileging of, 'biological' factors in explanations of the social condi-tions of women. 'One is not born, but rather becomes, a woman' de Beauvoir wrote in 1949 (1988: 295), and it is in this now famous line that, Donna Haraway argues, 'all the mod-ern feminist meanings of gender have [their] roots' (1991: 131). Regardless of its factic-ity, biological sex, for de Beauvoir, could not *in itself* limit the position of women. Instead, 'it is civilization as a whole that produces this creature' (1988: 295). This conceptual dis-tinction – on to which sex and gender have, rightly or wrongly, been roughly mapped (cf. Sandford 1999) – enabled feminists to contest the belief that women's social inequal-ity is rooted in, indeed justified by, (their) biology. The sex/gender paradigm which dominated feminism in the 1960s and 1970s served the useful purpose of restricting the concept of sex 'to biological sex, implicitly or explicitly specified in terms of anatomical, hormonal or chromosomal criteria,' while gender, by contrast, referred 'to all other "socially constructed characteristics" attributed to women and men' (Oudshoorn 1994: 2).

This trajectory (which is not in fact totalising, and contains its own nuanced contra-dictions) provides a partial explanation as to why the interest in the body in contemporary feminism – and there can be no doubting that interest – is confined for the most part to the body 'as a social, cultural, experiential, or psychical object that touches on the biological realm only lightly, discretely, hygienically' (Wilson 1998: 15). Forays *in* to the (biological) body, as the emphasis on the qualifying proviso 'strategic' in strategic essentialism indicates, continue to require at least 'minimal reassurance that [such] incursions…will be temporary and provisional – a "tactical" or "strategic" necessity that justifies the risks'

(Kirby 1997: 73).[1] 'Risks', because the biological body is often believed to be politically and materially *static*, while political and material *malleability* is reserved for the 'cultural' body (Wilson 1998: 203). Should we be comfortable with these distinctions however? Do they hold? (Have they ever held?). It is notable, for example, that the change and trans-formation associated with 'the cultural body' takes place for the most part on its *surface*, on the skin, and in other visible places. In this respect, the distinction between (cultural) bodies that can change and (biological) bodies that cannot redoubles the division between the interior and exterior, whereby the 'interior' body remains largely as the eighteenth and nineteenth centuries left it: closed and impenetrable.

Our purpose here is not to criticise feminism in particular, which has in fact long had to negotiate a relation with the 'uses and abuses' of biology, and has done so with sophis-tication and inventiveness. It is, rather, to be wary of characterising (biology) reductively, in the haste to critique reductionism. What if some aspects of the biological sciences could be credited with all the 'invention, imagination, intentionality and freely engaged passion [that is] mobilised in order to establish that there is one interpretation only, the "objec-tive one," owing nothing to invention, imagination, and passion' (Stengers 2002: 251)? If this were the case, then *what*, we ask, *is a body?* How, and with what conceptual imple-ments, do we go about addressing that question? Our intentions in raising these issues in a context that seems to put sociology 'at risk' are not to deliberately provoke (by imply-ing that biology has at least some of the 'answers'), but rather to risk the *possibility* of different kinds of relations with the 'others' of sociology.

Bodies and social (dis)order

Social theory is fundamentally concerned with the problem of social order, and this concern is reflected in both why and how the body has come to the attention of social sci-entists. Broadly conceived, the problem of social order refers to the classic question of how society itself is possible, that is, what conditions and mechanisms are presupposed by the existence and endurance of a social collective. This broad description includes many more specific problems, concerning for example how we may account for structural pat-terns of vertical stratification (e.g. castes or classes) or of horizontal differentiation (e.g. subcultures); or, at a micro-level, how we may account for the relatively predictable char-acter of face-to-face interaction. All these questions, in turn, involve thinking about the nature of social regulation and social control: does this occur spontaneously, or is it imposed? What objects or processes does regulation apply to, and with what effects?

The problem of social order is fundamental literally in the sense that it involves think-ing about foundations, or the bases on which both theories and societies rest. For exam-ple, the classification of phenomena into binary categories may be described as a basic mechanism through which both social scientists and different cultures make sense of the complexity of the world. The traditional assumption in social theory has been that the body *qua* biological organism constitutes a sort of conceptual counterpoint to the category of society, on the one hand because it exists as an *individual*, and on the other hand because it represents a form of existence given in, and as, *nature* (rather than culture). As we have seen, for sociology traditionally this meant that the body was not a properly sociological object, and one that the discipline could safely ignore. Acknowledging the biological or 'natural' dimension of individual bodies, however, may be the precondition for a study of how societies differ in the forms of interpretation and regulation they imprint on bodily substances and bodily processes, and how these are correlated with different forms of social structure. The extract by Mary Douglas included in this volume argues, for example, that the polarisation and opposition of the individual, physical body versus society, and the extent to which a tension is perceived between them, is a function of the degree of social complexity and social control characteristic of any one specific society or culture. Higher degrees of social complexity and control tend to correspond, she claims, to an attempt 'progressively to disembody or etherealise the forms of expression', such that 'social intercourse pretends to take place between disembodied spirits' (this volume, p. 100). Douglas' point has the great merit of allowing for a radical shift in perspective: not only the perceived antagonism between the individual/biological and the social body, but also the fundamental contrast between nature and culture it suggests, are socially and culturally specific.

This is broadly Bryan Turner's proposition, when he writes that 'the idea that the body is the location of anti-social desire is...not a physiological fact but a cultural construct which has significant political implications' (1996: 65). This construct has been powerfully articulated throughout the Western tradition, particularly in terms of religious discourse first, and of secularised medical expertise later. Bodies in this perspective are theoretically conspicuous for their capacity to exceed, escape, defy or threaten social order, and for requiring training or disciplining as a precondition of social life. '[A] sociology of the body' writes Turner '...can be organized around four issues. These are the reproduction and regulation of populations in time and space, and the restraint and representation of the body as a vehicle of the self. These four issues presuppose the existence in Western society of an opposition between the desires and reason, which I have suggested articulates with a further set of dichotomies, especially the private/public, female/male dichotomies. The control over the body is thus an "elementary" "primitive" political struggle' (1996: 68).

The theme of a logical antagonism between the natural dispositions of individuals and the requirements of social co-existence, such that instinct (e.g. sexuality, aggression) must be frustrated for civilisation to become possible, was addressed by Sigmund Freud in his *Civilization and Its Discontents* (1985 [1930]). When Freud wrote that 'civilized man has exchanged a portion of his possibilities for happiness for a portion of security' (1985 [1930]: 306), he reiterated a concept found much earlier in the social contract theory of Thomas Hobbes (Lessnoff 1990), whilst explicitly addressing the problem in terms of its biological preconditions and psychodynamic effects. As in Hobbes' *Leviathan*, the presentation of Freud's argument in terms of a transition from something like a 'state of nature' to a 'state of civilisation' is inherently historical in form, but the events to which this history refers appear intelligible only as a mythical or a hypothetical construct. In the work of Norbert Elias, the historical specificity of this theme receives full empirical treatment, including a historicisation of Freud's own ideas (see Elias 1994; 1998a,b). Significantly, the body and its elementary physiological functions constitute the focus of Elias' empirical analysis and theoretical demonstration. In his studies on the sociogenesis and psychogenesis of modern European civilisation Elias surveyed manner books from the late

Middle Ages to the Victorian period, demonstrating a progressive increase over this period in the disciplining of functions such as eating, urinating, defecating, spitting or blowing one's nose. He then correlated these changes with long-term social-structural changes related to processes of state formation on the one hand and, on the other hand, with the rise of a particular form of self-perception typical of modern individuals. This perception is precisely that of an irremediable contrast between self and society, and between society and nature: 'The advance of civilisation at certain stages' wrote Elias in *The Society of Individuals* 'is . . . increasingly accompanied by the feeling in individuals that in order to maintain their social positions in the human network they must allow their true nature to wither. They feel constantly impelled by the social structure to violate their "inner truth". . . . [To a modern individual] only that part of himself which [he] can explain by his "nature" seems entirely his own' (1991: 30,57). Elias' point here is useful in stressing how the nature/culture opposition is not universal, but specific to particular societies where social interaction has become increasingly disembodied (or, to use Elias' expression, 'psychologised').[2]

Even in the context of European history, the dispositions of the body and those of society have not always been regarded as essentially contradictory. A rather different assumption, Turner reminds us (1996), represented the dominant mode of theorising polit- ical arrangements and behaviour in Western thought until the seventeenth century. Theories of the 'body politic' in this tradition took the human body as the blueprint for order or regulation and conceived these as occurring spontaneously, like physiological functions, following a preordained purpose or design, whether divine or natural. The human body was thus addressed as a *metaphor* for society, with the various organs cor- responding to different institutions or social structures. The organic metaphor reflected and reinforced the belief that social hierarchies are both fixed and legitimate, and that communities constitute stable harmonious wholes where, as St Augustine put it, no per- son should wish to change their station 'any more than a finger should wish to be the body's eye' (quoted in Baumeister 1987: 169). It is with this analogy in mind that we may appreciate the subversive power of the carnivalesque, a genre whose primary trope is that of *inversion* (Stallybrass and White 1986): during the carnival lowly body parts and their functions are revered and grossly exhalted, in a celebration that dramatically enacts the possibility of upturning and transforming social hierarchies. In much more recent times, the organic metaphor became a key element in early sociological discourse. August Comte, for example, explicitly assimilated society to an organism in his *Cours de Philosophie Positive* (1838), borrowing concepts from the Hippocratic medical tradition to describe principles of social coordination, although he carefully qualified this view in subsequent publications. In England, Herbert Spencer similarly employed an 'organic analogy' to refer to social functions. In these examples of nineteenth-century positivism, the organic metaphor is thoroughly secularised in a form of biologism.

One of the most careful analyses of the relation between the concepts of organism and organisation, and of the possibility of assimilating social processes and structures to biological ones, has been offered by the philosopher and historian Georges Canguilhem (to whom we shall return in connection with several of the themes addressed in this Reader). Canguilhem takes the analogy seriously — unlike some who dismiss it in princi- ple, on the basis of the political undesirability of its implications — but stresses that while social regulation 'mimics' organic regulation, it differs from it in at least one fundamental respect:

> in a social organization, the rules for adjusting the parts into a collective which is more or less clear as to its own final purpose... are external to the adjusted multiple. Rules must be represented, learned, remembered, applied, while in a living organism the rules for adjusting the parts among themselves are immanent, presented without being represented, acting with neither deliberation nor calculation.... the fact that one of the tasks of the entire social organization consists in informing itself as to its possible purposes... seems to show clearly that, strictly speaking, it has no intrinsic finality. In the case of society, regulation is a need in search of its organ and norms of exercise. On the other hand, in the case of the organism the fact of need expresses the existence of a regulatory apparatus.
>
> (Canguilhem 1989: 252)

Society, therefore, has no self-evident unity of purpose, no 'optimum state of functioning' about which every one of its members could automatically and unambiguously agree. Rather, society must work at defining, representing, and transmitting a purpose for its structure and institutions, and this is what radically distinguishes it from a biological organism. At the same time, the proposition that social regulation tends towards organic regulation, albeit without ever functioning in quite the same way, suggests an approach to the problem of social order that eschews the customary dichotomy between consensus-based and conflict-based theory.

Bodies and identities

Is there a relation between the body and identity? If so, then what is the 'nature' (precisely) of that relation? We are immediately on contested terrain. For what appears to be absolutely given – one body, one self – turns out to be an historical event that dates from the Renaissance, and was consolidated with the Enlightenment. The sovereign subject: that ostensibly autonomous being whose autonomy is manifest not only in the exercise of individual will, agency, and choice, but in a bounded corporeality that is assumed to 'end' with the skin. And so it is that, despite the numerous angles from which this topic could be approached, we will narrow the focus substantially and *begin* with the skin. For in the tradition of discourses which are largely guided by a visual paradigm (Jay 1994) – where 'what you see is what you know' – material bodies, encoded with the ostensibly 'seeable' signs of identity, are often assumed to carry their 'truths', overtly and irrefutably, on their surfaces. The question is: can these bodies be trusted? Should they be?

On the terrain of identity politics during the late twentieth century, 'looking like what you are' has undoubtedly proven to be a powerful tool: 'Privileging visibility has become a tactic', Lisa Walker writes, 'in which participants often symbolise their demands for social justice by celebrating visual signifiers of difference that have historically targeted them for discrimination' (1993: 868). Although this risks the metonymic reduction of the visible signifiers of an identity with the signified identity, the ability to capture a complex system of signs in a single trope – 'Out and Proud,' 'Black is Beautiful' – packs a hefty punch, in part on account of the intuitive accessibility of visibility. On the other hand however, the complexities of disclosure ensure that, as Eve Sedgwick notes, 'no one person can take control over all the multiple, often contradictory codes by which information about . . . identity and activity can seem to be conveyed' (1991: 79). This too can be a source of political leverage. The drag artists at the heart of Judith Butler's *Gender Trouble* (1990) for example, are challenging precisely insofar as they contest the relation between what we see and what we know; or, to put that slightly differently, between the inside/outside binary that is productive of coherent gender identities. As Butler writes:

> The heterosexualization of desire requires and institutes the production of discrete and asymmetrical oppositions between 'feminine' and 'masculine', where these are understood as expressive attributes of 'male' and 'female'. The cultural matrix through which gender identity has become intelligible requires that certain kinds of 'identities' cannot 'exist' – that is, those in which gender does not follow from sex and those in which the practices of desire do not 'follow' from either sex or gender.
>
> (Butler 1990: 17)

Drag, then, is a double inversion of the assumption that the 'outer' male or female body is an expression of the 'inner' masculine or feminine self.

Although Butler illustrates how the sexual styles of drag queens and butch lesbians challenge the categories of sex and gender by producing signs of nonconformity with heterosexual bodily norms, she does arguably install something of a *political* coherence and intelligibility upon these figures. To what extent however, can these dimensions of subjectivity really be aligned? Those identified (by themselves and/or by others) as anorexic are particularly well known for the 'misalliance' of identity, oppression, power, and politics that they visibly embody. In her classic work on anorexia, Susan Bordo argues that '[p]aradoxically – and often tragically – these pathologies of female "protest" . . . actually function as if in collusion with the cultural conditions that produced them' (1995: 159):

> They are involved in an absolutely contradictory state of affairs, a totally no-win game: . . . the anorexic, who associates her relentless pursuit of thinness with power and control . . . in fact destroys her health and imprisons her imagination. She is surely the most startling and stark illustration of how cavalier power relations are with respect to the motivations and goals of individuals, yet how deeply they are etched on our bodies, and how well our bodies serve them.
>
> (1995: 164)[3]

In his analysis of Black hair/style politics, Kobena Mercer critiques the conflation of political, moral, and aesthetic judgements, and the 'psychologizing' of self-image that often accompanies this. He notes, for instance, how reactions to Michael Jackson's transformations

> have sparked off a range of everyday critiques on the cultural politics of 'race' and 'aesthetics.' The apparent transformation of his racial features through the glamorous violence of surgery has been read by some as the bizarre expression of a desire to achieve fame by 'becoming white' – a deracializing sell-out, the morbid symptom of a psychologically mutilated black consciousness.
>
> (1990: 247)

Against such claims, Mercer insists that bodily stylisations are a specifically cultural activity and practice, and that the meanings that accrue to particular styles are themselves historically situated. In relation to black hairstyles, he writes: 'What is at stake, I believe, is the difference between two logics of black stylization – one emphasizing "natural" looks, the other involving straightening to emphasise "artifice" ' (1990: 251). Although the relations between nature and artifice are deemed especially crucial in this context, this does not make them any the less contingent. Mercer argues that the 'naturalistic' logic that informed the body politics of the Afro and Dreadlocks during the 1960s and 1970s – that is, their redefinition of blackness as a positive attribute in terms of a reconstitutive link with Africa and the Caribbean – in fact spoke more of a critical dialogue between black and white Americans than between black Americans and Africans. For in what he calls an ' "African aesthetic", artifice is valued in its own right as a mark of both invention and tradition' (1990: 256). Where the Afro and Dreadlocks are overtly oppositional, the emphasis on artifice and ambiguity represents a ' "covert" logic of cultural struggle operating "in and against" hegemonic cultural codes' (Mercer 1990: 260). These are differently articulated 'responses' to the historical forces that have invested the materiality of the texture of black hair with personal and political significance.

Although the link (and especially the visual link) between bodies and identities has been useful in some areas then, in others it has been questioned and complexified. Consider, for example, Sarah Ahmed's challenge to the empiricism attributed to the visual field. As she points out, the reduction of race to skin colour ('chromotism') involves *investing* skin colour 'with the meaning of racial difference', a difference which 'may fix the object of the gaze into a logic of inclusion (you are white like me) or exclusion (you are black like them)' (1996: 10). Black and White skins thus become the vehicles through which subject and object, self and other, are established. However, the boundaries between these positions are not always straightforward. Ahmed has herself been identified by White policemen as first Aboriginal (Black like them) and then sun tanned (White like me). Passing as tanned, her body also passes as 'safe' (as opposed to 'criminal') because its colour is temporary, 'literally a detachable signifier, a "mask" that can be put on and taken off, inessential to the subject, and hence acceptable' (Ahmed 1996: 17).[4] Identifying herself as *both* Black *and* tanned, Ahmed questions her reader's construction of either. In this way, she illustrates Lisa Walker's claim that 'subjects who can "pass" exceed the categories of visibility that establish identity' (1993: 868. On passing, see also Phelan 1993; Tyler 1994).

Contemporary work on the body shows, in other words, that bodies may be 'marked' without also being either fixed by identity or defined by an essence (for a useful summary of different kinds of essentialisms, see Grosz 1995). If arguments which rest on essentialist claims have a particular force, this is now understood to derive not from the power of essentialism, but from the discursive power of the claim. Essentialism is stripped of its very essence, as theorists have argued that 'essence *as* irreducible has been *constructed* to be irreducible' (Fuss 1990: 4). Or, in a more sophisticated analysis (and one that pertains to the sex/gender paradigm), one might say that ontology, which is the form of essentialism to which Butler refers in *Gender Trouble*,[5] is an effect of performativity: 'The presumption here is that the "being" of [identity] is *an effect*, an object of a genealogical investigation that maps out the political parameters of its construction in the mode of ontology' (Butler in Sandford 1999: 23). With these and other theoretical manoeuvres, the foundations of identity politics have had to be reformulated. Often, they are cast not in terms of shared bodily characteristics but on the basis of political kinship. Thus Heidi Safia Mirza writes that 'being "black" in Britain is about a state of "becoming" (racialised); ... to be black in Britain is to share a common structural location; a racial location' (1997: 3).

In the final example that we want to address briefly in this section, a specifically posthuman identity promises not merely to challenge the essential foundations of the body, but to threaten it with 'extinction'. Here we are entering cyberspace – which is associated, in many representations, with a shift away from the 'constraints' of matter in favour of information (cf. Barry 2004):

> the electronic frontier is 'a world that is both everywhere and nowhere, but it is not where bodies live.' By our body, such visionaries [extreme Net enthusiasts] seem to mean not only our physical body with its front and back, arms and legs, and ability to move around in the world, but also our moods that make things happen to us, our location in a particular context where we have to cope with things and people, and the many ways we are exposed to disappointment and failure as well as to injury and death.
>
> (Dreyfus 2001: 4)

For some, this vision is profoundly threatening. Drawing on Merleau-Ponty's notion of 'intercorporeality', Hubert Dreyfus argues that, insofar as 'the devil is in the phenomenological details' (2001: 65), to lose one's body would be to lose one's grip on a distinctly (human) reality. And yet in her seminal critique and development of the concept of the posthuman, N. Katherine Hayles argues that it is precisely embodiment – the different embodiments of intelligent machines and humans – that puts a limit on just *how* seamlessly they could ever be welded together. It would be not only foolish, Hayles claims, but also unnecessary to underestimate the thousands of years of sedimented history that are incarnated in the body. Why, she asks, should a posthuman identity involve downloading oneself onto a computer in order to obtain the ultimate privilege of immortality? Unless one believes that consciousness constitutes the essence of who 'we' are, posthumanism might instead involve rethinking human identity in terms of a distributed system:

> This vision is a potent antidote to the view that parses virtuality as a division between an inert body that is left behind and a disembodied subjectivity that

inhabits the virtual realm... By contrast... it is not a question of leaving the body behind but rather of extending embodied awareness in highly specific, local, and material ways that would be impossible without electronic prosthesis.

(Hayles 1999: 290–1)

For Hayles, the posthuman is a way of challenging the liberal humanist subject (the subject with whom our comments on this topic began). Identified primarily with the rational mind, this subject appears to *possess* a body but not to *be* a body, and it is this split (between body and mind/self) that renders it 'possible to claim for the liberal subject its notorious universality, a claim that depends on erasing markers of bodily difference, including sex, race, and ethnicity' (Hayles 1999: 4–5). Like the feminist, post-colonial, and postmodern analyses of the relations between bodies and identities outlined above – which seek to explore the materiality of these markers, and the power relations within which they are situated – Hayles considers cyberspace and cybernetics to be an opportunity to keep 'flesh' in the picture. As she summarises it, '[i]f my nightmare is a culture inhabited by posthumans who regard their bodies as fashion accessories rather than the ground of being, my dream is a version of the posthuman that... understands human life [to be] embedded in a material world of great complexity, one on which we depend for our continued survival' (1999: 5).

Normal bodies (or not)

In a recent television advertisement campaign designed to re-launch the Marks and Spencers (M&S) clothing label among British consumers, a woman runs naked in open fields, reaching the top of a hill against a vast and windy sky. The image is one of freedom, or better: liberation. The hill is like a platform for her nudity and her feelings, which are evidently a mixture of pride and relief. As she reaches the top, arms stretching outwards, the camera takes off above her and around her, the image turning and reverberating itself like a wind – and like the woman's voice, which now rises in a long, powerful tone, shouting to the world: *I'm normal!*

This scene plays on the manifold meanings and feelings associated with the concept of 'normality' and of normal bodies. The crucial detail is that the woman running naked looks very different from a fashion model: she is, one would guess, probably a size 16 rather than a size 8; her running makes the difference obvious not only in terms of size but also in terms of the consistency of her flesh. And she is normal, we are told, which means, in this context, that she is not large. Her demeanour and the setting remind us, however, that this is far from stating the obvious. That she is not large is a discovery, a vindication, a source – precisely – of pride and relief (the hilltop now a podium, for display and celebration). Such can be the power of declaring something 'normal'.

What the concept of normality does for us, writes Ian Hacking, is to close the gap between fact and value, between *is* and *ought*: 'one can... use the word "normal" to say how things are, but also to say how they ought to be' (1990: 163). It is precisely the ambition of this M&S advertisement to erase the profound contradiction between an obvious fact and an equally obvious value: most ordinary women are in fact much larger than most fashion models; yet models, as the noun implies, represent a collective value in the sense that they set a dominant standard for how women 'ought to be'. In declaring that she is *normal*, the woman running naked up the hill is saying she is not large, in two very different senses. First, in the factual sense that she is probably of average size, in terms of the wider population of women. But second, and more importantly, she is not large in the sense that declaring her normality means setting *herself* as the standard against which size is to be measured. Others – including fashion models – may be large or small in relation to her, but she herself is neither large nor small, she is just as she (as one) ought to be.

This double function of the concept of normality, descriptive and evaluative, is already evident in its etymological roots, which must be traced back to classical geometry. In Latin, *norma* means a T-square, so that normal means that which is perpendicular, at right angles. As Hacking puts it: '[a] line may be orthogonal or normal (at right angles to the tangent of a circle, say) or not. This is a description of the line. But the evaluative "right" lurks in the background of right angles. It is just a fact that an angle is a right angle, but it is also a "right" angle, a good one' (1990: 163). The Greek-derived *orthogonal* is synonymous with the Latin *normalis*, and it provides the origin for the adjective *orthodox*. Like the normal, the orthodox conforms to a set of sanctioned, valued standards, and becomes in turn 'the reference for objects or facts which have yet to be in a position to be called such' (Canguilhem 1989: 239). A discourse organised around notions of the 'normal' thus has the effect (and is designed to have the effect) of devaluing all phenomena that fall outside or differ from the norm, designating them as modes of being in need of correction. Normality and the normal, therefore, are concepts that *represent* for the purpose of *intervention*. The idea of the normal is intimately bound with that of a normative intention, a plan and an experience of normalisation.

The normal is thus a 'dynamic and polemical' concept (Canguilhem 1989: 239) in the sense that it implies resistance and contradiction, in the form of a world outside the norm that stands to be corrected. As such, it is a concept whose political significance is great and yet not immediately obvious, because the exercise of judgement is here intrinsically coupled with that of factual, 'objective' description. In the tradition of sociological thought developed in the wake of Michel Foucault, the emergence of discourses opposing the normal to the abnormal is regarded as symptomatic of a change in the way power was conceived and exercised within European states, particularly from the late eighteenth century onwards (Burchell, Gordon and Miller 1991; Foucault 1979; Rose 1989, 1998). No longer identified with the negative prerogative to take life away, power in this new configuration became invested in the fostering of life and in the pursuit of optimal performance – chiefly in economic and military terms – through the disciplining of individual bodies and through the regulation of populations. This is the context in which the modern human sciences developed, spurred by important institutional reforms that began with hospitals and pedagogical establishments. The development of anatomo-clinical medicine and of physiology – the science of normal vital functions – were particularly important in inaugurating a secular rationality based on the normal/abnormal (or, here specifically, the normal/pathological) distinction. From the nineteenth century, the term 'normal' has been used to designate the state of organic health. There is therefore an intimate historical connection between the modern use of the concept of normality and the modern scientific study of the body in terms of its functions, development, anatomy and morphology.

Not only in medicine but in many other fields, from pedagogy and psychology to economics, the normal/abnormal distinction gradually replaced the one based on the notions of good and evil, or on equally dogmatic conceptions of 'human nature'. The reference to human nature (or to the good, for that matter) has not disappeared, but has since tended to assume the connotations of the concept of normality itself. For example, we say it is 'natural' for something to occur when we mean it is 'normal' – that is, regular, typical, and not deviant or pathological. In this case, 'human nature' and the 'natural' no longer refer to a set of dogmatic presuppositions, but to mechanisms and processes conceived as open to positive empirical investigation, of which knowledge of the normal is the product (for more on 'human nature' in the history of philosophy and scientific theory, see Stevenson 1981). Particularly in the nineteenth and in the early part of the twentieth century, bodily norms – concerning the size and shape of the skull, for example – came to provide the 'objective', positive and material standard of reference to determine normality or deviance in a variety of other discourses, such as criminology or psychiatry.

Another important source of the modern use of the concept 'normal' is explicitly related to the social regulation, or *normalisation*, of the technical means of education, health, warfare, or the transportation of people and goods. Across a wide variety of fields, the modern period saw the establishment of norms designed to standardise practice and production across a given national territory, stimulated by the demands of national defense and of industrialisation: for example, norms of training to regulate the practice of pharmacy, veterinary medicine or surgery; morphological norms informing the selection of army conscripts and horses; norms defining standard measurements of equipment or patterns for the purpose of industrial assembly, and so on. It may be difficult at first to see how the establishment of industrial or technological norms can be of interest to the social scientific study of bodies. It becomes more apparent, however, as soon as we consider what Canguilhem describes as the 'correlativity' of norms, which means simply that the definition of a norm in any one field tends to presuppose and interact with the norms that already exist in other fields. A technological norm will be concerned with the 'choice and determination of material, the forms and dimensions of an object whose characteristics from then on become necessary for consistent manufacture' (Canguilhem 1989: 246). The definition of a technological norm has to accommodate the logic and interests of industry, but also those of the economy and of the consumers – embodied consumers – to whom products are ultimately directed. Among other things, the definition of a technological norm thus presupposes the definition or the knowledge of 'normal' bodies, for which it relies on separate and superficially unrelated domains of practice, chiefly scientific and medical. This is immediately apparent in the norms regulating the built environment, which (still) reflect an assumption of able-bodiness as the norm of reference and, in so doing, simultaneously reinforce able-bodiness as a superior social value.

The correlativity of norms, however, may also work the other way around, in the sense that technical normalisation may itself contribute to changing the definition or the perception of what a 'normal' body is: 'the logic of normalization', that is to say, 'can be pushed as far as the normalization of needs [and bodies] by means of the persuasion of advertising' (Canguilhem 1989: 247; our addition within brackets). Taking 'advertising' in its broadest sense to include information and visibility, the example of the built environment might serve us once again: the more that architectural features catering for wheelchair users become ubiquitous, the more wheelchair users themselves are able to function 'normally' and indeed cease to be perceived and defined as individuals with 'abnormal' bodies. A less positive example might be the effect of advertising on the perception of appetite, the quintessential bodily 'need', both in terms of what appears (or is made to appear) appetising, and in terms of whether appetite is something to be indulged or suppressed – with attendant consequences on body image, eating behaviour, and body weight (Bordo 1995; Gordon 1990). This takes us back to the M&S advertisement with which we started, which was commented in the British news as part of general reporting on the financial status of the company. And here is the second half of that story: for, at least judging by those commentaries, the ad was not particularly successful at persuading its target audience of its message. It seems that ordinary women in the real world either did not believe their size and shape was normal, or did not find the idea of taking themselves rather than fashion models as the norm particularly attractive and worthy of celebration. Bearing in mind that the M&S advertisement was like the proverbial drop in an ocean of contrary advertising messages, we may perhaps consider it as the exception that confirms, and reveals, the rule.

Georges Canguilhem, who dedicated his intellectual brilliance to the concepts of norm and the normal, warns us however not to assume too quickly that 'need is an object of possible normalization', since it may equally be regarded as 'the subject obliged to invent norms' (1989: 247). The question here concerns the origin of norms, and whether these – as in the case of normalisation – must always be presumed to stem from a *social* regulatory power. As a historian and philosopher of medicine, Canguilhem was particularly concerned with biological norms, that is, with norms of biological value, which he believed were not the product of a theoretically arbitrary social judgement. Commenting on the definition of the 'normal' given in Lalande's *Vocabulaire technique et critique de la philosophie*, where the concept is taken to designate 'at once a fact and "a value attributed to this fact by the person speaking, by virtue of an evaluative judgement for which he takes responsibility"', Canguilhem writes:

> The entry [in the *Vocabulaire*]...seems to assume that value can be attributed to a biological fact only by 'him who speaks', obviously a man. We, on the other hand, think that the fact that a living man reacts to a lesion, infection, functional anarchy by means of a disease, expresses the fundamental fact that life is not indifferent to the conditions in which it is possible, that life is polarity and thereby even an unconscious position of value.
>
> (1989: 126)

The notion that value or preferences may be inherent in biological life, rather than the effect of a social judgement superimposed on neutral facts, presents a particularly difficult challenge in the context of contemporary social theory. This is because, on the one hand, social theorists have become accustomed to thinking of value in relation to biology in terms of the *value-ladenness* (or bias) of biological descriptions, whose (pseudo-) scientificity served to legitimise relations of inequality or oppression. Conversely, the value of subordinate or oppressed subject positions has often been reclaimed precisely by abstracting from biology, or deeming biological concepts to be irrelevant, on account of the presumed neutrality of biological realities. The attempt to (re)think the relation between matter, life, and value is among the most current, creative and uncertain aspects of social scientific theorising.

Bodies in health and disease

'If anything makes the collectivity we call the body somehow primordial', writes Thomas Osborne, 'it is not so much that we possess a body, but that one of its fundamental attributes is that it can go wrong, or at least that we perceive that it can' (Osborne 1996: 196). The body becomes conspicuous in the event of disease. We notice our body when the sudden or progressive impairment of one of its functions interferes with our daily activities, disturbing an order we take for granted. A leg that will no longer walk, an eye that will no longer see, a heart that strains to run a familiar stretch, impose themselves on our attention as they transform our customary relation to the world. The same point holds also in a broader sense, on the scale of peoples and centuries rather than individuals and their biographies: it is in connection with the multiple practices of medicine that the body has come to be interrogated, and its properties defined; through methods that range from the observation of reactions to specific treatments (or non-treatments), all the way to the dissection, measurement, and laboratory analysis of organs and tissues. As Henri Michaux has put it: '... the body (its organs and its functions) has become known and revealed not through the prowess of the strong, but through the troubles of the weak, the ill, the infirm, the wounded (for health is silent, the source of that immensely mistaken impression that *tout va de soi*) ...' (quoted in Canguilhem 2002: 50).

We owe it to Canguilhem to have highlighted how consistently, at least among modern physicians and philosophers, health has been defined as lack of bodily awareness, as a 'silence of the organs' (the expression is by the French surgeon René Leriche). At the same time, following Kant, Canguilhem stresses that the concept of health is not a scientific concept, but a commonsense one. We can *feel* well, but it is impossible to *know*, on the basis of this feeling, that we are well (see Jackie Stacey's personal account of this experience, 1997: 137–140). The silence of the organs, in other words, is 'silence' in at least two senses: first, in the sense that the body is subjectively experienced as quiet and unremarkable; and second, in the sense that this experience actually *says nothing* to the scientifically minded physician, it is silent with regard to whether one truly is healthy or not.

This proposition broadly agrees with the analysis given by Michel Foucault of the emergence of anatomo-clinical medicine in eighteenth-century France. The anatomo-clinical method allowed for the constitution of an expert truth of health and illness by referring not to the body of lived experience – so unreliable in its subjectivity – but to the dead body pried open in dissection. Corpses are static, and therefore 'stable, visible, legible' (Foucault 1973: 196) in a way that live, active bodies are not. It is the primary passivity of the corpse that, according to Foucault, allowed the human body to be regarded as an *object*, granting sovereign power to the empirical gaze of positive science. Death 'spoke retroactively the truth of disease' (1973: 158) by indexing this truth to signs, or lesions, that were demonstrable in the anatomical theatre. The sick living body, in this rational framework, can be read as the anticipation of the corpse it is likely to become: otherwise it remains unintelligible, opaque.

That modern biomedicine tends to treat bodies as objects, by working to neutralise subjectivity in clinical interaction and in the diagnostic process, has been the focus of critique on the part of social scientists and philosophers for decades (e.g. Jewson 1976; Illich 1977; Reiser 1978; Engel 1981; cf. Osborne 1992). But equally long-standing, if not equally well known, is the medical thematisation of the body as the ultimate site of expression, or revelation, of the self. If health is the 'silence of the organs', might organs *speak* in the event of illness or disease, rather than just make noise? Might sickness express an *intention*, that is, the meaning of relationships between a subject and the objects that constitute its environment? Might disease be an act of *creative expression*, rather than merely a fact of destruction; might it be a way of solving problems as well as being a problem itself? These are the kinds of questions articulated by early followers of Sigmund Freud, who saw in psychoanalysis the opportunity to transform medicine as a whole (e.g. Deutsch 1959; Ferenczi 1955; Groddeck 1977; for contemporary versions of psychoanalytic psychosomatics see Chiozza 1998a and 1998b; McDougall 1989; Taylor 1987). The versions of psychoanalysis they proposed were unorthodox and sometimes idiosyncratic, certainly at odds with both the medical and the psychoanalytic establishment. But the problematic they addressed, although marginal in terms of its social recognition, is not marginal in an epistemological sense: it may be described, in fact, as the photographic negative of the dominant biomedical paradigm – the dark side of the biomedical moon. Instead of being regarded as a morally neutral, 'natural' event, disease in this discourse appears existentially meaningful and ethically consequential. The body, in turn, is imagined as something capable of language, and of translating abstract meanings into material signs and symbols.

The attribution (or recognition) of meaning to illness is often, although not necessarily, related to the idea that the body can be a medium of expression instrumentally available to the 'mind', for the purpose of obtaining what is known as a 'secondary gain' from the sick status or role. This is Edward Shorter's assumption in his study of how psychosomatic symptoms – by which Shorter means bodily symptoms produced by the mind, without an organic cause – tend to vary historically, following changes in medical and in general culture. 'The unconscious mind', he writes, 'desires to be taken seriously and not be ridiculed. It will therefore strive to present symptoms that always seem, to the surrounding culture, legitimate evidence of organic disease. This striving introduces a historical dimension. As the culture changes its mind about what is legitimate disease and what is not, the pattern of psychosomatic illness changes' (Shorter 1992: x). Historical and cultural specificity, however, run deeper than Shorter supposes. Whilst Western (biomedical) culture may periodically change its mind as to the legitimacy of certain bodily signs and symptoms, the fact of conceiving illness as something whose 'legitimacy' needs to be ascertained through objective parameters is itself by no means self-evident or universal. On the contrary, this approach is indissociable from the structure of health care provision and therapeutic relationships within modern Western societies, and ultimately from the value and meaning ascribed to illness episodes within this particular culture. As Parsons began to argue over fifty years ago, the sick role is itself culturally specific in its predicament of excusing the patient for his or her condition, as well as being 'functional' to a specific socio-economic organisation (cf. Parsons 1951). Equally culturally specific, therefore, is what we might describe as the 'forensic' role the body-object performs in relation to the problem of establishing the legitimacy of a person's claim to the benefits associated with the sick role.

In Western culture, the presence of pathological signs in the form of biochemical or tissue alterations thus has the theoretical effect of foreclosing questions relating to the possible motives and moral standing of the sick person.[6] By implication, these questions are always either at the forefront, or at least lurking close in the background, whenever the material signs of disease are absent (in the sense that they cannot be ascertained). This is borne out by the deep ambivalence of modern Western culture towards the status of psychiatric and psychosocial problems, problems that appear suspended in a situation of permanent undecidability as to whether they ultimately constitute (or stem from) forms of pathology or deviance (cf. Foucault 1989; Lemert 1967; Szasz 1974). In Western society and culture, therefore, suffering that is unwarranted by organic findings is defined as psychiatric or psychosocial by default and, as such, it is always related to the hypothesis of deviance. This situation, it has been argued, produces the peculiarly adaptive phenomenon of 'somatoform disorders': illnesses that either mimick the presence of non-existing lesions (such as the ones described by Shorter), or that are defined by the patient's conviction that lesions or biochemical alternations are present when they are not (Kirmayer et al. 1994; Fabrega 1990).

Viewed from a global perspective, however, the behaviour of those who 'somatise' – or who express their suffering in bodily terms – appears ordinary rather than conspicuous or psychopathological. The expectation that suffering can and should be expressed in psychological terms is peculiar to Western(ised) middle- and upper class, urban populations (Borens et al. 1977; Kirmayer 1987; Kleinman 1986; Posse and Hallstrom 1999; Salminen et al. 1999). Medical anthropologists and historians, on their part, have long been demonstrating how different practices of medicine involve different conceptions of the body, and correspondingly different idioms of suffering. A particularly well-researched comparison is that between Western biomedicine and traditional Chinese medicine (see e.g. Ots 1990, 1994; Kleinman and Good 1985). Ots has argued, for example, that Chinese medical thought is also structured by a profound dualism, but one where 'somatic functions and emotions are not strictly separated. Emotions are merely understood as pathogenic factors which cause disturbances of the organs and their functions. There exists a long tradition of expressing emotions in somatic metaphors. . . . The difference between the Western and the Chinese view is not that of a dichotomised Western and a supposedly holistic Chinese view of the body-mind. The difference lies in the Chinese assessment of an emotional body' (1990: 26). The dualism in Chinese culture does not oppose the body to the mind, at least insofar as '[t]here exists no equivalent of our construct of psyche in Chinese language' (Ots 1994: 119). The opposition is rather between what we might call two different modes of existence of the body itself: that is, between the heart (xin) as the seat of cognition and virtue, and the body in (e)motion and turmoil. Although it does involve the stigmatisation of emotional expressions and behaviour – which itself leads to an emphasis on the somatic aspects of illness – the Chinese dichotomy does not involve a general subordination of the body to the mind. The body, in other words, is not essentially, ontologically divorced from the seat of knowledge and, as a result, the Chinese 'are culturally trained to "listen" within their body' (Ots 1990: 26). This subordination, by contrast, is apparent in the very etymology of the English terms 'body' and 'embodiment', both of which stem from the old Saxon *bodig* meaning 'vessel'; the implication here is that the body is the mere carrier or container for the soul or mind.[7]

The notion that bodily, physical, material disease constitutes a natural and thus morally neutral event, however fundamental this notion may be to the epistemology and vocation of Western biomedicine, must be somewhat re-qualified in the context of contemporary society and culture. As the medical emphasis has shifted from cure to health promotion and prevention through specific lifestyle choices, disease itself can be increasingly perceived and addressed as evidence of deviant behaviour. In an article published in the *New England Journal of Medicine*, Faith Fitzgerald asks whether we are establishing a 'tyranny of health in which those who are unwell are assumed to have misbehaved (with certain areas of misbehavior forgiven and others condemned)' (1994: 197). This prompts the question of whether, in the contemporary climate of heightened health-consciousness, the diseased body may be stigmatised in a generic sense, and not (only) on account of the particular character of the specific condition it bears (on stigma, see Goffman 1963). In a world that many would describe as characterised by moral relativism, the value of health has come to replace other values in securing moral consensus and seemingly unconditional approval. In a global context, however, the unreflexive pursuit of utopian ideals of health raises serious ethical questions – such as those that emerge in connection with the global traffic in human organs (see discussion of bodies in consumer culture, below).

Bodies and technologies

'Tool-making man makes tools that imitate his own functions' (Poster 1992: 437), Mark Poster writes. He also goes on to suggest, in his analysis of the film *Robocop*, that what distinguishes postindustrial society from other tool-making eras is that here it is not only the (human) body which is reproduced by tools/machines, but the brain too: 'As the functions of the brain are progressively added to the robot, the social world progressively includes new species of cyborgs and androids' (1992: 437). Robocop is one such cyborg. A policeman who neither eats nor sleeps, he is understood to be the answer to the crime problem. In this film, '[s]cience remodels the human body to suit the needs of capitalism, which, of course, in turn serves to benefit humanity' (Poster 1992: 439).

The context in which the word first appeared in print, in a 1960 issue of the journal *Astronautics*, certainly suggests that cyborgs, in fact as well as in science fiction, are bound up with capitalism and science. Having been asked by NASA to 'do something psychopharmaceutical for astronauts' (Hacking 1998: 209), the psychopharmacologist Nathan Kline, along with the musician and scientist Manfred Clynes, decided that the most important issue raised by space travel was the dependence of human beings on their environment:

> If man in space must constantly be checking things and making adjustments merely in order to keep himself alive, he becomes a slave to the machine. The purpose of the Cyborg ... is to provide an organizational system in which such robot-like problems are taken care of automatically and unconsciously, leaving man free to explore, to create, to think, and to feel.
>
> (Clynes and Kline in Hacking 1998: 209)

Clynes and Kline were quite the 'Cartesian' dualists. Only the body was to be affected by its incorporation into a cybernetic feedback loop. The mind, representing all that is human about human 'nature', was assumed to remain untouched.

These two brief sketches draw attention to some of the relations between capitalism, science, nature, body, mind and technology that contemporary theorists, and especially those who address themselves to cyborgs, as well as to science and technology more generally, seek to interrogate. Science studies scholars for example, contest that most common-sense assumption (evident in *Robocop*, as well as in the story of Clynes and Kline), that technological 'progress' is the product of science and scientific knowledge over and above other cultural practices. Rather differently, in her ground-breaking book *Primate Visions*, Donna Haraway shows how primatology developed not (solely) along the lines of rationality and reason, but was also informed by 'the relationship between human and animal, nature and culture, anthropology and biology, First and Third World' (Haraway 2000: 137). The primate body 'may be read as a map of power' (Haraway 1989: 10). It is one of a number of boundary creatures that populate Haraway's texts. As she describes them: 'animal–human for primate; machine-organic for cyborg; and nature and labor for OncoMouse^{TM}' (Haraway 2000: 140). What is important here is that, rather than conceive of the body (human or otherwise) in terms of an authentic or 'pure' identity, all 'corporealizations' are, for Haraway, indubitably 'mixed up' with other things, including technology. Simply put: 'one is not born an organism' (Haraway 1991: 208).

But what is *technological* specifically? What are the technologies with which bodies are mixed? As Mike Michael notes, although 'cyborgology' is often bound up with 'exotic' technologies – technologies which, in challenging the organisation of society and selfhood, are frequently the objects of extended academic reflection – 'mundane' technologies (in his book, walking boots, the car, the television remote control, and the dog lead) also play an important role in sustaining and sometimes subverting local configurations. In his analysis of the 'Hudogledog' for example – a single entity derived from Hu(man) + Dogle(ad) + Dog – Michael illustrates how this assemblage of human, animal, and technology is constituted in ways that displace the human as the privileged source of agency (see also Birke 1994; Birke, Brown and Michael 1998). The dog lead:

> serves as a channel or conduit of communication in several senses: tactile, kinaesthetic, aural and visual. What is important here is that it allows for a mutuality between dog and human – that is, a process of *joint action*... Via the medium of the dog-lead, the human, for example, reads on behalf of the dog (e.g. warning signs, traffic lights) and the dog, for example, reads on behalf of the human (e.g. danger, dog mess, quarry, evidence).... this co(a)gency is enabled by the wider nexus of associations – representational, institutional, legal, commercial, veterinary, and so on.
>
> (Michael 2000: 129)

Although the distinction between the exotic and the mundane may ultimately be considered to be spurious (exotic technologies depend, after all, on mundane ones and vice versa), in drawing attention to it, Michael implicitly invites the question as to why 'some objects (gadgets, machines, systems) [are] marked as explicitly technical and others are not'

(Mackenzie 2002: 217). In a similar vein, Bruno Latour (1993) contests – or more accurately, displaces – the common assumption that, in the modern era, (at least some) bodies and lives are 'more' deeply imbricated in the technological than ever before (cf. Latour 1994).

The distinction between the natural and the social is especially significant with respect to the relations between bodies and technologies because, regardless of contemporary claims to the contrary, '[w]e have all been taught a strong contrast between artefacts and living things' (Hacking 1998: 205). Technologies are made, bodies are not. And yet Georges Canguilhem, writing fifty-odd years before the cyborg promised to meld human bodies and technologies together, does not think it matters. As Ian Hacking summarises his position: '[w]hether there is a sharp distinction between the made and the born or not, tools and machines are *extensions of the body*' (Hacking 1998: 205). Canguilhem is suggesting, in other words, not that tools are an imitation of the body, or that they are mixed up with the body, but rather that '*machines can be considered as organs of the human species*. A tool or a machine is an organ, and organs are tools or machines' (Canguilhem 1992: 55, emphasis in the original). This claim is certainly persuasive with regards to those tools which are held close to, on, or about the body (contact lenses, pacemakers, and prosthetics spring to mind here), but it is more difficult to accept in relation to those which are free-standing: 'if machines are organs, is the spinning jenny an organ? Or an organism?' (Hacking 1998: 207). Perhaps one of the most significant aspects of Canguilhem's argument is that it encourages his reader to resist the assumption that machine and organism are fundamentally opposed, or that machines are 'other,' or different, to human beings. In order to cut across this distinction, Canguilhem suggests that machines are a part of life, that they are an 'extension of vitality, of living force' (Hacking 1998: 207).

This is not quite the same as saying that 'life' has *become* intensely technological. This common-place belief often runs thus:

> 'life,' from the supermarket tomato, through genetically altered rabbit viruses,
> to cloned sheep and attempts at human somatic gene therapy, has undergone
> a fairly literal technological rendering. Life, as we are told constantly, is now
> being explicitly designed or engineered . . . Numerous warnings about new bio-
> medical and biotechnological practices and the effect they could have on our
> norms (nature, kinship, family and health) are now taking place.
>
> (Mackenzie 2002: 171)

The link between life and technology seems to be most clearly constituted and demonstrated in relation to information. Importantly, contra the assumption that *today* is more techno-logical, this association of life and technology is not a new one. Biological understandings of life were informatic, Adrian Mackenzie argues, long before Watson and Crick's discovery of the double helix structure of DNA, and they continue to be so even though the notion that information flows from the DNA to proteins has been repudiated: 'the informatic metaphor, rather than falling away, has now clearly extended well beyond the genetic material to include the whole cell, if not the whole organism. . . . understanding life as an information system entails taking a far more complicated view of information' (Mackenzie 2002: 180).

Of course there are competing conceptions of information and its implications (Kay 1995, 1997; see also the discussion of N. Katherine Hayles' work earlier). In communication theory for instance, information is understood to be a measure of the degree of uncertainty in a series of signals, whereas genetic information, at its most reductive, is believed to be contained in the 'code' from which instructions with regards to the living organism unfold over time. Cybernetic and genetic conceptions of information often overlap however: as noted earlier, an organism may be considered *to be* an information system. Indeed, with the reduction of life to the gene and gene to information, heredity is often conceptualised in terms of communication, guidance and control. Nevertheless, this confusion of different metaphors and, often, of metaphors with materiality, is not in itself necessarily problematic. Mackenzie argues that it may be a productive, 'enabling error': 'Information is not just a metaphor that reduces the complexity of life as an object of biological knowledge, it is also a set of technical–economic practices which trace certain paths and not others' (2002: 181). Notably, objections to the informatic metaphor in the social sciences do not usually turn on the claim that it violates some notion of a specifically *human* essence that cannot be reduced to an informatic programme. On the contrary, they are more likely to highlight how the reduction of life to information does not take account of the vast array of 'distributed, heterogeneous work processes' (some scientific, some technical, others not) that enable particular conceptions of life – of life as information, say – to be materialised in particular ways.

If Robocop emerged, as Mark Poster claims, out of the gap between the dead and the living, contemporary biotechnology is arguably characterised by the co-implication of living and non-living elements:

> Biotechnological objects in their current forms, whether 'rationally designed drugs', genetically modified bacteria, goats or cows used for 'pharming' custom-designed drugs, genetically modified crops and food products, prospective somatic or germline therapies for disease, or genetically modified bacteria for breaking down crude oil, draw on an ensemble of technical elements, both living and non-living. These include electrophoresis gels, immortal cell lines, stem cells, sequencing robots, PCR assays, DNA microarrays, etc.
>
> (Mackenzie 2002: 192)

For Mackenzie, what distinguishes contemporary biotechnology is that it is no longer possible to imagine that it is the living thing that animates technology or, conversely, that living things are reduced to non-living processes. Instead, biotechnology is *enabled* precisely insofar as it thrives on the tension, and exploits the links, between living and non-living processes. In place of questions regarding the admixture of human and non-human elements then, and against the notion that biotechnology is distinguished solely by its *interference* in living processes, we might address the specific points at which information is laced into different realities. Mackenzie asks, for example, how the relations between living and non-living entities are stabilised, how living processes (patterns of reproduction, growth and death) are accelerated and suspended, and how connections between and within living things are interrupted and reorganised in historically specific ways (see also Franklin 2000). In this way, accounts of contemporary biotechnology that are characterised by polarised positions (such as the claim that biotechnology advances 'progress' versus biotechnology as contributor to further exploitation, or the fear that biotechnology will ultimately control living processes as opposed to the belief in living processes as always able to elude biotechnology) are displaced. Technicity, from this perspective, is originary: it is impossible to think about the body outside of it. Rather than identifying the differences *between* what is human and non-human, living and non-living, we might more productively look towards and analyze the differences – spatial, temporal, and topological – *within* particular corporealisations.

Bodies in consumer culture

All cultures are material cultures, and consumption is central, as Don Slater (2003) notes, to all social and cultural reproduction. *Consumer culture* however, is a specific form of material culture, usually associated with Euro-American modern market society.[8] Here,

> key social values, identities and processes are negotiated through the figure of 'the consumer' (as opposed to, say, the worker, the citizen or the devotee); central modern values such as freedom, rationality and progress are enacted and assessed through consumerist criteria (range of choice, price calculations and rising affluence, respectively); and the cultural landscape seems to be dominated by commercial signs (advertising, portrayals of 'lifestyle' choices through the media, obsessive concern with the changing meanings of things).
>
> (Slater 2003: 147)

The consumption of images is a crucial aspect in this context, with images of the body in particular predominating. In fact in a consumer culture, the material fabric of everyday life – social space – seems to be specifically designed in order to facilitate the display of the body (open-plan spaces, mirrors and glass in restaurants, shops and shopping centres, for example) (Jameson 1985), thus engendering greater bodily self-consciousness and self-scrutiny. The image, Rachel Bowlby argues, 'is useful for thinking about consumer forms of subjectivity' (Bowlby 1985: 29). Looking itself is the commodity for which one frequently pays. Looking is the site of desire, pleasure, and objectification.

The objectification of women is particularly intense in this context (although see Edwards 1997 for an analysis of men in consumer culture). For women are not only the principle targets of many consumer goods (goods which are integral, for instance, to the work of femininity, in which each and every part of the body can be broken down and rebuilt), but are also the privileged sign in commodity aesthetics. Subject and object, women are both consumer and consumed, consumers, indeed, of themselves (as commodities) (Lury 1996: 135). This double position is perfectly captured in the moment of suspension before a purchase, the moment when, as Bowlby argues, the consumer is 'just looking' – just looking, that is, at how the object for sale would look on the looker: '[c]onsumer culture transforms the narcissistic mirror into a shop window, the *glass* which reflects an idealised image of the woman (or man) who stands before it, in the form of the model she could buy or become. Through the glass, the woman sees what she wants and what she wants to be' (1985: 32).

Like Bowlby, Mike Featherstone also links the consumer to the 'tragedy' of Narcissus. Consumer culture coincides with a culture of narcissism, Featherstone suggests, and a 'new' conception of the self, a 'performing self', which 'places greater emphasis on appearance, display and the management of impressions' (1982: 27). Of course an ethics or aesthetics of the self is hardly new, as Michel Foucault has clearly illustrated (see the section on 'body ethics' below). However, where early Christian technologies of the self demanded for the most part a *renunciation* of the self, the eighteenth century brought with it a decisive break, a 'discontinuity' as Foucault would have it, after which time such techniques are employed to 'constitute, positively, a new self' (Foucault 1988: 49). In this respect, one might say that the emergence of consumer culture coincides not only with a culture of narcissism, but with the reflexive development of the self in modernity (Giddens 1991), a development which is also a *government* of the self (Rose 1989). One of the key sites of such governance is the body. For while on the one hand work on the body is encouraged as a form of self-expression (here commodities play an important role in the project of self-actualisation), it is at the same time a disciplining force, placing ever greater burdens on individuals. Body maintenance for example, can be understood to be an instrumental strategy in a context where '[s]elf preservation depends upon the preservation of the body...[and where] the body is the passport to all that is good in life. Health, youth, beauty, sex, fitness are the positive attributes which body care can achieve and preserve' (Featherstone 1982: 26). Although the individual in consumer culture might be encouraged to enjoy a hedonistic lifestyle, it is a 'calculating hedonism' (Jacoby in Featherstone 1982: 27) in which he or she is expected to be able to Just Do it *and* to Just Say No. This is arguably especially so in the sphere of health, where the turning of patients into consumers encourages the pursuit of health as a form of consumption, which bleeds into a *duty* to be healthy with all the attendant expectations and responsibility that this entails (Coward 1989).

In a consumer culture, commodity relations have been extended to all facets of life. Commodities mediate – stand in for, indeed – social relationships, including the relationship of the self to the self. Perhaps it is here that the significance of consumer culture is really felt on a daily basis: as a resource for the creation and transformation of the self, and especially the body. But if it is the case that 'I shop therefore I am', as the artist Barbara Kruger put it, then what identities are available for purchase? Susan Willis asks: 'is mass culture by its very definition white culture?' (1990: 80). For Willis, consumer society is characterised by a contradiction, 'between the ideology...that would have everyone believe that we all trade equally in commodities, and the reality of all marginalized people for whom translation into the dominant white model is impossible' (1990: 83). The popularity of 'beige' fashion models for example, she argues, 'is the industry's metaphor for the magical erasure of race as a problem in our society':

> To understand how this is achieved we have only to compare the look of racial homogeneity to the look of gender homogeneity. For some time now the fashion industry has suggested that all women... whether they are 12 years old or 45, are equally gendered.... Now, the suggestion that women with the proper 'look' are equally 'raced'. Such a look denies the possibility for articulating cultural diversity precisely because it demonstrates that difference is only a matter of fashion.
>
> (1990: 87)

This is not to suggest that difference in consumer culture is only ever, or must be understood *solely* in terms of, commodity seriality however. In a complex analysis of the numerous physical transformations that Michael Jackson has undergone (transformations that cast 'race' as a surgical rather than biological identity), Willis argues that while, on the one hand, Jackson's body is analogous to 'Ford's yearly productions of its "new" models', it is also informed by an entirely different tradition, the blackface worn by nineteenth century minstrel performers. Like blackface – 'the original metaphor for transformation [in the black American entertainment tradition]' (Willis 1990: 89) – Willis argues that Jackson too is a trademark, whose physical mutations are 'a means for bringing all the sexual tensions and social contradictions present in blackface into a contemporary form' (1990: 91). And yet like the dancer Juba, Jackson is also able (at least in some of his performances) to separate himself from blackface, 'out-moonwalk[ing] the commodity form of himself' (Willis 1990: 94).

Bodies then, like and as commodities, can both encapsulate and efface social contradictions. As zones of contention, they necessarily raise questions about power and resistance. To what extent does making *a* spectacle (of oneself and one's body) for example, confirm and reproduce *the* spectacle (Debord 1977; Plant 1992)? As Lois McNay puts it:

> in a society in which the behaviour of individuals is often governed by an incitement to consumption, it may be necessary to determine the point at which the construction of one's life as a work of art ceases to be an act of conspicuous consumption – or in Bourdieu's terms a sign of 'distinction' – and becomes a gesture of resistance.
>
> (1994: 155)

The debate over the political efficacy of 'lipstick lesbianism,' and whether gay people are accepted as consuming rather than social subjects is a pertinent example here (Clark 1993). The theatrical performances of the queer body that often accompany queer activism have also come under considerable scrutiny. Saalfield and Navarro for instance, ask whether ACT UP's 'obsessive relationship with its own image in the media' represents anything other than an exercise in conspicuous 'lifestyle' consumption: 'Is going to an ACT UP demo like buying Calvin Klein underwear?' (1991: 362). In short, one might ask to what extent a *politics* based on the body in consumer culture will be able to distinguish itself from the widespread 'aestheticization of everyday life' (Featherstone 1991). As Michel Maffesoli notes:

> [w]hether trendy exercises in sensory isolation, or various forms of body-building, or jogging, or Eastern techniques of one sort or another, the body is being constructed as a value ... even in its most private aspects, *the body is being constructed only in order to be seen*; it is theatralized to the highest degree. Within advertising, fashion, dance, the body is adorned only to be made into a spectacle.
>
> (1991: 18–19, our emphasis added)

Commodity fetishism – the notion that the value of the commodity resides in the physical object (its signification or meaning) rather than in the human labour that goes into producing it, and the social relations that are its conditions – is a key feature of consumer culture.[9] Perhaps it is also arguable therefore, that despite the accent on visibility (as described by Maffesoli and others), consumer culture also contributes to the 'invisibilisation' of differences between bodies, of the different values ascribed to particular bodies, as well as the invisibilisation of unequal power relations. We end the discussion with an example of this, in the context of the worldwide traffic in body parts or organs. As Rosi Braidotti notes, the commercialisation of living matter is based on 'the perverse notion' that all organs are equal to each other and interchangeable, that all organs are *the same* (1994: 64). Braidotti invites her reader to consider this problematic assumption in the context of intragenerational procreation, asking if it really is the case that a uterus is a uterus...or whether, instead, this 'flattening out' of the object serves to conceal differences between 'real' and 'whole' women, differences (of age, 'race', and class) which have implications for the roles women are called upon to play in the reproductive industry. Like the emphasis on lifestyles and commodities, the focus solely on the physical object/organ itself, at the expense of the social context from which it emerges, can displace or hide important differences between individuals which are structured by social inequality.

Body ethics

The term 'ethics' refers to a variety of meanings probably as complex as the term 'body' itself: equally varied are the possibilities of their interrelationship. At a commonsense level, however, the association of ethics and the body appears very far fetched indeed. In a culture (still) characterised, as we have seen, by a fundamental dualism, ethics would appear to sit firmly on the side of things mental or spiritual. It is common to hear the reference to ethical *principles* or ethical *reasoning*, for example, but few would find a recognisable meaning in an expression such as ethical *bodies*. In what ways, then, do bodies intersect with ethics? An obvious place to start might be by considering the field of 'bioethics', where the reference to a biological dimension that would include the body is explicit. The field of bioethics in general, and of biomedical ethics in particular, considers the moral or ethical dimension of research and practice in medicine and the life sciences – most often with the purpose of providing frameworks or guidelines for decision making in relation to various medical or research situations. Since the second half of the twentieth century (in the aftermath of the trials, held at Nuremberg between 1946 and 1949, that addressed the horrors perpetrated by Nazi medicine) the field of bioethics has expanded and complicated enormously, in proportion with the speed of technological, scientific and other social developments. Although the types of theory involved in bioethics are multiple – Beauchamp and Childress (1994) list eight types, for example, ranging from utilitarian or consequence-based theory to principle-based common-morality theories – it is probably fair to say that in all of these the body tends to figure as an incidental object to the theory. In other words, the theory is primarily concerned with the definition of ethical concepts (such as *right, obligation, virtue, justification, autonomy, beneficence, responsibility, sympathy*, etc.), and of norms or principles that apply to circumstances in which bodies are – happen to be – involved. Is organ donation acceptable on the part of minors or mentally incompetent persons? Should aborted human foetuses be used as research material? Under what circumstances should patients on life-support machines be allowed to die? These are some examples of questions involving bodies, but where bodies appear as the passive object of an abstract moral reasoning that stems from a seemingly disembodied subject. The disembodied style of ethical reasoning that is typical especially of a certain Anglo-American philosophy has been effectively described by Martha Nussbaum as 'correct, scientific, abstract, hygienically pallid...a kind of all-purpose solvent in which philosophical issues of any kind at all could be efficiently disentangled, any and all conclusions neatly disengaged' (Nussbaum 1990: 19).

This dominant approach in bioethics has become the focus of much criticism in recent times, in the wake of both postmodernist and postcolonial theory. As Howard Brody has put it, '[t]he dominant, principlist approach to bioethics says that the voice worth listening to is the one that expresses itself in terms of certain abstract ethical concepts. The patient's life experience has to be translated somehow into autonomy, beneficence, nonmaleficence, and justice before we can draw any moral conclusions – and it is hard to imagine the average patient being able to carry out that translation unaided by experts' (1997: 23). Brody is one of a growing number of advocates of an alternative, narrative approach, both to ethics in general and in the context of health and illness in particular (see Brody 2003; Lindemann Nelson 1997). It is in the work of Arthur Frank, however, that narrative ethics are explicitly discussed as embodied ethics, or ethics premised on the fact of embodiment (Frank 1995). In Frank's account, stories, and particularly illness stories, are not only or primarily *about* bodies as they are *told by* bodies, which testify values through their being and their presence. One of the many testimonies Frank discusses in detail is that of Gail, a chronic pain sufferer. Gail describes herself and other pain sufferers as people with access to different experiences and knowledges, thanks to which they see how precious various aspects of life are, how worthy of being given priority both at an individual and at a social level. She is 'convinced only sick people know what health is. And they know it by its very loss', and asks '[w]hat would happen if we all knew what it really meant and we all lived as if it really mattered, which it does' (quoted in Frank 1995: 141). Frank stresses how different Gail's 'knowledge' is from what we ordinarily understand by that term: '...embodiment is the essence of witness. Gail's knowledge and the difference it could make emanate from the site of her pain, which is the source of this knowledge. Her testimony is her body, and ultimately her body can only be apprehended through all the senses of another body' (1995: 142).

Testimony is connoted by the impossibility of detachment and abstraction: unlike other reports, it 'implicates others in what they witness', and transforms them into witnesses in turn (Frank 1995: 143). The testimony is not a message that can be taken away, moved on from – for, as Brody puts it, 'the patient cannot ultimately escape from his own story' (1997: 20). This means that truly receiving the story involves *staying with* the embodied teller, and offering embodied presence to *commune* (or live in and with) the other's pain/knowledge. Bodies, in this perspective, can be thought of as ethical in at least two ways: first of all, insofar as their very being is the source of particular values, and value-judgements; and second, insofar as they are able and ready to be implicated in relationships of testimony, or to become what Frank refers to as 'communicative bodies'. As Gail's own words suggest ('what would happen if we all...lived as if it really mattered, which it does'), an ethics of testimony implies a social ethic, involving 'not some reorganisation of "service delivery" or enhanced "communication skills" among physicians...[but]

nothing less than changing the cultural milieu so that people like Gail are *seen* for what their bodies testify to' (Frank 1995: 145).

The narrative approach thus involves moving away from a conception of ethics as a set of true propositions leading to moral precepts, and – as Frank's own example illustrates – may be loosely counted among forms of ethics based on bodily specificity. In the words of Rosalyn Diprose, these are accounts that 'locate the body as the site of one's habitat or subjectivity – where the body is constituted by a dynamic relation with other bodies in a social context of power, desire and knowledge' (1991: 66). Feminist theorists, among others, have been important contributors to this tradition (besides Diprose, see e.g. Braidotti 1989; Gatens 1996; Irigaray 1984). Generally speaking, as soon as ethics is conceived as stemming from *processes* of being and encountering – and not as the relationship between a pre-constituted moral subject applying criteria to equally pre-constituted objects – the connection between ethics and bodies appears far less improbable. This is evident in the late work of Michel Foucault, which turned to the practices of Greek and Roman antiquity to challenge the rigid separation of ethics and aesthetics that characterises contemporary (post-Kantian) ethical thinking. In Foucault's work, ethics is described as a practice of the constitution of the self as a subject, and as the 'deliberate form assumed by liberty' (1988a: 4). Liberty here is closely associated with power – Foucault refers to it also as 'freedom-power' – and with the bringing of power to bear upon one's self: 'Just as in the household it was the man who ruled, and in the city it was right that only men should exercise power, and not slaves, children, or women, so each man was supposed to make his manly qualities prevail within himself. Self-mastery was a way of being a man with respect to oneself ... a way of being active in relation to what was by nature passive and ought to remain so' (Foucault 1986: 82–3). Among the Greeks and Romans, Foucault argued further, the ethical practice of freedom involved an aesthetics of existence – a stylisation of conduct – whose primary focus was the body and its pleasures.

Andrew Thacker among others has highlighted several ambiguities and problems in Foucault's use of the concept of aesthetics (Thacker 1993; see also Eagleton 1990; Wolin 1986). These difficulties concern, primarily, whether and how the classical model outlined by Foucault can serve as the blueprint for a reconfiguration of contemporary ethics in a post-Kantian world. Regardless of the 'applicability' of the Greco-Roman model to the present, Foucault's studies of classical antiquity highlight the possibility of a very different role for aesthetic judgements in the sphere of ethics, where the body (or the corporeal) does not appear as the passive object of a soul or philosophical mind, but as the active instance of aesthetic balance and as a source of wisdom and knowledge. In this configuration, unlike that of the dominant versions of contemporary bioethics, it was thought that medicine should direct philosophy at least as much as the reverse (Foucault 1988b).

This last proposition – that medicine should direct philosophy – should not be confused with the notion that ethics can or should be founded on scientific knowledge (and is therefore contingent on, and subject to, instruction by scientists). It is related, on the contrary, to a legitimate problematisation of the extent to which the ethos and the knowledge of medicine can be identified with those of science (cf. Diprose 1991). Hans Jonas' characterisation of the organism as 'a substantial entity enjoying a sort of *freedom* with respect to its own substance, an independence from that same matter of which it nonetheless wholly consists' (see p. 76, this volume), is suggestive of a material world permeated with value, a world in relation to which questions are always already ethical in character. Here is thus a further sense in which bodies are linked to the domain of ethics: bodies are especially conspicuous witnesses to a reality of matter whose freedom never loses its power to surprise us, to suspend our certainties, to demand our engagement in forms that are, to use the phrase employed by Isabelle Stengers, *relevant* – which means both responsive and responsible:

> The intrinsic complexity of living beings...imposes...the necessity for an intelligent experimentation, which assumes the risky responsibility of asking relevant questions. Every question is a wager concerning what the interrogated object is sensitive to, and no method is neutral with respect to this problem. The problem of relevance does not lead to irrationalism, but to the ever-present risk of 'silencing' the very thing one is interrogating.
>
> (1997: 17)

The expression 'body ethics', in this regard, points to the general implication of responsibility in the relations and forms of interaction we establish not only among humans, but with the material world in a broad sense.

Reformulating the agenda

In his introduction to the first edition of *The Body and Society* (1984) – a text that was seminal in setting the agenda for a sociology of the body twenty years ago – Bryan Turner wrote:

> The study of the body is of genuine sociological interest and it is unfortunate that so much of the field is already cluttered by trivial or irrelevant intrusions – neo-Darwinism, sociobiology, biologism. By contrast, there have been important developments in phenomenology, anthropology and existential philosophy which converge on the notion of human embodiment and which provide a basis for a sociology of social being.
>
> (1984: 6)

And also:

> In writing this study of the body, I have become increasingly less sure of what the body is. The paradoxes illustrate this confusion. The body is a material organism, but also a metaphor; it is the trunk apart from head and limbs, but also the person (as in 'anybody' and 'somebody'). The body may also be an aggregate of bodies, often with legal personality as in 'corporation' or in 'the mystical body of Christ'. Such aggregate bodies may be regarded as legal fictions or as social facts which exist independently of the 'real' bodies which happen to constitute them....
>
> (1984: 7–8)

The notion that we might reformulate the sociological agenda in relation to the body is perhaps misleading, because it suggests that the questions or topic-domains articulated only two decades ago have been superseded or exhausted. We do not find this to be the case – there is still much room and much interest for the study of bodies under each of the aspects listed above, among others, by Turner. What perhaps can be gleaned by reflecting on the rapid expansion of studies of the body in the last twenty years is not the need for a radically new agenda, but the need for a more concentrated and exacting attention on aspects that, whilst being in a sense foundational, remained at the margins of the old one – a change of focus, as it were, rather than a change of field. If we refer to the second of the two paragraphs above, for example, we might reflect on the fact that, in 1984, stating that one had 'become increasingly less sure of what the body is' had good reasons to function as a prelude to a long list of the surprising ways in which 'the body' could be addressed – as a material entity, as a metaphor, as a legal fiction, as a collectivity, and so on. At the time, the list had yet to be articulated, let alone be systematically researched. Today, however, rather than adding to that list we might adjust our focus on the introductory phrase about being 'increasingly less sure of what the body is', to assess and engage with the full weight of its implications. Are we content with our uncertainty, that is, with an answer (to the question of 'what the body is') that comes in the form of a list? If so, what is the character of that list, what are our reasons for defining it so, and how do these impact and interact with the reasons of other practices of knowledge – most immediately, perhaps, those of biology and medicine? What world do these interactions create?

Similarly, if we look at the first quotation, we might want to focus not so much on the substantives (*neo-Darwinism, sociobiology, biologism* or *phenomenology, anthropology, existential philosophy*) as on the terms that describe the modes of their mutual relation: 'cluttered', 'trivial', 'irrelevant', 'intrusion'. These terms, we suggest, are the repositories of deeply held assumptions about the nature of boundaries and relationships between different practices of knowledge. As such, they are also the repositories of definite, if implicit, assumptions concerning what a 'biological' body is and can or cannot do. It is to the continuing relevance of these, in fact rather old, questions concerning disciplinary boundaries and the environment of knowledge that we would like to point the reader. This continuing relevance, we believe, is evident in a number of interrelated themes that have emerged for reflection in the course of preparing this Introduction, which we could summarise as follows:

1   the problem of conflating *biology* with *biologism*: that is, the problem of holding reductive assumptions concerning what biology has to say about bodies, and concerning its relevance to both the politics and the social scientific study of (the same) bodies. This problem is compounded by the fact that individual biologists may themselves produce partial or reductive accounts of their own discipline (as well as of the social sciences); that is, they may be far more creative in the practice of their biological work than in how they articulate the implications of that practice (and of their discipline more generally) for society and social theory. Accordingly,

2   the need to *engage* with the biological dimension of the body. The term *engage* here is used deliberately to suggest not a non-polemical relation of parallel coexistence between biologists and sociologists, but rather an active interest in developing a relationship capable of acknowledging both the variety and the significance of what one might term the 'biological imagination'. Evidently, the premises for a possible

reciprocity of interest must pass though a problematisation of the social sciences' own role in constructing what now appears like an unbridgeable gulf, flaring at times into a climate of hostility, between the worlds of biology and social science. It should be stressed, moreover, that *engagement* here is not meant in the linear sense of an 'interdisciplinary collaboration', whereby sociologists would simply defer to biologists the description of a portion (or an aspect) of the reality of bodies, whilst claiming to retain the 'right' to an autonomous and independent description of other portions of that reality. It means rather seeking to understand and to articulate in specific and precise ways where and how the problems that interest sociologists and those that interest (at least some) biologists are mutually relevant in a theoretical sense.

3   Above all, and most importantly, this need for engagement arises within the context of a more general problematic that goes beyond the 'body' as a field of research, but that appears particularly evident and urgent in this field. This problematic concerns how to think about material entities in ways that are true both to their material-reality and to the fact that they are relations embodied (see Fraser *et al.* 2004).

These are questions to be seriously engaged with, and which demand that we take that engagement seriously. Not, however, at the expense of humour! On the contrary, being engaged – or 'the taste to be interested', as Isabelle Stengers puts it – is indissociable from the freedom to laugh at what one is engaged *in*. It is the quality of the laughter that is important here however, as Stengers also points out:

> I do not want a mocking laughter, or a laughter of derision, an irony that always and without risk recognizes the same thing beyond the differences. I would like to make possible the laughter of humor, which comprehends and appreciates without waiting for salvation, and can refuse without letting itself terrorize. I would like to make possible a laughter that does not exist at the expense of scientists, but one that could, ideally, be shared with them.
>
> (Stengers 2000: 17.8)

Perhaps when we ask 'what is a body?' then, we are really asking with whom it is we want to laugh.

Using the Reader

This Introduction is substantive, but our intentions have been modest. We hope we have provided a clarification of the key points of debate in relation to the body, a starting point from which to enter into these debates, and an invitation to explore further the variety and complexity of issues that are at stake. The shorter Introductions which open each of the parts that follow are informed by this general discussion. In them, however, we are mainly concerned with outlining the principal arguments of the chosen authors. We have also included an annotated Guide to further reading at the end of this volume, with lists that correspond to each of the eight parts. While it would surely be impossible to offer even a snapshot of what is a continuously changing – and challenging – field, we have nevertheless tried to include within this Guide a wide range of texts that capture the diversity of theoretical and empirical work on the body in different contexts. We hope that the important work that is included in the Guide will help the reader to pursue the themes introduced here in a structured and organised way.

Please note that the use of ellipses in square brackets indicates where the original text has been edited.

NOTES

1   For an extensive analysis of those risks in a legal setting, see Halley (1994). Halley's account points to the complexity of the use of 'strategic essentialism', in a context where culture and choice may be cast as essences, and biology and genetics as open to manipulation.

2   Elias' work, with its emphasis on the development of emotional controls, points to another important way in which the relationship between the body and social order has been theorised. Sociologists of emotion have described embodied emotion in terms of a 'social energy' produced by the social structure, which in turn sustains it (Collins 1990; see also Kemper 1984); from a micro-sociological perspective, emotions have been theorised as the key to understanding how individuals come to experience social control as exterior and constraining (Scheff 1997).

3   The provocation of the anorexic body has recently been further intensified with the pro ana (pro anorexia) and pro mia (pro bulimia) groups (and their sub-groups, such as the pro ana suicide society) that are flourishing, particularly on the world wide web.

4   That Ahmed is passed off as White illustrates the unmarked, and therefore assumed, nature of Whiteness. Richard Dyer (1988, 1997) argues that this is precisely where the power of Whiteness lies – not in its representation as superiority, but rather as 'normality'.

5   There is no reason to assume that ontology must necessarily be understood to be essentialist, or that it should be conflated, as Sandford claims it is in *Gender Trouble*, with 'a substance, in the traditional philosophical sense of the word' (Sandford 1999: 20).

6   This, of course, is not the case in absolute terms. Susan Sontag in her very well known *Illness as Metaphor* (1978), for example, illustrated the many moral connotations of diseases that bear particular cultural significance, such as cancer. Sontag's argument, however, confirms the Western epistemological assumption that *real* (i.e. physical) disease is a neutral natural occurrence that need not, and should not, be burdened with cultural and moral meanings.

7   See Ots (1994) for a useful introduction to the German concept of *Leib* – a term that has no equivalent in English. The term is widely used in the work of the German phenomenologists and 'refers to the living body, to my body with feelings, sensations, perceptions, and emotions' (1994: 116).

8   For a compelling analysis of what does or does not count as *material*, and how this is defined in relation to gender and class, see Lawler (2000).

9   As Rosemary Hennessey notes, the human labour that is 'materially embodied in [commodities]...is not visible in the objects themselves as a physical property' (1995: 161). The material, in other words, exceeds the physical, tangible, 'seeable' object.

REFERENCES

Adkins, A. and Lury, C. (2000) 'Making bodies, making people, making work', in L. McKie and N. Watson (eds), *Organising Bodies: Institutions, Policy and Work*, Basingstoke: Macmillan.

Ahmed, S. (1996) 'Tanning the body: skin, colour and gender'. Paper presented at Lancaster Women's Studies Dayschool on 'Passsing.' See also however Ahmed, S. (1998) 'Animated borders: skin, colour and tanning', in M. Shildrick and J. Price (eds), *Vital Signs: Feminist Configurations of the Bio/logical Body*, Edinburgh: Edinburgh University Press.

Baker, G. and Morris, K. J. (1996) *Descartes' Dualism*, London and New York: Routledge.

Barry, A. (2004) 'Pharmaceutical matters: the invention of informed materials', *Theory, Culture and Society*, forthcoming.

Baumeister, R. F. (1987) 'How the self became a problem: a psychological review of historical research', *Journal of Personality and Social Psychology* 52: 163–76.

Beauchamp, T. L. and Childress, J. F. (1994) *Principles of Biomedical Ethics*, 4th edition, Oxford and New York: Oxford University Press.

Birke, L. (1994) *Feminism, Animals and Science: The Naming of the Shrew*, Buckingham: Open University Press.

Birke, L., Brown, N. and Michael, M. (1998) 'The heart of the matter: animal bodies, ethics and species boundaries', *Society and Animals* 6: 245–61.

Bordo, S. (1995) *Unbearable Weight: Feminism, Western Culture, and the Body*, Berkeley, Los Angeles, London: University of California.

Borens, R., Grosse-Schulte, E., Jaensch, W. and Kortemme, K. H. (1977) 'Is "alexithymia" but a social phenomenon?', *Psychotherapy and Psychosomatics* 28: 193–8.

Bowlby, R. (1985) *Just Looking: Consumer Culture in Dreiser, Gissing and Zola*, New York and London: Methuen.

Braidotti, R. (1989) 'The politics of ontological difference', in T. Brennan (ed.), *Between Feminism and Psychoanalysis*, London and New York: Routledge.

Braidotti, R. (1994) *Nomadic Subjects: Embodiment and Sexual Difference in Contemporary Feminist Theory*, New York: Columbia University Press.

Braun, M. (1992) *Picturing Time: The Work of Etienne-Jules Marey (1830–1904)*. Chicago: University of Chicago Press.

Brody, H. (1997) 'Who gets to tell the story? Narrative in postmodern bioethics', in H. Nelson Lindemann (ed.), *Stories and Their Limits: Narrative Approaches to Bioethics*, New York and London: Routledge.

Brody, H. (2003) *Stories of Sickness*, New York and Oxford: Oxford University Press.

Burchell, G., Gordon, C. and Miller, P. (eds) (1991) *The Foucault Effect: Studies in Governmentality*, Brighton: Harvester Wheatsheaf.

Butler, J. (1990) *Gender Trouble: Feminism and the Subversion of Identity*, London and New York: Routledge.

Canguilhem, G. (1989) *The Normal and the Pathological*, New York: Zone.

Canguilhem, G. (1992) 'Machine and organism', in J. Crary and S. Kwinter (eds), *Incorporations*, New York: Zone.

Canguilhem, G. (2002) 'La santé: concept vulgaire et question philosophique', in *Ecrits sur la médecine*, Paris: Editions du Seuil.

Chiozza, L. (1998a) *Hidden Affects in Somatic Disorders*, Madison, Conn.: Psychosocial Press.

Chiozza, L. (1998b) *Why Do We Fall Ill? The Story Hiding in the Body*, Madison, Conn.: Psychosocial Press.

Clark, D. (1993) 'Commodity Lesbianism', in H. Abelove *et al.* (eds), *The Lesbian and Gay Studies Reader*, London: Routledge.

Cockburn, C. (1981) 'The material of male power', *Feminist Review* 9: 41–58.

Collins, R. (1990) 'Stratification, emotional energy, and the transient emotions', in T. D. Kemper (ed.), *Research Agendas in the Sociology of Emotions,* Albany: State University of New York Press.

Coward, R. (1989) *The Whole Truth: The Myth of Alternative Medicine,* London: Faber and Faber.

de Beauvoir, S. (1988) *The Second Sex*, London: Picador.

Debord, G. (1977) *The Society of the Spectacle*, Detroit: Black and Red Press.

Descartes, R. (1985) *The Philosophical Writings of Descartes*, 2 vols. Cambridge: Cambridge University Press.

Descartes, R. (1991) *The Philosophical Writings of Descartes*, 3rd vol. with Anthony Kenny. Cambridge: Cambridge University Press.

Deutsch, F. (1959) *On the Mysterious Leap from the Mind to the Body: A Workshop Study on the Theory of Conversion*, New York: International Universities Press.

Diprose, R. (1991) 'A "genethics" that makes sense', in R. Diprose and R. Ferrell (eds), *Cartographies – Poststructuralism and the Mapping of Bodies and Spaces*, Sydney: Allen & Unwin.

Donzelot, J. (1979) *The Policing of Families*, London: Random House.

Dreyfus, H. L. (2001) *On the Internet*, London and New York: Routledge.

Dyer, R. (1988) 'White' *Screen* 29, 4: 44–64.

Dyer, R. (1997) *White*, London: Routledge.

Eagleton, T. (1990) The *Ideology of the Aesthetic*, Oxford: Basil Blackwell.

Edwards, T. (1997) *Men in the Mirror: Men's Fashion, Masculinity and Consumer Society*, London: Cassell.

Elias, N. (1991) *The Society of Individuals*, Oxford: Basil Blackwell.

Elias, N. (1994) 'Synopsis', in *The Civilizing Process*, Oxford: Blackwell.

Elias, N. (1998a) 'Civilization and rationalization', in J. Goudsblom and S. Mennell (eds), *The Norbert Elias Reader*, Oxford: Blackwell.

Elias, N. (1998b) 'An interview in Amsterdam', in J. Goudsblom and S. Mennell (eds), *The Norbert Elias Reader*, Oxford: Blackwell.

Engel, G. L. (1981) 'The need for a new medical model: a challenge for biomedicine', in H. T. Engelhardt, A. L. Kaplan and J. McCartney (eds), *Concepts of Health and Disease*, London: Addison.

Fabrega, I. (1990) 'The concept of somatization as a cultural and historical product of Western medicine', *Psychosomatic Medicine* 52: 653–72.

Featherstone, M. (1982) 'The Body in Consumer Culture', *Theory, Culture and Society* 1, 2: 18–33. Also reprinted in Featherstone, M., Hepworth, M. and Turner, B. S. (eds) (1991), *The Body: Social Process and Cultural Theory*, London: Sage.

Featherstone, M. (1991) *Consumer Culture and Postmodernism*, London: Sage.

Featherstone, M., Hepworth, M., and Turner, B. S. (1991) *The Body: Social Process and Cultural Theory*, London: Sage.

Ferenczi, S. (1955) *Final Contributions to the Problems and Methods of Psychoanalysis*, New York: Basic Books.

Fitzgerald, F. T. (1994) 'The tyranny of health', *New England Journal of Medicine* 331: 196–8.

Foster, S. L. (1995) *Corporealities: Dancing Knowledge, Culture and Power*, London and New York: Routledge.

Foucault, M. (1973) *The Birth of the Clinic*, London: Routledge.

Foucault, M. (1979) *Discipline and Punish: The Birth of the Prison*, London: Peregrine.

Foucault, M. (1980) 'The politics of health in the eighteenth century', in C. Gordon (ed.), *Power/Knowledge*, Brighton: Harvester.

Foucault, M. (1986) *The Use of Pleasure: The History of Sexuality,* vol. 2, London: Penguin.

Foucault, M. (1988) 'Technologies of the self', in L. H. Martin, H. Gutman and P. H. Hutton (eds), *Technologies of the Self: A Seminar with Michel Foucault*, London: Tavistock.

Foucault, M. (1988a) 'The ethic of care of the self as a practice of freedom', in J. Bernauer and D. Rasmussen (eds), *The Final Foucault*, Cambridge, Mass.: MIT Press.

Foucault, M. (1988b) *The Care of the Self: The History of Sexuality,* vol. 3, London: Penguin.

Foucault, M. (1989) *Madness and Civilization*, London: Routledge.

Fox Keller, E. (1992) *Secrets of Life, Secrets of Death: Essays on Language, Gender and Science*, New York: Routledge.

Frank, A. (1990) 'Bringing bodies back in: a decade review', *Theory, Culture and Society* 7: 131–62.

Frank, A. (1995) *The Wounded Storyteller*, Chicago: University of Chicago Press.

Franklin, S. (2000) 'Life itself: global nature and the genetic imaginary', in S. Franklin, C. Lury and J. Stacey (eds), *Global Nature, Global Culture*, London: Sage.

Fraser, M., Kember, S. and Lury, C. (2004) *Material processes/virtual life*, Special issue of Theory, Culture and Society.

Freud, S. (1985 [1930]) 'Civilization and Its Discontents', in S. Freud. *Civilization, Society and Religion*, Pelican Freud Library, vol. 12, London: Penguin Books.

Freund, P. (1988) 'Bringing society into the body', *Theory and Society* 17: 839–64.

Fuss, D. (1990) *Essentially Speaking: Feminism, Nature and Difference*, London: Routledge.

Gatens, M. (1996) *Imaginary Bodies: Ethics, Power and Corporeality*, London and New York: Routledge.

Giddens, A. (1991) *Modernity and Self-Identity: Self and Society in the Late Modern Age*, Cambridge: Polity Press.

Giddens, A. (1991a) *The Transformation of Intimacy: Sexuality, Love, and Eroticism in Modern Societies*, Stanford, California: Stanford University Press.

Goffman, E. (1963) *Stigma*, New York: Simon & Schuster.

Gordon, R. A. (1990) *Anorexia and Bulimia: Anatomy of a Social Epidemic*, New York: Blackwell.

Groddeck, G. (1977) *The Meaning of Illness*, London: Karnac Books.

Grosz, E. (1995) 'Sexual difference and the problem of essentialism', in *Space, Time and Perversion*, London: Routledge.

Hacking, I. (1990) *The Taming of Chance*, Cambridge: Cambridge University Press.

Hacking, I. (1998) 'Canguilhem amid the cyborgs', *Economy and Society* 27, 2+3: 202–16.

Halley, J. E. (1994) 'Critiquing immutability', *Stanford Law Review* 46: 503–68.

Haraway, D. (1989) *Primate Visions: Gender, Race, and Nature in the World of Modern Science*, New York and London: Routledge.

Haraway, D. (1991) *Simians, Cyborgs, and Women: The Reinvention of Nature*, London: Free Association Books.

Haraway, D. (1997) *Modest_Witness@Second_Millennium.FemaleMan©_Meets_OncoMouse*™, New York and London: Routledge.

Haraway, D. (2000) *How Like a Leaf: An Interview with Thyrza Nichols Goodeve*, New York and London: Routledge.

Harding, S. (1986) *The Science Question in Feminism*, Ithaca, New York: Cornell University Press.

Hayles, K. N. (1999) *How We Became Posthuman: Virtual Bodies in Cybernetics, Literature, and Informatics*, Chicago: University of Chicago Press.

Hennessey, R. (1995) 'Queer visibility in commodity culture', in L. Nicholson and S. Seidman (eds), *Social Postmodernism: Beyond Identity Politics*, Cambridge: Cambridge University Press.

Illich, I. (1977) *Medical Nemesis*, New York: Pantheon Books.

Irigaray, L. (1984) *Ethique de la Difference Sexuelle*, Paris: Minuit.

Jay, M. (1994) *Downcast Eyes: The Denigration of Vision in Twentieth-Century French Thought*, Berkeley: University of California Press.

Jameson, F. (1985) 'Postmodernism and consumer culture', in H. Foster (ed.), *Postmodern Culture*, London: Pluto.

Jewson, N. (1976) 'The disappearance of the sick man from medical cosmology, 1770–1870', *Sociology* 10: 225–44.

Jordanova, L. J. (1989) *Sexual Visions: Images of Gender in Science and Medicine between the Eighteenth and Twentieth Centuries*, New York and London: Harvester Wheatsheaf.

Kay, L. (1995) 'Who wrote the book of life? Information and the transformation of molecular biology, 1945–55', *Science in Context* 8, 4: 609–34.

Kay, L. (1997) 'Cybernetics, information, life: The emergence of scriptural representations of heredity', *Configurations* 5: 23–91.

Kemper, T. D. (1984) 'Power, status, and emotions: a sociological contribution to a psychophysiological domain', in K. Scherer and P. Ekman (eds), *Approaches to Emotion*, Hillsdale, N. J.: Erlbaum.

Kirby, V. (1997) *Telling Flesh: The Substance of the Corporeal*, New York and London: Routledge.

Kirmayer, L. J. (1987) 'Languages of suffering and healing: alexithymia as a social and cultural process', *Transcultural Psychiatric Research Review* 24: 119–36.

Kirmayer, L. J. *et al.* (1994) 'Somatoform disorders: personality and the social matrix of somatic distress', *Journal of Abnormal Psychology* 103: 125–36.

Kleinman, A. (1986) *Social Origins of Distress and Disease*, New Haven: Yale University Press.

Kleinman, A. and Good, G. (eds) (1985) *Culture and Depression*, Berkeley: University of California Press.

Latour, B. (1993) *We Have Never Been Modern*, Translated by Catherine Porter. London and New York: Harvester Wheatsheaf.

Latour, B. (1994) 'On technical mediation: philosophy, sociology, genealogy', *Common Knowledge* 3, 2: 29–64.

Lawler, S. (2000) 'Escape and escapism: representing working class women', in S. Munt (ed.), *Cultural Studies and the Working Class*, London: Cassell.

Lessnoff, M. (ed.) (1990) *Social Contract Theory*, New York: New York University Press.

Lemert, E. M. (1967) *Human Deviance, Social Problems and Social Control*, Englewood Cliffs, NJ: Prentice Hall.

Lindemann N. H. (ed.) (1997) *Stories and Their Limits*, New York and London: Routledge.

Lury, C. (1996) *Consumer Culture*, New Brunswick, NJ: Rutgers University Press.

Mackenzie, A. (2002) *Transductions: Bodies and Machines at Speed*, London and New York: Continuum.

Maffesoli, M. (1991) 'The ethic of aesthetics', *Theory, Culture and Society* 8: 7–21.

McDougall, J. (1989) *Theatres of the Body*, London: Free Association Books.

McNay, L. (1994) *Foucault: A Critical Introduction*, Cambridge: Polity.

Mercer, K. (1990) 'Black hair/style politics', in R. Ferguson, M. Gever, T. T. Minh-ha and C. West (eds), *Out There: Marginalisation and Contemporary Cultures*, Cambridge, Mass.: MIT Press.

Merchant, C. (1990) *The Death of Nature: Women, Ecology and the Scientific Revolution*, San Francisco: Harper.

Michael, M. (2000) *Reconnecting Culture, Technology and Nature: From Society to Heterogeniety*, London and New York: Routledge.

Mirza, H. S. (1997) 'Introduction: mapping a genealogy of Black British feminism', in H. S. Mirza (ed.), *Black British Feminism: A Reader*, London and New York: Routledge.

Nussbaum, M. (1990) *Love's Knowledge: Essays on Philosophy and Literature*, New York: Oxford University Press.

O'Neill, J. (1985) *Five Bodies: The Human Shape of Modern Society*, Ithaca: Cornell University Press.

Osborne, T. (1992) 'Medicine and epistemology: Michel Foucault's archaeology of clinical reason', *History of the Human Sciences* 5: 63–93.

Osborne, T. (1996) 'Body amnesia: comments on corporeality', in D. Owen (ed.), *Sociology After Postmodernism*, London: Sage.

Ots, T. (1990) 'The angry liver, the anxious heart, and the melancholy spleen: the phenomenology of perceptions in Chinese culture', *Culture, Medicine and Psychiatry* 14: 21–58.

Ots, T. (1994) 'The silenced body – the expressive *Leib*: on the dialectic of mind and life in Chinese cathartic healing', in T. J. Csordas (ed.), *Embodiment and Experience: The Existential Ground of Culture and Self*, Cambridge: Cambridge University Press.

Oudshoorn, N. (1994) *Beyond the Natural Body: An Archaeology of Sex Hormones*, London and New York: Routledge.

Parsons, T. (1968 [1937]) *The structure of social action: a study in social theory, with special reference to a group of recent European writers*, New York: Free Press.

Parsons, T. (1951) 'Illness and the role of the physician', *American Journal of Orthopsychiatry* 21: 452–60.

Phelan, P. (1993) *Unmarked: The Politics of Performance*, London: Routledge.

Plant, S. (1992) *The Most Radical Gesture*, London: Routledge.

Posse, M. and Hallstrom, T. (1999) 'The prevalence of alexithymia in primary care patients', *European Journal of Psychiatry* 13: 5–11.

Poster, M. (1992) 'Robocop', in J. Crary and S. Kwinter (eds), *Incorporations*, New York: Zone.

Reiser, S. J. (1978) *Medicine and the Reign of Technology*, Cambridge: Cambridge University Press.

Rose, N. (1989) *Governing the Soul: The Shaping of the Private Self*, London: Routledge.

Rose, N. (1998) *Inventing Our Selves: Psychology, Power, and Personhood*, Cambridge: Cambridge University Press.

Rose, S. (1998) *Lifelines: Biology, Freedom, Determinism*, London: Penguin.

Saalfield, C. and Navarro, R. (1991) 'Shocking pink praxis: race and gender on the ACT UP frontlines', in D. Fuss (ed.), *Inside/Out*, London: Routledge.

Salminen, J. K., Saarijärvi, S., Äärelä, E., Toikka, T., and Kauhanen, J. (1999) 'Prevalence of alexithymia and its association with sociodemographic variables in the general population of Finland', *Journal of Psychosomatic Research* 46: 75–82.

Sandford, S. (1999) 'Contingent ontologies: sex, gender and "woman" in Simone de Beauvoir and Judith Butler', *Radical Philosophy* 97: 18–29.

Scheff, T. (1997) *Emotions, the Social Bond, and Human Reality*, Cambridge: Cambridge University Press.

Sedgwick, E. K. (1991) *The Epistemology of the Closet*, Hemel Hempstead: Harvester Wheatsheaf.

Shapin, S. (1998) 'The philosopher and the chicken: on the dietetics of disembodied knowledge', in C. Lawrence and S. Shapin (eds), *Science Incarnate: Historical Embodiments of Natural Knowledge*, Chicago and London: University of Chicago Press.

Shilling, C. (1993) *The Body and Social Theory*, London: Sage.

Shorter, E. (1992) *From Paralysis to Fatigue: A History of Psychosomatic Illness in the Modern Era*, New York: Free Press.

Slater, D. (2003) 'Cultures of consumption', in K. Anderson, M. Domosh, S. Pile and N. Thrift (eds), *Handbook of Cultural Geography*, London: Sage.

Sontag, S. (1978) *Illness as Metaphor*, New York: Farrar, Straus & Giroux.

Stacey, J. (1997) *Teratologies: A Cultural Study of Cancer*, London and New York: Routledge.

Stallybrass, P. and White, A. (1986) *Politics and Poetics of Transgression*, London: Menthuen.

Stengers, I. (1997) *Power and Invention*, Minneapolis/London: University of Minnesota Press.

Stengers, I. (2000) *The Invention of Modern Science*, Minneapolis/London: University of Minnesota Press.

Stengers, I. (2002) 'Beyond conversation: the risks of peace', in C. Keller and A. Daniell (eds), *Process and Difference: Between Cosmological and Poststructuralist Postmodernisms*, Albany: State University of New York Press.

Stevenson, L. (1981) *The Study of Human Nature – Readings*, Selected and introduced by Stevenson, L., New York and Oxford: Oxford University Press.

Synnott, A. (1993) *The Body Social: Symbolism, Self and Society*, London: Routledge.

Szasz, T. (1974) *The Myth of Mental Illness*, New York: Harper & Row.

Taylor, G. J. (1987) *Psychosomatic Medicine and Contemporary Psychoanalysis*, Madison, Ill.: International Universities Press.

Thacker, A. (1993) 'Foucault's aesthetics of existence', *Radical Philosophy* 63: 13–21.

Thomas, H. (2003) *The Body, Dance and Cultural Theory*, Palgrave Macmillan.

Turner, B. (1984) *The Body and Society: Explorations in Social Theory*, Oxford: Blackwell.

Turner, B. (1996) *The Body and Society*, Second edition. London: Sage.

Tyler, C.-A. (1994) 'Passing: narcissism, identity, and difference', *Differences: A Journal of Feminist Cultural Studies* 6, 2+3: 212–48.

Walker, L. (1993) 'How to recognize a lesbian: the cultural politics of looking like what are', *Signs: Journal of Women in Culture and Society* 18, 4: 866–91.

Whitehead, A. N. (1938) *Modes of Thought*, Cambridge: Cambridge University Press.

Willis, S. (1990) 'I want the black one: is there a place for afro-american culture in commodity culture?', *New Formations* 10: 77–97.

Wilson, E. A. (1998) *Neural Geographies: Feminism and the Microstructure of Cognition*, New York and London: Routledge.

Wilson, E. A. (1999) 'Introduction: somatic compliance – feminism, biology and science', *Australian Feminist Studies* 14, 29: 7–18.

Wolin, R. (1986) 'Foucault's aesthetic decisionism', *Telos*. 67: 71–110.

PART ONE

What is a body?

INTRODUCTION

THE BODY READER OPENS with Elizabeth Grosz's summary of the some of the
principal ways in which Western philosophical traditions have shaped contemporary
conceptions of the body. Each of the texts that follow in this section are informed by that
inheritance but also, importantly, seek to challenge it. Grosz's piece begins by addressing
the somatophobia that underpins the distinction between bodies and minds, and which
constitutes the body as a 'danger' to reason. She briefly traces this legacy in Plato,
Aristotle and in the Christian tradition. In each case, the body/mind dualism maps onto
other binaries, such as mother (woman) and father (man), matter and form, mortal and
immortal. Importantly, Grosz also shows how Cartesianism, by separating the mind from
nature and the world, established a scientific discourse premised on impersonality and
objectivity. This premise continues to shape the biological and medical sciences, as well as
the human and social sciences. It is an assumption that makes it particularly difficult to
address the important question of the relations between 'two apparently incompossible
substances', the body and mind. Reductionism cannot help here, Grosz argues, for it only
inverts the hierarchy such that the mind is understood in terms of the body (most commonly, today, in terms of the brain). In this way the interaction between the two is
explained *away*, rather than explained. Indeed each of the heirs of Cartesianism that
Grosz examines fail, she claims, to account for the complexity of the body, its corporeality and its agency. This is a piece that lays down the gauntlet.

Merleau-Ponty's contribution is fundamental, for he seeks neither to privilege body
over mind, nor to unify them in an overarching theory. Instead, he exploits the concepts
of experience and perception in order to illustrate that the body is never *either* a subject *or*
an object, mind *or* body, transcendental *or* immanent. For Merleau-Ponty, knowledge of
one's own body and knowledge of the world can be accessed only *through* the body. This

is what he seeks to address: the experience of the body, and the way that the body shapes experience. In the extract we have chosen here, taken from the classic text *Phenomenology of Perception* (originally published in 1945), Merleau-Ponty pursues this issue by exploring and contesting the notion that the body is an object like any other. For the body is *not* an object, he argues, but is rather the condition through which it is possible to have relations *with* objects, with, that is, the world. Importantly, this conception of the body also changes the meaning of 'world': no longer a collection of determinate things, Merleau-Ponty argues, it is instead a 'horizon' that is 'latent in all our experience'. Or to put that differently: the body's relations with the world are not those of cause and effect but are rather the result of meanings, meanings which cannot be solely explained by either psychology or physiology. One of the key implications of this argument is that the individual body cannot be considered to be a strictly atomistic and bounded entity; it is not neatly divided off from the world. It is impossible to stand back from the world, and to look at it from 'the outside', because it is impossible to stand outside of one's own body. I cannot get an outside perspective *on* my body, for it is the vehicle through which my perspective comes into being. Our relationships with objects, and with our own bodies, are therefore always partial. We cannot know them absolutely.

Where Merleau-Ponty interrogates the notion of permanence in relation to objects, Hans Jonas discusses endurance in relation to the identity of a living thing. Both proceed with reference to the relation between the individual body and the external world – or, in Jonas's vocabulary, the environment. For Jonas this relation, of both independence *and* dependence, is crucial. It is a defining property of life, marking out the difference between 'mere' substance and organic matter. How so? Jonas begins with a question to ontology: 'How does an ordinary physical thing … endure?' And he answers: it does not endure simply by being the same thing over time. On the contrary, if a biologist were to find that a body *was* the same over a period of time, if it was found to be have identical components, then it would most likely be considered to be a corpse. The question mark that hangs over the difference between a corpse and a living body exemplifies Jonas's compelling take on issues that theorists have asked of the body again and again: how is it possible to reconcile (if reconciliation is what is required) the fact that the identity of a living entity is *not* reducible to its component parts, and yet is at the same time 'grounded in transactions' among them? Those transactions, moreover, do not occur only within the bounded limits of the body 'itself'. A living thing, Jonas reminds his reader, is always exchanging matter with its environment. Indeed it *depends* on this exchange, a fact which serves to qualify or anchor any notion of an absolute independence from matter: 'the freedom which the living thing enjoys', Jonas writes, 'is rather a stern *necessity*'. This, he concludes, is what is unique to a living entity: its active dependence upon the environment. 'Doing' is what is required 'to be' – the possibility of doing, a possibility which is always haunted by the possibility of *not* doing (of ceasing to be, of death). Life, Jonas concludes, is 'at the mercy of its own performance'.

Perhaps one of the most important aspects of the piece we have included by Gilles Deleuze is that it challenges any notion of the body as a bounded corporeality endowed with an origin, interiority and depth. The body, for Deleuze, is not a unified entity, nor is it organised around a central governor. It is not defined by intentionality, biology or by a psyche. It is not a property of the subject, nor is it an expression of subjectivity. It is not a locus of meaning. Indeed, a body is not to be deciphered or interpreted at all. Instead, the convergences between bodies (whether they be human or non-human, organic or not, natural or artificial) are there to be made and surveyed: mapped. For Deleuze is a cartographer, who situates all bodies on the same, flat, ontological plane (the plane of immanence), and defines them by what he calls longitude and latitude. Drawing on Spinoza, Deleuze argues that a body must be understood not in terms of a form or functions, but with reference instead to its relations of speed and slowness (longitude), and to what it can *do*, by its capacity to affect and to be affected (latitude).

This understanding of bodies cuts across genus and species. On the basis of its affective capacities, the plough horse, for instance, is found to have more in common with the ox than it does with the race horse. A body is not a 'thing', but a becoming, a series of processes, movements, intensities and flows. It is a mobile assemblage of connections which might be extended, but which might equally be severed. This is one of the exciting aspects of Deleuze's ethology. To define a body by its affective capacities means that 'you do not know beforehand of what good or bad you are capable; you do not know beforehand what a body or a mind can do, in a given encounter'. *In a given encounter* is a vital qualifier here. For what a body can do will depend upon its relations with 'the world' (relations which are, like the boundaries of a body itself, necessarily contingent). In this respect, Deleuze's ethology is also an ethics, an ethics which turns on the question of whether, in a particular set of circumstances (or rather, a particular set of connections), a body's capacities will be increased or diminished, and its relations of speed accelerated or slowed down. Importantly, once again, there is no privileged sphere (such as 'nature' or 'culture' for example) in relation to which that potentiality or capacity can or should unfold.

If Judith Butler and Gilles Deleuze have anything in common, it is perhaps that they both conceive of bodies in terms of *processes*. For Butler, however, the process of materialisation is highly constrained. It is limited by regulatory norms, and especially by the norm of heterosexuality which 'ontologizes and fixes that gendered matrix in its place' (Butler 1993: 29). This is where we end the first Part of the Reader, appropriately enough, with an extract from a book that is in large part a response to 'those whose patience with constructionist arguments is close to exhaustion' (Kirby 1997: 105). Interestingly, *Bodies that Matter* is also intended as a clarification of Butler's *own* use of the term 'construction' in the earlier *Gender Trouble* (1990), in which she claims that she 'overrode the category of sex too quickly' (Butler in Sandford 1999: 26). The result is neither a theory of the cultural construction of gender, nor of 'the materiality of sex'. Instead, Butler writes of the 'sex of materiality', in which 'materiality [is] the site at which a certain drama of sexual difference plays itself out' (Butler 1993: 49).

In order to negotiate the tension between a critique of constructionist positions on the one hand, and a recognition on the other that without direct access to 'facticity' any conception of matter is necessarily interpretative, Butler suggests a 'return' to a differently figured conception of matter 'not as a surface or site', but rather 'as a process of materialization that stabilises over time to produce the effect of boundary, fixity, and surface we call matter' (emphasis omitted). Matter will no longer refer to an inert substance or a blank slab upon which discourse inscribes itself, but is instead a process which itself constitutes the static 'matter' of bodies. Crucially, *as* a process, materialization must necessarily be temporal. Matter does not 'exist' in and of itself, for *all* time, but is instead repeatedly produced *over* time through performativity (performativity is that which brings into being or enacts what it names). While it may therefore seem certain that 'I am a woman', this identity is in fact never fixed, and is always unstable. The subject may *appear* to have 'an identity', an identity which is resolutely written on the body, but this is only because reiteration 'conceals or dissimulates the conventions of which it is a repetition' (Butler 1993: 12).

The contributions in this section offer demanding and sometimes provocative reformulations of some of the more conventional and perhaps intuitive understandings of what a body 'is'. If these pieces are challenging, it is surely because they are faced with the hardest of tasks: engaging with and contesting the legacy of dualisms that haunt Western philosophy. Each of these texts, in their different (and more or less explicit) ways, have implications for the relations between 'nature' and 'culture', substance and matter, mind and body, and subject and object. These are among the most important themes that will be recurring in different contexts throughout the Body Reader.

REFERENCES

Butler, J. (1990) *Gender Trouble: Feminism and the Subversion of Identity*, London and New York: Routledge.

Butler, J. (1993) *Bodies that Matter: On the Discursive Limits of 'Sex'*, London and New York: Routledge.

Kirby, V. (1997) *Telling Flesh: The Substance of the Corporeal*, New York and London: Routledge.

Sandford, S. (1999) 'Contingent ontologies: sex, gender and "woman" in Simone de Beauvoir and Judith Butler', *Radical Philosophy* 97: 18–29.

Chapter 1

Elizabeth Grosz

REFIGURING BODIES

From E. Grosz (1994) *Volatile Bodies,* Bloomington: Indiana University Press.

Philosophy and the body

SINCE THE INCEPTION OF PHILOSOPHY as a separate and self-contained discipline in ancient Greece, philosophy has established itself on the foundations of a profound somatophobia. While I cannot here preset an adequate or detailed discussion of the role of the body in the history of philosophy, I can at least indicate in a brief sketch some of the key features of the received history that we have inherited in our current conceptions of bodies. The body has been regarded as a source of interference in, and a danger to, the operations of reason. In the *Cratylus*, Plato claims that the word body (*soma*) was introduced by Orphic priests, who believed that man was a spiritual or noncorporeal being trapped in the body as in a dungeon (*sēma*). In his doctrine of the Forms, Plato sees matter itself as a denigrated ad imperfect version of the Idea. The body is a betrayal of and a prison for the soul, reason, or mind. For Plato, it was evident that reason should rule over the body and over the irrational or appetitive functions of the soul. A kind of natural hierarchy, a self-evident ruler–ruled relation, alone makes possible a harmony within the state, the family, and the individual. Here we have one of the earliest representations of the body politic. Aristotle, in continuing a tradition possibly initiated by Plato in his account of *chora* in *Timaeus* where maternity is regarded as a mere housing, receptacle, or nurse of being rather than a co-producer, distinguished matter or body from form, and in the case of reproduction, he believed that the mother provided the formless, passive, shapeless matter which, through the father, was given form, shape, and contour, specific features and attributes it otherwise lacked. The binarization of the sexes, the dichotomization of the world and of knowledge has been effected already at he threshold of Western reason.

The matter/form distinction is refigured in terms of the distinction between substance and accident and between a God-given soul and a mortal, lustful, sinful carnality. Within the Christian tradition, the separation of mind and body was correlated with the distinction between what is immortal and what is mortal. As long as the subject is alive, mind and soul form an indissoluble unity, which is perhaps best exemplified in the figure of Christ himself. Christ was a man whose soul, whose immortality, is derived from God but whose body and mortality is human. The living soul is, in fact, a part of the world, and above all, a part of nature. Within Christian doctrine, it is as an experiencing, suffering, passionate being that generic man exists. This is why moral characteristics were given to various physiological disorders and why punishments and rewards for one's soul are administered through corporeal pleasures and punishments. For example, in the Middle Ages, leprosy was regarded as the diseased consequence of lechery ad covetousness, a corporeal signifier of sin.

What Descartes accomplished was not really the separation of mind from body (a separation which had already been long anticipated in Greek philosophy since the time of Plato) but the separation of soul from nature. Descartes distinguished two kinds of substances: a thinking substance (*res cogitans*, mind) from an extended substance (*res extensa*, body); only the latter, he believed, could be considered part of nature, governed by its physical laws and ontological exigencies. The body is a self-moving machine, a mechanical device, functioning according to causal laws and the laws of nature. The mind, the thinking substance, the soul, or consciousness, has no place in the natural world. This exclusion of the soul from nature, this evacuation of consciousness from the world, is the prerequisite for founding a knowledge, or better, a science, of the governing principles of nature, a science which excludes and is indifferent to considerations of the subject. Indeed, the impingements of subjectivity will, from Descartes's time on, mitigate the status and value of scientific formulations. Scientific discourse aspires to impersonality, which it takes to be equivalent to objectivity. The correlation of our ideas with the world or the reality they represent is a secondary function, independent of the existence of consciousness, the primary, indubitable self-certainty of the soul. Reality can be attained by the subject only indirectly, by inference, deduction, or projection. Descartes, in short, succeeded in linking the mind/body opposition to the foundations of knowledge itself, a link which places the mind in a position of hierarchical superiority over and above nature, including the nature of the body. From that time until the present, subject or consciousness is separated from and can reflect on the world of the body, objects, qualities.

Dualism

Descartes instituted a dualism which three centuries of philosophical thought have attempted to overcome or reconcile. Dualism is the assumption that there are two distinct, mutually exclusive and mutually exhaustive substances, mind and body, each of which inhabits its own self-contained sphere. Taken together the two have incompatible characteristics. The major problem facing dualism and all those positions aimed at overcoming dualism has been to explain the interactions of these two apparently incompossible substances, given that, within experience and everyday life, there seems to be a manifest connection between the two in willful behavior and responsive psychical reactions. How can something that inhabits space affect or be affected by something that is nonspatial? How can consciousness ensure the body's movements, its receptivity to conceptual demands and requirements? How can the body inform the mind of its needs and wishes? How is bilateral communication possible? Dualism not only poses irresolvable philosophical problems; it is also at least indirectly responsible for the historical separation of the natural sciences from the social sciences and humanities, the separation of physiology from psychology, of quantitative analysis from qualitative analysis, and the privileging of mathematics and physics as ideal models of the goals and aspirations of knowledges of all types. Dualism, in short, is responsible for the modern forms of elevation of consciousness (a specifically modern version of the notion of soul, introduced by Descartes) above corporeality.

This separation, of course, has its costs. Since the time Descartes, not only is consciousness positioned outside of the world, outside its body, outside of nature; it is also removed from direct contact with other minds and a sociocultural community. At its extreme, all that consciousness can be sure about is its own self-certain existence. The existence of other minds must be inferred from the apparent existence of other bodies. If minds are private, subjective, invisible, amenable only to first-person knowledge, we can have no guarantee that our inferences about other minds are in fact justified. Other bodies may simply be complex automata, androids or even illusions, with no psychical interior, no affective states or consciousness. Consciousness becomes, in effect, an island unto itself. Its relations to others, to the world, and its own body are the consequences of mediated judgments, inferences, and are no longer understood as direct and unmediated.

Cartesian dualism establishes an unbridgeable gulf between mind and matter, a gulf most easily disavowed, however problematically, by reductionism. To reduce either the mind to the body or the body to the mind is to leave their interaction unexplained, explained away, impossible. Reductionism denies any interaction between mind and body, for it focuses on the actions of either one of the binary terms at the expense of the other. Rationalism and idealism are the results of the attempt to explain the body and matter in terms of mind, ideas, or reason; empiricism and materialism are the results of attempts to explain the mind in terms of bodily experiences or matter (today most commonly the mind is equated with the brain or central nervous system). Both forms of reductionism assert that either one or the other of the binary terms is "really" its opposite and can be explained by or translated into the terms of its other.

There are not only good philosophical but also good physiological reasons for rejecting reductionism as a solution to the dualist dilemma. As soon as the terms are defined in mutually exclusive ways, there is no way of reconciling them, no way of understanding their mutual influences or explaining their apparent parallelism. Moreover, attempts to correlate ideas or mental processes with neurological functions have thus far failed, and the project itself seems doomed.

Cartesianism

There are at least three lines of investigation of the body in contemporary thought which may be regarded as the heirs of Cartesianism. [...]

In the first line of investigation, the body is primarily regarded as an object for the natural sciences, particularly for the life sciences, biology and medicine; and conversely, the body is amenable to the humanities and social sciences, particularly psychology (when, for example, the discipline deals with "emotions," "sensations," "experiences," and "attitudes"), philosophy (when, for example, it deals with the body's ontological and epistemological status and implications), and ethnography (where, for example, the body's cultural variability, its various social transformations, are analyzed). The body either is understood in terms of organic and instrumental functioning in the natural sciences or is posited as *merely* extended, *merely* physical, an object like any other in the humanities and social sciences. Both, in different ways, ignore the specificity of bodies in their researches.

The more medicalized biologistic view implies a fundamental continuity between man and animals, such that bodies are seen to have a particularly complex form of physiological organization, but one that basically differs from organic matter by degree rather than kind. In a sense, this position is heir to the Christian concept of the human body being part of a natural or mundane order. As an organism, the body is merely a more complex version of other kinds of organic ensembles. It cannot be qualitatively distinguished from other organisms: its physiology poses general questions similar to those raised by animal physiology. The body's sensations, activities, and processes become "lower-order" natural or animal phenomena, part of an interconnected chain of organic forms (whether understood in cosmological or ecological terms). The natural sciences tend to treat the body as an organic system of interrelated parts, which are themselves framed by a larger ecosystemic order. The humanities reduce the body to a fundamental continuity with brute, inorganic matter. Despite their apparent dissimilarity, they share a common refusal to acknowledge the distinctive complexities of organic bodies, the fact that bodies construct and in turn are constructed by an interior, a psychical and a signifying view-point, consciousness or perspective.

The second line of investigation commonly regards the body in terms of metaphors that construe it as an instrument, a tool, or a machine at the disposal of consciousness, a vessel occupied by an animating willful subjectivity. For Locke and the liberal political tradition more generally, the body is seen as a possession, a property of a subject, who is thereby dissociated from carnality and makes decisions and choices about how to dispose of the body ad its powers (in, for example, the labor market). Some models, including Descartes', construe the body as a self-moving automaton, much like a clock, car, or ship (these are pervasive but by no means exclusive images), according to the prevailing modes of technology. This understanding of the body is not unique to patriarchal philosophies but underlies some versions of feminist theory which see patriarchy as the system of universal male right to the appropriation of women's bodies (MacKinnon, Dworkin, Daly, and Pateman), a position that has been strongly criticized by other feminists (e.g. Butler and Cornell). In many feminist political struggles (those, for example, which utilize the old slogan "get your laws off my body") which are openly and self-consciously about women's bodies and their control by women (e.g. campaigns around such issues as sexual harassment and molestation, rape, the control of fertility, etc.), the body is typically regarded as passive and reproductive but largely unproductive, an object over which struggles between its "inhabitant" and others/exploiters may be possible. Whatever agency or will it has is the direct consequence of animating, psychical intentions. Its inertia means that it is capable of being acted on, coerced, or constrained by external forces. (This is not of course to deny that there are real, and frequent, form of abuse and coercive mistreatment of women's bodies under the jealous and mutilating hostility of some men, but rather to suggest that frameworks within which women's bodies must be acknowledged as active, viable, and autonomous must be devised so that these practices can no longer be neatly rationalized or willfully reproduced.) As an instrument or tool, it requires careful discipline and training, and as a passive object it requires subduing and occupation. Such a view also lies behind the models of "conditioning" and "social construction" that are popular in some feminist circles, especially in psychology and sociology (Gilligan, Chodorow).

In the third line of investigation, the body is commonly considered a signifying medium, a vehicle of expression, a mode of rendering public and communicable what is essentially private (ideas, thoughts, beliefs, feelings, affects). As such, it is a two-way conduit: on one hand, it is a circuit for the transmission information from outside the organism, conveyed through the sensory apparatus; on the other hand, it is vehicle for the expression of an otherwise sealed and self-contained, incommunicable psyche. It is through the body that the subject can express his or her interiority, and it is through the body that he or she can receive, code, and translate the inputs of the "external" world. Underlying this view too is a belief in the fundamental passivity and transparency of the body. Insofar as it is seen as a medium, a carrier or bearer of information that comes from elsewhere (either "deep" in the subject's incorporeal interior or from the "exterior" world), the specificity and concreteness of the body must be neutralized, tamed, made to serve other purposes. If the subject is to gain knowledge about the external world, have any chance of making itself understood by others, or be effective in the world on such a model, the body must be seen as an unresistant pliability which minimally distorts information, or at least distorts it in a systematic and comprehensible fashion, so that its effects can be taken into account and information can be correctly retrieved. Its corporeality must be reduced to a predictable, knowable transparency; its constitutive role in forming thoughts, feelings, emotions, and psychic representations must be ignored, as must its role as threshold between the social and the natural.

These seem to be some of the pervasive, unspoken assumptions regarding the body in the history of modern philosophy and in conceptions of knowledge considered more generally.

[…]

Chapter 2

Maurice Merleau-Ponty

THE EXPERIENCE OF THE BODY AND CLASSICAL PSYCHOLOGY

From M. Merleau-Ponty (2002) *Phenomenology of Perception,* London and New York: Routledge.

I N ITS DESCRIPTIONS OF THE BODY from the point of view of the self, classical psychology was already wont to attribute to its 'characteristics' incompatible with the status of an object. In the first place it was stated that my body is distinguishable from the table or the lamp in that I can turn away from the latter whereas my body is constantly perceived. It is therefore an object which does not leave me. But in that case is it still an object? If the object is an invariable structure, it is not one *in spite* of the changes of perspective, but in *that* change or *through* it. It is not the case that ever-renewed perspective simply provide it with opportunities of displaying its permanence, and with contingent ways of presenting itself to us. It is an object, which means that it is standing in front of us, only because it is observable: situated, that is to say, directly under our hand or gaze, indivisibly overthrown and re-integrated with every movement they make. Otherwise it would be true like an idea and not present like a thing. It is particularly true that an object is an object only insofar as it can be moved away from me, and ultimately disappear from my field of vision. Its presence is such that it entails a possible absence. Now the permanence of my own body is entirely different in kind: it is not at the extremity of some indefinite exploration; it defies exploration and is always presented to me from the same angle. Its permanence is not a permanence in the world, but a permanence on my part. To say that it is always near me, always there for me, is to say that it is never really in front of me, that I cannot array it before my eyes, that it remains marginal to all my perceptions, that it is *with* me. It is true that external objects too never turn one of their sides to me without hiding the rest, but I can at least freely choose the side which they are to present to me. They could not appear otherwise than in perspective, but the particular perspective which I acquire at each moment is the outcome of no more than physical necessity, that is to say, of a necessity which I can use and which is not a prison for me: from my window only the tower of the church is visible, but this limitation simultaneously holds out the promise that from elsewhere the whole church could be seen. It is true, moreover, that if I am a prisoner the church will be restricted, for me, to a truncated steeple. If I did not take off my clothes I could never see the inside of them, and it will in fact be seen that my clothes may become appendages of my body. But this fact does not prove that the presence of my body is to be compared to the *de facto* permanence of certain objects, or the organ compared to a tool which is always available. It shows that conversely those actions in which I habitually engage incorporate their instruments into themselves and make them play a part in the original structure of my own body. As for the latter, it is my basic habit, the one which conditions all the others, and by means of which they are mutually comprehensible. Its permanence near to me, its unvarying perspective are not a *de facto* necessity, since such necessity presupposes them: in order that my window may impose upon me a point of view of the church, it is necessary in the first place that my body should impose upon me one of the world; and the first necessity can be merely physical only in virtue of the fact that the second is metaphysical; in short, I am accessible to factual situations only if my nature is such that there are factual situations for me. In other words, I observe external objects with my body, I handle them, examine them, walk round them, but my body itself is a thing, which I do not observe: in order to be able to do so, I should need the use of a second body which itself would be unobservable. When I say that my body is always perceived by me, these words are not to be taken in a purely statistical sense, for there must be, in the way my own body presents itself, something which makes its absence or its variation inconceivable. What can it be? My head is presented to my sight only to the extent of my nose end and the boundaries of my eye-sockets. I can see my eyes in three mirrors, but they are the eyes of someone observing, and I have the utmost difficulty in catching my living glance when a mirror in the street unexpectedly reflects my image back at me. My body in the mirror never stops following my intentions like their shadow, and if observation consists in varying the point of view while keeping the object fixed, then is escapes observation and is given to me as a simulacrum of my tactile body since it imitates the body's actions instead of responding to them by a free unfolding of perspectives. My visual body is certainly an object as far as its parts far removed from my head are concerned, but as we come nearer to the eyes, it becomes divorced from objects, and reserves among them a quasi-space to which they have no access, and when I try to fill this void by recourse to the image in the mirror, it refers me back to an original of the body which is not out there among things, but in my own province, on this side of all things seen. It is no difference, in spite of what may appear to be the case, with my tactile body, for if I can, with my left hand, feel my right hand as it touches an object, the right hand as an object is not the right hand as it touches: the first is a system of bones, muscles and flesh brought down at a point of space, the second shoots through space like a rocket to reveal the external object in its place. Insofar as it sees or touches the world, my body can therefore be neither seen nor touched. What prevents its ever being an object, ever being 'completely constituted'[1] is that it is that by which there are objects. It is neither tangible nor visible insofar as it is that which sees and touches. The body therefore is not one more among external objects, with the peculiarity of always being there. If it is permanent, the permanence is absolute and is the ground for the relative permanence of disappearing objects, real objects. The presence and absence of external objects are only variations within a field of primordial presence, a perceptual domain over which my body exercises power. Not only is the permanence of my body not a particular case of the permanence of external objects in the world, but the second cannot be understood except through the first: not only is the perspective of my body not a particular case of that of objects, but furthermore, the presentation of objects in perspective cannot be understood except through the resistance of my body to all variation of perspective. If objects may never show me more than one of their facets, this is because I am myself in a certain place from which I see them and others, which I cannot see. If nevertheless I believe in the existence of their hidden sides and equally in a world which embraces them all and co-exists with them, I do so insofar as my body, always present for me, and yet involved with them in so many objective relationships, sustains their co-existence with it and communicates to them all the pulse of its duration. Thus the permanence of one's own body, if only classical psychology had analyses it, might have led it to the body no longer conceived as an object of the world, but as our means of communications with it, to the world no longer conceived as a collection of determinate objects, but as the horizon latent in all our experience and itself ever-present and anterior to every and anterior to every determining thought.

[…]

Note

1   Husserl, *Idden* T. II (unpublished). We are indebted to Mgr Noël and the Institut Supérieur de Philosophies of Louvain, trustees of the collected *Nachlass*, and particularly to the kindness of the Reverend Father Van Bréda, for having been able to consult a certain amount of unpublished material.

Chapter 3

Hans Jonas

THE BURDEN AND BLESSING
OF MORTALITY

From H. Jonas (1996) *Mortality and Morality – A Search for the Good after Auschwitz*, Evanston, Ill.: Northwestern University Press.

[...]

OUR OPENING OBSERVATION IS that organisms are entities whose being is their own doing. That is to say that they exist only in virtue of what they do. And this in the radical sense that the being they earn from this doing is not a possession they then own in separation from the activity by which it was generated, but is the continuation of that very activity itself, made possible by what it has just performed. Thus, to say that the being of organisms is their own doing is also to say that doing what they do is their being itself; being for them consists in doing what they have to do in order to go on to be. It follows directly that *to cease doing it* means *ceasing* to be; and since the requisite doing depends not on themselves alone, but also on *the compliance of an environment* that can either be granted or denied, the peril of cessation is with the organism from the beginning. Here we have the basic link of life with death, the ground of mortality in its very constitution.

What we have couched so far in the abstract terms of being and doing, the language of ontology, can now be called by its familiar name: *metabolism*. This concretely is the "doing" referred to in our opening remark about entities whose being is their own doing, and metabolism can well serve as the defining property of life: all living things have it, no nonliving thing has it. What is denotes is this: to exist by way of exchanging matter with the environment, transiently incorporate it, use it, excrete it again. The German *Stoffwechsel* expresses it nicely. Let us realize how unusual, nay unique a trait this is in the vast world of matter. How does an ordinary physical thing – a proton, a molecule, a stone, a planet – endure? Well, just by being there. Its being now is the sufficient reason for its also being later, if perhaps in a different place. This is so because of the constancy of matter, one of the prime laws of nature ever since, soon after the Big Bang, the exploding chaos solidified into discrete, highly durable units. In the universe hence evolving, the single stubborn particle, say a proton, is simply and fixedly what it is, identical with itself over time, and with no need to maintain that identity by anything it does. Its conservation is mere remaining, not a reassertion of being from moment to moment. It is there once and for all. Saying, then, of a composite, macroscopic body – this stone in our collection – that it is the same as yesterday amounts to saying that it still consists of the same elementary parts as before.

Now by this criterion a living organism would have no identity over time. Repeated inspections would find it to consist less and less of the initial components, more and more of new ones of the same kind that have taken their place, until the two compared states have perhaps no components in common anymore. Yet no biologist would take this to mean that he is not dealing with the same organic individual. On the contrary, he would consider any other finding incompatible with the sameness of a living entity qua living: if it showed the same inventory of parts after a long enough interval, he would conclude that the body in question has soon after the earlier inspection ceased to live and is in that decisive respect no longer "the same," that is, no longer a "creature" but a corpse. Thus we are faced with the ontological fact of an identity totally different from inert physical identity, yet grounded in transactions among items of that simple identity. We have to ponder this highly intriguing fact.

It presents something of a paradox. On the one hand, the living body is a composite of matter, and at any one time its reality totally coincides with its contemporary stuff – that is, with one definite manifold of individual components. On the other hand, it is not identical with this or any such simultaneous total, as this is forever vanishing downstream in the flow of exchange; in this respect it is different from its stuff and not the sum of it. We have thus the case of a substantial entity enjoying a sort of *freedom* with respect to its own substance, an independence from that same matter of which it nonetheless wholly consists. However, though independent of the sameness of this matter, it is dependent on the exchange of it, on its progressing permanently and sufficiently, and there is no freedom in this. Thus, the exercise of the freedom which the living things enjoys is rather a stern *necessity*. This necessity we call "need," which has a place only where existence is unassured and its own continual task.

With the term *need* we have come upon a property of organic being unique to life and unknown to all the rest of reality. The atom is self-sufficient and would continue to exist if all the world around it were annihilated. By contrast, nonautarky is of the very essence of organism. Its power to use the world, this unique prerogative of life, has its precise reverse in the necessity of having to use it, on pain of ceasing to be. The dependence here in force is the cost incurred by primeval substance in venturing upon the career of organic – that is, self-constituting – identity instead of merely inert persistence. Thus the need is with it from the beginning and marks the existence gained in this way as a hovering between being and not-being. The "not" lies always in wait and must be averted ever anew. Life, in other words, carries death within itself.

Yet if it is true that with metabolizing existence not-being made its appearance in the world as an alternative embodied in the existence itself, it is equally true that thereby to be first assumes an emphatic sense: intrinsically qualified by the threat of its negative it must affirm itself, and existence affirmed is existence as a *concern*. Being has become a task rather than a given state, a possibility ever to be realized anew in opposition to its ever-present contrary, not-being, which inevitably will engulf it in the end.

With the hint at inevitability, we are ahead of our story. As told so far in these musings of mine, we can sum up the inherent dialectics of life somewhat like this: committed to itself, put at the mercy of its own performance, life must depend on conditions over which it has no control and which may deny themselves at any time. Thus dependent on the favor or disfavor of outer reality, life is exposed to the world from which it has set itself off and by means of which it must yet maintain itself. Emancipated from the identity with matter, life is yet in need of it; free, yet under the whip of necessity; separate, yet in indispensable contact; seeking contact, yet in danger of being destroyed by it and threatened no less by its want – imperiled thus from both sides, importunity and aloofness of the world, and balanced on the narrow ridge between the two. In its process, which must not cease, liable to interference; in the straining of its temporality always facing the imminent no-more: thus does the living form carry on its separatist existence in matter – paradoxical, unstable, precarious, finite, and in intimate company with death. The fear of death, with which the hazard of this existence is charged, is a never-ending comment on the audacity of the original venture upon which substance embarked in turning organic.

[...]

Chapter 4

Gilles Deleuze

ETHOLOGY: SPINOZA AND US

From G. Deleuze (1992) 'Ethology: Spinoza and us', in J. Crary and S. Kwinter (eds), *Incorporations*, translated by Robert Hurley, New York: Zone.

'SPINOZA AND US' – this phrase could mean many things, but among other things, it means 'us in the middle of Spinoza'. To try to perceive and to understand Spinoza by way of the middle. Generally one begins with the first principle of a philosopher. But what counts is also the third, the fourth or the fifth principle. Everyone knows the first principle of Spinoza: one substance for all the attributes. But we also know the third, fourth or fifth principle: one Nature for all bodies, one Nature for all individuals, a nature that is itself an individual varying in an infinite number of ways. What is involved is no longer the affirmation of a single substance, but rather the laying out of a *common plane of immanence* on which all bodies, all minds and all individuals are situated. This plane of immanence or consistency is a plan, but not in the sense of a mental design, a project, a program; it is a plan in the geometric sense: a section, an intersection, a diagram.[1] Thus, to be in the middle of Spinoza is to be on this model plane, or rather to install oneself on this plane – which implies a mode of living, a way of life. What is this plane and how does one construct it? For at the same it is fully a plane of immanence, and yet it has to be constructed if one is to live a Spinozist manner.

How does Spinoza define a body? A body, of whatever kind, is defined by Spinoza in two simultaneous ways. In the first place, a body, however small it may be, is composed of an infinite number of particles; it is the relations of motion and rest, of speeds and slownesses between particles that define a body, the individuality of a body. Second, a body affects other bodies, or is affected by other bodies; it is this capacity for affecting and being affected that also defines a body in its individuality. These two propositions appear to be very simple; one is kinetic and the other dynamic. But if one truly installs oneself in the midst of these propositions, if one lives them, things are much more complicated and one finds that one is a Spinozist before having understood why.

Thus, the kinetic proposition tells us that a body is defined by relations of motion and rest, of slowness and speed between particles. That is, it is not defined by a form or by functions. Global form, specific form and organic functions depend on relations of speed and slowness. Even the development of a form, the course of development of a form, depends on these relations, and not the reverse. The important thing is to understand life, each living individuality, not as form or a development of form but as a complex relation between differential velocities, between deceleration and acceleration of particles. A composition of speeds and slownesses on a plane of immanence. In the same way, a musical form will depend on a complex relation between speeds and slownesses of sound particles. It is not just a matter of music but of how to live: it is by speed and slowness that one slips in among things, that one connects with something else. One never commences; one never has a tabula rasa; one slips in, enters in the middle; one takes up or lays down rhythms.

The second proposition concerning bodies refers us to the capacity for affecting and being affected. You will not define a body (or a mind) by its form, nor by its organs or functions, and neither will you define it as a substance or a subject. Every reader of Spinoza knows that for him bodies and minds are not substances or subjects, but modes. It is not enough, however, merely to think this theoretically. For, concretely, a mode is a complex relation of speed and slowness, in the body but also in thought, and it is a capacity for affecting and being affected, pertaining to the body or to thought. Concretely, if you define bodies and thoughts as capacities for affecting and being affected, many things change. You will define an animal or a human being not by its form, its organs and its functions and not as a subject either; you will define it by the affects of which it is capable. Affective capacity, with a maximum threshold and a minimum threshold, is a constant notion in Spinoza. Take any animal and make a list of affects, in any order. Children know how to do this: Little Hans, in the case reported by Freud, makes a list of affects of a draft horse pulling a cart in a city (to be proud, to have blinders, to go fast, to pull a heavy load, to collapse, to be whipped, to kick up a racket, and so on). For example, there are greater differences between a plow horse or a draft horse and a racehorse than between an ox and a plow horse. This is because the racehorse and the plow horse have neither the same affects nor the same capacity for being affected; the plow horse has affects in common, rather, with the ox.

It should be clear that the plane of immanence, the plane of Nature that distributes affects, does not make any distinction at all between things that might be called natural and things that might be called artificial. Artifice is fully a part of Nature, since each thing, on the immanent plane of Nature, is defined by the arrangements of motions and affects into which it enters, whether these arrangements are artificial or natural. Long after Spinoza, biologists and naturalists will try to describe animal worlds defined by affects and capacities for affecting and being affected. For example, Jakob von Uexküll will do this for the tick, an animal that sucks the blood of mammals. He will define this animal by three affects: the first has to do with light (climb to the top of a branch); the second is olfactive (let yourself fall onto the mammal that passes beneath the branch); and the third is thermal (seek the area without fur, the warmest spot). A world with only three affects, in the midst of all that goes on in the immense forest. An optimal threshold and a pessimal in the capacity for being affected: the gorged tick that will die, and the tick capable of fasting for a very long time.[2] Such studies as this, which define bodies, animals or humans by the affects they are capable of, founded what is today called *ethology*. The approach is no less valid for us, for human beings, than for animals, because no one knows ahead of time the affects one is capable of; it is a long affair of experimentation, requiring a lasting prudence, a Spinozan wisdom that implies the construction of a plane of immanence or consistency. Spinoza's ethics has nothing to do with a morality; he conceives it as an ethology, that is, a composition of fast and slow speeds, of capacities for affecting and being affected on this plane of immanence or consistency. That is why

Spinoza calls out to us in the way that he does: you do not know beforehand what good or bad you are capable of; you do not know beforehand what a body or a mind can do, in a given encounter, a given arrangement, a given combination.

Ethology is first of all the study of the relations of speed and slowness, of the capacities for affecting and being affected that characterize each thing. For each thing these relations and capacities have an amplitude, thresholds (maximum and minimum) and variations or transformations that are peculiar to them. And they select, in the world or in Nature, that which corresponds to the thing; that is, they select what affects or is affected by the thing, what moves or is moved by it. For example, given an animal, what is the animal unaffected by in the infinite world? What does it react to positively or negatively? What are its nutriments and its poisons? What does it 'take' in its world? Every point has its counterpoints: the plant and the rain, the spider and the fly. So an animal, a thing, is never separable from its relations with the world. The interior is only a selected exterior, and the exterior, a projected interior. The speed or slowness of metabolisms, perceptions, actions and reactions link together to constitute a particular individual in the world.

Further, there is also the way in which these relations of speed and slowness are realized according to circumstances, and the way in which these capacities for being affected are filled. For they always are, but in different ways, depending on whether the present affects threaten the thing (diminish its power, slow it down, reduce it to the minimum), or strengthen, accelerate and increase it: poison or food? – with all the complications, since a poison can be a food for part of the thing considered.

Lastly, ethology studies the compositions of relations or capacities between different things. This is another aspect of the matter, distinct from the preceding ones. Heretofore, it was only a question of knowing how a particular thing could decompose other things by giving them a relation that was consistent with one of its own or, on the contrary, how it risks being decomposed by other things. But now it is a question of knowing whether relations (and which ones?) can compound directly to form a new, more 'extensive' relation, or whether capacities can compound directly to constitute a more 'intensive' capacity or power. It is no longer a matter of utilizations or captures, but of sociabilities and communities. How do individuals enter into composition with one another in order to form a higher individual, ad infinitum? How can a being take another being into its world, while preserving or respecting the other's own relations and world? And in this regard, what are the different types of sociabilities, for example? What is the difference between the society of human beings and the community of rational beings? . . . Now, we are concerned not with a relation of point to counterpoint, nor with the selection of a world, but with a symphony of Nature, the composition of a world that is increasingly wide and intense. In what order and in what manner will the powers, speeds and slownesses be composed?

A plane of musical composition, a plane of Nature, insofar as the latter is the fullest and most intense Individual, with parts that vary in an infinity of ways. Uexküll, one of the main founders of ethology, is a Spinozist when first he defines the melodic lines or contrapuntal relations that correspond to each thing, and then describes a symphony as an immanent higher unity that takes on breadth and fullness ('natural composition'). This musical composition comes into play throughout the *Ethics*, constituting it as one and the same Individual whose relations of speed and slowness do not cease to vary, successively and simultaneously. Successively: the different parts of the *Ethics* are assigned changing relative velocities, until the absolute velocity of thought is reached in the third kind of knowledge. And simultaneously: the propositions and the scholia do not proceed at the same pace, but compose two movements that intercross. The *Ethics* is a composition whose parts are all carried forward by the greatest velocity, in the fullest movement. In a very fine text, Lagneau spoke of this velocity and amplitude, which caused him to compare the *Ethics* to a musical work: a lightning 'speed of thought', a 'wide-ranging power', a 'capacity for discerning in a single act the relationship of the greatest possible number of thoughts.'[3]

In short, if we are Spinozists we will not define a thing by its form, nor by its organs and its functions, nor as a substance or a subject. Borrowing terms from the Middle Ages, or from geography, we will define it by *longitude* and *latitude*. A body can be anything; it can be an animal, a body of sounds, a mind or an idea; it can be a linguistic corpus, a social body, a collectivity. We call longitude of a body the set of relations of speed and slowness, of motion and rest, between particles that compose it from this point of view, that is, between *unformed elements*.[4] We call latitude the set of affects that occupy a body at each moment, that is, the intensive states of an *anonymous force* (force for existing, capacity for being affected). In this way we construct the map of a body. The longitudes and latitudes together constitute Nature, the plane of immanence or consistency, which is always variable and is constantly being altered, composed and recomposed, by individuals and collectivities.

[. . .]

Notes

1   The French word *plan*, used by the author throughout this essay, covers virtually all the meanings of the English 'plan' and 'plane'. To preserve the major contrast that Deleuze sets up here, between *plan d'immanence ou de consistance and plan de transcendance ou d'organisation*, I use 'plane' for the first term, where the meaning is, roughly, a conceptual-affective continuum, and 'plan' for the second term. The reader should also keep in mind that 'plan' has the meaning of 'map' in English as well (TRAN).

2   Jakob von Uexküll, *Mondes animaux et monde humain* (Gonthier).

3   Jules Lagneau, *Célèbres leçons et fragments* (2nd ed., Paris: P.U.F., 1964), pp. 67–8. This is one of the great texts on Spinoza. Similarly, Romain Rolland, when he speaks of the velocity of thought and the musical order in Spinoza: *Empédocle d'Agrigente, suivi de l'Eclair de Spinoza* (Editions du Sablier, 1931). As a matter of fact, the theme of a velocity of thought greater than any given velocity can be found in Empedocles, Democritus or Epicurus.

4   See what Spinoza calls 'the simplest bodies'. They have neither number nor form nor figure, but are infinitely small and always exist as infinities. The only bodies having a form are the composite bodies, to which the simple bodies belong according to a particular relation.

Chapter 5

Judith Butler

BODIES THAT MATTER

From J. Butler (1993) *Bodies That Matter: On the Discursive Limits of "Sex,"*
New York: Routledge.

I S THERE A WAY TO LINK THE QUESTION of the materiality of the body to the performativity of gender? And how does the category of "sex" figure within such a relationship? Consider first that sexual difference is often invoked as an issue of material differences. Sexual difference, however, is never simply a function of material differences which are not in some way both marked and formed by discursive practices. Further, to claim that sexual differences are indissociable from discursive demarcations is not the same as claiming that discourse causes sexual difference. The category of "sex" is, from the start, normative; it is what Foucault has called a "regulatory ideal." In this sense, then, "sex" not only functions as a norm, but is part of a regulatory practice that produces the bodies it governs, that is, whose regulatory force is made clear as a kind of productive power, the power to produce – demarcate, circulate, differentiate – the bodies it controls. Thus, "sex" is a regulatory ideal whose materialization is compelled, and this materialization takes place (or fails to take place) through certain highly regulated practices. In other words, "sex" is an ideal construct which is forcibly materialized through time. It is not a simple fact or static condition of a body, but a process whereby regulatory norms materialize "sex" and achieve this materialization through a forcible reiteration of those norms. That this reiteration is necessary is a sign that materialization is never quite complete, that bodies never quite comply with the norms by which their materialization is impelled. Indeed, it is the instabilities, the possibilities for rematerialization, opened up by this process that mark one domain in which the force of the regulatory law can be turned against itself to spawn rearticulations that call into question the hegemonic force of that very regulatory law.

But how, then, does then notion of gender performativity relate to this conception of materialization? In the first instance, performativity must be understood not as a singular or deliberate "act," but, rather, as the reiterative and citational practice by which discourse produces the effects that it names. [...] [T]he regulatory norms of "sex" work in a performative fashion to constitute the materiality of bodies and, more specifically, to materialize the body's sex, to materialize sexual difference in the service of the consolidation of the heterosexual imperative.

In this sense, what constitutes the fixity of the body, its contours, its movements, will be fully material, but materiality will be rethought as the effect of power, as power's most productive effect. And there will be no way to understand "gender" as a cultural construct which is imposed upon the surface of matter, understood either as "the body" or its given sex. Rather, once "sex" itself is understood in its normativity, the materiality of the body will not be thinkable apart from the materialization of that regulatory norm. "Sex" is, thus, not simply what one has, or a static description of what one is: it will be one of the norms by which the "one" becomes viable at all, that which qualifies a body for life within the domain of cultural intelligibility.

At stake in such a reformulation of the materiality of bodies will be the following:

(1)   the recasting of the matter of bodies as the effect of a dynamic of power, such that the matter of bodies will be indissociable from the regulatory norms that govern their materialization and the signification of those material effects;

(2)   the understanding of performativity not as the act by which a subject brings into being what she/he names, but, rather, as that reiterative power of discourse to pro- duce the phenomena that it regulates and constrains;

(3)   the construal of "sex" no longer as a bodily given on which the construct of gender is artificially imposed, but as a cultural norm which governs the materialization of bodies;

(4)   a rethinking of the process by which a bodily norm is assumed, appropriated, taken on as not, strictly speaking, undergone *by a subject*, but rather that the subject, the speaking, "I," is formed by virtue of having gone through such a process of assuming a sex; and

(5)   a linking of this process of "assuming" a sex with the question of *identification*, and with the discursive means by which the heterosexual imperative enables certain sexed identifications and forecloses and/or disavows other identifications.

This exclusionary matrix by which subjects are formed thus requires the simulaneous production of a domain of abject beings, those who are not yet "subjects," but who form the constitutive outside to the domain of the subject. The abject designates here precisely those "unlivable" and "uninhabitable" zones of social life which are nevertheless densely populated by those who do not enjoy the status of the subject, but whose living under the sign of the "unlivable" is required to circumscribe the domain of the subject. This zone of uninhabitability will constitute the defining limit of the subject's domain; it will consti- tute that site of dreaded identification against which – and by virtue of which – the domain of the subject will circumscribe its own claim to autonomy and to life. In this sense, then, the subject is constituted through the force of exclusion and abjection, one which produces a constitutive outside to the subject, an abjected outside, which is, after all, "inside" the subject as its own founding repudiation.

[…]

From construction to materialization

The relation between culture and nature presupposed by some models of gender "construc- tion" implies a culture or an agency of the social which acts upon a nature, which is itself presupposed as a passive surface, outside the social and yet its necessary counterpart. One question that feminists have raised, then, is whether the discourse which figures the action of construction as a kind of imprinting or imposition is not tacitly masculinist, whereas the figure of the passive surface, awaiting that penetrating act whereby meaning is endowed, is not tacitly or – perhaps – quite obviously feminine. Is sex to gender as feminine is to masculine?

Other feminist scholars have argued that the very concept of nature needs to rethought, for the concept of nature has a history, and the figuring of nature as the blank and lifeless page, as that which is, as it were, always already dead, is decidedly modern, linked perhaps to the emergence of technological means of domination. Indeed, some have argued that a rethinking of "nature" as a set of dynamic interrelations suits both feminist and ecological aims (and has for some produced an otherwise unlikely alliance with the work of Gilles Deleuze). This rethinking also calls into question the model of construction whereby the social unilaterally acts on the natural and invests it with its parameters and its meanings. Indeed, as much as the radical distinction between sex and gender has been crucial to the de Beauvoirian version of feminism, it has come under criticism in more recent years for degrading the natural as that which is "before" intelligibility, in need of the mark, if not the mar, of the social to signify, to be known, to acquire value. This misses the point that nature has a history, and not merely a social one, but, also, that sex is positioned ambiguously in relation to that concept and its history. The concept of "sex" is itself troubled terrain, formed through a series of contestations over what ought to be decisive criterion for distinguishing between the two sexes; the concept of sex has a history that is covered over by the figure of the site or surface of inscription. Figured as such a site or surface, however, the natural is construed as that which is also without value; moreover, it assumes its value at the same time that it assumes its social character, that is, at the same time that nature relinquishes itself as the natural. According to this view, then, the social construction of the natural presupposes the cancellation of the natural by the social. Insofar as it relies on this construal, the sex/gender distinction founders along parallel lines; if gender is the social significance that sex assumes within a given culture – and for the sake of argument we will let "social" and "cultural" stand in an uneasy interchangeability – then what, if anything, is left of "sex" once it has assumed its social character as gender? At issue is the meaning of "assumption," where to be "assumed" is to be taken up into a more elevated sphere, as in "the Assumption of the Virgin." If gender consists of the social meanings that sex assumes, then sex does not *accrue* social meanings as additive properties but, rather, *is replaced by* the social meanings it takes on; sex is relinquished in the course of that assumption, and gender emerges, not as a term in a continued relationship of opposition to sex, but as the term which absorbs and displaces "sex," the mark of its full substantiation into gender or what, from a materialist point of view, might constitute a full *de*substantiation.

When the sex/gender distinction is joined with a notion of radical linguistic constructivism, the problem becomes even worse, for the "sex" which is referred to as prior to gender will itself be a postulation, a construction, offered within languages, as that which is prior to language, prior to construction. But this sex posited as prior to construction will, by virtue of being posited, become the effect of that very positing, the constructed of construction. If gender is the social construction of sex, and if there is no access to this "sex" except by means of its construction, then it appears not only that sex is absorbed by gender, but that "sex" becomes something like a fiction, perhaps a fantasy, retroactively installed at a prelinguistic site to which there is no direct access.

But is it right to claim that "sex" vanishes altogether, that it is a fiction over and against what is true, that it is a fantasy over and against what is reality? Or do these very oppositions need to be rethought such that if "sex" is a fiction, it is one within whose necessities we live, without which life itself would be unthinkable? And if "sex" is a fantasy, is it perhaps a phantasmatic field that constitutes the very terrain of cultural intelligibility? Would such a rethinking of such conventional oppositions entail a rethinking of "constructivism" in its usual sense?

[...]

What I would propose in place of these conceptions of construction is a return to the notion of matter, not as site or surface, but as *a process of materialization that stabilizes over time to produce the effect of boundary, fixity, and surface we call matter*. That matter is always materialized has, I think, to be thought in relation to the productive and, indeed, materializing effects of regulatory power in the Foucaultian sense. Thus, the question is no longer, How is gender constituted as and through a certain interpretation of sex? (a question that leaves the "matter" of sex untheorized), but rather, Through what regulatory norms is sex itself materialized? And how is it that treating the materiality of sex as a given presupposes and consolidates the normative conditions of its own emergence?

Crucially, then, construction is neither a single act nor a causal process initiated by a subject and culminating in a set of fixed effects. Construction not only takes places *in* time, but is itself a temporal process which operates through the reiteration of norms; sex is both produced and destabilized in the course of this reiteration. As a sedimented effect of a reiterative or ritual practice, sex acquires its naturalized effect, and, yet, it is also by virtue of this reiteration that gaps and fissures are opened up as the constitutive instabilities in such constructions, as that which escapes or exceeds the norm, as that which cannot be wholly defined or fixed by the repetitive labor of that norm. This instability is the *de*constituting possibility in the very process of repetition, the power that undoes the very effects by which "sex" is stabilized, the possibility to put the consolidation of the norms of "sex" into a potentially productive crisis.

[...]

PART TWO

Bodies and social (dis)order

INTRODUCTION

THIS SECTION INCLUDES A SELECTION of texts in social theory that have
come to be regarded as 'classic' in stating the fundamental importance of the body
to the problems of social order, social control and social stratification. They tend to agree
in one observation, namely, that the body at first appears *inconspicuous* as a sociological
object and as an object of social regulation, but also that regulatory effects are all the
more powerful thanks precisely to this inconspicuousness.

Marcel Mauss' chapter 'Techniques of the Body', first published in 1935 and
celebrated as a pioneering text, still conveys with fresh immediateness the process of
articulating – and thus, in a sense, discovering – the thoroughly social character of bodily
actions, probably for the first time in the history of social science. Mauss begins by observing ordinary bodily actions such as swimming, walking, digging, resting or throwing, and
how the manner of performing these differs across societies and across generations. It is
only through cultural and generational variation that these actions become sociologically
conspicuous, that is, visible as *social* actions. Otherwise they appear to the social scientist, as indeed they do to the social actor, to be '*actions of a mechanical, physical or
physico-chemical order*', outside the remit of culture and of social scientific interest.
Mauss reflects on the fact that this particular assumption typically applies to traditional
actions an anthropologist would classify as *techniques* rather than rites. Viewed from an
anthropological perspective, of course, both types of action (rites and techniques) bear the
marks of a specific culture, of particular traditions. From the native's perspective,
however, technical actions (such as grinding grain or carrying water through particular
implements) appear devoid of any cultural specificity or meaning; they are experienced in
purely physical and mechanical terms, and pursued with physical and mechanical aims in
view. Mauss argues that, when it comes to considering everyday bodily actions, the

anthropological perspective can be as blind to the role of culture as the perspective of a native. Mauss writes: 'I made, and went on making for several years, the fundamental mistake of thinking that there is technique only when there is an instrument.' His mistake was to suppose that physical action could be classified as a technique, or as a cultural practice, only when mediated by an artificial object, an instrument – that is, a visible token of 'culture'. By implication, the naked body, the body acting without instrumental mediation, would appear to be a purely 'natural' object, independent of social relations of authority and power. These assumptions are powerfully challenged by Mauss' claim that the body is 'man's first and *most natural technical object*' (our emphasis).

The problem of classification, and of how to understand the relation between nature and culture in connection with bodily phenomena, is also central to Mary Douglas' work. In the chapter included here, Douglas addresses what she sees as limits in the contrasting approaches of Mauss, on the one hand, and structural anthropologist Lévi-Strauss on the other. In Douglas' view, Mauss' focus on bodily action as technique placed too exclusive an emphasis on cultural variation, to the point of generating the mistaken impression that there is no such thing as natural behaviour. Lévi-Strauss, on the other hand, was intent on 'discovering' universal symbolic structures corresponding to the structure of the human mind, which he believed informed how human bodies and their activities are socially controlled. Unlike Mauss, Lévi-Strauss focused on symbolic universals that left little room to account for local and specific cultural variations. Against this background Douglas carves an original and deeply influential explanatory model, designed to accommodate local differences whilst making substantive claims with regard to universals. In this model, the categories of nature and culture are displaced from their customary locations: they do not map on to the physical body, on the one hand, and to society on the other. Douglas argues that what is 'natural', in the sense that it is universally found across cultures, is not the physico-biological body as such, but rather a certain principle of correspondence between *two bodies*, the physico-biological or individual body and the social body. What is universal is a 'drive to achieve consonance in all levels of experience' which, Douglas claims, 'produces concordance among the means of expression, so that the use of the body is coordinated with other media'. There is therefore a kind of parallelism and mutual reinforcement between messages (or meanings) relative to the physico-biological, individual body, and messages (or meanings) relative to the social body. The physical body is never immediately perceived, but always experienced through the mediation of cultural categories; social preoccupations and concerns – typically in relation to the demarcation of boundaries or hierarchies – translate into preoccupations and concerns regarding flows to and from bodily apertures, or the relation between different bodily organs in the upper and lower body. Such concerns are materialised through techniques of control, ranging from the control of physiological processes (such as excretion) to that of posture, movement and appearance. This is the sense in which 'the physical body is a microcosm of society', its experience always sustaining a particular set of cultural meanings, a particular social order. The body is also a *natural* symbol, in the sense that it universally expresses the relation of parts (or individuals) to a whole (or society).

Mauss and Douglas articulate the social character and significance of the body in the idiom of anthropology, where variations across cultures constitute perhaps the main focus of explanatory interest. With Goffman and Bourdieu we are in quintessentially sociological terrain, where one of the main concerns is with how social order and stratification are internally maintained and reproduced, at a micro- and a macro-sociological level. In the text included here, Goffman focuses on the body as an instrument of communication that conveys information about a person's membership to, or exclusion from, a given situational order. Embodied information is a crucial condition of face-to-face interaction, and defines such interaction as marked by a profound symmetry or mutuality: '... to use our naked senses is to use them nakedly and to be made naked by their use. ... Copresence renders persons uniquely accessible, available, and subject to one another.' For this reason, the question of how society is possible can be thought of, at a micro-level, as having to do with the normative regulation of situational presence and of interpersonal accessibility. Situational presence signals social membership, in the sense that it signals the readiness and willingness to participate in a commonly defined interaction. Such presence, however, is not simply given – it must be demonstrated through the appropriate bodily demeanour. The body and its expressions have to be managed so as to indicate concern and interest in the setting and its participants. Correspondingly, disruptions or breakdowns of the interaction typically become conspicuous as/in bodily manifestations (e.g. blushing, yawning, etc.).

In this extract from Bourdieu's *Logic of Practice*, practical sense – our intuitive and implicit beliefs concerning how the world works – also figures as a condition of membership to a given social field, and one which is implicitly demonstrated through 'countless acts of recognition'. Somewhat counter-intuitively, Bourdieu describes practical sense or practical belief as 'a state of the body'. Social values are literally incorporated, in the sense that they are '*made* body', through 'seemingly innocuous details of bearing or physical and verbal manners'. In this way, social values (and the ordered social structure to which they correspond) become invisible as aspects of culture, and appear instead to be perfectly natural. What is 'learned by the body' is therefore something that does not properly figure as knowledge and does not become an object of consciousness; it is inconspicuous as a form of training, and it involves an 'implicit pedagogy' enacted through participation in play and ritual, rather than the teaching of explicit precepts and rules. Accordingly, embodied practical sense is not something the individual can stand before, contemplate, and possibly reject; it is something the individual *is*, or has become. For Bourdieu, practical sense speaks not only of situational membership, but of membership to a particular structural segment of society – such as class or gender.

In the work of Mikhail Bakhtin the concern with boundaries and hierarchies, and with how these correspond to expressions and representations of the body, becomes explicitly political. The focus here is on the body as a locus of transgression and a revolutionary tool, one by which social hierarchies can be destabilised, inverted, mocked and satirised. To illustrate this potential for the body to act as a site of resistance, Bakhtin focused on particular occasions in social existence when control of the body is ritually abandoned: carnivals, fairs, festivals, masquerades, banquets and spectacles all enact challenges to the established order of things, in the form of ritual inversions. In the course of a carnival men would dress as women, paupers would be crowned kings, peasants would abuse nobles, and everyone would swear, curse, sing, and most importantly, laugh. In this momentary suspension of the customary rules of social conduct, the body invaded the social scene as its most conspicuous actor, unrivalled in performing distortion and exaggeration – in other words, in the task of turning the world upside-down.

In this extract, Bakhtin discusses the grotesque, or carnivalesque body in contrast to what he calls the 'new bodily canon' to be found increasingly prevailing in European literature starting from the sixteenth century. The chief point is that in the grotesque mode or genre '[t]he confines between the body and the world and between separate bodies are drawn ... quite differently than in the classic and naturalist images'. The grotesque body is a body whose boundaries are uncertain and always changeable, since its most conspicuous features are its apertures and the flows they allow. The grotesque body is thus open, protruding, bulging, extending and secreting; it is wet, bloody, sweaty and odorous. Above all, it is connected to the world, and to other bodies, in such a way that it is difficult to consider it as an individual. This is probably the main point of contrast between the grotesque and the classical body of the new canon, whose surface is closed and smooth, an 'impenetrable façade'. The classical body is a finished body, that is 'self-sufficient and speaks in its name alone'. It is a body from which all ambiguity has been purged, whose features stress the demarcation between self and other, self and society.

The emergence of the classical body as a new 'canon' around the sixteenth century corresponds, in European history, to the emergence of new standards of refinement and delicacy, as well as new thresholds of disgust, shame and embarrassment. Bakhtin's periodisation here broadly agrees with that provided by Norbert Elias in his studies of the history of manners, in connection with what he called the 'civilising process' (see Elias 1994). Like Bakhtin, Elias stresses that the experience of the self as an enclosed individual, standing opposite other individuals and society rather than merging with them, is correlated with changes in the quality and degree of control exerted over bodily functions, activities and expressions. These changes, in turn, are linked to large-scale structural transformations such as the progressive centralisation of political authority within nationally defined territories, resulting in the pacification of social relations. The text included here is from a previously unpublished lecture that Elias delivered to a congress of physicians specialising in psychosomatic medicine – the branch of medicine that studies the role of psychological factors in physical illness and disease. As well as offering an outline of the essential features of the civilising process, the text links this process explicitly to an increase in so-called psychosomatic disorders in the modern period. The civilising process involves a process of internalisation of tension and conflict: whereas previously these manifested themselves as physical violence *between* individuals or groups, over time they disappear from the social scene. Instead, as individuals learn to exercise increasing amounts of self-control over their emotions and behaviour, tension and conflict become infrapsychic and tend to play themselves out *within* the individual. A particularly interesting claim being made in this text is that the features of social order, and the different forms of bodily regulation they imply, produce patterns not only at the level of behaviours and demeanours, but also at the level of the body's internal functioning, namely our physiology.

The last reading in this section is an extract from Foucault's *Discipline and Punish* – a text that, perhaps more than any other, is associated with placing the body at the centre of a new sociological agenda. The reason for this is that Foucault's analysis of the body in terms of its 'political investment' involved a simultaneous change of perspective not only on the body itself, but also on the relationship between power and knowledge. This was a conceptual shift of broad significance to the social sciences as a whole; in this text, the body is the occasion demonstrating the necessity of this shift. Unlike other authors included in this section, Foucault stresses how the body is involved in relations that are political not only in an implicit sense, but explicitly and consciously so. The body is an object of techniques and strategies that bear on its materiality in order to channel it, train it, mould it and subject it, rendering the body 'docile' for economic or military purposes. Foucault names 'political technology of the body' a form of knowledge that is at once politically interested, and yet true to the materiality it seeks to affect. To imagine such a knowledge is to contradict a long-standing assumption according to which 'knowledge can exist only where power relations are suspended', and interest is deemed antithetical to truth insofar as it constitutes a 'bias'. Foucault here demonstrates how power and knowledge mutually imply each other, rather than cancelling each other out.

Chapter 6

Marcel Mauss

TECHNIQUES OF THE BODY[1]

From M. Mauss (1973 [1936]) 'Techniques of the body', translated by Ben Brewster, *Economy and Society* 2: 70–88.

[…]

WHEN A NATURAL SCIENCE makes advances, it only ever does so in the direction of the concrete, and always in the direction of the unknown. Now the unknown is found at the frontiers of the sciences, where the professors are at each other's throats, as Goethe put it (though Goethe was not so polite). It is generally in these ill-demarcated domains that the urgent problems lie. Moreover, these uncleared lands are marked. In the natural sciences at present, there is always one obnoxious rubric. There is always a moment when, the science of certain facts not being yet reduced into concepts, the facts not even being organically grouped together, these masses of facts receive that posting of ignorance: 'Miscellaneous'. This is where we have to penetrate. We can be certain that this is where there are truths to be discovered: first because we known that we are ignorant, and second because we have a lively sense of the quantity of the facts. For many years in my course in descriptive ethnology, I have had to teach in the shadow of the disgrace and opprobrium of the 'miscellaneous' in a matter in which in ethnography this rubric 'miscellaneous' was truly heteroclite. I was well aware that walking or swimming, for example, and all sorts of things of the same type, are specific to determinate societies; that the Polynesians do not swim as we do, that my generation did not swim as the present generation does. But what social phenomena did these represent? They were 'miscellaneous' social phenomena, and, as this rubric is a horror, I have often thought about this 'miscellaneous', at least as often as I have been obliged to discuss it and often in between times.

[…]

An example will put us in the picture straight away: us, the psychologists, as well as the biologists and sociologists. Previously we were taught to dive after having learnt to swim. And when we were learning to dive, we were taught to close our eyes and then to open them under water. Today the technique is the other way round. The whole training begins by getting the children used to keeping their eyes open under water. Thus, even before they can swim, particular care is taken to get the children to control their dangerous but instinctive ocular reflexes, before all else they are familiarised with the water, their fears are suppressed, a certain confidence is created, suspensions and movements are selected. Hence there is a technique of diving and a technique of education in diving which have been discovered in my day. And you can see that it really is a technical education and, as in every technique, there is an apprenticeship in swimming. On the other hand, here our generation has witnessed a complete change in technique: we have seen the breast-stroke with the head out of the water replaced by the different sorts of crawl. Moreover, the habit of swallowing water and spitting it out again has gone. In my day swimmers thought of themselves as a king of steam-boat. It was stupid, but in fact I still do this: I cannot get rid of my technique. Here then we have a specific technique of the body, a gymnic art perfected in our own day.

But this specificity is characteristic of all techniques. An example: during the War I was able to make many observations on this spcificity of techniques. E.g. the technique of *digging*. The English troops I was with did not know how to use French spades, which forced us to change 8000 spades a division when we relieved a French division, and vice versa. This plainly shows that a manual knack can only be learnt slowly. Every technique, properly so-called, has its own form.

But the same is true of every attitude of the body. Each society has its own special habits.

[...]

A kind of a revelation came to me in hospital. I was ill in New York. I wondered where previously I had seen girls walking as my nurses walked. I had the time to think about it. At last I realised that it was at the cinema. Returning to France, I noticed how common this gait was, especially in Paris; the girls were French and they too were walking in this way. In fact, American walking fashions had begun to arrive over here, thanks to the cinema. This was an idea I could generalise. The positions of the arms and hands while walking form a social idiosyncracy, they are not simply a product of some purely individual, almost completely psychical arrangements and mechanisms. For example: I think I can also recognise a girl who has been raised in a convent. In general she will walk with her fists closed. And I can still remember my third-form teacher shouting at me: 'Idiot! why do you walk around the whole time with your hands flapping wide open?' Thus there exists an education in walking, too.

Another example: there are polite and impolite *positions for the hands* at rest. Thus you can be certain that if a child at table keeps his elbows in when he is not eating he is English. A young Frenchman has no idea how to sit up straight; his elbows stick out sideways; he puts them on the table, and so on.

Finally, in *running*, too, I have seen, you all have seen, the change in technique. Imagine, my gymnastics teacher, one of the top graduates of Joinville around 1860, taught me to run with my fists close to my chest: a movement completely contradictory to all running movements; I had to see the professional runners of 1890 before I realised the necessity of running in a different fashion.

Hence I have had this notion of the social nature of the 'habitus' for many years. Please note that I use the Latin word – it should be understood in France – habitus. The word translates infinitely better than 'habitude' (habit or custom), the 'exis', the 'acquired ability' and 'faculty' of Aristotle (who was a psychologist). It does not designate those metaphysical *habitudes*, that mysterious 'memory', the subjects of volumes or short and famous theses. These 'habits' do not just vary with individuals and their imitations, they vary especially between societies, educations, proprieties and fashions, prestiges. In them we should see the techniques and work of collective and individual practical reason rather than, in the ordinary way, merely the soul and its repetitive faculties.

[…]

Another series of facts impressed itself upon me. In all these elements of the art of using the human body, the facts of *education* were dominant. […] The child imitates actions of adults, which have succeeded and which he has seen successfully performed by people in whom he has confidence and who have authority over him. The action is imposed from without, from above, even if it is an exclusively biological action, involving his body. The individual borrows the series of movements which constitute it from the action executed in front of him or with him by others.

It is precisely this notion of the prestige of the person who performs the ordered, authorised, tested action *vis-à-vis* the imitating individual that contains all the social element. The imitative action which follows contains the psychological element and the biological element. But the whole, the ensemble, is conditioned by the three elements indissolubly mixed together.

[…]

I made, and went on making for several years, the fundamental mistake of thinking that there is technique only when there is an instrument. I had to go back to ancient notions, to the Platonic position on technique, for Plato spoke of a technique of music and in particular of a technique of the dance, and extend these notions.

I call technique an action which is *effective* and *traditional* (and you will see that in this it is no different from a magical, religious or symbolic action). It has to be *effective* and *traditional*. There is no technique and no transmission in the absence of tradition. This above all is what distinguishes man from the animals: the transmission of his techniques and very probably their oral transmission.

Allow me, therefore, to assume that you accept my definitions. But what is the difference between the effective traditional action of religion, the symbolic or juridical effective traditional action, the actions of life in common, moral actions on the one hand and the traditional actions of technique on the other? It is that the latter are felt by the author as *actions of a mechanical, physical or physico-chemical order* and that they are pursued with that aim in view.

In this case all that need be said is quite simply that we are dealing with *techniques of the body*. The body is man's first and most natural instrument. Or more accurately, not to speak of instruments, man's first and most natural technical object, and at the same time technical means, is his body. Immediately this whole broad category of what I classified in descriptive sociology as 'miscellaneous' disappeared from that rubric and took shape and body: we now know where to range it.

Before instrumental techniques there is the ensemble of techniques of the body. […] The constant adaption to a physical, mechanical or chemical aim (e.g. when we drink) is pursued in a series of assembled actions, and assembled for the individual not by himself alone but by all his education, by the whole society to which he belongs, in the place he occupies in it.

Moreover, all these techniques were easily arranged in a system which is common to us, the notion basic to psychologists, [...] of the symbolic life of the mind; the notion we have of the activity of the consciousness as being above all a system of symbolic assemblages.

I should never stop if I tried to demonstrate to you all the facts that might be listed to make visible this concourse of the body and moral or intellectual symbols. Here let us look for a moment at ourselves. Everything in us all is under command. I am a lecturer for you; you can tell it from my sitting posture and my voice, and you are listening to me seated and in silence. We have a set of permissible or impermissible, natural or unnatural attitudes. Thus we should attribute different values to the act of staring fixedly: a symbol of politeness in the army, and of rudeness in everyday life.

[...]

What emerges very clearly...is the fact that we are everywhere faced with physio-psycho-sociological assemblages of series of actions. These actions are more or less habitual and more or less ancient in the life of the individual and the history of the society.

Let us go further: one of the reasons why these series may more easily be assembled in the individual is precisely because they are assembled by and for social authority. As a corporal this is how I taught the reason for exercise in close order, marching four abreast and in step. I ordered the soldiers not to march in step drawn up in ranks and in two files four abreast, and I obliged the squad to pass between two of the trees in the courtyard. They marched on top of one another. They realised that what they were being made to do was not so stupid. In group life as a whole, there is a kind of education of movements in close order.

In every society, everyone knows and has to know and learn what he has to do in all conditions. Naturally, social life is not exempt from stupidly and abnormalities. Error may be a principle. The French Navy only recently began to teach its sailors to swim. By example and order, that is the principle. Hence there is a strong sociological causality in all these facts.

On the other hand, since these are movements of the body, this all presupposes an enormous biological and physiological apparatus. What is the breadth of the linking psychological cog-wheel? I deliberately say cog-wheel. A Comtian would say that there is no gap between the social and the biological. What I can tell you is that there I see psychological facts as connecting cogs and not as causes, except in moments of creation or reform.

[...]

I believe that this whole notion of the education of races that are selected on the basis of a determinate efficiency is one of the fundamental moments of history itself: education of the vision, education in walking – ascending, descending, running. It consists especially of education in composure. And the latter is above all a retarding mechanisms, a mechanism inhibiting disorderly movements; this retardation subsequently allows a co-ordinated response of co-ordinated movements setting off in the direction of a chosen goal. This resistance to emotional seizure is something fundamental in social and mental life. It separates out, it even classifies the so-called primitive societies; according to whether they display more brutal, unreflected, unconscious reactions or on the contrary more isolated, precise actions governed by a clear consciousness.

It is thanks to society that there is an intervention of consciousness. It is not thanks to unconsciousness that there is an intervention of society. It is thanks to society that there is the certainty of pre-prepared movements, domination of the conscious over emotion and unconsciousness. It is right that the French Navy is now to make it obligatory for its sailors to learn to swim.

[...]

Note

1   This lecture was given at a meeting of the Société de Psychologie, May 17th, 1934 and published in the *Journal de psychologie normal et patholigique*, Paris, Année XXXII, 1935, pp. 271–93. Reprinted in Marcel Mauss, *Sociologie et Anthropologie* (with introduction by Claude Levi-Strauss), 4th edition, Paris: Presses Universitaires de France, 1968, pp. 364–86.

Chapter 7

Mary Douglas

THE TWO BODIES

From M. Douglas (1996 [1970]) 'The two bodies', in *Natural Symbols: Explorations in Cosmology,* London and New York: Routledge.

THE SOCIAL BODY CONSTRAINS the way the physical body is perceived. The physical experience of the body, always modified by the social categories through which it is known, sustains a particular view of society. There is a continual exchange of meanings between the two kinds of bodily experience so that each reinforces the categories of the other. As a result of this interaction the body itself is a highly restricted medium of expression. The forms it adopts in movement and repose express social pressures in manifold ways. The care that is given to it, in grooming, feeding and therapy, the theories about what it needs in the way of sleep and exercise, about the stages it should go through, the pains it can stand, its span of life, all the cultural categories in which it is perceived, must correlate closely with the categories in which society is seen insofar as these also draw upon the same culturally processed idea of the body.

Marcel Mauss, in his essay on the techniques of the body (1936), boldly asserted that there can be no such thing as natural behaviour. Every kind of action carries the imprint of learning, from feeding to washing, from repose to movement and, above all, sex. Nothing is more essentially transmitted by a social process of learning than sexual behaviour, and this of course is closely related to morality.

[...]

Whereas Mauss was concerned to emphasize the culturally learnt control of the body, other scholars, before and after, have noticed unconscious correspondences between bodily and emotional states. Psychoanalysis takes considerable account of what Freud called 'conversion' of the emotional into the physical condition. This insight has had immense therapeutic and theoretical importance.

[...]

[But] such observations do not remotely approach a general sociological theory such as Mauss was seeking.

[...]

To be useful, the structural analysis of symbols has somehow to be related to a hypothesis about role structure. From here the argument will go in two stages. First, the drive to achieve consonance in all levels of experience produces concordance among the means of expression, so that the use of the body is co-ordinated with other media. Second, controls exerted from the social system place limits on the use of the body as medium.

[...]

Hence we would always expect some concordance between social and bodily expressions of control, first because each symbolic mode enhances meaning in the other, and so the ends of communication are furthered, and second because, as we said earlier, the categories in which each kind of experience is received are reciprocally derived and mutually reinforcing. It must be impossible for them to come apart and for one to bear false witness to the other except by a conscious, deliberate effort.

Mauss's denial that there is any such thing as natural behaviour is confusing. It falsely poses the relation between nature and culture. Here I seek to identify a natural tendency to express situations of a certain kind in an appropriate bodily style. Insofar as it is unconscious, insofar as it is obeyed universally in all cultures, the tendency is natural. It is generated in response to a perceived social situation, but the latter must always come clothed in its local history and culture. Therefore the natural expression is culturally determined.

[...]

[T]he human body is always treated as an image of society and ... there can be no natural way of considering the body that does not involve at the same time a social dimension. Interest in its apertures depends on the preoccupation with social exits and entrances, escape routes and invasions. If there is no concern to preserve social boundaries, I would not expect to find concern with bodily boundaries. The relation of head to feet, of brain and sexual organs, of mouth and anus are commonly treated so that they express the relevant patterns of hierarchy. Consequently I now advance the hypothesis that bodily control is an expression of social control – abandonment of bodily control in ritual responds to the requirements of a social experience which is being expressed. Furthermore, there is little prospect of successfully imposing bodily control without the corresponding social forms. And lastly, the same drive that seeks harmoniously to relate the experience of physical and social, must affect ideology. Consequently, when once the correspondence between bodily and social controls is traced, the basis will be laid for considering co-varying attitudes in political thought and in theology.

[...]

So far we have given two rules: one, the style appropriate to a message will co-ordinate all the channels; two, the scope of the body acting as a medium is restricted by the demands of the social system to be expressed. As this last implies, a third is that strong social control demands strong bodily control. A fourth is that along the dimension from weak to strong pressure the social system seeks progressively to disembody or etherealize the forms of expression; this can be called the purity rule. The last two work together, so I shall deal briefly with purity first, before illustrating how they dictate the bodily media of expression.

Social intercourse requires that unintended or irrelevant organic processes should be screened out. It equips itself therefore with criteria of relevance and these constitute the universal purity rule. The more complex the system of classification and the stronger the pressure to maintain it, the more social intercourse pretends to take place between disembodied spirits. Socialization teaches the child to bring organic processes under control. Of these, the most irrelevant and unwanted are the casting-off of waste products. Therefore all such physical events, defecation, urination, vomiting and their products, uniformly carry a pejorative sign for formal discourse. The sign is therefore available universally to interrupt such discourse if desired [...]. Other physiological processes must be controlled if they are not part of the discourse, sneezes, sniffs or coughs. If not controlled, formal framing-off procedures enable them to be shorn of their natural meaning and allow the discourse to go on uninterrupted. Lastly, and derived from the purity rule, are two physical dimensions for expressing social distance; one is the front-back dimension, the other the spatial. Front is more dignified and respect-worthy than back. Greater space means more formality, nearness means intimacy. By these rules an ordered pattern is found in the apparently chaotic variation between diverse cultures. The physical body is a microcosm of society, facing the centre of power, contracting and expanding its claims in direct accordance with the increase and relaxation of social pressures. Its members, now riveted into attention, now abandoned to their private devices, represent the members of society and their obligations to the whole. At the same time, the physical body, by the purity rule, is polarized conceptually against the social body. Its requirements are not only subordinated, they are contrasted with social requirements. The distance between the two bodies is the range of pressure and classification in the society. A complex social system devises for itself ways of behaving that suggest that human intercourse is disembodied compared with that of animal creation. It uses different degrees of disembodiment to express the social hierarchy. The more refinement, the less smacking of the lips when eating, the less mastication, the less the sound of breathing and walking, the more carefully modulated the laughter, the more controlled the signs of anger, the clearer comes the priestly aristocratic image. Since food takes a different place in different cultures this general rule is more difficult to see at work in table manners than in habits of dress and grooming.

The contrast of smooth with shaggy is a member of the general set of symbolic contrasts expressing formal/informal. Shaggy hair, as a form of protest against resented forms of social control, is a current symbol in our own day. There is no lack of pop-sociology pointing a moral which is fully compatible with my general thesis. Take the general run of stockbrokers or academics; stratify the professional sample by age; be careful to distinguish length of hair from unkempt hair; relate the incidence of shagginess in hair to sartorial indiscipline. Make an assessment under the division smooth/shaggy of other choices, preferred beverages, preferred meeting-places and so on. The prediction is that where the choices for the shaggy option cluster, there is least commitment to the norms of the profession. Or compare the professions and trades one against another. Those which are aiming at the centre top, public relations, or hair dressing, and those which have long been fully committed to the main morality, chartered accountants and the law, they are predictably against the shaggy option and for the smooth drink, hair style, or restaurant. Art and academia are potentially professions of comment and criticism on society: they display a carefully modulated shagginess according to the responsibilities they carry. But how shaggy can they get? What are the limits of shagginess and bodily abandon? It seems that the freedom to be completely relaxed must be culturally controlled.

[...]

[T]he social experience of disorder is expressed by powerfully efficacious symbols of impurity and danger. Recently I have argued that the joke is another such natural symbol (Douglas 1968). Whenever in the social situation, dominance is liable to be subverted, the joke is the natural and necessary expression, since the structure of the joke parallels the structure of the situation. In the same sense, I here argue that a social structure which requires a high degree of conscious control will find its style at a high level of formality, stern application of the purity rule, denigration of organic process and wariness towards experiences in which control of consciousness is lost.

[...]

Natural symbols will not be found in individual lexical items. The physical body can have universal meaning only as a system which responds to the social system, expressing it as a system. What it symbolizes naturally is the relation of parts of an organism to the whole. Natural symbols can express the relation of an individual to his society at that general systemic level. The two bodies are the self and society; sometimes they are so near as to be almost merged; sometimes they are far apart. The tension between them allows the elaboration of meanings.

References

Douglas, Mary (1968) *Social Control of Cognition. Factors in Joke Perception.* Man, N.S. 3. 3, pp. 361–7.
Mauss, Marcel (1936) Les techniques du corps, *Journal de la Psychologie.* 32, Mar–Apr.

Chapter 8

Erving Goffman

EMBODIED INFORMATION IN
FACE-TO-FACE INTERACTION

From E. Goffman (1963) *Behavior in Public Places: Notes on the Social Organization of Gatherings*, Free Press of Glencoe, Collier-Macmillan.

T HE EXCHANGE OF WORDS and glances between individuals in each other's presence is a very common social arrangement, yet it is one whose distinctive communication properties are difficult to disentangle. Pedantic definitions seem to be required.

An individual may give information through the linguistic means formally established in society for this purpose, namely, speech or recognized speech substitutes such as writing and pictorial signs or gestures. One speaks here of an individual sending messages to someone who receives them. But the individual may also give information expressively, through the incidental symptomatic significance of events associated with him. In this case one might say that he emits, exudes, or gives off information to someone who gleans it.

[...]

The information that an individual provides, whether he sends it or exudes it, may be *embodied* or *disembodied*.[1] A frown, a spoken word, or a kick is a message that a sender conveys by means of his own *current* bodily activity, the transmission occurring only during the time that this body is present to sustain this activity. Disembodied messages, such as the ones we receive from letters and mailed gifts, or the ones hunters receive from the spoor of a now distant animal, require that the organism do something that traps and holds information long after the organism has stopped informing. This study will be concerned only with embodied information.

[...]

In everyday thinking about the receiving senses, it is felt that ordinarily they are used in a "naked" or "direct" way. This apparently implies a restriction on boosting devices — mechanical, chemical, or electrical — except as these raise the faulty sense of a particular individual to average unassisted strength: glasses, for example, but not binoculars; hearing aids but not microphones. Electric lighting would have to be allowed as merely raising a room to day-time standards.

When one speaks of experiencing someone else with one's naked senses, one usually implies the reception of embodied messages. This linkage of naked senses on one side and embodied transmission on the other provides one of the crucial communication conditions of face-to-face interaction. Under this condition any message that an individual sends is likely to be qualified and modified by much additional information that others glean from him simultaneously, often unbeknownst to him; further, a very large number of brief messages may be sent.

Now the individual can, of course, receive embodied messages by means of his naked senses without much chance of these communication roles being reversed, as when he spies on persons through a crack in the wall or overhears them through a thin partition.[2] Such asymmetrical arrangements may even be established as part of an occupational setting, as in the procedure by which psychoanalysts or priests observe their clients without being as easily observed in return. Ordinarily, however, in using the naked senses to receive embodied messages from others, the individual also makes himself available as a source of embodied information for them (although there is always likely to be some differential exploitation of these monitoring possibilities). Here, then, is a second crucial communication condition of face-to-face interaction: not only are the receiving and conveying of the naked and embodied kind, but each giver is himself a receiver, and each receiver is a giver.

The implications of this second feature are fundamental. First, sight begins to take on an added and special role. Each individual can *see* that he is being experienced in some way, and he will guide at least some of this conduct according to the perceived identity and initial response of his audience.[3] Further, he can be seen to be seeing this, and can see that he has been seen seeing this. Ordinarily, then, to use our naked senses is to use them nakedly and to be made naked by their use. We are clearly seen as the agents of our acts, there being very little chance of disavowing having committed them; neither having given nor having received messages can be easily denied, at least among those immediately involved.[4]

The factor emerges, then, that was much considered by Adam Smith, Charles Cooley, and G. H. Mead; namely, the special mutuality of immediate social interaction. That is, when two persons are together, at least some of their world will be made up out of the fact (and consideration for the fact) that an adaptive line of action attempted by one will be either insightfully facilitated by the other or insightfully countered, or both, and that such a line of action must always be pursued in this intelligently helpful and hindering world. Individuals sympathetically take the attitude of others present, regardless of the end which they put the information thus acquired.[5]

[...]

Copresence renders persons uniquely accessible, available, and subject to one another. Public order, in its face-to-face aspects, has to do with the normative regulation of this accessibility. Perhaps the best explored face-to-face aspect of public order as traditionally defined is what is sometimes called "public safety." Its basic rules are few and clear, and, in Western society today, heavily reinforced by police authority.

[...]

For our present purposes, the aspect of public order having to do with personal safety will be passed by. I will be concerned with the fact that when persons are present to one another they can function not merely as physical instruments but also as communicative ones. This possibility, no less than the physical one, is fateful for everyone concerned and in every society appears to come under strict normative regulation, giving rise to a kind of communication traffic order.

[...]

In American society, it appears that the individual is expected to exert a kind of discipline or tension in regard to his body, showing that he has his faculties in readiness for any face-to-face interaction that might come his way in the situation.

[...]

One of the most evident means by which the individual shows himself to be situationally present is through the disciplined management of personal appearance or "personal front," that is, the complex of clothing, make-up, hairdo, and other surface decorations he carries about on his person. In public places in Western society, the male of certain classes is expected to present himself in the situation neatly attired, shaven, his hair combed, hands and face clean; female adults have similar and further obligations. It should be noted that with these matters of personal appearance the obligation is not merely to possess the equipment but also to exert the kind of sustained control that will keep it properly arranged. (And yet, in spite of these rulings, we may expect to find, in such places as the New York subway during the evening rush hour, that some persons, between scenes, as it were, may let expression fall from their faces in a kind of temporary uncaring and righteous exhaustion, even while being clothed and made up to fit a much more disciplined stance.)

I have already suggested that a failure to present oneself to a gathering in situational harness is likely to be taken as a sign of some kind of disregard for the setting and its participants.

[...]

An interesting expression of the kind of interaction tonus that lies behind the proper management of personal appearance is found in the constant care exerted by men in our society to see that their trousers are buttoned and that an erection bulge is not showing.[6] Before entering a social situation, they often run through a quick visual inspection of the relevant parts of their personal front, and once in the situation they may take the extra precaution of employing a protective cover, by either crossing the legs or covering the crotch with a newspaper or book, especially if self-control is to be relaxed through comfortable sitting. A parallel to this concern is found in the care that women take to see that their legs are not apart, exposing their upper thighs and underclothing. The universality in our society of this kind of limb discipline can be deeply appreciated on a chronic female ward where, for whatever reason, women indulge in zestful scratching of their private parts and in sitting with legs quite spread, causing the student to become conscious of the vast amount of limb discipline that is ordinarily taken for granted. A similar reminder of one's expectations concerning limb discipline can be obtained from the limb movements required of elderly obese women in getting out of the front seat of a car. Just as a Balinese would seem ever to be concerned about the direction and height of his seat, so the individual in our society, while "in situation," is constantly oriented to keeping "physical" signs of sexual capacities concealed. And it is suggested here that these parts of the body when

exposed are not a symbol of sexuality merely, but of a laxity of control over the self –
evidence of an insufficient harnessing of the self for the gathering.

[…]

One of the most delicate components of personal appearance seems to be the composition of the face. A very evident means by which the individual shows himself to be situationally present is by appropriately controlling through facial muscles the shape and
expression of the various parts of this instrument. Although this control may not be
conscious to any extent, it is nonetheless exerted. We have party faces, funeral faces, and
various kinds of institutional faces.

[…]

An interesting fact about proper composition of the face is that the ease of maintaining it in our society would seem to decline with age, so that, especially in the social class
groupings whose women long retain an accent on sexual attractiveness, there comes to
be an increasingly long period of time after awakening that is required to get the face into
shape, during which the individual in her own eyes is not "presentable." A point in age is
also reached when, given these youthful standards of what a face in play should look like,
there will be viewing angles from which an otherwise properly composed face looks to
have insufficient tonus.

The disciplined ordering of personal front is one way, then, in which the individual
is obliged to express his aliveness to those about him.

Notes

1   Compare the usage by T. S. Szasz, *The Myth of Mental Illness* (New York: Hoeber-Harper,
     1961), p. 116 ff.
2   An asymmetrical communication relation of this kind, Polonius notwithstanding, is of
     course more practical when boosting devices, such as concealed microphones, are
     employed. In Shetland Isle pocket telescopes were commonly used for the purpose of
     observing one's neighbors without being observed in the act of observing. In this way
     it was possible to check constantly what phase of the annual cycle of work one's neigh-
     bors were engaged in, and who was visiting whom. This use of the telescope was appar-
     ently related to the physical distance between crofts, the absence of trees and other
     blocks to long-distance perception, and the strong maritime tradition of the Islands. It
     may be added that every community and even work place would seem to have some
     special communication arrangements of its own.
3   In the asymmetrical case, where a person is being spied upon by direct or indirect
     means, he may greatly modify his conduct if he suspects he is being observed, even
     though he does not know the identity of the particular audience that might be observ-
     ing him. This is one of the possibilities celebrated in Orwell's *1984*, and its possibility
     is one of the force operative is socially controlling persons who are alone.
4   When two-way television is added to telephones, the unique contingencies of direct
     interaction will finally be available for those who are widely separated. In any case these
     mediated 'point-to-point' forms of communication can be characterized by the degree
     to which they restrict or attenuate the communicative possibilities discussed here.

5   As R. E. Park suggested in "Human Nature and Collective Behavior," *American Journal of Sociology*, 32 (1927), 738:

> In human society every act of every individual tends to become a gesture, since what one does is always an indication of what one intends to do. The consequence is that the individual in society lives a more or less public existence, in which all his acts are anticipated, checked, inhibited, or modified by the gestures and the intentions of his fellows. It is in this social conflict, in which every individual lives more or less in this mind of every other individual, that human nature and the individual may acquire their most characteristic and human traits.

6   The difficulty of engaging in this kind of protective concealment is one of the contingencies apparently faced by men with leg paralysis. See E. Henrich and L. Kriegel (eds) *Experiments in Survival* (New York: Association for the Aid of Crippled Children, 1961), p. 192.

Chapter 9

Pierre Bourdieu

BELIEF AND THE BODY

From P. Bourdieu (1984) 'Belief and the body', in *The Logic of Practice*, Oxford: Blackwell.

PRACTICAL SENSE IS A QUASI-BODILY involvement in the world which presupposes no representation either of the body or of the world, still less of their relationship. It is an immanence in the world through which the world imposes its immanence, things to be done or said, which directly govern speech and action. It orients 'choices' which, though not deliberate, are no less systematic, and which, without being ordered and organized in relation to an end, are nonetheless charged with a kind of retrospective finality. A particularly clear example of practical sense as a proleptic adjustment to the demands of a field is what is called, in the language of sport, a 'feel for the game'. This phrase (like 'investment sense', the art of 'anticipating' events, etc.) gives a fairly accurate idea of the almost miraculous encounter between the *habitus* and a field, between incorporated history and an objectified history, which makes possible the near-perfect anticipation of the future inscribed in all the concrete configurations on the pitch or board.

[...]

In a game, the field (the pitch or board on which it is played, the rules, the outcome at stake, etc.) is clearly seen for what it is, an arbitrary social construct, an artefact whose arbitrariness and artificiality are underlined by everything that defines its autonomy — explicit and specific rules, strictly delimited and extra-ordinary time and space. Entry into the game takes the form of a quasi-contract, which is sometimes made explicit (the Olympic oath, appeals to 'fair play', and, above all, the presence of a referee or umpire) or recalled to those who get so 'carried away by the game' that they forget it is 'only a game'. By contrast, in the social fields, which are the products of a long, slow process of autonomization, and are therefore, so to speak, games 'in themselves' and not 'for themselves', one does not embark on the game by a conscious act, one is born into the game, with the game; and the relation of investment, *illusio*, investment, is made more total and unconditional by the fact that it is unaware of what it is. As Claudel put it, 'connaître, c'est naître avec', to know is to be born with, and the long dialectical process, often described as 'vocation', through which the various fields provide themselves with agents equipped with the *habitus* needed to make them work, is to the learning of a game very much as the acquisition of the mother tongue is to the learning of a foreign language. In the latter case, an already constituted disposition confronts a language that is perceived as such, that is, as an arbitrary game, explicitly constituted as such in the form of grammar, rules and exercises, expressly taught by institutions expressly designed for that purpose. In the case of primary learning, the child learns at the same time to speak the language (which is only ever presented in action, in his own or other people's speech) and to think *in* (rather than with) the language. The earlier a player enters the game and the less he is aware of the associated learning (the limiting case being, of course, that of someone born into, born with the game), the greater is his ignorance of all that is tacitly granted through his investment in the field and his interest in its very existence and perpetuation and in everything that is played for in it, and his unawareness of the unthought presuppositions that the game produces and endlessly reproduces, thereby reproducing the conditions of its own perpetuation.

Belief is thus an inherent part of belonging to a field. In its most accomplished form — that is, the most naive form, that of native membership — it is diametrically opposed to what Kant, in the *Critique of Pure Reason*, calls 'pragmatic faith', the arbitrary acceptance, for the purposes of action, of an uncertain proposition (as in Descartes's paradigm of the travelers lost in a forest who stick to an arbitrary choice of direction). Practical faith is the condition of entry that every field tacitly imposes, not only by sanctioning and debarring those who would destroy the game, but by so arranging things, in practice, that the operations of selecting and shaping new entrants (rites of passage, examinations, etc.) are such as to obtain from them that undisputed, pre-reflexive, naive, native compliance with the fundamental presuppositions of the field which is the very definition of doxa.[1] The countless acts of recognition which are the small change of the compliance inseparable from belonging to the field, and in which collective misrecognition is ceaselessly generated, are both the precondition and the product of the functioning of the field. They thus constitute investments in the collective enterprise of creating symbolic capital, which can only be performed on condition that the logic of the functioning of the field remains misrecognized. That is why one cannot enter this magic circle by an instantaneous decision of the will, but only by birth or by a slow process of co-option and initiation which is equivalent to a second birth.

One cannot really *live* the belief associated with profoundly different conditions of existence, that is, with other games and other stakes, still less give others the means of reliving it by the sheer power of discourse. [...] Practical belief is not a 'state of mind', still less a kind of arbitrary adherence to a set of instituted dogmas and doctrines ('beliefs'), but rather a state of the body. Doxa is the relationship of immediate adherence that is established in practice between a *habitus* and the field to which it is attuned, the pre-verbal taking-for-granted of the world that flows from practical sense. [...] Practical sense, social necessity turned into nature, converted into motor schemes and body automatisms, is what causes practices, in and through what makes them obscure to the eyes of their producers, to be *sensible*, that is, informed by a common sense. It is because agents never know completely what they are doing that what they do has more sense than they know.

Every social order systematically takes advantage of the disposition of the body and language to function as depositories of deferred thoughts that can be triggered off at a distance in space and time by the simple effect of re-placing the body in an overall posture which *recalls* the associated thoughts and feelings, in one of the inductive states of the body which, as actors know, give rise to states of mind. Thus the attention paid to staging great collective ceremonies derives not only from the concern to give a solemn representation of the group (manifest in the splendour of baroque festivals) but also, as many uses of singing and dancing show, from the less visible intention of ordering thoughts and suggesting feelings through the rigorous marshalling of practices and the orderly disposition of bodies, in particular the bodily expression of emotion, in laughter or tears. Symbolic power works partly through the control of other people's bodies and belief that is given by the collectively recognized capacity to act in various ways on deep-rooted linguistic and muscular patterns of behaviour, either by neutralizing them or by reactivating them to function mimetically.

Adapting a phrase of Proust's, one might say that arms and legs are full of numb imperatives. One could endlessly enumerate the values given body, *made* body, by the hidden persuasion of an implicit pedagogy which can instil a whole cosmology, through injunctions as insignificant as 'sit up straight' or 'don't hold your knife in your left hand', and inscribe the most fundamental principles of the arbitrary content of a culture in seemingly innocuous details of bearing or physical and verbal manners, so putting them beyond the reach of consciousness and explicit statement. The logic of scheme transfer which makes each technique of the body a kind of *pars totalis*, predisposed to function in accordance with the fallacy of *pars pro toto*, and hence to recall the whole system to which it belongs, gives a general scope to the apparently most circumscribed and circumstantial observances. The cunning of pedagogic reason lies precisely in the fact that it manages to extort what is essential while seeming to demand the insignificant, such as the respect for forms and forms of respect which are the most visible and most 'natural' manifestation of respect for the established order, or the concessions of politeness, which always contain political concessions.[2]

Bodily hexis is political mythology realized, *em-bodied*, turned into a permanent disposition, a durable way of standing, speaking, walking, and thereby of feeling and thinking. The opposition between male and female is realized in posture, in the gestures and movements of the body, in the form of the opposition between the straight and the bent, between firmness, uprightness and directness (a man faces forward, looking and striking directly at his adversary), and restraint, reserve and flexibility.

[…]

In other words, when the elementary acts of bodily gymnastics (going up or down, forwards or backwards, etc.) and, most importantly, the specifically sexual, and therefore biologically preconstructed, aspect of this gymnastics (penetrating or being penetrated, being on top or below, etc.) are highly charged with social meanings and values, socialization instils a sense of the equivalences between physical space and social space and between movements (rising, falling, etc.) in the two spaces and thereby roots the most fundamental structures of the group in the primary experiences of the body which, as is clearly seen in emotion, takes metaphors seriously.[3] For example, the opposition between the straight and the bent … is central to most of the marks of respect or contempt that politeness uses in many societies to symbolize relations of domination. On the one hand, lowering or bending the head or forehead as a sign of confusion or timidity, lowering the eyes in humility or timidity, and also shame or modesty, looking down or underneath, kneeling, curtseying, prostration (before a superior or a god); on the other hand, looking up, looking someone in the eyes, refusing to bow the head, standing up to someone, getting the upper hand … Male, upward movements and female, downward movements, uprightness versus bending, the will to be on top, to overcome, versus submission – the fundamental oppositions of the social order, whether between the dominant and the dominated or between the dominant-dominant and the dominated-dominant – are always sexually overdetermined, as if the body language of sexual domination and submission had provided the fundamental principles of both the body language and the verbal language of social domination and submission.[4]

[...]

[T]he process of acquisition – a practical *mimesis* (or mimeticism) which implies an overall relation of identification and has nothing in common with an *imitation* that would presuppose a conscious effort to reproduce a gesture, an utterance or an object explicitly constituted as a model – and the process of reproduction – a practical reactivation which is opposed to both memory and knowledge – tend to take place below the level of consciousness, expression and the reflexive distance which these presuppose. The body believes in what it plays at: it weeps if it mimes grief. It does not represent what it performs, it does not memorize the past, it *enacts* the past, bringing it back to life. What is 'learned by body' is not something that one has, like knowledge that can be brandished, but something that one is.

[...]

So long as the work of education is not clearly institutionalized as a specific, autonomous practice, so long as it is the whole group and a whole symbolically structured environment, without specialized agents or specific occasions, that exerts an anonymous, diffuse pedagogic action, the essential part of the *modus operandi* that defines practical mastery is transmitted through practice, in the practical state, without rising to the level of discourse. The child mimics other people's action rather than 'models'. Body hexis speaks directly to the motor function, in the form of a pattern of postures that is both individual and systematic, being bound up with a whole system of objects, and charged with a host of special meanings and values. But the fact that schemes are able to pass directly from practice to practice without moving through discourse and consciousness does not mean that the acquisition of *habitus* is no more than a mechanical learning through trial and error.

[...]

Between learning through sheer familiarization, in which the learner insensibly and unconsciously acquires the principles of an 'art' and an art of living, including those that are not known to the producer of the practices or artefacts that are imitated, and explicit and express transmission by precept and prescription, every society provides structural exercises which tend to transmit a particular form of practical mastery.

[...]

The world of objects, a kind of book in which each thing speaks metaphorically of all others and from which children learn to read the world, is read with the whole body, in and through the movements and displacements which define the space of objects as much as they are defined by it.[5] The structures that help to construct the world of objects are constructed in the practice of a world of objects constructed in accordance with the same structures. The 'subject' born of the world of objects does not arise as a subjectivity facing an objectivity: the objective universe is made up of objects which are the product of objectifying operations structured according to the same structures that the *habitus* applies to them. The *habitus* is a metaphor of the world of objects, which is itself an endless circle of metaphors that mirror each other *ad infinitum*.

[...]

In a society divided into classes, all the products of a given agent, by an essential overdetermination, speak inseparably and simultaneously of his/her class – or, more precisely, his/her position and rising or falling trajectory within the social structure – and of his/her body – or, more precisely, of all the properties, always socially qualified, of which he/she is the bearer: sexual ones, of course, but also physical properties that are praised, like strength or beauty, or stigmatized.

Notes

1   The term *obsequium* used by Spinoza to denote the 'constant will' produced by the conditioning through which 'the State fashions us for its own use and which enables it to survive' (Matheron 1969: 349) could be used to designate the public testimonies of recognition that every group requires of its members (especially at moments of co-option), i.e. the symbolic tributes due from individuals in the exchanges that are set up in every group between the individuals and the group. Because, as in gift exchange, the exchange is an end in itself, the tribute demanded by the group generally comes down to a matter of trifles, that is, symbolic rituals (rites of passage, the ceremonials of etiquette, etc.) formalities and formalisms which 'cost nothing' to perform and seem such 'natural' things to demand ('It's the least one can do...', 'it wouldn't cost him anything to...') that abstention amounts to a challenge.

2   Thus, practical mastery of the rules of politeness and, in particular, the art of adjusting each of the available formulae (e.g. at the end of a letter) to the various classes of possible recipients presupposes implicit mastery, and therefore recognition, of a set of oppositions constituting the implicit axiomatics of a given political order: oppositions between men and women, between younger and older, between the personal, or private, and the impersonal (administrative or business letters), between superiors, equals and inferiors.

3   Like hysteria which, according to Freud, 'takes expressions literally, really feeling the heart-rending or the smack in the face which a speaker refers to metaphorically'.

4   The opposition between the sexes can also be organized on the basis of the opposition, which is used intensively in gestural or verbal insults, between the front (of the body), the site of sexual difference, and the behind, which is sexually undifferentiated, feminine and submissive.

5   This means to say that the 'learning by doing' hypothesis, associated with the name of Arrow (1962), is a particular case of a very general law: every made product – not least, symbolic products, such as works of art, games, myths, etc. – exerts by its very functioning, particularly by the use made of it, an educative effect which helps to make it easier to acquire the dispositions required for its adequate use.

References

Arrow, K. J. 1962: The economic implications of learning by doing. *Review of Economic Studies*, 39, pp. 155–73.

Matheron, A. 1969: *Individu et société chez Spinoza*. Paris: Éditions de Minuit.

Chapter 10

Mikhail Bakhtin

THE GROTESQUE IMAGE OF THE BODY AND ITS SOURCES

From M. M. Bakhtin (1984) *Rabelais and His World*, translated by Helene Iswolsky, Bloomington, IN: Indiana University Press.

[...]

WE FIND AT THE BASIS of grotesque imagery a special concept of the body as a whole and of the limits of this whole. The confines between the body and the world and between separate bodies are drawn in the grotesque genre quite differently than in the classic and naturalist images.

[...]

Of all the features of the human face, the nose and mouth play the most important part in the grotesque image of the body; the head, ears, and nose also acquire a grotesque character when they adopt the animal form or that of inanimate objects. The eyes have no part in these comic images; they express an individual, so to speak, self-sufficient human life, which is not essential to the grotesque. The grotesque is interested only in protruding eyes. [...] It is looking for that which protrudes from the body, all that seeks to go out beyond the body's confines. Special attention is given to the shoots and branches, to all that prolongs the body and links it to other bodies or to the world outside. Moreover, the bulging eyes manifest a purely bodily tension. But the most important of all human features for the grotesque is the mouth. It dominates all else. The grotesque face is actually reduced to the gaping mouth; the other features are only a frame encasing this wide-open bodily abyss.

The grotesque body, as we have often stressed, is a body in the act of becoming. It is never finished, never completed; it is continually built, created, and builds and creates another body. More-over, the body swallows the world and is itself swallowed by the world (let us recall the grotesque image in the episode of Gargantua's birth on the feast of cattle-slaughtering). This is why the essential role belongs to those parts of the grotesque body in which it outgrows its own self, transgressing its own body, in which it conceives a new, second body: the bowels and the phallus. These two areas play the leading role in the grotesque image, and it is precisely for this reason that they are predominantly subject to positive exaggeration, to hyperbolization; they can even detach themselves from the body and lead an independent life, for they hide the rest of the body, as something secondary (The nose can also in a way detach itself from the body). Next to the bowels and the genital organs is the mouth, through which enters the world to be swallowed up. And next is the anus. All these convexities and orifices have a common characteristic; it is within them that the confines between bodies and between the body and the world are overcome: there is an interchange and an interorientation. This is why the main events in the life of the grotesque body, the acts of the bodily drama, take place in this sphere. Eating, drinking, defecation and other elimination (sweating, blowing of the nose, sneezing), as well as copulation, pregnancy, dismemberment, swallowing up by another body – all these acts are performed on the confines of the body and the outer world, or on the confines of the old and new body. In all these events the beginning and end of life are closely linked and interwoven.

Thus the artistic logic of the grotesque image ignores the closed, smooth, and impenetrable surface of the body and retains only its excrescences (sprouts, buds) and orifices, only that which leads beyond the body's limited space or into the body's depths. Mountains and abysses, such is the relief of the grotesque body; or speaking in architectural terms, towers and subterranean passages.

Grotesque images may, of course, present other members, organs and parts of the body (especially dismembered parts), but they play a minor role in the drama. They are never stressed unless they replace a leading image.

Actually, if we consider the grotesque image in its extreme aspect, it never presents an individual body; the image consists of orifices and convexities that present another, newly conceived body. It is a point of transition in a life eternally renewed, the inexhaustible vessel of death and conception.

As we have said, the grotesque ignores the impenetrable surface that closes and limits the body as a separate and completed phenomenon. The grotesque image displays not only the outward but also the inner features of the body: blood, bowels, heart and other organs. The outward and inward features are often merged into one.

We have already sufficiently stressed the fact that grotesque imagery constructs what we might call a double body. In the endless chain of bodily life it retains the parts in which one link joins the other, in which the life of one body is born from the death of the preceding, older one.

[...]

This boundless ocean of grotesque bodily imagery within time and space extends to all languages, all literatures, and the entire system of gesticulation; in the midst of it the bodily canon of art, belles lettres, and polite conversation of modern times is a tiny island. This limited canon never prevailed in antique literature. In the official literature of European peoples it has existed only for the last four hundred years.

We shall give a brief characterization of the new canon, concerning ourselves less with the pictorial arts than with literature. We shall build this characterization by comparing it to the grotesque conception and bringing out the differences.

The new bodily canon, in all its historic variations and different genres, presents an entirely finished, completed, strictly limited body, which is shown from the outside as something individual. That which protrudes, bulges, sprouts, or branches off (when a body transgresses its limits and a new one begins) is eliminated, hidden, or moderated.

All orifices of the body are closed. The basis of the image is the individual, strictly limited mass, the impenetrable façade. The opaque surface and the body's 'valleys' acquire an essential meaning as the border of a closed individuality that does not merge with other bodies and with the world. All attributes of the unfinished world are carefully removed, as well as all the signs of its inner life. The verbal norms of official and literary language, determined by the canon, prohibit all that is linked with fecundation, pregnancy, childbirth. There is a sharp line of division between familiar speech and 'correct' language.

The fifteenth century was an age of considerable freedom in France. In the sixteenth century the norms of language become more strict, and the borderline between the different norms grew more evident. This process intensified at the end of the century, when the canon of polite speech that was to prevail in the seventeenth century was definitely formed. At the end of the century Montaigne protested in his *Essays* against these prohibitions.

> What harm has the genital act, so natural, so necessary, and so lawful, done to humanity, that we dare not speak of it without shame, and exclude it from serious and orderly conversation? We boldly utter the words, *kill, rob, betray*: and the other we only dare utter under our breath. Does this mean that the less of it we breathe in words, the more are we at liberty to swell our thoughts with it? For it is amusing that the words which are least used, least written, and most hushed up should be the best known and the most generally understood. There is no person of any age or morals but knows them as well as he knows the word *bread*. They are impressed upon each of us, without being expressed, without voice and without form. (And the sex that does it most is charged to hush it up.)[1]

In the new canon, such parts of the body as the genital organs, the buttocks, belly, nose and mouth cease to play the leading role. Moreover, instead of their original meaning they acquire an exclusiveness; in other words, they convey a merely individual meaning of the life of one single, limited body. The belly, nose, and mouth, are of course retained in the image and cannot be hidden, but in an individual, completed body they either fulfill purely expressive functions (this is true of the mouth only) or the functions of characterization and individualization. There is no symbolic, broad meaning whatever in the organs of this body. If they are not interpreted as a characterization and an expressive feature, they are referred to on the merely practical level in brief explanatory comments. Generally speaking, all that does not contain an element of characterization in the literary image is reduced to a simple bodily remark added to speech or action.

In the modern image of the individual body, sexual life, eating, drinking, and defecation have radically changed their meaning: they have been transferred to the private and psychological level where their connotation becomes narrow and specific, torn away from the direct relation to the life of society and to the cosmic whole. In this new connotation they can no longer carry on their former philosophical functions.

In the new bodily canon the leading role is attributed to the individually characteristic and expressive parts of the body: the head, face, eyes, lips, to the muscular system, and to the place of the body in the external world. The exact position and movements of this finished body in the finished outside world are brought out, so that the limits between them are not weakened.

The body of the new canon is merely one body; no signs of duality have been left. It is self-sufficient and speaks in its name alone. All that happens within it concerns it alone, that is, only the individual, closed sphere. Therefore, all the events taking place within it acquire one single meaning: death is only death, it never coincides with birth; old age is torn away from youth; blows merely hurt, without assisting an act of birth. All actions and events are interpreted on the level of a single, individual life. They are enclosed within the limits of the same body, limits that are the absolute beginning and end and can never meet.

In the grotesque body, on the contrary, death brings nothing to an end, for it does not concern the ancestral body, which is renewed in the next generation. The events of the grotesque sphere are always developed on the boundary dividing one body from the other and, as it were, at their points of intersection. One body offers its death, the other its birth, but they are merged in a two-bodied image.

In the new canon the duality of the body is preserved only in one theme, a pale reflection of its former dual nature. This is the theme of nursing a child. But the image of the mother and the child is strictly individualized and closed, the line of demarcation cannot be removed. This is a completely new phase of the artistic conception of bodily interaction.

Finally, the new canon is completely alien to hyperbolization. The individualized image has no place for it. All that is permitted is a certain accentuation of expressive and characterized features. The severance of the organs from the body or their independent existence is no longer permitted.

We have roughly sketched the basic outlines of the modern canon, as they generally appear in the norms of literature and speech.

[…]

Note

1   Montaigne, 'Essays', III, Chapter 5. Translated by George B. Ivez, Copyright Harvard University Press, 1925.

Chapter 11

Norbert Elias

CIVILIZATION AND PSYCHOSOMATICS

From N. Elias (unpublished) 'Civilisation and Psychosomatics'.

A T A TIME WHEN THE TENDENCY towards apartheid of biological and social sciences is still very great, it is a rare honour, but also a pleasure and a rewarding task for a social scientist to be called upon to address this congress of specialists in psychosomatic medicine. The unity and interdependence of all scientific disciplines concerned with human beings is difficult to deny, and it is essential for the advance of knowledge of ourselves, of human beings, to broaden the common ground. In my own work that is what I have often tried to do. Particularly my theory of civilization, cannot be confined to any special human science. It is concerned with problems of personal and social constraint, of changes in the manner people regulate their own and each other's conduct and sentiment.

Hence, in my talk I shall be concerned with comparisons between different stages in the development of societies which may have an influence on the incidence and cause of psychosomatic diseases. This can be easily understood as a historical interest in human beings. That would be a mistake. The historian's approach to the human past, with some notable exceptions, often leaves me with the impression of a walk through a museum. The social science approach to the human past is different. It is not concerned with the history, but with the development of present societies. It seeks to explain aspects of the present which remain unexplainable and perhaps invisible without references to the past. The concept of a civilizing process itself has, among other things, an explanatory function. It focusses attention on *changes* in the social standards of human conduct and sentiment and thus also of illnesses connected with them.

Let me take as an example a prescription characteristic of a different phase of a civilizing process: 'Don't spit over the table, spit under the table.' Compare this with the later prescription 'Please use the spittoon.' Still later one could find in public transport vehicles the laconic prescription: 'spitting prohibited'. Finally, the custom of spitting itself has largely vanished. One need not doubt that considerations of hygiene played a part in that change, but it is at most a part explanation.

Spitting, like kissing, is not a biological need, but a social custom. At earlier stages of development it is often regarded as a symbol of manliness to assemble sputum in one's mouth and to dispose of it by spitting. In contemporary industrial societies it is not usual to collect surplus sputum in one's mouth and to ejaculate it aimfully or at random.

Instead, it has become customary to swallow it mostly without being aware of it as it comes along. This technique very much corresponds to the manner in which members of industrial society regulate emotional impulses and to their general reticence with regard to the bodily functions of other people. It points in the same direction as the so-called 'internalization' of emotional impulses which is a characteristic of one of the later stages of a civilizing process.

Take as another example the development of physical violence. It was once ubiquitous. The ruins of castles and of the fortress walls of cities bear witness to the fact that the central control of physical violence performed by a king or his representatives or, in other words, the internal pacification of society was very ineffectual in the feudal period. It became more effectual when sword and armour gave way to fire weapons and the armoured knight, part of a cavalry formation and doing his duty to an overlord, gave way to the wage earning foot soldier. They enabled their master, emperor, king or prince, to collect the taxes more regularly and effectively, or to borrow money on future taxes. A small part of the prince's tax income, in principle, came regularly back to the soldier as wages. Thus, as the social development moves from feudal state to absolute state and from absolute state to the parliamentary multiparty state, intra-state pacification became more effective while inter-state wars became more destructive. [...]

Armed conflict was more or less endemic in a society with an upper-class of warrior nobles, but physical conflict was not confined to armed men. In a sixteenth century book with rules for women one can read: 'If he beats you and you escape by the front door, come home again by the back door.' Beating one's wife was at that time a fairly normal event. Today, as a result of the state's monopoly of physical violence, every form of physical violence not licenced by the state calls for an intervention of state authorities. If a husband beats his wife, neighbours may call the police.

In conjunction with the greater effectiveness of violence control within these states people's self-control and sensitivity with regard to acts of physical aggression has grown. News about acts of violence arouse curiously ambivalent feelings. On the one hand, doing the forbidden thing, arouses people's interest. It evokes, on the other hand, a kind of repugnance. People's sensitivity with regard to acts of violence has greatly increased. In this case too, detached reflection which one might call rational is fused with strong emotion. Even the beating of children which survived the mounting abhorrence longer than most other acts of physical violence has now been largely banished from home and school. A child's conduct may be very trying, yet the child's father would earn disapproval if he boxed the child's ear. Teachers who did that might lose their job. Attempts at breaking the state's monopoly of violence usually catch wide attention, but they also show how great the power resources are which a state administration can marshal in order to protect its privileged position with regard to the use of violence.

One can easily forget the price that has to be paid by individuals for intra-state pacification and individual self-regulation in accordance with the state monopoly of physical violence and of taxation. Present discussions of problems such as this are marred with the widely used concept of aggressiveness. Eminent scientists, such as Freud and Lorenz, have added the weight of their opinion to the view that human beings by attacking and perhaps destroying each other follow an inborn and thus inalterable instinct. Their main opponents are behaviouristic schools of thought which present all tendencies of human beings to attack and perhaps to destroy each other as tendencies acquired by people through learning, and wholy independent of the genetic constitution of humans.

In accordance with the prevailing standards of speaking and thinking, opinions are divided on simple polar lines. The incidence of violence among human beings is explained either in terms of changeable social or natural conditions usually represented by the key-concept 'environment' or in terms of unchangeable human nature usually represented by the key-concept 'instinct of aggressiveness'. Freud called it *Todestrieb* or drive towards death. They are made to appear as the only two alternatives from which one can choose in this context. In actual fact the seemingly exclusive opposition between such antagonists as instinct and environment are simply reflections of the antagonism between two social groups.

There is no evidence for the assumption that acts of aggression satisfy a universal human need in the same way in which drinking a glass of water may satisfy the natural instinct of thirst. There is good evidence for the assumption that human beings share with their more animalistic ancestors a genetically determined alarm reaction. In case of danger the whole organism is put into a different gear. It is automatically prepared for flight or fight. One can imagine that some people are more or less permanently geared for the emergency of a flight or fight situations without being able to use their motoric equipment in the manner for which it is prepared by this reaction of the automatic branch of their nervous system. Their face or perhaps their stomach receives permanently less than its normal supply of blood. Arms and legs are geared for an action they are never called upon to perform. Such discrepancies between activities of the central nervous system in normal and emergency situations and activities of the vegetative branch of the nervous system anticipating an emergency situation (perhaps a coming attack or a conflict which may exist only in a person's imagination) may well give rise to psychosomatic disorders. It has sometimes been assumed that the various sections of the human organism in general and those of the nervous system in particular always work in peace and harmony with each other, but that is not the case. Discrepancies are far from rare. Those connected with an emergency which fails to materialize or which exists only in a person's imagination are not the only examples. It is possible that a person's recurrent tendencies to attack others form part of a feeling of being attacked by others or, more generally, of being in danger. The incidence and pattern of the use of violence in human relations has changed quite drastically. In spite of all fluctuations, the control of acts of aggression within states has become more thorough. Compared with feudal societies the centralization and monopolization of the use of physical violence in contemporary industrial states has become much more efficient. In conjunction with the greater effectiveness of violence control within these states, as I have mentioned before, people's self-control and sensitivity with regard to acts of physical aggression has grown. It is difficult to argue for or against the existence of a universal human instinct of aggressiveness as long as one does not take such changes in the standards of social and self-regulation with regard to acts of physical violence into account. At present that is seldom done.

[…]

As one may recognize, the direction of change brought to light by a long-term comparison between stages in the development of the state organization bears some relationship to the direction of change in the custom of spitting revealed by a comparison of relevant samples from different stages in the development of societies. It bears some relationship too to the direction of change in the attitude towards violence. To put it briefly the three sequences — first: feudal state, absolute state, parliamentary state; second: spitting under the table, using a spittoon, keeping sputum to oneself and third: the sequence leading from endemic violence, living in fortified castles and walled cities to the normally almost complete disappearance of intra-state physical violence — run on more or less parallel lines. They indicate what the term 'civilization' means if it is understood as representing not a political or philosophical ideal, but a factual process.

Especially the increasingly effective curbing of state-internal violence suggests an hypothesis with regard to psychosomatic disorders. As is well known, illnesses of this type have a strong element of self-aggression. The hypothesis is that in societies in which one is forbidden to inflict physical pain on others, the incidence of those who instead inflict physical pain upon themselves is likely to be high. Inflicting pain on others is strictly forbidden. Inflicting pain upon oneself is not forbidden and not punishable. The question that suggests itself is that of a possible connection between the high effectiveness which the monopoly of physical violence has attained in most parliamentary nation-states and the high incidence of psychosomatic disorders.

[…]

At the end a word of caution may be appropriate. The human difficulties which I have tried to put before you may give rise to illnesses, but they themselves are not illnesses. A precise concept is lacking. I myself conceptualize them as difficulties of the social habitus or the social personality structure of people. The often heard complaint 'I cannot express my emotions' or 'I cannot express my feelings' point to difficulties of this type. They are difficulties of members of specific societies, of representatives of a particular stage in their development. If one likes, one may call them 'disorders of a period'. At the moment it must be enough to bring such conceptual problems into the open.

Societies are not entirely without remedy in the face of difficulties of this type. Almost blindly, that is, without any purposeful and concerted steerage, some very old social institutions have developed in a way which can and in fact quite often do act as antidote against the tensions produced by the inability to discharge strong drives or affective impulses in the form of motoric actions or, in the simpler language of every day, to express one's feelings. To give an example, many and perhaps most of our leisure time occupations are opportunities for experiencing and in some cases for acting out strong feelings often, if not always, without doing serious harm either to others or to oneself. The function and character of leisure time occupations within the human universe and especially their connection with other types of social activities have not found and, indeed, hardly find the attention they would deserve if significance for human beings were the determining factor of the selection of topics of sociological or, for that matter, of medical research. One can well imagine that at some future date doctors in care of patients with psychosomatic complaints will routinely ask such questions as: 'What are your leisure time occupations? Do you enjoy them?'

Chapter 12

Michel Foucault

THE POLITICAL INVESTMENT
OF THE BODY

From M. Foucault (1979) *Discipline and Punish: The Birth of the Prison*, translated by Alan Sheridan, New York: Random House.

HISTORIANS LONG AGO BEGAN to write the history of the body. They have studied the body in the field of historical demography or pathology; they have considered it as the seat of needs and appetites, as the locus of physiological processes and metabolisms, as a target for the attacks of germs or viruses; they have shown to what extent historical processes were involved in what might seem to be the purely biological base of existence; and what place should be given in the history of society to biological 'events' such as the circulation of bacilli, or the extension of the life-span (cf. Le Roy-Ladurie). But the body is also directly involved in a political field; power relations have an immediate hold upon it; they invest it, mark it, train it, torture it, force it to carry out tasks, to perform ceremonies, to emit signs. This political investment of the body is bound up, in accordance with complex reciprocal relations, with its economic use; it is largely as a force of production that the body is invested with relations of power and domination; but, on the other hand, its constitution as labour power is possible only if it is caught up in a system of subjection (in which need is also a political instrument meticulously prepared, calculated and used); the body becomes a useful force only if it is both a productive body and a subjected body. This subjection is not only obtained by the instruments of violence or ideology; it can also be direct, physical, pitting force against force, bearing on material elements, and yet without involving violence; it may be calculated, organized, technically thought out; it may be subtle, make use neither of weapons nor of terror and yet remain of a physical order. That is to say, there may be a 'knowledge' of the body that is not exactly the science of its functioning, and a mastery of its forces that is more than the ability to conquer them: this knowledge and this mastery constitute what might be called the political technology of the body. Of course, this technology is diffuse, rarely formulated in continuous, systematic discourse; it is often made up of bits and pieces; it implements a disparate set of tools or methods. In spite of the coherence of its results, it is generally no more than a multiform instrumentation. Moreover, it cannot be localized in a particular type of institution or state apparatus. For they have recourse to it; they use, select or impose certain of its methods. But, in its mechanisms and its effects, it is situated at a quite different level. What the apparatuses and institutions operate is, in a sense, a micro-physics of power, whose field of validity is situated in a sense between these great functionings and the bodies themselves with their materiality and their forces.

Now, the study of this microphysics presupposes that the power exercised on the body is conceived not as a property, but as a strategy, that its effects of domination are attributed not to 'appropriation', but to dispositions, manoeuvres, tactics, techniques, functionings; that one should decipher in it a network of relations, constantly in tension, in activity, rather than a privilege that one might possess; that one should take as its model a perpetual battle rather than a contract regulating a transaction or the conquest of a territory. In short this power is exercised rather than possessed; it is not the 'privilege', acquired or preserved, of the dominant class, but the overall effect of its strategic positions – an effect that is manifested and sometimes extended by the position of those who are dominated. Furthermore, this power is not exercised simply as an obligation or a prohibition on those who 'do not have it'; it invests them, is transmitted by them and through them; it exerts pressure upon them, just as they themselves, in their struggle against it, resist the grip it has on them. This means that these relations go right down into the depths of society, that they are not localized in the relations between the state and its citizens or on the frontier between classes and that they do not merely reproduce, at the level of individuals, bodies, gestures and behaviour, the general form of the law or government; that, although there is continuity (they are indeed articulated on this form through a whole series of complex mechanisms), there is neither analogy nor homology, but a specificity of mechanism and modality. Lastly, they are not univocal; they define innumerable points of confrontation, focuses of instability, each of which has its own risks of conflict, of struggles, and of an at least temporary inversion of the power relations. The overthrow of these 'micro-powers' does not, then, obey the law of all or nothing; it is not acquired once and for all by a new control of the apparatuses nor by a new functioning or a destruction of the institutions; on the other hand, none of its localized episodes may be inscribed in history except by the effects that it induces on the entire network in which it is caught up.

Perhaps, too, we should abandon a whole tradition that allows us to imagine that knowledge can exist only where the power relations are suspended and that knowledge can develop only outside its injunctions, its demands and its interests. Perhaps we should abandon the belief that power makes mad and that, by the same token, the renunciation of power is one of the conditions of knowledge. We should admit rather that power produces knowledge (and not simply by encouraging it because it serves power or by applying it because it is useful); that power and knowledge directly imply one another; that there is no power relation without the correlative constitution of a field of knowledge, nor any knowledge that does not presuppose and constitute at the same time power relations. These 'power-knowledge relations' are to be analysed, therefore, not on the basis of a subject of knowledge who is or is not free in relation to the power system, but, on the contrary, the subject who knows, the objects to be known and the modalities of knowledge must be regarded as so many effects of these fundamental implications of power-knowledge and their historical transformations. In short, it is not the activity of the subject of knowledge that produces a corpus of knowledge, useful or resistant to power, but power-knowledge, the processes and struggles that traverse it and of which it is made up, that determines the forms and possible domains of knowledge.

To analyse the political investment of the body and the microphysics of power presupposes, therefore, that one abandons – where power is concerned – the violence–ideology opposition, the metaphor of property, the model of the contract or of conquest; that – where knowledge is concerned – one abandons the opposition between what is 'interested' and what is 'disinterested', the model of knowledge and the primacy of the subject. Borrowing a word from Petty and his contemporaries, but giving it a different meaning from the one current in the seventeenth century, one might imagine a political 'anatomy'. This would not be the study of a state in terms of a 'body' (with its elements, its resources and its forces), nor would it be the study of the body and its surroundings in terms of a small state. One would be concerned with the 'body politic', as a set of material elements and techniques that serve as weapons, relays, communication routes and supports for the power and knowledge relations that invest human bodies and subjugate them by turning them into objects of knowledge.

[...]

Let us take the ideal figure of the soldier as it was still seen in the early seventeenth century. To begin with, the soldier was someone who could be recognized from afar; he bore certain signs: the natural signs of his strength and his courage, the marks, too, of his pride; his body was the blazon of his strength and valour; and although it is true that he had to learn the profession of arms little by little – generally in actual fighting – movements like marching and attitudes like the bearing of the head belonged for the most part to a bodily rhetoric of honour; 'The signs for recognizing those most suited to this profession are a lively, alert manner, an erect head, a taut stomach, broad shoulders, long arms, strong fingers, a small belly, thick thighs, slender legs and dry feet, because a man of such a figure could not fail to be agile and strong'; when he becomes a pikebearer, the soldier 'will have to march in step in order to have as much grace and gravity as possible, for the pike is an honourable weapon, worthy to be borne with gravity and boldness' (Montgommery, 6 and 7). By the late eighteenth century, the soldier has become something that can be made; out of a formless clay, an inapt body, the machine required can be constructed; posture is gradually corrected; a calculated constraint runs slowly through each part of the body, mastering it, making it pliable, ready at all times, turning silently into the automatism of habit; in short, one has 'got rid of the peasant' and given him 'the air of a soldier' (ordinance of 20 March 1764). Recruits become accustomed to 'holding their heads high and erect; to standing upright, without bending the back, to sticking out the belly, throwing out the chest and throwing back the shoulders; and, to help them acquire the habit, they are given this position while standing against a wall in such a way that the heels, the thighs, the waist and the shoulders touch it, as also do the backs of the hands, as one turns the arms outwards, without moving them away from the body ... Likewise, they will be taught never to fix their eyes on the ground, but to look straight at those they pass ... to remain motionless until the order is given, without moving the head, the hands or the feet ... lastly to march with a bold step, with knee and ham taut, on the points of the feet, which should face outwards' (ordinance of 20 March 1764).

The classical age discovered the body as object and target of power. It is easy enough to find signs of the attention then paid to the body – to the body that is manipulated, shaped, trained, which obeys, responds, becomes skilful and increases its forces. The great book of Man-the-Machine was written simultaneously on two registers: the anatomico-metaphysical register, of which Descartes wrote the first pages and which the physicians and philosophers continued, and the technico-political register, which was constituted by a whole set of regulations and by empirical and calculated methods relating to the army, the school and the hospital, for controlling or correcting the operations of the body. These two registers are quite distinct, since it was a question, on the one hand, of submission and use and, on the other, of functioning and explanation: there was a useful body and an intelligible body. And yet there are points of overlap from one to the other. La Mettrie's *L'Homme-machine* is both a materialist reduction of the soul and a general theory of *dressage*, at the centre of which reigns the notion of 'docility', which joins the analysable body to the manipulable body. A body is docile that may be subjected, used, transformed and improved. The celebrated automata, on the other hand, were not only a way of illustrating an organism, they were also political puppets, small-scale models of power: Frederick II, the meticulous king of small machines, well-trained regiments and long exercises, was obsessed with them.

What was so new in these projects of docility that interested the eighteenth century so much? It was certainly not the first time that the body had become the object of such imperious and pressing investments; in every society, the body was in the grip of very strict powers, which imposed on it constraints, prohibitions or obligations. However, there were several new things in these techniques. To begin with, there was the scale of the control: it was a question not of treating the body, *en masse*, 'wholesale', as if it were an indissociable unity, but of working it 'retail', individually; of exercising upon it a subtle coercion, of obtaining holds upon it at the level of the mechanism itself – movements, gestures, attitudes, rapidity: an infinitesimal power over the active body. Then there was the object of the control: it was not or was no longer the signifying elements of behaviour or the language of the body, but the economy, the efficiency of movements, their internal organization; constraint bears upon the forces rather than upon the signs; the only truly important ceremony is that of exercise. Lastly, there is the modality: it implies an uninterrupted, constant coercion, supervising the processes of the activity rather than its result and it is exercised according to a codification that partitions as closely as possible time, space, movement. These methods, which made possible the meticulous control of the operations of the body, which assured the constant subjection of its forces and imposed upon them a relation of docility-utility, might be called 'disciplines'. Many disciplinary methods had long been in existence – in monasteries, armies, workshops. But in the course of the seventeenth and eighteenth centuries the disciplines became general formulas of domination. They were different from slavery because they were not based on a relation of appropriation of bodies; indeed, the elegance of the discipline lay in the fact that it could dispense with this costly and violent relation by obtaining effects of utility at least as great. They were different, too, from 'service', which was a constant, total, massive, non-analytical, unlimited relation of domination, established in the form of the individual will of the master, his 'caprice'. They were different from vassalage, which was a highly coded, but distant relation of submission, which bore less on the operations of the body than on the products of labour and the ritual marks of allegiance. Again, they were different from asceticism and from 'disciplines' of a monastic type, whose function was to obtain renunciations rather than increases of utility and which, although they involved obedience to others, had as their principal aim an increase of the mastery of each individual over his own body. The historical moment of the disciplines was the moment when an art of the human body was born, which was directed not only at the growth of its skills, nor at the intensification of its subjection, but at the formation of a relation that in the mechanism itself makes it more obedient as it becomes more useful, and conversely, what was then being formed was a policy of coercions that act upon the body, a calculated manipulation of its elements, its gestures, its behaviour. The human body was entering a machinery of power that explores it, breaks it down and rearranges it. A 'political anatomy', which was also a 'mechanics of power', was being born; it defined how one may have a hold over others' bodies, not only so that they may do what one wishes, but so that they may operate as one wishes, with the techniques, the speed and the efficiency that one determines. Thus discipline produces subjected and practised bodies, 'docile' bodies. Discipline increases the forces of the body (in economic terms of utility) and diminishes these same forces (in political terms of obedience). In short, it dissociates power from the body; on the one hand, it turns it into an 'aptitude', a 'capacity', which it seeks to increase; on the other hand, it reverses the course of the energy, the power that might result from it, and turns it into a relation of strict subjection. If economic exploitation separates the force and the product of labour, let us say that disciplinary coercion establishes in the body the constricting link between an increased aptitude and an increased domination.

PART THREE

Bodies and identities

INTRODUCTION

THE TEXTS IN THIS SECTION explore how the body figures in relation to a variety of identities, including gender, class, 'race', sexuality, and age. The key issues that inform these pieces (more or less explicitly) concern how, in what way, and with what implications, the relations between identities and bodies are constituted: how do identities mark bodies, and bodies shape identities? In what ways are bodies and identities co-produced?

Barbara Creed begins from the premise that all female bodies are threatening to patriarchal heterosexual culture. Unlike the male body, she writes, 'the proper female body is penetrable, changes shape, swells, gives birth, contracts, lactates, bleeds. Woman's body reminds man of his "debt to nature" and as such threatens the boundary between human and animal, civilized and uncivilized' (Creed 1995: 87. See also Bakhtin, this volume, p. 112). In the extract that we have included here, Creed argues that lesbian bodies in particular, in male fantasies and stereotypes, are distinguished from the bodies of other women. Perceived as uniquely threatening, they must be immediately visible, and instantly recognisable. Creed explores the nature of their threat (especially as it jeopardises the boundaries between male and female, active and passive, animal/nature, and human/culture), and how it is portrayed across a range of representations, including pre-Freudian historical and sexological texts, psychoanalytic works, fairy tales, and literary and filmic narratives. These representations, she argues, function as 'ideological litmus paper': in warning and policing non-lesbian women, they speak not of the lesbian body as it 'really' is, but of the culture that produces such images.

Where Creed's focus lies on images *of* bodies of women, Nicola Diamond, in the second extract in this section, considers how particular images – specifically, images of thinness – have real effects *on* the bodies of women. Diamond takes issue with

Susie Orbach's (1981) book *Fat is a Feminist Issue* which, she argues, implicitly posits fat 'itself' as a problem (and weight loss as the solution). Against this view – in which fat acquires the status of an individual psychoanalytic and/or medical symptom – Diamond argues that fat is a socially constructed term without a fixed referent. It is produced in relation to thinness, and cross-cut by cultural ideas of femininity. She urges her readers therefore to consider instead the *social* meanings that shape how fat and thin (and indeed health) are understood, as well as the material bodies of women, their experiences of their bodies, body image, eating, and food: 'the very experience of "physical hunger" ', Diamond writes, 'is stimulated and patterned by social responses' (Diamond 1985: 57–8).

Diamond is concerned with the relations between the social, the psychological, and the physiological. For her, feminist strategies around the body can only be successful if they move 'away from definitions of the "natural" and back into the political/social arena of struggle' (Diamond 1985: 59–60). This does raise the question however, of where the limits of 'the social' (and social constructionism) might lie – a point that Gilleard and Higgs, in the third extract in this section, consider in relation to ageing. As the authors note, ageing seems to represent a kind of biological ground zero, an immutable and inevitable fact that challenges the notion that there is, no longer, a 'natural' to speak of. Certainly, anti-ageing products, practices, and the ambitions of high-tech anti-ageing medicine can claim to have rolled back some of nature's frontiers. Indeed Gillieard and Higgs argue that, in fracturing the associations between the visible appearance of age and disability and death, and in so making ageing a less dissatisfactory experience, they may (even) have established a real distance between chronological age and decline and death. Nevertheless, this so-called triumph over nature will not necessarily combat the ways in which ageing is publicly valued (or not valued), and may even increase the social dread of getting older. This is significant, Gilleard and Higgs claim, for it is not only biological and physiological changes that shape the ageing body, but also the economic, psychological, and social effects of *ageism* that affect the physical well-being of the aged.

As these extracts illustrate, the focus on bodies and identities inevitably seems to raise the complex issue of the relation between essentialism and constructivism. The problem with these two terms however, Michael Moon and Eve Sedgwick argue, especially when they are set up in opposition to each other, is that they often collapse the question of phylogeny – 'the centuries-long processes ... by which ... identities are or are not invented' – with that of ontogeny, which concerns itself with the more limited lifespan of an individual. When the latter is privileged over the former, the great burden of identity (its construction, adoption, rejection, and/or deconstruction) is placed at the feet of the individual. Moreover, to ignore the sedimentation over years of bodies and identities, the authors continue, is to fall prey to the logic of the capitalist/consumer market in which identities are understood to be *either* an absolute choice – comparable to an object to be purchased (see especially Lury, this volume, p. 288) – *or* an absolute compulsion, an addiction. Rather than try to distinguish between these different temporal horizons, Moon and Sedgwick explore instead their points of collision and departure. In doing so, they draw attention to the ways in which the organisation of identities are inextricably entangled in each other. The relationships between size, shape, and gendered bodies, the magnetism of the diva figure and complexities of transvestism, the role of the 'large' body in the political economy of health, work, and waste – these are among the many connections that the authors turn over in this extract.

In the course of their analysis of the emotional and historical linkages (and 'dislinkages') between gay men and fat women, Sedgwick and Moon briefly discuss the notion of glamour, which they suggest functions as an interface between abjection and defiance. In the fifth extract in this section, Beverley Skeggs also considers this issue and, although her analysis refers to a very different group of people (White working class women[1] in the north of England), here too glamour pertains to 'the interlocking histories of stigma, self-constitution, and epistemological complication' (as Sedgwick and Moon describe it) that inform particular identities. Skeggs begins by illustrating how, in the eighteenth and nineteenth centuries, an 'ideal' of femininity emerged that was explicitly White and middle class and that, importantly, divided sexuality from femininity. Although Black working class women 'forged models of womanhood that continually and dramatically challenge prevailing notions of femininity', Skeggs argues that White working class women have more commonly tried to disidentify themselves from an identity that has many negative associations and connotations. In their alternative bid for 'respectability', the women in her study sought to disavow sexual experience and conduct, which was opposed to the feminine. This is where glamour comes in: Skeggs illustrates that glamour, with all the complexities that it brings with it, was the vehicle by which the women negotiated the tension between sexuality and respectability. In this respect it *is* an interface, a 'style of flesh' that mediates the relations between gender, sexuality and class.

In their different ways, each of the pieces in this section deconstruct (in a loose sense) the notion that identities 'naturally' inhere in the body. We have included an extract from Allacquère Rosanne Stone's book here not only because it spells out the assumptions that underpin this conventional relationship, but because it illustrates the profound sense of pain and loss that can occur when the links between bodies and identities are threatened and even severed. Stone tells of Julie Graham, an apparently severely disabled woman, who was a popular and dominating member of a virtual on-line community. Unknown to the participants of that community however, in 'real' life Julie Graham was Sanford Lewin, an able-bodied man and psychiatrist. As the story runs its course, it raises a number of issues pertaining to gender, to cross-dressing and to disability. It also, importantly, raises the ethics of taking the bodies of 'others' upon oneself. As Stone illustrates, to have Julie exposed as a 'construct' was, for some of her friends, a violation likened to sexual assault, and more emotionally staggering than learning of her near-death.

'Julie Graham' implicitly draws attention to the crucial role that visibility plays in establishing, or not, bodily identities. In the final extract, Judith Butler renders that role absolutely explicit as she considers the video footage of the beating of Rodney King, a black man, by a group of white policeman in 1991. Her analysis of the way that this footage was seen and received by the jurors in a Simi Valley courtroom illustrates how racially saturated the visual field is, and how charged. Her purpose is to challenge the notion that the events depicted on the tape 'speak for themselves', or that what one sees there is in any way self-evident. Instead, Butler argues that the visual episteme is itself a powerful racial formation, that produces bodies and identities in particular ways. From Fanon through to King, Butler shows how the black male body is constituted as – is *seen to be* – a site and source of danger and violence prior to any action on his part. She argues that this beating could only be considered legitimate, even justified, in the context of a white paranoia that sought to punish King 'for the blows he never delivered, but which he is, by virtue of his blackness, always about to deliver'.

It is not that there is no pleasure to be had in 'having' an identity: Creed's brief analysis of a lesbian community's play with fashion in the 1970s, Sedgwick and Moon's celebration of an attitude of 'divinity', and Skeggs' account of glamour are all testimonies to this fact. What Stone and Butler, in their different ways, also remind us however, is that 'being' (seen as) a particular body, or passing as a particular identity, can also be about mourning and loss, violence, deception, and death.

NOTE

1   Importantly, Skeggs notes that when she imposes the categories 'White and working class' on the women she interviewed, she is not identifying their subjectivities, but rather the 'economic, social and discursive relations' (Skeggs 1997: 165) in which they are positioned. As she notes, there are plenty of reasons why the women may or *may not* choose to recognise, or identify with, this discursive positioning.

REFERENCES

Creed, B. (1995) 'Lesbian bodies: tribades, tomboys and tarts', in E. Grosz and E. Probyn (eds), *Sexy Bodies: The Strange Carnalities of Feminism*, London and New York: Routledge.

Diamond, N. (1985) 'Thin is the feminist issue', *Feminist Review* 19: 46–64.

Orbach, S. (1981) *Fat is a Feminist Issue*, London: Hamlyn.

Skeggs, B. (1998) *Formations of Class and Gender*, London: Sage.

Chapter 13

Barbara Creed

LESBIAN BODIES

Tribades, tomboys and tarts

From B. Creed (1995) 'Lesbian bodies: tribades, tomboys and tarts', in E. Grosz and E. Probyn (eds), *Sexy Bodies: The Strange Carnalities of Feminism*, London and New York: Routledge.

[...]

REGARDLESS OF HER SEXUAL preferences, woman in whatever form – whether heterosexual or lesbian – has been variously depicted as narcissist, sex-fiend, creature, tomboy, vampire, maneater, child, nun, virgin. One does not need a specific kind of body to become – or to be seen as – a lesbian. All female bodies represent the threat or potential – depending how you see it – of lesbianism. [...] If it is the female body in general – rather than specifically the lesbian body – which signifies the other, how, then, does the lesbian body differ from the body of the so-called 'normal' woman?

There are at least three stereotypes of the lesbian body which are so threatening they cannot easily be applied to the body of the non-lesbian. These stereotypes are: the lesbian body as active and masculinized; the animalistic lesbian body; the narcissistic lesbian body. Born from a deep-seated fear of female sexuality, these stereotypes refer explicitly to the lesbian body, and arise from the nature of the threat lesbianism offers to patriarchal heterosexual culture.

The central image used to control representations of the potentially lesbian body – to draw back the female body from entering the dark realm of lesbian desire – is that of the tomboy. The narrative of the tomboy functions as a liminal journey of discovery in which feminine sexuality is put into crisis and finally recuperated into the dominant patriarchal order – although not without first offering the female specta-tor a series of contradictory messages which may well work against their overtly ideological purpose of guiding the young girl into taking up her proper destiny. In other words, the well-known musical comedy, *Calamity Jane*, which starred Doris Day as the quintessential tomboy in love with another woman, could be recategorized most appro-priately, in view of its subversive subtextual messages about the lure of lesbianism, as a 'lesbian western', that ground-breaking subgenre of films so ardently championed by Hollywood.

The masculinized lesbian body

There is one popular stereotype about the nature of lesbianism which does posit a recognizable lesbian body. This view, which has been dominant in different historical periods and is still prevalent today, is that the lesbian is really a man trapped in a woman's body. The persistent desire to see the lesbian body as a pseudo male body certainly does not begin with Freud's theory of penis envy. We find evidence of the masculinized lesbian body in a number of pre-Freudian historical and cultural contexts: Amazonian society in which the Amazon is seen as a masculinized, single-breasted, man-hating warrior; cross-cultural woman-marriage (Cavin 1985: 129–37) whereby women don men's clothes and marry other women: female transvestism or cross-dressing; and the history of tribadism and female sodomy. It is the last category I wish to discuss in some detail.

In earlier centuries, prior to the invention (Katz 1990: 7–34) in the mid-nineteenth century of the homosexual and heterosexual as a person with a specific identity and lifestyle, women and men who engaged in same-sex relations – presumed to consist primarily of sodomy – were described as sodomites. Sodomites – heterosexual and homosexual – were 'guilty' of carrying out a specific act, not of being a certain kind of person with readily identifiable characteristics. Specifically, women were thought to take part in sodomy with other women in one of two ways: through clitoral penetration of the anus or with the use of diabolical instruments. In general terms, however, the term sodomite was used to refer to anyone engaged in unorthodox practices.

[…]

The solution to the female body which threatens to confuse gender boundaries is either legal ('she really is a man') or surgical ('cut her back to size') or lethal ('burn the witch'). In all three instances the offending body challenges gender boundaries in terms of the active/passive dualism, a dichotomy which is crucial to the definition of gender in patriarchal culture.

[…]

The tribade is the woman who assumes a male role in sexual intercourse with another woman – either because she is the one 'on top' or because she has a large clitoris and can engage in penetration. She threatens because she is active, desiring, hot. Theo van der Meer argues that the tribade does not really fit into the world of romantic, but asexual female friendships, nor into the tradition of female transvestism. Van de Meer claims that perhaps the tribades, with their overtly sexual desires, 'may represent the more – if not the most – important and direct predecessors of the modern lesbian' (1990: 209). I have used the word tribade for the early modern period, because, not only did the term 'lesbian' not exist in the eighteenth century, but 'lesbian' also conveys the idea of a sexual identity which was not really invented for the female homosexual until the mid-nineteenth century. According to Barbara Walker (1983: 536), in Christian Europe, lesbianism was 'a crime without a name'. The sixteenth-century definition of the tribade as a pseudo male has much in common with Freud's later definition of the homosexual woman as one suffering from unresolved penis-envy. Both definitions adopt male anatomy as the defining norm. The difference is that Freud's model of sexual difference is based on the two-sex theory; in this, woman is not an ill-formed man, she is the 'other' – a creature who has already (in male eyes) been castrated.

The lesbian body of Freudian theory is one that attempts to overcome its 'castration' by assuming a masculine role in life and/or masculine appearance through clothing, gesture, substitution.

[...]

Freud's narrative of woman's sexual journey from clitorial pubescence into mature vaginal bliss is a bit like the transformation fairy tales in which the ugly duckling matures into a beautiful swan and marries the handsome cygnet. Literary and filmic narratives replay this scenario of female fulfilment through the figure of the tomboy. The tomboy's journey is astonishingly similar to that of the clitoris. During the early stage, the tomboy/clitoris behaves like a 'little man' enjoying boy's games, pursuing active sports, refusing to wear dresses or engage in feminine pursuits; on crossing into womanhood the youthful adventurer relinquishes her earlier tomfoolery, gives up boyish adventures, dons feminine clothes, grows her hair long and sets out to capture a man whose job it is to 'tame' her as if she were a wild animal.

[...]

The liminal journey of the tomboy — one of the few rites of passage stories available to women in the cinema — is a narrative about the forging of the proper female identity. It is paralleled by Freud's anatomical narrative about the journey of the clitoris which is, at base, a narrative about culture. The tomboy who refuses to travel Freud's path, who clings to her active, virile pleasures, who rejects the man and keeps her horse is stigmatized as the lesbian. She is a threatening figure on two counts. First, her image undermines patriarchal gender boundaries that separate the sexes. Second, she pushes to its extreme the definition of the active heterosexual woman — she represents the other side of the heterosexual woman, her lost phallic past, the autonomy she surrenders in order to enter the heritage of the Freudian womb. In this context, it is the lesbian — not woman in general — who signifies the 'ruin of representation'.

Animalistic lesbian body

The stereotype that associates lesbianism with bestiality also pushes representation to its limits. [...] [w]oman is, in the popular (male) imagination, associated more with the world of abject nature because of her procreative and birth-giving functions. In religious discourse, her sinful nature makes her a natural companion of the serpent. The embodiment of mother nature, woman represents the fertile womb. the Freudian hearth of domestic bliss. Whereas woman's function is to replicate that of the natural world, man's function is to control and cultivate that world for his own uses. Like the animal world, woman has an insatiable sexual appetite that must be controlled by man. Modern pornography depicts woman's link with nature in images of women posed in the 'doggy' position or engaged in sex with animals — particularly horses and dogs.

[...]

If women in general were associated with the animal world, the lesbian was an animal. Dijkstra [...] refers to the work of Havelock Ellis to support his argument. Drawing on Darwin's view that animals could become sexually excited by the smell of women, Havelock Ellis argued that 'the animal is taught to give gratification by cunnilinctus.

In some cases there is really sexual intercourse between the animal and the woman'. Apparently, Ellis drew connections between lesbianism in young girls and 'later predilection for encounters with animals' (Dijkstra 1986: 297). The association of homosexuality with bestiality, however, extends much further back than Victorian England. One of the most widely read books of the medieval period, said to be as popular as the Bible, was the *Physiologus*, also known as 'the medieval bestiary'. It consisted of a collection of stories, many without any accuracy whatsoever, about animal behaviour and its relationship to human behaviour. It was widely translated, and its influence felt for centuries. According to Boswell it was a 'manual of piety, a primer of zoology, and a form of entertainment' (1980: 141).

[...]

Another popular image of the lesbian as non-human creature appeared in stories of the female vampire. A seductive creature of the night, the lesbian vampire – still a popular monster of the horror film – not only attacked young girls but also men whose blood she drank in order to assume their masculine virility. Like an animal, the lesbian vampire was prey to her own sexual lusts and primitive desires.

The tomboy, the girl whose sexual identity is androgynous, is almost always associated with animals, particularly the horse and dog. The image of the lesbian as part of the natural world – as distinct from the civilized – might repel some, but it is also immensely appealing.

Narcissistic lesbian body

A popular convention of *fin-de-siècle* painting, the cinema and fashion photography is the image of two women, posed in such a way as to suggest one is a mirror-image of the other. We see the image of the lesbian as narcissist in films about lesbianism. After the two women in *Les Biches* begin a relationship they start to imitate each other in dress and appearance; the women in *Persona* also wear identical clothes and beach hats, making it almost impossible to tell them apart; in *Single White Female* the mentally disturbed girl, in love with her flatmate, deliberately vampirizes her appearance and behaviour until they look like identical twins. In lesbian vampire horror films, such as *Vampyres*, the female fiends are also depicted as identical, even the blood that smears their lips seems to trickle from identical mouths and fangs.

[...]

Like masturbation, lesbianism was seen as inextricably linked to self-absorption and narcissism. Men were shut out from this world – hence they understood the threat offered by the lesbian couple. (According to popular male mythology, what the lesbian really needs is a good fuck, that is, a phallic intrusion to break up the threatening duo.) The representation of the lesbian couple as mirror-images of each other constructs the lesbian body as a reflection or an echo. Such an image is dangerous to society and culture because it suggests there is no way forward – only regression and circularity are possible. [...] The threat offered by the image of the lesbian-as-double is not specifically related to the notion of sexual penetration. Instead, the threat is associated more with auto-eroticism and exclusion.

Representations of the lesbian double — circulated in fashion magazines, film and pornography — draw attention to the nature of the image itself, its association with the feminine, and the technologies that enable duplication and repetition. The lesbian double threatens because it suggests a perfectly sealed world of female desire from which man is excluded, not simply because he is a man, but also because of the power of the technology to exclude the voyeuristic spectator. But exclusion is also part of the nature of voyeuristic pleasure which demands that a distance between the object and the subject who is looking should always be preserved. Photographic technology, with its powers of duplication, reinforces a fear that, like the image itself, the lesbian couple-as-double will reduplicate and multiply.

The lesbian body/community

The body is both so important in itself and yet so clearly a sign or symbol referring to things outside itself in our culture. So far I have discussed the representation of the lesbian body in terms of male fantasies and patriarchal stereotypes. Historically and culturally, the lesbian body — although indistinguishable in reality from the female body itself — has been represented as a body in extreme: the pseudo-male, animalistic and narcissistic body. Although all of these deviant tendencies are present in the female body, it is the ideological function of the lesbian body to warn the 'normal' woman about the dangers of undoing or rejecting her own bodily socialization. This is why the culture points with most hypocritical concern at the mannish lesbian, the butch lesbian, while deliberately ignoring the femme lesbian, the woman whose body in no way presents itself to the straight world as different or deviant. To function properly as ideological litmus paper, the lesbian body must be instantly recognizable. In one sense, the femme lesbian is potentially as threatening — although not as immediately confronting — as the stereotyped butch because she signifies the possibility that all women are potential lesbians. Like the abject, the stereotyped mannish/animalistic/auto-erotic lesbian body hovers around the borders of gender socialization, luring other women to its side, tempting them with the promise of deviant pleasures.

Within the lesbian community itself, however, a different battle has taken place around the definition of the lesbian body. This battle has nothing to do with the size of the clitoris, animals or self-reflecting mirrors. Preoccupied with the construction of the properly socialized feminine body, lesbian-feminism of the 1970s became obsessed with appearance, arguing that the true lesbian should reject all forms of clothing that might associate her image with that of the heterosexual woman and ultimately with patriarchal capitalism.

[…]

A recent film, *Framing Lesbian Fashion* (Karen Everett, 1991), […] makes one thing very clear: most women enjoyed wearing the different 'uniforms' such as flannel, leather, lipstick because it gave them a sense of belonging to a community, the gang, the wider lesbian body. They speak of having a sense of family and shared identity via their common forms of dress. The need to construct a sense of community, through dress and appearance, suggests quite clearly that there is no such thing as an essential lesbian body — lesbians themselves have to create this body in order to feel they belong to the larger lesbian community, recognizable to its members not through essentialized bodily forms but through representation, gesture and play. The 1990s lesbian is most interested in playing with appearance and with sex roles. Women interviewed in *Framing Lesbian Fashion* were very clear about the element of parody in their dress styles. One woman who cross-dressed even wore a large dildo in her leather pants ('packing it') to simulate the penis – the male penis as well as the one that male fantasy has attributed throughout the centuries to the lesbian and her tribade forebears. Unlike Calamity Jane, whose outfit would have caused a sensation at *Club Q*, the 1990s lesbian refuses to exchange her whip and leathers for home, hearth and the seal of social approval. She has a body that is going places.

References

Boswell, J. (1980) *Christianity, Social Tolerance, and Homosexuality*. Chicago, Ill. and London: University of Chicago Press.

Cavin, S. (1985) *Lesbian Origins*. San Francisco, CA: Ism Press Inc.

Dijkstra, B. (1986) *Idols of Perversity: Fantasies of Feminine Evil in Fin-de-Siècle Culture*. New York: Oxford University Press.

Katz, J. N. (1990) 'The Invention of Heterosexuality', *Socialist Review*, 20, 1: pp. 7–34.

Walker, B. (1983) *The Woman's Encyclopedia of Myths and Secrets*, San Francisco, CA: Harper & Row.

Chapter 14

Nicky Diamond

THIN IS THE FEMINIST ISSUE

From N. Diamond (1985) 'Thin is the feminist issue', *Feminist Review* 19: 45–64.

[...]

T HE QUESTION FAT IS A FEMINIST ISSUE (*FIFI*) asks is 'why do women compulsively eat and because of this become fat'? 'Fat is a social disease, and fat is a feminist issue' (Orbach, 1981: 18). Orbach argues that compulsive eating and fatness occur for two related reasons. First, women's natural hunger mechanism is subjected to a process of social and psychological distortion. Second, women's conscious desires to become 'thin' are undermined by the unconscious desire to be 'fat', thus serving an unconscious defence strategy. Both processes emerge as a result of women's social oppression.

[...]

Is 'Fat' the issue?

FIFI assumes without question that 'fat' is part of the problem, hence the emphasis upon losing it. It will be argued that such a proposition – in setting up 'fat' as the problem – in effect reproduces those cultural ideals of femininity which define 'fat' as the social problem for feminity and 'thin' as the ideal (definitions that Orbach as a feminist, at times seeks to criticize). The point to be made is that a feminist analysis needs to think in alternative terms to those which already limit our possible notions of women's body imagery.

Contrary to the overt proposals contained in *FIFI*, 'fat' is actually posited with inherent attributes. This is because 'fat' can only be thought of as a specific kind of symptom, and so, in consequence, it becomes both the issue and the problem. There are two ways in which this happens in *FIFI*. First, a psychoanalytic concept of symptom is evoked when 'fat' (the symptom) is understood as an effect of unconscious processes. However, just as an hysterical symptom can take the form of a cough (see Freud, 1977), this does not mean that all coughs are hysterical symptoms for, by definition, psychical processes do not arise and develop from the intrinsic physical properties of the symptom as such. Yet *FIFI* makes the psychical meanings intrinsic to the 'fat', because they are immediately read off from the literal physical state.

Second, a medical notion of the symptom is employed when 'fat' is posed as the consequence of biological distortion (reflecting a malfunction of the hunger mechanism). A disease model is assumed because an abberration from an organic norm is implied. The logical conclusion of this position is that 'fat' is an unnatural pathological state for women (hence the *FIFI* stress on thinness and weight loss as natural). Such an equation, 'fat' – symptom – pathology (mental) and (physical) does not help us as women to think out of the way in which our bodies have already been defined. Instead, women have 'weight problems' and 'fat is a social disease' (Orbach, 1980: 18). Ultimately for *FIFI*, it is 'fat' that is a social disease that women in particular suffer, rather than the social making 'fat' into a disease for women in particular.

FIFI's analysis puts psychical perceptions of body size and eating by the way-side. It starts with the presumption that actual fatness and compulsive eating are the problem. In failing to consider the way in which social definitions construct what is conceived as fatness and over-eating *FIFI* forecloses an exploration of the social conditions which made it possible for us to think that 'fat' is a terrible problem for and to women.

The terms 'fat', as well as 'thin', are both assumed as given and are used repeatedly throughout the text. This repetition has the effect of solidifying a social opposition (which poses female 'fat' as the problem and 'thin' as the ideal) set up by forms of media practice and the diet industry. In providing no definition for the terms 'fat' and 'thin', these terms are consequently left open to definitions set by the aforementioned practices (which relatively fix the imagery and meanings of these terms).

In order to do justice to *FIFI* it is necessary to look at the way the terms 'fat' and 'thin' operate in the text. Insofar as the categories are taken for granted, they are presumed to be obvious, objective descriptions which thus have absolute meanings. This has the effect of making meaning which is socially produced appear as if it is an essential part of the natural order. This not only allows social definitions of 'the natural' to prevail, but also prohibits differing psychical perceptions from entering the account.

It could, however, be argued that Orbach purposefully does not define her terms in order to allow space for subjective perceptions. This argument only leads to further difficulties, as the uncritical use of categories like 'fat' and 'thin' can have the effect of reinforcing psychical perceptions of fatness and eating too much, rather than permitting such perceptions to be questioned. Finally to solve confusions over what 'fat' and 'thin' mean cannot be a matter of simply clarifying terms. A prescribed opposition between 'fat' and 'thin' circumscribes the way we conceive a problem and its solutions: 'fat' is set up as part of the problem and 'thin' as part of the solution. A feminist intervention needs to work at constructing alternatives instead of thinking within such a binary opposition.

To criticize this opposition we need to also question the level of 'experience'. For the social structuration of meanings forms the way we think of ourselves. It does not seem plausible to suggest that there is an individual enclave of self, separate from the social. For even if we accept this as a possibility prior to the social constitution of the subject, then in what sense can we maintain that this self is pre-social once constituted? This appears to be an immediate contradiction. Yet *FIFI* assumes that the way a woman really feels is closer to her 'true self'. In the end, a woman's desire to lose weight is not questioned; in fact if this is what she 'really desires' then it is endorsed as a therapeutic aim. However, if we are to account for the production of subjectivity and social meaning then experiences of being – feeling 'fat' and wanting to be 'thin' need to be the place where feminist investigation begins, not where it ends.

References

Freud, S. (1977) 'Fragment of an analysis of a case of hysteria ('Dora')', *Case Histories I*. The Pelican Freud Library, vol. 8, London: Penguin Books.
Orbach, S. (1981) *Fat is a Feminist Issue*, London: Kamlyn.

Chapter 15

Chris Gilleard and Paul Higgs

AGEING AND ITS EMBODIMENT

From C. Gilleard and P. Higgs (2000) *Cultures of Ageing: Self, Citizen and the Body*, London: Prentice Hall.

The body as the 'true' foundation of ageing: confronting physicality

WHILE PUBLIC POLICIES CONTRIBUTE much to the social construction of old age, there is a strong perception in people's minds that ageing is really a bodily affair. This viewpoint is evident in gerontology where the body has been a central reference point from which to study and understand 'the ageing process'. Perhaps the bulk of gerontologists would argue that ageing is, in the end, a matter of biology, best defined by an increasing risk of irremediable physical disability and death. Most gerontologists – indeed most social gerontologists – accept ageing as an immutable fact, one that is fundamentally unaffected by how the productive processes are organized and how goods, services and capital are distributed. The only arena for human agency is in equalizing the quality of life for each age group and for each category of physical and mental frailty.

It seems incontestable that there are limits to every lifespan. The more social environments support and enable everyone to reach old age, the more evident are these limits. In the process of constructing a more equitable old age, what becomes evident is that age itself is unfair; that, in the end, age impoverishes more than poverty ages. Removing the skeins of social disadvantage exposes the greater disadvantage that is woven into our own imperfect DNA.

This kind of foundationalist position raises several questions for social gerontologists particularly when they adopt a 'social constructionist' account of old age as a product of social policy. The biological finitude of ageing is taken as setting the limits to the social construction of old age. The physicality that is the essence of old age seems to wipe away the imprint of class, gender and race that is so salient in earlier life. This view is illustrated in a comment made by Kathleen Woodward in her book *Aging and Its Discontents*: 'As we approach the extremity of old age we approach in the West the limit of the pure cultural construction of aging.'[1]

Faced with the physicality of old age – the changes in appearance and function that are seen socially as defining adult ageing – it seems impossible to argue that ageing can be understood as rooted not in the domain of biology but in social relations. It is in the biological materiality of the body that the 'cultural' approach toward understanding ageing meets its greatest challenge.

[…]

But now, at the start of a new century and a new millennium, drenched in the hyper-real cyber-cultures that promise endless human possibilities, discernible elements of 'modern' culture can be identified that continue to shape the body across the lifecourse. It is to these current cultural and technological practices that influence both the external appearance and the inner mechanisms of 'ageing' that we wish to turn our attention. Highlighting such considerations serves to challenge any straightforwardly foundational-ist position that seeks to establish the body as the unquestionable 'bottom line' in the dis-course on ageing, enabling an examination of how the ageing body might be, and we would argue, is culturally differentiated.

Anti-ageing and the aesthetics of the body

Cosmetic surgery is available only to a limited number of people. It is not funded within either taxation-based or insurance-based health-care systems. There are still relatively few people whose lives create sufficient dissonance between their public and private selves that they would go so much out of their way to realize a wish to look younger. Anti-ageing medicine remains very much a private business. Nevertheless, the rising popularity of cosmetic surgery has more than merely iconic value in demonstrating the plasticity of the ageing body. That a significant minority of people – usually those with considerable mate-rial resources – do choose to have aesthetic surgery to rejuvenate their appearance shows what the many without those resources might also do had they similar opportunities.

Much of the work of cosmetic surgeons concentrates primarily upon 'anti-ageing' procedures. These are becoming more various and more technically sophisticated year on year. Current practice includes chemical skin peels to rejuvenate the appearance of the skin, scleropathy (removing distended veins on the legs), hair transplantation, facelifts and tucks, forehead lifts and blepharoplasty (correction of drooping eyelids). New techniques are constantly being introduced such as laser hair transplanting and 'botox' injections to relax lined and wrinkled skin. These developments are driven by market forces originat-ing largely from the baby-boomer generation. What is surprising is that 'anti-ageing' cos-metic surgery is sought not only by the middle-aged/third-age population but also by significant numbers of people in their twenties and thirties. […] '[A]ge concerns' have spread across significant sections of the adult population. Surveys conducted in 1998 and 1999 in the United States indicate that the majority of 20-year-olds, 30-year-olds, 40-year-olds, 50-year-olds and 60-year-olds 'approve' of cosmetic surgery. Only after age 65 do the approval ratings decline. Equally significant, though less surprising, is the finding that approval ratings are lower, the lower the individual's income.

It seems probable that these cohort effects will persist, and cosmetic surgery and related procedures will become part of everyday life, providing more and more people with the opportunity to mould their appearance to how they would like to be. Surgeons themselves see techniques improving as they become more widely used and the growth of computerized systems using photographs of patients that were taken in their youth in order to 'redesign' the face in advance of surgery offers further evidence of what Baudrillard termed the simulation and hyperreality of modern life.

[...]

In the absence of an inner logic to ageing, the play of signification that is involved in choosing how and when to age offers a wide scope for the marketing of desire. Skin peels, tummy tucks, forehead lifts, hair transplants, botox injections and facial fat grafting do not 'restore' a youthful appearance so much as improve the 'aesthetic' appearance of the ageing face. To that extent cosmetic surgery is less about anti-ageing and more to do with a general desire felt by many people to improve on their 'natural' appearance. The public appearance of 'agedness' is no deep signifier of incipient disability or closeness to death. It is in that sense exquisitely concerned with the surface plane of 'signification'. However, without this connectivity to the interior pathways of old age, the increasing lifestyle aestheticization exemplified by anti-ageing cosmetic surgery might seem a cultural epiphenomenon of the commodification and marketing of health rather than posing a serious challenge to the foundationalist position of bio-ageing. At the same time, dissatisfaction with ageing is highly predictive of mortality amongst older adults – even after taking account of chronological age, socioeconomic status, health and other risk factors.[2] If aesthetic surgery succeeds in reducing such dissatisfaction it may contribute quite incidentally to distancing chronological agedness from both decline and death.

Other anti-ageing technologies offer a more direct route toward preventing or delaying bio-ageing. Continuing medical research into various steroids, steroid-like compounds, vitamins and related nutrients (dehydroepiandrosterone (DHEA); estrogens and phytoestrogens; coenzyme Q-10; vitamin E; superoxide dismutase (SOD); etc.) suggests small but measurable benefits in terms of later-life disease prevention. Cross-national and temporal variations in the age-specific rates of cardiovascular disease and various cancers also suggest that there is scope for further gains in 'healthy years of life' by modification of lifestyle and dietary habits. More radical proposals exist.

[...]

The ageing body is rapidly becoming a key element in the postmodern uncertainty over what constitutes the natural. While cosmetic surgery exploits the possibilities of surgical technology to re-aestheticize the ageing body in one swift act, it remains a private and risky enterprise that currently possesses a rather limited social value. Consumption of over-the-counter medicines and all the various 'anti-ageing' cosmeceuticals and nutraceuticals offers a less risky strategy but requires sustained lifestyle changes with little obvious to show for them. Both practices nevertheless represent the active choices of consumers. Other aspects of anti-ageing medicine relate less to consumerism and the health market. Rather they seek to derive their status from their ability to represent themselves as a continuing part of medicine's modernist 'triumph over nature'. Prophylactic high-technology surgery is a small but significant component of a largely private health-care industry that actively promotes itself as 'anti-ageing medicine'. The evidence base for such practices is extremely limited and often rather tenuously linked to experimental gerontological research. In fact, much of the secular and cross-national variation in age-specific morbidity seems to derive not from variations in access to the latest technology but from variation in lifestyle and environment. The claims of anti-ageing medicine represent more an aspirational science which has flourished within postmodern culture than traditional 'modern medicine'. Indeed all three elements of 'anti-ageing' health care can be seen as deriving from and reinforcing that particular form of 'ageism' ushered in by modernity.

[...]

Ageism: the personal and the public

Using cosmetic surgery to determine whether and how to 'age' is not just a matter of personal aesthetics. It reflects the public valuing of 'agedness'. Expenditure of over US$15 billion on anti-ageing nutritional compounds in the USA is not just a matter of consumer choice. It represents a massive social dread of old age. While negative attitudes toward old age have been in evidence for centuries, they have rarely played the role that they do in contemporary society. What is unique about the ageism of modernity is that it is represented in numerous institutional practices that treat 'agedness' as a proxy for poverty, neediness and proximity to death. Therefore, we shall argue, current ageist assumptions constitute more than mere cultural by-products of particular economic and biological power relations. They exercise a direct and proximal influence upon the processes of bio-ageing itself.

Three routes mediate the effects of ageism on bio-ageing. In the first place secular changes in the economy have resulted until relatively recently in older adults occupying positions of lowered socioeconomic status. This position of socioeconomic disadvantage enhances their risks of ill-health, disability and death. Second, the internalization of negative attitudes about ageing and old age undermines the confidence of older adults in their dealings with the physical and social world, leading them to entertain lower expectations of themselves as agents. Such self-imposed limitations lead in turn to poorer health and fitness, increased risk of disability and ultimately a reduced chance of survival. Finally, institutional ageism limits access to those facilities and resources that promote health and well-being, prevent disease and facilitate recovery. Although this is most obvious in relation to health-care practices, it applies to a much wider set of institutions including the workplace, personal finance institutions and the educational system.

In short, ageism has economic, psychological and social effects that potentially impact upon the physical well-being of retired people.

[...]

Is it ageism, in short, that causes people to undergo cosmetic surgery – or is it ageism that prevents or restricts the accessibility of such surgery; is it ageism that seeks to set limits on how old a woman can be to receive fertility treatments; that asserts that death should be the appropriate fate of 'old' people but not 'young' people? Resolutions of these dilemmas will not arise from the shrinking postmodern state. Creating viable cultures of ageing depends upon establishing a sufficient economic base to sustain a level of consumption that will enable them to be expressed through the strength of individual demand. For most older people, the body is still too dangerous to serve such ends and after all consumer culture is not really about instilling physical self-confidence. Its success comes from achieving the very opposite. Our bodies are still too little our own. Retired people are establishing an increasing variety of post-work lifestyles, yet the body remains problematic, occupying a complex and contradictory position in relation to ageing and its cultural possibilities.

Notes

1   Woodward, K. (1991) *Aging and Its Discontents: Frend and Other Fictions*, Bloomington IN: Indiana University Press, p. 194.
2   See Maier, H. and Smith, J. (1999) 'Psychological predictors of mortality in old age', *Journal of Gerontology*, 54B, table 2.

Chapter 16

Michael Moon and Eve Kosofsky Sedgwick

DIVINITY

A dossier, a performance piece, a little-understood emotion

From M. Moon and E. K. Sedgwick (1994) "Divinity: a dossier, a performance piece, a little-understood emotion," in E. K. Sedgwick (ed.), *Tendencies*. London and New York: Routledge.

EKS: **THIS IS A DREAM I HAD** a couple of years ago. I was shopping for clothes for myself at a store that was nominally Bloomingdale's. I was dubious about whether they would have any clothes that would be big enough for me, but a saleswoman said they did, adding that rather than being marked by size numbers, each size-group of clothes was gathered under a graphic symbol: over here, she said, were the clothes that would fit me. "Over here" referred to a cluster of luscious-looking clothes, hung on a rack between two curtained dressing-rooms. The graphic symbol that surmounted them was a pink triangle.

I woke up extremely cheerful.

MM: My love of opera as a proto-gay child growing up in rural Oklahoma in the fifties had at least as much to do with the available "visuals" as it did with the music – opening nights at the Met photographed in living color in *Life* and *Look* and on television, featuring befurred and bejeweled divas, usually fat, radiating authority and pleasure, beaming out at cameras from the midst of tuxedoed groups of what I remember one of the slick newsmagazines of the time calling "hipless" men. I was struck by the strangeness of that locution even when I read it at age eleven or twelve; like so many other bits of knowingly inflected pseudo-information about adults, their bodies, and their mystifying sexualities, all I could figure out about what it meant for a reporter to call an elegant group of men in evening clothes "hipless" was that it must be another bit of code for doing what was called at the time "impugning their masculinity." It was a deep fear of mine as a twelve-year-old boy putting on pubescent weight that after having been a slender child, I was at puberty freakishly and unaccountably developing feminine hips and breasts. My anxieties on this count made me a fierce discriminator of the prevailing representational codes of bodies and body parts, but everything about this urgent subject seemed hopelessly confused and confusing. Why was John Wayne's big flabby butt taken as yet another sign of his virility while my aging male piano teacher's very similarly shaped posterior was read as that of a "fat-ass pansy" by some of my nastier agemates? What was the difference between a hermaphrodite – a figure still presented in freakshows at the local county fair in my childhood – and a male movie star like Victor Mature who was considered hypermasculine despite his overdeveloped and to my and many other childish eyes quite feminine-looking breasts? Was a man supposed to have hips or not? What regimen of diet, exercise, and character-building could possibly produce the apparently unattainable ideal of right-sized and -shaped male hips on my seemingly out-of-control body – a body that was supposed to be neither "hipless," that is, gay, or "fat-assed," that is, gay?

For many gay men, as for such diverse modern avatars of male sexual and social styles as Byron and Wilde and Henry James and Marlon Brando and Elvis, dramatic weight-gain and -loss have played a highly significant, much remarked but almost completely unanalyzed part in the formation of our identities. One happy aspect of the story of my own and many other gay men's formations of our adolescent and adult body-images is that the fat, beaming figure of the diva has never been entirely absent from our *imaginaire* or our fantasies of ideal bodies; besides whatever version or versions of the male "power-body" of the seventies and eighties we may have cathected, fantasized about, developed or not developed, and, in our time, pursued down countless city streets, the diva's body has never lost its representational magnetism for many of us as an alternative body-identity fantasy, resolutely embodying as it does the otherwise almost entirely anachronistic ideal, formed in early nineteenth-century Europe, of the social dignity of corpulence, particularly that of the serenely fat bourgeois matron.

EKS: Catherine Gallagher has written on the complex representational functions of the image of the large human body in political economy after Malthus. By Gallagher's account, Malthus in 1798 inaugurated a representational regime in which the healthy working body both continued, on the one hand, to function – as it had for millennia – as a symbol and prerequisite for the health of the social and economic body as a whole; and at the same time the same substantial and hence procreative individual body began, on the other hand, through the newly activated specter of overpopulation, to represent the constitutive and incurable *vitiation from within* of that same economic totality. After Malthus, she concludes, "a general sense of the body's offensiveness spreads out" from the large body "and permeates the whole realm of organic matter."[1]

The labor of concentrating and representing "a general sense of the body's offensiveness" is not a form of employment that will seem archaic or exotic to large women in modern American society. It permeates the mise-en-scène of my dream – the store where "I was dubious about whether they would have any clothes that would be big enough for me" – whose implicit tension and dread must be resonant for almost any fat woman in this culture. The confrontation of the complex labor of representing offense with the female-homosocial marketplace of gendered visibility – the materialization of a fat woman in a clothing store – lights up the works of a pinball machine of economic, gender, and racial meanings, at the same time as it is likely to register on the steeled body itself as an insult, concussion, ejection. To that woman the air of the shadowbox theater of commerce thickens continually with a mostly unspoken sentence, with what becomes, under capitalism, the primal denial to anyone of a stake in the symbolic order: "There's nothing here for you to spend your money on." Like the black family looking to buy a house in the suburbs, the gay couple looking to rent an apartment, the handicapped high-school kid visiting a barrierridden college in the Ivy League: who and what you are means that there's nothing here for you; your money is not negotiable in this place. Distinct from the anxiety of never *enough* money, the anxiety that there won't be any roof for my head, food for my hunger, doctor for my illness – the more awful anxieties whose energy, however, at least knows how to be commandeered with a fluency just as awful into the capitalist circulation of meaning – this is instead the precipitation of one's very body as a kind of cul-de-sac blockage or clot in the circulation of economic value. My permeability to offensive meanings in such a situation comes, to follow Gallagher's argument, from the double and contradictory value exacted from my bodily representation. Visible on the one hand, in this scene, as a disruptive *embolism* in the flow of economic circulation, the fat female body functions on the other hand more durably (and through the same etymologic route) as the very *emblem* of that circulation.[2] Like the large, dangerous bodies in Malthus, the twentieth-century fat female body represents both the efflorescence and the damaging incoherence of a social order, its function sharpened by representational recastings and by the gender specification, class complication, and racial bifurcation that accompanied the shifts from nineteenth-century European to twentieth-century US models. Its consequence: that what I put on to go shopping is in the brittle armor of a membrane-thin defiance whose verso is stained with abjection.

MM: We have for some time been collaboratively compiling a dossier on a feeling or attitude we call "divinity." The presiding figure for these meditations has been, naturally, Divine, the late star of many John Waters films. As a huge man who repeatedly created the role of "the most beautiful woman in the world," Divine seems to offer a powerful condensation of some emotional and identity linkages – historically dense ones – between fat women and gay men. Specifically, a certain interface between abjection and defiance (what Divine referred to as "glamor fits" and which may more broadly be hypothesized to constitute a subjectivity of glamor itself, especially in the age of the celebrity) seems to be related to interlocking histories of stigma, self-constitution, and epistemological complication proper to fat women and gay men in this century. This combination of abjection and defiance often produces a divinity-effect in the subject, a compelling belief that one is a god or a vehicle of divinity. The subjectivities from which we ourselves are enabled to speak are, it goes without saying, my own experiences of divinity as a fat woman, and Eve's as a gay man.

EKS: John Waters and Divine were a celebrated gay-man-and-diva couple who, until Divine's death in 1987, pursued powerfully mutually enabling careers in film and performance. That Divine, the eponymous diva in question, was not a woman but a biologically male transvestite is important to our project, but so is the way Waters's and Divine's respective body-types play themselves out in the representational world of their films, writings, performances, and interviews. Like his mock-sleazy moustache, Water's body is pencil-thin, what some would call "hipless." Divine's, by contrast, was that of a three-hundred-pound man not trapped in but scandalously and luxuriously corporeally cohabiting with the voluptuous body of a fantasy Mae West or Jayne Mansfield.

MM: In the film and theater of the past two decades, as well as in the body of critical gender theory and performance theory that has arisen during the same period, transvestism has often been trivialized and domesticated into mere "crossdressing," as if its practice had principally to do with something that can be put on and off as easily as a costume. In fact, influential essays like Elaine Showalter's "Critical Cross-Dressing"[3] have allowed transvestism to become *the* dominant image in feminist theory for the purely discretionary or arbitrary aspects of gender identity. As such, it is sometimes treated as sinister — when men are seen as being empowered by a pretense of femininity they can doff at will, leaving their underlying gender identity and privilege untouched or indeed enhanced.[4] Alternatively, a very similar understanding of transvestism can take on a utopian tinge: as a denaturalizing and defamiliarizing exposure of the constructed character of *all* gender; as a translation of what are often compulsory gender behaviors to a caricatural, exciting, *chosen* plane of arbitrariness and free play.

But the social field in which this universalizing, discretionary "theory" of transvestism gets mobilized is already structured by a very different, overlapping set of transvestite knowledges thereby repressed but by no means deactivated.

EKS: That some people can crossdress convincingly and others can't.

MM: That some people's bodies make more sense to themselves and others when they're crossdressed than when they aren't.

EKS: That some people get turned on when they crossdress and others just feel at home.

MM: That crossdressing crosses between public and private differently for different people.

EKS: That for some people, crossdressing signifies their hetero-, and for other people their homo-, sexual identity.

MM: That the embeddedness of crossdressing in routines, in work, in spectacle, in ritual, in celebration, in self-formation, in bodily habitus, in any sexuality, can vary infinitely from one person to another.

EKS: That some people's crossdressing is consistently treated as a form of aggression and responded to with violence.

MM: Divine's performances forcibly remind us of what so many treatments of transvestism require that we forget: that "drag" (as Esther Newton has suggested) is inscribed not just in dress and its associated gender codes but in the body itself: in habitual and largely unconscious physical and psychological attitudes, poses, and styles of bodily relation and response — not just on the body's clothed and most socially negotiable and discretionary surfaces. In addition, it depends on, even as it may perceptually reorganize, the already culturalized physical givens of the body, among them characteristics – size, color, gestural scale – that may have near-ineffaceable associations of power or stigma or both. In stark contrast with the performance style of a relatively "respectable" "female impersonator" like Charles Pierce doing a characteristic turn as Carol Channing or Barbra Streisand in an upscale nightclub, Divine's fiercely aggressive performances do not conceal or disavow what a dangerous act drag can be, onstage and off. Nor do they gloss over how obnoxious many viewers find the act, especially if it is not hedged on all sides with halftruths about why performers "do drag" and why audiences enjoy it – for example, it's merely a performing skill like any other; it's a classic theatrical tradition; it allows performer and spectator to let off steam without really challenging predominant gender-and sex-roles for either. Divine's "loud and vulgar" (to use her terms for it) drag style flings the open secrets of drag performance in the faces of her audience: that unsanitized drag disgusts and infuriates many people, and that it is not wearing a wig or skirt or heels that is the primary sign of male drag performance but rather a way of inhabiting the body with defiant effeminacy – or, the effeminate body itself. And, finally, that it is just this conjunction of effeminacy and defiance in male behavior that can make a man the object of furious punitive energies, of gaybashing threatened or carried out rather than applause.

[...]

EKS: We'd like to say a word at this point about the kind of intervention we are trying to make in the current uses of crossdressing as a condensed emblem for the whole project of gender and social constructivism. Nothing could be further from our intent than to push backward against the constructivist trajectory in the name, or even in the direction, of an essentialism whose killing effects we take to have been amply documented. But we do fear that the choice of crossdressing as emblem for the constructivist project may, along with the real progress it is still enabling (in, for example, the recent work of Judith Butler), also further a dangerous conflation of issues in the current framings of the debate on "constructivism" versus "essentialism." Briefly, as regards gender and sexual identities, we fear a conflation of the question of what might be called phylogeny with that of individual ontogeny. (The origin of this conflation probably has something to do with the double disciplinary genealogy of constructivism itself: on the one hand through a Foucauldian historicism designed to take the centuries vertiginously in stride, on the other through an interactional communications theory whose outermost temporal horizon is, in practice, the individual life span.) The *phylogenic* question, which asks about the centuries-long processes – linguistic, institutional, intergenerational – by which such identities are or are not invented, manipulated, and altered, gets asked under the rubric of "constructivism" as if it were identical to the *ontogenic* question: the question "how did *such-and-such-a person* come to be," shall we say, gay rather than straight.

We see three problems with this tacit devolution from constructivism-as-phylogeny to constructivism-as-ontogeny, a devolution that seems to be facilitated by some current uses of the topos of crossdressing. The first is simply the cognitive loss, a certain vulgarization involved in the ideational collapse. The second, as we have mentioned, is the frightening ease with which anything that our capitalist/consumer culture does not figure as absolute *compulsion* (e.g. addiction), it instead recasts as absolute *choice* through the irresistible metaphor of the marketplace. One, but only one terrible effect of this marketplace imagery is the right-wing demand that gays who wish to share in human rights and dignities must (and *can*) make the free-market choice of becoming *ex-gays* – an abuse of the constructivist analysis to which there absolutely must be some response stronger than the currently popular gay-politicos' retreat into the abjectly essentialist, "We deserve rights and dignity because *we were born this way and can't help it.*"

Finally, there is a reason to be nostalgic for the exhilaration of that founding moment of gay-liberation ideology, the moment when the question of gay ontogeny – "What makes Johnny gay?" – got dislinked, seemingly once and for all, from the assertion of the gay subject's claims on the resources and support of the society in which she must exist. The project of gay/lesbian liberation was possible *only* when the fascination, the consequentiality of the riddle of individual ontogeny had been shattered. So there is a clear (not to say prohibitive) risk in the reviving demand for *any* form of narrative in the ontogenic framework.

[...]

MM: Interestingly, it is in the nascent unfolding of a movement much younger than gay/lesbian liberation, namely the fat liberation movement, that the liberatory moment of ontogenic *dis*linkage is currently being enacted. New science (much of it being done by gay men scientists) is finally getting around to demonstrating the commonplace – discursively valueless so long as it was spoken only by fat people – that fat people do not actually eat more than thin people. At any rate, whether or not *because* of this "scientific development," the issue of *being fat* is able to be, even today *is being*, severed thrillingly (though still with an unstanchable incompleteness) from the moralizing discourses of greed or the medicalizing discourses of "eating disorders" – to be established instead in the assertive, anti-ontogenic space of an emergent identity politics. That the politicized insistence on a willed agnosticism about individual *causes*, the anti-ontogenic crux moment in fat liberation, rhymes so closely with the analogous moment in gay liberation, records a profound and unacknowledged historical debt. It might point as well to the political need for a historicizing, phylogenic, anti-essentialist construction of size – which is indeed already under way in such work as that of Hillel Schwartz as well as in our present work.

EKS: The ontogenic dis-linkage of fat is, however, the farthest thing from the obsessive mind of John Waters; indeed, it is his absolute refusal of such a move that makes the center-of-gravity of his inimitably heft thematics. In a late-capitalist world economy of consumption, the problematics of waste and residue, hitherto economically marginal, tend increasingly to assume an uncanny centrality. The concept of "ecology" itself, with its profoundly, permanently destabilizing anthropomorphization of the planet as a single living body, emerged in the seventies much less from the question of how to feed the earth's inhabitants than from that of how to contain or innocuously to recirculate their wastes. At the level of the disciplines surrounding the supposed individual body, the recent strange career of cholesterol in the medical and public imagination suggests that to the conflict between virological and immunological body models which is dramatized in discourses around cancer and AIDS, there must be added a muted but potent third term involving not just cardiovascular medicine but the discipline that has come to be called garbology. The issue (in many ways a startlingly new one) of the very viability of our planet has emerged as the need not merely to limit waste but – no doubt you'll pick up on the paradox involved – to eliminate it. Which, paradoxically again, can only mean to consume it.

One consequence of these developments has been that the Enlightenment western fantasy-imperative of the hygienic has, not come to an end, but come under increasing and transformative stress. At the moment when Mary Douglas can construct an *anthropology* of hygiene, at least the transcendent self-evidence of the expulsive, projective hygienic project must be nearing its close.[5] If an ecological system includes no "out there" to which the waste product can, in fantasy, be destined, then it makes sense that the meaning-infused, diachronically rich, perhaps inevitably nostalgic chemical, cultural, and material garbage — our own waste in whose company we are destined to live and die — is accruing new forms of interpretive magnetism and new forms, as well, of affective and erotic value.

[...]

Notes

1   Catherine Gallagher, "The Body Versus the Social Body in the Works of Thomas Malthus and Henry Mayhew," *Representations* 14 (Spring 1986): 102.

2   Embolism: cf. embolus < Gk *embolos* stopper = *em* + *bolos* a throw, akin to *ballein* to throw. Emblem: < Gk something to put on = *em* + *blema* something thrown or put, cf. *emballein* to throw in or on. Cf. also abject < L *abjectus* thrown down.

3   Elaine Showalter, "Critical Cross-Dressing: Male Feminists and the Woman of the Year," most readily available in Alice Jardine and Paul Smith (eds), *Men in Feminism* (New York: Methuen, 1987), pp. 116–32.

4   A trenchant critique of the presumptions of Showalter's essay — which has unfortunately failed to prevent their being replicated almost endlessly on the feminist critical scene — is Craig Owen's "Outlaws: Gay Men in Feminism," in Jardine and Smith, pp. 217–32.

5   Mary Douglas, *Purity and Danger: An Analysis of Concepts of Pollution and Taboo* (New York: Praeger, 1966).

Chapter 17

Beverley Skeggs

AMBIVALENT FEMININITIES

From B. Skeggs (1998) 'Ambivalent Femininities', in *Formations of Class and Gender: Becoming Respectable,* London: Sage.

[...]

Classed femininities

POOVEY (1984) CHARTS HOW the emergence of femininity as an ideal was produced through textuality in the eighteenth century. The femininity produced had an affinity with the habitus of the upper classes, of ease, restraint, calm and luxurious decoration. It was produced as a sign of difference from other women. Conduct books and magazines encapsulated this habitus with the concept of the 'lady' which equated conduct with appearance. This ideal of the lady continued to be reproduced into the nineteenth century where both textual and visual technologies operated as a strong marker for the development of gendered notions of sexual propriety (Lury, 1993; Nead, 1988; Pollock, 1989). Through the development of the textually mediated feminine ideal the visual became the site where values were allocated to groups of women and the construction of appearance as a sign of value became established. White middle-class femininity was defined as the ideal but also as the most passive and dependent of femininities. It was always coded as respectable.

By the end of the nineteenth century femininity had become established as a (middle-) classed sign, a sign of a particular form of womanhood. It was, Walkerdine (1989) argues, a projection of male fantasy. Femininity was seen to be the *property* of middle-class women who could *prove* themselves to be respectable through their appearance and conduct. Because femininity developed as a classed sign it became imbued with different amounts of power, as Ware (1992) has shown. White middle-class women could use their proximity to the sign of femininity to construct distinctions between themselves and others. Investments in the ideal of femininity enabled them to gain access to limited status and moral superiority. It was their desire for value that led them to evaluate others. Their take-up of their positioning and their display of it through appearance enabled them to judge those who were lacking in femininity, hence respectability. This generated struggles over respectable appearance and conduct. Hall (1979) shows how middle- and upper-class women, in the name of evangelicalism, would visit the houses of the poor in an attempt to redeem them from themselves, that is from themselves as a sign of dangerous, disruptive, sexual women.

Working-class women were coded as inherently healthy, hardy and robust (whilst, also paradoxically as a source of infection and disease) against the physical frailty of middle-class women. They were also involved in forms of labour that prevented femininity from ever being a possibility. For working-class women femininity was never a given (as was sexuality); they were not automatically positioned by it in the same way as middle- and upper-class White women. Femininity was always something which did not designate them precisely. Working-class women – both Black and White – were coded as the sexual and deviant other against which femininity was defined (Gilman, 1992). Ware (1992) shows how the categories of White middle-class womanhood were constructed against those of potentially dangerous Black women. And Davis (1995) notes how African-American women have, as a result of these different significations, historically forged models of womanhood that continually and dramatically challenge prevailing notions of femininity.

The distance that is drawn between the sexual and the feminine was drawn onto the bodies of working-class women. 'This dynamic of representation is not "women" as a sign but femininity as (dis)simulation, a mask of non-identity, a bodily submission to "ideas about herself" ' (Lury, 1993: 204). It is more difficult for working-class women to make a bodily submission to ideas about herself, for herself and her body is of a different class, within a different cultural and material economy. This is why when they do try on femininity they often feel it is the wrong size. It was designed for someone with a different bodily shape. This is not just metaphoric play: White working-class bodies are generally smaller, less healthy and live shorter lives (The Black Report, 1982; Bourke, 1994). Moreover, the White female working-class body is often represented as out of control, in excess, such as that of *Roseanne*. Rowe (1995) argues that working-class women have often been associated with the lower unruly order of bodily functions such as that of expulsion and leakage (and reproduction) which signified lack of discipline and vulgarity. And, as Bourdieu (1986) shows, working-class women are considered to be distanced from having 'taste'. Rowe refers to a representation of working-class women by Alan King as:

> The hopeless underclass of the female sex. The polyester-class, overweight occupants of the slow track. Fast food waitresses, factory workers, housewives-members of the invisible pink-collar army. The despised, the jilted, the underpaid.
>
> (Rowe, 1995: 57)

Femininity requires the display of classed dispositions, of forms of conduct and behaviour, different forms of cultural capital, which are not part of their cultural baggage: they are unlikely to display 'divine composure', which include the components of femininity as silent, static, invisible and composed (Cixous, 1980). Working-class women's relationship to femininity has always been produced through recourse to vulgarity. It is in the desire to avoid being positioned by the vulgar, pathological, tasteless and sexual, in order to prove their respectability, that the women of the study make investments in femininity. Even though they are positioned at a distance from femininity, investments in the forms of femininity to which they have access enable a movement away from the sexual; they offer routes into respectability, but not without incurring costs and implicating women in circuits of exchange. To do femininity they have to both appear and *be* feminine.

The division between the sexual and the feminine was most carefully coded at the level of conduct where appearance became the signifier of conduct: to look was *to be*. Appearance and conduct became markers of respectability, although these had to be coded in the correct way: too much concentration on appearance was seen to be a sign of female deviancy, as Lury (1993) notes: no good girl can afford to appear bad. This legacy remains. Throughout this research value judgements were made on the basis of appearance. Appearance became the means by which the women felt they could know and place others. The hierarchy of placement was based on respectability. Ortner (1991) notes, for instance, how a group of middle-class college women interpreted the hairstyles of a group of working-class women as a sign of lack of sexual restraint. It is against this constant marking and positioning that the women make investments.

[...]

Glamour, desirability and confirmation of value

[...] [F]or working-class women the sexual has to be disavowed. Glamour, however, is a way of holding together sexuality and respectability, but it is difficult to achieve. Pearce (1995) argues that glamour is always read as 'degrading' unless 'protected' and defended by other marks of middle-class respectability (such as education or wealth). The women have to negotiate being glamorous and desirable — to which they all aspire — whilst not being marked as rough and common. Whilst the women were keen not to be associated with the sexual, they also knew that carefully coded displays of sexuality could generate value (such as their use of flirting). They knew that their sexuality had a value that could be traded in their local circuits of exchange. This value was based on a conglomeration of variables, including: physically corresponding to dominant ideals of femininity, wearing locally designated appropriate clothing; limiting their sexual activity to avoid a reputation; not being aggressive, vulgar or domineering. These could all be negotiated through glamour. The women had to carefully code, display and conduct themselves to generate value. Glamour is the mechanism by which the marks of middle-class respectability are transposed onto the sexual body, a way in which recognition of value is achieved.

Stacey (1994) charts the historical association of glamour with Americanness. She argues that glamour was defined against British respectability in the 1950s in which it was understood to signify confidence, sophistication and self-assurance, but that by the 1980s it had been tempered by British middle-class restraint and respectability. Sherratt (1983) notes how by the 1970s glamour had moved into the British mainstream becoming a centralized concern for young women. She argues:

> Glamour was being conceptualized as a style of life, defined on the one hand as essentially the obverse of their own 'boring' present existence, whatever that may be; and on the other hand in terms of qualities of being.
>
> (1983: 54)

Glamour offers the ability to appear as something different from the mundane. It is an escape route. When discussing glamour, the following responses were evoked:

> Well when I said she looked really glam what I meant was that she looked gorgeous, you know quite stunning, like you'd really notice her, not because she was displaying herself, which is the main way to get attention, but because she looked really good. She looked, well, glamorous, well fanciable without turning it on too much.
>
> (Diane, 1988)

> You know it when you see it, sort of well put together and looking sexy but not tarty or obvious. There's nothing vulgar about being glamorous. It's good when it works, if it doesn't you just look stupid. I think it's also about attitude and the way you do it. I think you have to feel good to look glamorous. It's also then about how confident you feel. You can always tell glamorous women, they're dead confident about themselves.
>
> (Fiona, 1988)

Glamour involves attitude as well as appearance, it is a 'structure of feeling' (Williams, 1961, 1977), albeit within the discourse of textually-mediated femininity. Whereas other forms of femininity are not experienced as subjectivity, the recognition of oneself as glamorous serves to engender an identification, enabling femininity to operate as a disposition *and* a form of cultural capital, even if only momentarily and always tied to performance. It is the attitude that makes the difference. It gives agency, strength and worth back to women and is not restricted to youth. They do glamour with style. Glamour is about a performance of femininity *with* strength:

> Yea I get glammed up, we all do. You have to be up for it though. There's no point if you're not in the mood or feeling down. You've got to feel you're invincible. Whistles, comments, chat-ups the lot, you've just got to look down your nose at them. I know when I look good. I make sure others do too.
>
> (Angela, 1992)

Glamour is a way of transcending the banalities of femininity which render women as passive objects, as signs of appearance without agency, as something which has to be done. This shows how femininity is fragmented in which some facets can be re-enacted with vision, pleasure and attitude in a way more appropriate to those for whom it was not designed. Femininity may be textually mediated, an artifice, a masquerade, a performance but through glamour it is also experienced as a temporary 'way of being'. To be feminine, as Butler (1990) argues, is a mode of enacting and re-enacting of received gender norms which surface as so many styles of the flesh. Glamour is one of the areas, one of the styles of the flesh, in which pleasure can be gained. Glamour enables the projection of desirability.

[...]

Conclusion

The concept of femininity is only partially adequate to encapsulate the experiences by which the women of the study occupied the category 'woman'. It is always over-layered with other categorizations such as class and race. Historically this is because working-class women (Black and White) have been positioned against femininity with the sexual. They were precisely what femininity was not. However, to claim respectability, disavowal of the sexual is necessary and constructions, displays and performances of feminine appearance and conduct are seen as necessary. The women are positioned at a distance from femininity but claim proximity to it. This ambivalent positioning informed their responses. The women made feminine performances appropriate to the situations they were in. These could be made across a range of sites, with differing value and potential (often produced through institutionalization (in the sexual division of labour; the legal system; the education system)). These were not masquerades employed to generate distance (that was already guaranteed) but tactical deployments of forms of femininity which protected their investments and gained cultural approval and validations. Their attempts to 'pass' as feminine were always in jeopardy of being read by others as representative of authentic femininity. To not make these performances would have seriously endangered their bids for respectability. Their awareness of their positioning by default as sexual, vulgar, tarty, pathological and without value meant that they felt they had to continually prove that they were different.

[...]

This suggests that femininity may indeed be an uninhabitable category, reproduced by White working-class women through necessity rather than volition, through their deployment of different forms of femininity. The women's performances did not engender identification because they did not recognize themselves addressed by the classed category of femininity. They do not know themselves as feminine. Aspects of femininity are, however, something which they have learnt to perform and from which they can sometimes take pleasure. The central problem with the reproduction of femininity was that there were few culturally valid and economically possible or potential alternatives available for enacting at a local level.

References

Black Report (1982) *Inequalities in Health*, P. Townsend and N. Davidson (eds), Harmondsworth: Penguin.

Bourdieu, P. (1986) *Distinction: A Social Critique of the Judgement of Taste*, London: Routledge.

Bourke, J. (1994) *Working Class Cultures in Britain: 1890–1960*, London: Routledge.

Butler, J. (1990) *Gender Trouble: Feminism and the Subversion of Identity*, London: Routledge.

Cixous, H. (1980) 'The laugh of the Medusa', trans. K. Cohen and P. Cohen, in E. Marks and I. de Courtivron (eds), *New French Feminisms*, Brighton: Harvester, pp. 90–9.

Davis, A. Y. (1995) 'I used to be your sweet mama: ideology, sexuality and domesticity in the blues of Gertrude "Ma" Rainey and Bessie Smith', in E. Grosz and E. Probyn (eds), *Sexy Bodies: The Strange Carnalities of Feminism*, London: Routledge, pp. 231–66.

Gilman, S. L. (1992) 'Black bodies, white bodies: towards an iconography of female sexuality in late nineteenth century art, medicine and literature', in J. Donald and A. Rattansi (eds), *'Race', Culture and Difference*, London: Sage, pp. 171–98.

Hall, C. (1979) 'The early formation of Victorian domestic ideology', in S. Burman (ed.), *Fit Work for Women*, London: Croom Helm, pp. 15–33.

Lury, C. (1993) *Cultural Rights: Technology, Legality and Personality*, London: Routledge.

Nead, L. (1988) *Myths of Sexuality: Representations of Women in Victorian Britain*, Oxford: Blackwell.

Ortner, S. (1991) 'Reading America: preliminary notes on class and culture', in G. R. Fox (ed.), *Recapturing Anthropology: Working in the Present*, Sante Fe, NM: School of American Research Press, pp. 163–91.

Pearce, L. (1995) Personal communication with the author, 9 December.

Pollock, G. (1989) *Vision and Difference: Femininity, Feminism and the Histories of Art*, London: Routledge.

Poovey, M. (1984) *The Proper Lady and the Woman Writer: Ideology as Style in the Works of Mary Wollstonecraft, Mary Shelly, and Jane Austen*, Chicago: University of Chicago Press.

Rowe, K. (1995) *The Unruly Woman: Gender and the Genres of Laughter*, Austin: University of Texas Press.

Sherratt, N. (1983) 'Girls, jobs and glamour', *Feminist Review*, 15: 47–62.

Stacey, J. (1994) *Star Gazing: Hollywood Cinema and Female Spectatorship*, London: Routledge.

Walkerdine, V. (1989) 'Femininity as performance', *Oxford Review of Education*, 15 (3): 267–79.

Ware, V. (1992) *Beyond The Pale: White Women, Racism and History*, London: Verso.

Williams, R. (1961) *Culture and Society 1780–1950*, Harmondsworth: Penguin.

Williams, R. (1977) *Marxism and Literature*, Oxford: Oxford University Press.

Chapter 18

Allucquère Rosanne Stone

IN NOVEL CONDITIONS
The cross-dressing psychiatrist

From A. R. Stone (1996) "In novel conditions: the cross-dressing psychiatrist," in *The War of Desire and Technology at the Close of the Mechanical Age*, Cambridge, MA and London, England: The MIT Press.

[…]

ONE OF OUR WESTERN industrialized cultural assumptions is that subjectivity is invariably constituted in relation to a physical substrate – that social beings, people, exist by virtue of possessing biological bodies through which their existence is warranted in the body politic. Another is that we know unproblematically what "body" is. Let me tell you a boundary story, a tale of the nets.

[…]

This one begins in 1982, on the CompuServe conference system. […] Most on-line conferences now offer what are called chat lines, which are virtual places where many people can interact simultaneously in real time. In the Internet world there are many such places with quite elaborately worked out geographies; these are known as multiple-user thisses-and-thats. […] It was on CompuServe, some time early in 1982, that a New York psychiatrist named Sanford Lewin opened an account.

In the conversation channels, particularly the real-time chat conferences such as CB, it is customary to choose an on-line name, or "handle," that may have no relationship to one's "real" name, which CompuServe does not reveal. Frequently, however, participants in virtual conversations choose handles that express some part of their personalities, real or imagined. Lewin, with his profession in mind, chose the handle "Doctor."

It does not appear to have dawned on him that the term was gender-neutral until a day not long after he first signed on. He had been involved in a general chat in public virtual space, had started an interesting conversation with a woman, and they had decided to drop into private mode for a few minutes. In private mode two people who have chosen to converse can only "hear" each other, and the rest of the people in the vicinity cannot "hear" them. The private conversation was actually under way for a few minutes before Lewin realized it was profoundly different from any conversation he'd been in before. Somehow the woman to whom he was talking had mistaken him for a *woman* psychiatrist. He had always felt that even in his most personal conversations with women there was always something missing, some essential connection. Suddenly he understood why, because the conversation he was now having was deeper and more open than anything he'd experienced. "I was stunned," he said later, "at the conversational mode. I hadn't known that women talked among themselves that way. There was so much more vulnerability, so much more depth and complexity. And then I thought to myself, Here's a terrific opportunity to help people, by catching them when their normal defenses are down and they're more able to hear what they need to hear."

Lewin reasoned, or claimed to have reasoned, that if women were willing to let down their conversational barriers with other women in the chat system, then as a psychiatrist he could use the chat system to do good. The obvious strategy of continuing to use the gender-neutral "Doctor" handle didn't seem like the right approach. It appears that he became deeply intrigued with the idea of interacting with women *as a woman*, rather than using a female persona as a masquerade. He wanted to become a female persona to such an extent that he could feel what it was like to be a woman in some deep and essential way. And at this point his idea of helping women by becoming an on-line woman psychiatrist took a different turn.

He opened a second account with CompuServe under the name Julie Graham.

[...]

Julie first signed on in 1982. She described herself as a New York neuropsychologist who, within the last few years, had been involved in a serious automobile accident caused by a drunken driver. Her boyfriend had been killed, and she had suffered severe neurological damage to her head and spine, in particular to Broca's area, which controls speech. She was now mute and paraplegic. In addition, her face had been severely disfigured, to the extent that plastic surgery was unable to restore her appearance. Consequently she never saw anyone in person. She had become a recluse, embittered, slowly withdrawing from life, and seriously planning suicide, when a friend gave her a small computer and modem and she discovered CompuServe.

After being tentatively on-line for a while, her personality began to flourish. She began to talk about how her life was changing, and how interacting with other women in the net was helping her reconsider her situation. She stopped thinking of suicide and began planning her life. Although she lived alone and currently held no job, she had a small income from an inheritance; her family had made a fortune in a mercantile business, so at least she was assured of a certain level of physical comfort. She was an atheist, who enjoyed attacking organized religion; smoked dope, and was occasionally quite stoned on-line late at night; and was bisexual, from time to time coming on to the men and women with whom she talked. In fact, as time went on, she became flamboyantly sexual. Eventually she was encouraging many of her friends to engage in net sex with her.

Some time during this period Julie changed her handle, or sign-on pseudonym, as a celebration of her return to an active social life, at least on the net. She still maintained her personal privacy, insisting that she was too ashamed of her disfigurements and her inability to vocalize, preferring to be known only by her on-line persona. People on the chat system held occasional parties at which those who lived in reasonable geographic proximity would gather to exchange a few socialities in biological mode, and Julie assiduously avoided these. Instead she ramped up her social profile on the net even further. Her standard greeting was a huge, expansive "HI!!!!!!!!!!!!!"

Julie started a women's discussion group on CompuServe. She also had long talks with women outside the group, and her advice was extremely helpful to many of them. Over the course of time several women confided to her that they were depressed and thinking about suicide, and she shared her own thoughts about her brush with suicide and helped them to move on to more life-affirming attitudes. She also helped several women with drug and chemical dependencies. An older woman confided her desire to return to college and her fear of being rejected; Julie encouraged her to go through with the application process. Once the woman was accepted, Julie advised her on the writing of several papers (including one on multiple personality "disorder" (MPD)) and in general acted as wise counsel and supportive sister.

She also took it upon herself to ferret out pretenders in the chat system, in particular men who masqueraded as women. As Van Gelder pointed out in her study of the incident, Julie was not shy about warning women about the dangers of letting one's guard down on the net. "Remember to be careful," Van Gelder quotes her as saying, "Things may not be as they seem."

There is a subtext here, which has to do with what I have been calling the on-line persona. Of course we all change personae all the time, to suit the social occasion, although with on-line personae the act is more purposeful. Nevertheless, the societal imperative with which we have been raised is that there is one primary persona, or "true identity," and that in the off-line world – the "real world" – this persona is firmly attached to a single physical body, by which our existence as a social being is authorized and in which it is grounded. The origin of this "correct" relationship between body and persona seems to have been contemporaneous with the Enlightenment, the same cultural moment that gave birth to what we like to call the sovereign subject. True, there is no shortage of examples extending far back in time of a sense of something in the body other than just meat. Usually this has to do with an impalpable soul or a similar manifestation – some agency that carries with it the seat of consciousness, and that normally may be decoupled from the body only after death. For many people, though, the soul or some impalpable avatar routinely journeys free of the body, and a certain amount of energy is routinely expended in managing the results of its travels. Partly the Western idea that the body and the subject are inseparable is a worthy exercise in wish fulfillment – an attempt to explain why ego-centered subjectivity terminates with the substrate and to enforce the termination. Recently we find in science fiction quite a number of attempts to refigure this relationship, notably in the work of authors like John Varley, who has made serious tries at constructing phenomenologies of the self (e.g. Varley 1986).

[…]

Julie, John, Joan – they are all wonderful examples of the war of desire and technology. Their complex virtual identities are real and productive interventions into our cultural belief that the unmarked social unit, besides being white and male, is a single self in a single body. MPD is another such intervention. As I tried to make clear in "Identity in Oshkosh," MPD is generally considered to be pathological, the result of trauma. But we can look to the construction and management of pathology for the circumstances that constitute and authorize the unmarked, so that we may take the pathologization of MPD and in general the management and control of any manifestations of body-self, other than the one body – one self norm, to be useful tools to take apart discourses of the political subject so we can see what makes them work. There are other interventions to be made, and here we interrogate a few Harawayan elsewheres – in this case, virtual space, the phantasmic "structure" within which real social interactions take place – for information. Of course, the virtual environment of the chat lines is just the beginning, a look at a single event when such events were still singular.

[…]

Jekyll and Julie. As her friendships deepened and simultaneously the imposture began to unravel, Lewin began to realize the enormity of his deception. And the simplicity of the solution. Julie had to die. And so events ground inexorably onward. One day Julie became seriously ill. […] For a few days she hovered between life and death, while Lewin hovered, setting up her demise in a plausible fashion.

The result was horrific. Lewin, as John, was deluged with expressions of shock, sorrow, and caring. People offered medical advice, offered financial assistance, sent cards, sent flowers. Some people went into out-and-out panic. The chat lines became jammed. So many people got seriously upset, in fact, that Lewin backed down. He couldn't stand to go through with it. He couldn't stand to engineer her death. Julie recovered and came home.

The relief on the net was enormous. Joyous messages were exchanged. Julie and John were overwhelmed with caring from their friends. In fact, sometime during the great outpouring of sympathy and concern, while Julie was at death's door, one of her friends managed to find out the name of the hospital where she was supposed to be staying. He called, to see if he could help out, and was told there was no one registered by that name.

[…]

The Julie persona began to come seriously unraveled. First the disabled women began to wonder aloud, then Lewin took the risk of revealing himself to a few more women with whom he felt he had built a friendship. Once he started the process, word of what was happening spread rapidly through the net. But just as building Julie's original persona had taken some time, the actual dismantling of it took several months, as more clearly voiced suspicions gradually turned to factual information and the information was passed around the conferences, repeated, discussed, and picked over.

[…]

Perhaps to everyone's surprise, the emotion that many of those in the chat system felt most deeply was mourning. Because of the circumstances in which it occurred, Julie's unmasking as a construct, a cross-dressing man, had been worse than a death. There was no focused instant of pain and loss. There was no funeral, no socially supported way to lay the Julie persona to rest, to release one's emotions and to move on. The help Julie had given people in that very regard seemed inappropriate in the circumstance. Whatever else Julie was or wasn't, she had been a good friend and a staunch supporter to many people in need, giving unstintingly of her time and virtual energy wherever it was required. Her fine sense of humor and ability to see the bright side of difficulties had helped many people, mostly women, over very difficult places in their lives. At least some of her charm and charisma should have rubbed off on Lewin. But it didn't. And, quite understandably, some of the women did not bounce back with forgiveness. At least one said that she felt a deep emotional violation which, in her opinion, was tantamount to sexual assault. "I felt raped," she said, "I felt as if my deepest secrets were violated. The good things Julie did ... were all done by deception." Some of the women formed a support group to talk about their sense of betrayal and violation, which they referred to wryly as "Julie-anon."

[...]

References

Van Gelder, Lindsy (1985) "The strange case of the electronic lover," *Ms.*, October, pp. 94–5.
Varley, John (1986) *Blue Champagne*, New York: Berkley.

Chapter 19

Judith Butler

ENDANGERED/ENDANGERING

Schematic racism and white paranoia

From J. Butler (1993) "Endangered/endangering: schematic racism and white paranoia," in R. Gooding-Williams (ed.), *Reading Rodney King/Reading Urban Uprising*, New York and London: Routledge.

THE DEFENSE ATTORNEYS FOR the police in the Rodney King case made the argument that the policemen were endangered, and that Rodney King was the source of that danger. The argument they made drew from many sources, comments he made, acts he refused to perform on command, and the highly publicized video recording taken on the spot and televised widely before and during the trial. During the trial, the video was shown at the same time that the defense offered a commentary, and so we are left to presume that some convergence of word and picture produced the "evidence" for the jurors in the case. The video shows a man being brutally beaten, repeatedly, and without visible resistance; and so the question is, How could this video be used as evidence that the body being beaten was *itself* the source of danger, the threat of violence, and, further, that the beaten body of Rodney King bore an intention to injure, and to injure precisely those police who either wielded the baton against him or stood encircling him? In the Simi Valley courtroom, what many took to be incontrovertible evidence *against* the police was presented instead to establish police vulnerability, that is, to support the contention that Rodney King was endangering the police. Later, a juror reported that she believed that Rodney King was in "total control" of the situation. How was this feat of interpretation achieved?

That it *was* achieved is not the consequence of ignoring the video, but, rather, of reproducing the video within a racially saturated field of visibility. If racism pervades white perception, structuring what can and cannot appear within the horizon of white perception, then to what extent does it interpret in advance "visual evidence"? And how, then, does such "evidence" have to be read, and read publicly, *against* the racist disposition of the visible which will prepare and achieve its own inverted perceptions under the rubric of "what is seen"?

[...]

To claim that King's victimization is *manifestly* true is to assume that one is presenting the case to a set of subjects who *know how to see*; to think that the video "speaks for itself" is, of course, for many of us, obviously true. But if the field of the visible is racially contested terrain, then it will be politically imperative to read such videos aggressively, to repeat and publicize such readings, if only to further an antiracist hegemony over the visual field. [...] The visual field is not neutral to the question of race; it is itself a racial formation, an episteme, hegemonic and forceful.

[...]

> "Look, a Negro!" It was an external stimulus that flicked over me as I passed by. I made a tight smile.
> "Look, a Negro!" It was true. It amused me.
> "Look, a Negro!" The circle was drawing a bit tighter.
> I made no secret of my amusement.
> "Mama, see the Negro! I'm frightened!" "Frightened!"
> Frightened! Now they were beginning to be afraid of me. I made up my mind to laugh myself to tears but laughter had become impossible.
>
> (Frantz Fanon, 1967)

Frantz Fanon offers here a description of how the black male body is constituted through fear, and through a naming and a seeing: "Look, a Negro!" where the "look" is both a pointing and a seeing, a pointing out what there is to see, a pointing which circumscribes a dangerous body, a racist indicative which relays its own danger to the body to which it points. Here the "pointing" is not only an indicative, but the schematic foreshadowing of an accusation, one which carries the performative force to constitute that danger which it fears and defends against. In his clearly masculinist theory, Fanon demarcates the subject as the black male, and the Other as the white male, and perhaps we ought for the moment to let the masculinist of the scene stay in place; for there is within the white male's racist fear of the black male body a clear anxiety over the possibility of sexual exchange; hence, the repeated references to Rodney King's "ass" by the surrounding policemen, and the homophobic circumscription of that locus of sodomy as a kind of threat.

In Fanon's recitation of the racist interpellation, the black body is circumscribed as dangerous, prior to any gesture, any raising of the hand, and the infantilized white reader is positioned in the scene as one who is helpless in relation to that black body, as one definitionally in need of protection by his/her mother or, perhaps, the police. The fear is that some physical distance will be crossed, and the virgin sanctity of whiteness will be endangered by that proximity. The police are thus structurally placed to protect whiteness against violence, where violence is the imminent action of that black male body. And because within this imaginary schema, the police protect whiteness, their own violence cannot be read as violence; because the black male body, prior to any video, is the site and source of danger, a threat, the police effort to subdue this body, even if in advance, is justified regardless of the circumstances. Or rather, the conviction of that justification rearranges and orders the circumstances to fit that conclusion.

What struck me on the morning after the verdict was delivered were reports which reiterated the phantasmatic production of "intention," the intention inscribed in and read off Rodney King's frozen body on the street, his intention to do harm, to endanger. The video was used as "evidence" to support the claim that the frozen black male body on the ground receiving blows was himself producing those blows, about to produce them, was himself the imminent threat of a blow and, therefore, was himself responsible for the blows he received. That body thus received those blows in return for the ones it was about to deliver, the blows which were that body in its essential gestures, even as the one gesture that body can be seen to make is to raise its palm outward to stave off the blows against it. According to this racist episteme, he is hit in exchange for the blows he never delivered, but which he is, by virtue of his blackness, always about to deliver.

Here we can see the splitting of that violent intentionality off from the police actions, and the investment of those very intentions in the one who receives the blows. How is this splitting and attribution of violent intentionality possible? And how was it *reproduced* in the defense attorneys' racist pedagogy, thus implicating the defense attorneys in a *sympathetic* racist affiliation with the police, inviting the jurors to join in that community of victimized victimizers? The attorneys proceeded through cultivating an identification with white paranoia in which a white community is always and only protected by the police, against a threat which Rodney King's body emblematizes, quite apart from any action it can be said to perform or appear ready to perform. This is an action that the black male body is always already performing within that white racist imaginary, has always already performed prior to the emergence of any video. The identification with police paranoia culled, produced, and consolidated in that jury is one way of reconstituting a white racist imaginary that postures *as if* it were the unmarked frame of the visible field, laying claim to the authority of "direct perception."

The interpretation of the video in the trial had to work the possible sites of identification it offered: Rodney King, the surrounding police, those actively beating him, those witnessing him, the gaze of the camcorder and, by implication, the white bystander who perhaps feels moral outrage, but who is also watching from a distance, suddenly installed at the scene as the undercover newsman. In a sense, the jury could be convinced of police innocence only through a tactical orchestration of those identifications, for in some sense, they *are* the white witness, separated from the ostensible site of black danger by a circle of police; they *are* the police, enforcers of the law, encircling that body, beating him, once again. They are perhaps King as well, but whitewashed: the blows he suffers are taken to be the blows they *would* suffer if the police were not protecting them from him. Thus, the physical danger in which King is recorded is transferred to them; they identify with that vulnerability, but construe it as their own, the vulnerability of whiteness, thus refiguring him as the threat. The danger that they believe themselves always to be in, by virtue of their whiteness (whiteness as an episteme operates despite the existence of two nonwhite jurors). This completes the circuit of paranoia: the projection of their own aggression, and the subsequent regarding of that projection as an external threat.

[...]

Is it precisely because this black male body is on the ground that the beating becomes intensified? For if white paranoia is also to some degree homophobia, then is this not a brutalization performed as a desexualization or, rather, as a punishment for a conjectured or desired sexual aggression? The image of the police standing over Rodney King with their batons might be read as a sexual degradation which ends up miming and inverting the imagined scene of sexual violation that it appears to want and to loathe; the police thus deploy the "props" and "positions" of that scene in the service of its aggressive denial.

The reversal and displacement of dangerous intention mentioned above continued to be reiterated after the verdict: first, in the violence that took place in Los Angeles in which the majority of individuals killed were black and in the streets, killed by the police, thus replaying, intensifying, and extending the scope of the violence against Rodney King. The intensification of police violence against people of color can be read as evidence that the verdict was taken as further state sanction for racist police violence; second, in remarks made by Mr. Bush on the day after the verdict was announced in which he condemned public violence, noting first the lamentability of public violence against property(!), and holding responsible, once again, those black bodies on the street, as if the figure of the brutalized black body had, as anticipated, risen and raised its forces against the police. The groups involved in street violence thus were construed paradoxically as the originators of a set of killings that may well have left those very bodies dead, thus exonerating the police and the state *again*, and performing an identification with the phantasmatic endangerment of the white community in Simi Valley; a third, in the media scanning of street violence, the refusal to read how and where and why fires were lit, stores burned, indeed, what was being articulated in and through that violence. The bestialization of the crowds, consolidated by scanning techniques which appeared to "hunt down" people of color and figure their violence as "senseless" or "barbaric," thus recapitulated the racist production of the visual field.

If the jury's reading of the video reenacted the phantasmatic scene of the crime, reiterating and re-occupying the always already endangered status of the white person on the street, and the response to the reading, now inscribed as verdict, was to re-cite the charge and to reenact and enlarge the crime, it achieved this in part through a transposition and fabrication of dangerous intention. This is hardly a full explanation of the causes of racist violence, but it does, perhaps, constitute a moment in its production. It can perhaps be described as a form of white paranoia which projects the intention to injure that it itself enacts, and then repeats that projection on increasingly larger scales, a specific social modality of repetition compulsion, which we still need to learn how to read, and which as a "reading," performed in the name of law, has obvious and consequential effects.

Reference

Fanon, Frantz (1967) "The fact of blackness," in *Black Skin; White Masks*, translated by Charles Lam Markmann, New York: Grove Press, pp. 111–12.

PART FOUR

Normal bodies (or not)

INTRODUCTION

THE TEXTS INCLUDED IN THIS SECTION illustrate a variety of problems and research areas relative to the concept of a 'normal' body and to bodily norms broadly conceived. The texts by Laqueur, Gould and Sekula are historical in character, and point to the use of new technologies and new scientific discourses in the construction of politically significant differences between 'races', sexes and classes.

Thomas Laqueur illustrates here a profound transformation in the conceptualisation of sexual difference occurring near the end of the eighteenth century, whose primary symptom was that women's orgasm ceased to be regarded necessary or relevant to generation. The new conceptualisation of the female orgasm signalled the passage from a form of biology rooted in classical Antiquity, where sexual difference was construed as difference of degree (in terms of bodily heat, or of the relative position of the two sexes in the hierarchy of beings), to a form of biology where the sexes appear as ontological opposites and therefore incommensurable. That generation should not require orgasm on the part of women marked their reproductive physiology – and therefore their physiology in general – as being radically different to that of men. Laqueur argues that this change cannot be attributed primarily to the logic of scientific development or progress – such as the discovery of previously unknown significant mechanisms or facts. Following Mary Douglas (see extract in this volume, p. 78), he proposes that this new representation of the body corresponds to a new way of constituting social realities, and should therefore be understood in the context of broader socio-cultural developments taking place in the same period. In particular, Laqueur refers here to the secularisation of political authorities and to the undermining of the traditional metaphysical foundations for the subordination of certain groups to others. If the subordination of women could previously be justified with reference to a preordained order of values, it now resorted to rational justification that appealed to observable biological facts. In this new horizon, the radical physiological differences posited between men and women would explain the radically different roles they tended to play in social practice; the polarity of sexes neatly mapped onto the rapidly configuring polarity of public and private life. This form of justification, moreover, rendered the value- and power-dimension of difference between the sexes implicit rather than explicit. Women were no longer conceived as 'lesser' men, but as value-neutral bodies simply characterised by different (but theoretically equal) capacities and dispositions.

The broader background context that Laqueur sketches in relation to the problem of gender is valid also in relation to patterns of domination in other domains, such as 'race' or class. In his chapter on craniometry, Stephen J. Gould illustrates how the discourses of evolutionary biology and of physical anthropology were also mobilised in an effort to justify the subordination of black people. In the mid-nineteenth century, Paul Broca produced a number of studies to demonstrate a correlation between increasing brain size and the progress of European civilisation. Gould's careful analysis of Broca's statistical procedures demonstrates how Broca constructed his arguments through facts that 'were reliable ... but [that] were gathered selectively and then manipulated unconsciously in the service of prior conclusions. By this route, the conclusions received not only the blessing of science, but the prestige of numbers'.

Instead of focusing on (pseudo-)scientific argument and theory, the extract by Sekula approaches the construction of normality and deviance, and the 'naturalisation' of class differences, through an analysis of the introduction of a new material technology – photography – particularly in the context of police and penal procedures. From around 1840, photography offered the promise of a form of legal evidence deemed more reliable on account of its visual realism. The photograph would provide a 'mute testimony' of the reality of the criminal or the pauper that would serve to supersede the far more ambiguous oral testimonies the individuals themselves could produce. The material and static objectness of the visual image would generate the illusion of neutral factuality, in stark contrast with verbal accounts that allowed greater scope for disguises, alibis and excuses. Although Sekula does not explicitly make this point here, the photographic documentation of prisoners should be considered in conjunction with the emergence, around the same period, of criminology, phrenology and physiognomy – disciplines that would use arguments and parameters similar to those of Broca (as mentioned earlier) for the specification of varieties of criminal character, and that would turn to photographic images of convicted criminals for the purposes of illustration. Sekula's broader point in this text, however, is that photography was simultaneously adopted in the context of working- and lower middle-class life, where it extended and popularised the traditional function of artistic portraiture, that is, the function of 'providing for the ceremonial [and honorific] presentation of the bourgeois self'. In conjunction with the forensic and pedagogical functions of photography in the contexts of law and science respectively, the introduction of this new medium produced therefore what might be described as a systematic mapping of bodies in society, broadly structured along class lines. This was a veritable archive eloquently illustrating the difference between respectable normal bodies, and those of the socially pathological or deviant.

The focus in Peter Freund's text is shifted from what is considered 'normal' in relation to bodies, to what is considered 'normal' in relation to the spatio-temporal environment. This piece thus tackles the theme of bodies in space, a theme that remains under-represented in this volume. Norms of functioning are incorporated into the design of public and private spaces, as well as into the design of timed devices such as traffic signals, automatically operated barriers, and so on. Spatio-temporal structures, in turn, are material factors that play an important role in the social construction of disability. Freund examines, for example, how 'Ca]n incompatibility between socially generated rhythms and the rhythms of various bodies can be produced in workplaces, traffic systems, etc., with disabling consequences'. Cities designed around the norm of car-ownership represent a 'disablist' organisation of space that tends to confine certain people (not only those with disabilities but also, for example, children) into private and/or institutional spaces. The social organisation of space, moreover, can produce disabling effects not only in a material or mechanically ergonomic sense but also in a phenomenological sense, that is, in terms of its impact on how one's body is experienced. For example, an increasing 'technisation' of the routines of daily life 'can be a source of stress, and can disenfranchise or put at risk those unwilling or unable to meet [the] demands [imposed by the use of potentially dangerous technologies and spaces]'. The extract concludes by highlighting how the socially sustained drive to normalise (or correct) bodies *rather* than normalising social space-time can lead to what Freund calls 'somatic false consciousness'.

Disability is also the focus of Lennard Davis' text. Like Freund, Davis operates here a fundamental reversal of premises: instead of asking what characteristics of a disabled person account for his or her disability, he asks what characteristics of 'normalcy' give rise to the phenomenon of disability as devalued existence. Using cultural analysis and psychoanalytic theory, Davis will conclude that disability 'is in some sense the basis on which the "normal" body is constructed: disability defines the negative space the body must not occupy'. To reach this conclusion, Davis starts by considering disability as a disturbance of the sensory field of the observer: disability somehow contradicts expectations of what a body should look, feel and sound like. Again, and crucially, this is regarded 'more as a question about the nature of the [gazing] subject than about the qualities of the object': the question, in other words, is one of why the perception of a disabled body should constitute such a source of distress and anxiety in the 'normal' subject, that it generates such a strong imperative to regulate, rationalise and contain it. Davis argues that, on one level, the disabled body is threatening because it is a reminder of the fragility of the self. In Lacanian terms, the formation of a self is contingent on the repression of the earliest experience of the body, which is of the body as fragmented. This process of repression generates the 'hallucination' of the self as corresponding to a whole and coherent body. In what Lacan called the 'mirror stage', 'the child recognizes (actually misrecognizes) that unified image [in the mirror] as his or her self. That identification is really the donning of an identity, an "armor" against the chaotic or fragmented body'.

Considered from this perspective, therefore, the disabled body generates anxiety because it is 'always the reminder of the whole body about to come apart at the seams'. The resurfacing of, or reversal to, chaos and fragmentation is always a possibility (see extract by Bakhtin, p. 112), while the 'normal' body requires a constantly renewed effort of the imagination to be held together. This effort is a polarising one: the threat of chaos is managed by instituting a binary order where all 'badness', all negative value, is concentrated on one side. Here Davis offers a very good example of the correlativity of norms (see discussion of Canguilhem on p. 38), or of the way that norms interact together in a system: unlike nearsightedness, deafness is considered a disability because of its association with aging, which is another negative value. Echoing the work of structural anthropologists such as Levi Strauss and Douglas (see extract by Douglas in this volume, p. 78), Davis describes the desire to split bodies and body parts into radically opposite categories as a primitive thought process found in all cultures. The ongoing imaginative effort to repress the fragmented body is evident in the idealised conventions relating to how bodies are supposed to look in artistic representation. The same effort is also evident in the attitude of art critics and historians faced with mutilated works of art, whose mutilation they do not register as disability. It is significant that this imaginative effort simultaneously represents an act of abstraction from the biological reality of bodies: 'there are no pregnant Venuses ... no paintings of Venuses who are menstruating, micturating, defecating'.

Last but not least, Davis stresses how the dialectic of normal and disabled bodies – however primitive the psychological processes it may be rooted in – is enforced and rendered practically consequential in the context of historically specific social situations. Disability, in this regard, has become most dysfunctional in the context of industrial and postindustrial societies, where the mechanisation of labour relies on the standardisation of tasks, leading to the exclusion of disabled people from the production process. The salience of the body to processes of production and consumption in industrial and postindustrial societies constitutes a powerful obstacle to the acknowledgment of the continuum that joins normalcy and disability.

The last text presented in this section, an essay on monstrosity and the monstruous by Georges Canguilhem, is published here in English for the very first time. Its theme works well as a follow on from Davis' piece, in that it similarly addresses the question of the relation of order to chaos, and the mediation of this relationship by anxiety. As its title indicates, the essay focuses on the relationship between monsters (or monstrosity) and the monstrous. In the first case we have a noun, designating an observable phenomenon; in the second case we have an adjective that refers to an 'imaginary, turbid, vertiginous world' of anti-values, to the perversion or inversion of the order of things, an anti-world. Are monsters monstruous? The proposition is only apparently tautological: the question concerns precisely whether the existence of monsters involves 'mere' difference (implying that monsters are actually mere anomalies, irregularities), or whether the difference is based on a significant polarity of values (in the sense that monsters embody negative, monstrous values). Canguilhem opens the discussion by observing and decoding a symptom: the existence of monsters provokes 'radical fear', 'panic terror'. That this should be so, he explains, is a reflection of our vulnerability and contingency as *living beings*. The apparent regularity of living phenomena – the apparent law-like way in which living beings reproduce, for example – makes us oblivious to the precariousness of life itself. Monsters negate the possibility of that obliviousness: through monsters, the precarious and contingent character of life stares us in the face; our own existence assumes the form of narrowly avoided failure, and one that could *yet* produce a monster. These points can be used to reflect on Davis' observation that the conventions for the artistic representation of ideal bodies exclude the reference to biological processes such as pregnancy, aging, menstruation or excretion (as mentioned earlier). Canguilhem's analysis suggests precisely that (the illusion of) ontological security can be afforded only by abstracting – or forgetting – our biology, that is, the contingent character of life which is expressed in the changes bodies undergo through time. The idealised body is a timeless body, accordingly incapable of change or processes suggesting temporality.

That we can explain why monsters should provoke radical fear – that is, why monsters can rightly be regarded as 'monstrous' – does not, however, definitively settle the question of whether monsters *are* monstrous or not. Our fear, as we have seen, is the function of a particular form of existence, a function, moreover, of the similarity of this form of existence to that of monsters themselves. The fear, in other words, is a function of the impossibility of detachment; it expresses the sense of an 'it could have been me'. In the remainder of this text Canguilhem surveys two different forms of the historical relation between monstrosity and the monstrous, broadly corresponding to the pre-scientific age and to that of positive science. In classical antiquity and particularly in the Middle Ages monstrosity was closely associated with the monstrous in the sense that it was identified with a violating intention, with a deliberate subversion of values. This means also that monstrosity appeared as a choice of perversion theoretically open to everyone, stressing the continuity between monsters and non-monsters. The monstrosity of monsters, as we have seen, is a function of the impossibility of detachment. In the age of positive teratology, by contrast, the monster is 'naturalised'. Through comparative anatomy and embryology, science provided explanations that dissociated monsters from the subversion or contradiction of rules and regarded them instead as neutral 'anomalies', or as the expression of biological variety. In this context, monsters no longer appear monstrous.

We would be mistaken once more, however, if we thought that scientific explanation finally settled the question of whether the monstrous is a mere category of the imagination, or the possibility of realisation of a negative value. As Canguilhem puts it, 'how can we resist the temptation of finding the monstrous ensconced once again at the very heart of the scientific world, from which it had supposedly been expelled, and of catching the biologist himself red-handed in the pursuit of Surrealism?'. The possibility of realising monstrous values, in other words, surfaces again through the technical capacities for intervention – for creating 'monsters' experimentally – that scientific understanding makes available. In this case what would have to be regarded as 'monstrous' are not the monsters themselves, but the intentions that may underlie their production.

Chapter 20

Thomas Laqueur

ORGASM, GENERATION, AND THE POLITICS OF REPRODUCTIVE BIOLOGY

From T. Laqueur (1987) "Orgasm, generation, and the politics of reproductive biology," in C. Gallagher and T. Laqueur (eds), *The Making of the Modern Body*, Berkeley: University of California Press.

[...]

N EAR THE END OF the century of Enlightenment, medical science and those who relied upon it ceased to regard the female orgasm as relevant to generation. Conception, it was held, could take place secretly, with no tell-tale shivers or signs of arousal. For women the ancient wisdom that "apart from pleasure nothing in mortal kind comes into existence" was uprooted. We ceased to regard ourselves as beings "compacted in blood, of the seed of man, and the pleasure that [comes] with sleep." We no longer linked the loci of pleasure with the mysterious infusing of life into matter. Routine accounts, like that in a popular Renaissance midwifery text of the clitoris as that organ "which makes women lustful and take delight in copulation," without which they "would have no desire, nor delight, nor would they ever conceive," came to be regarded as controversial if not manifestly stupid.[1]

Sexual orgasm moved to the periphery of human physiology. Previously a deeply embedded sign of the generative process – whose existence was no more open to debate than was the warm, pleasurable glow that usually accompanies a good meal – orgasm became simply a feeling, albeit an enormously charged one, whose existence was a matter for empirical inquiry or armchair philosophizing. Jacques Lacan's provocative characterization of female orgasm, "la jouissance, ce qui ne sert a rien," is a distinctly modern possibility.[2]

The new conceptualization of the female orgasm, however, was but one formulation of a more radical eighteenth-century reinterpretation of the female body in relation to that of the male. For several thousand years it had been a commonplace that women have the same genitals as men, except that, as Nemesius, bishop of Emesa in the sixth century, put it: "Theirs are inside the body and not outside it."

[...]

By 1800 this view, like that linking orgasm to conception, had come under devastating attack. Writers of all sorts were determined to base what they insisted were fundamental difference between male and female sexuality, and thus between man and woman, on discoverable biological distinctions. In 1803, for example, Jacques Moreau de la Sarthe, one of the founders of "moral anthropology," argued passionately against the nonsense written by Aristotle, Galen, and their modern followers on the subject of women in relation to men.[3] Not only are the sexes different, they are different in every conceivable respect of body and soul, in every physical and moral aspect. To the physician or the naturalist the relation of woman to man is "a series of oppositions and contrasts." Thus the old model, in which men and women were arrayed according to their degree of metaphysical perfection, their vital heat, along an axis whose telos was male, gave way by the late eighteenth century to a new model of difference, of biological divergence. An anatomy and physiology of incommensurability replaced a metaphysics of hierarchy in the representation of women in relation to men.[4]

[…]

The shift in the interpretation of the male and female body, however, cannot have been due, even in principle, primarily to scientific progress. In the first place the "oppositions and contrasts" between the female and the male have been self-evident since the beginning of time: the one gives birth and the other does not, to state the obvious. Set against such momentous truths, the discovery, for example, that the ovarian artery is not, as Galen would have it, the homologue of the vas deferens is of relatively minor significance. Thus, the face that at one time male and female bodies were regarded as hierarchically, that is vertically, ordered and that at another time they came to be regarded as horizontally ordered, as opposites, as incommensurable, must depend on something other than one or even a set of real or supposed "discoveries."

In addition, nineteenth-century advances in developmental anatomy (germlayer theory) pointed to the common origins of both sexes in a morphologically androgenous embryo and thus not to their intrinsic difference. Indeed the Galenic homologies were by the 1850s reproduced at the embryological level: the penis and the clitoris, the labia and the scrotum, the ovary and the testes shared common origins in fetal life. Finally, and most tellingly, no one was very interested in looking at the anatomical and concrete physiological differences between the sexes until such differences became politically important. It was not, for example, until 1797 that anyone bothered to reproduce a detailed female skeleton in an anatomy book so as to illustrate its difference from the male. Up to this time there had been one basic structure for the human body, the type of the male.[5]

Instead of being the consequence of increased scientific knowledge, new ways of interpreting the body were rather, I suggest, new ways of representing and indeed of constituting social realities.

[…]

The anatomy and physiology of hierarchy

The existence of female sexual pleasure, indeed the necessity of pleasure for the successful reproduction of humankind, was an unquestioned commonplace well before the elaboration of ancient doctrines in the writings of Galen, Soranus, and the Hippocratic school.

[...]

Heat is of critical importance in the Galenic account. It is, to begin with, the sign of perfection, of one's place in the hierarchical great chain of being. Humans are the most perfect of animals, and men are more perfect than women by reason of their "excess of heat." Men and women are, in this model, not different in kind but in the configuration of their organs; the male is a hotter version of the female, or to use the teleologically more appropriate order, the female is the cooler, less perfect version of the male.[6] Understanding the machinery of sex thus becomes essentially an exercise in topology:

Understanding the machinery of sex thus becomes essentially an exercise in topology: "Turn outward the woman's, turn inward, so to speak, and fold double the man's, and you will find the same in both in every respect."

[...]

In fact, Galen argues, "You could not find a single male part left over that had not simply changed its position." And, in a blaze of rhetorical virtuosity, he elaborates a stunning and unsuspected simile to make all this more plausible: the reproductive organs of women are like the eyes of the mole. Like other animals' eyes, the mole's have "vitreous and crystalline humors and the tunics that surround [them]"; yet, they do not see. Their eyes do not open, "nor do they project but are left there imperfect." Likewise, the womb itself is an imperfect version of what it would be were it projected outward. But like the eyes of a mole, which in turn "remain like the eyes of other animals when these are still in the uterus," the womb is forever as if still in the womb![7]

If the female is a replica of the male, with the same organs inside than outside the body, why then, one might ask, are women not men? Because they have insufficient heat to extrude the organs of reproduction and, as always for Galen, because form befits function. Nature in her wisdom has made females cooler, allowing their organs to remain inside and providing there a safe, guarded place for conception and gestation. Moreover, if women were as hot as men, semen planted in the womb would shrivel and die like seed cast upon the desert; of course, the extra nutriment needed by the fetus would likewise burn off. The fact remains that women, whatever their special adaptations, are but variations of the male form, the same but lower on the scale of being and perfection.[8]

[...]

Male and female bodies in these Renaissance accounts were, as is perhaps obvious, still very much those of Galen. Consider Leonardo's drawings, or the far more influential engravings in Andreas Vesalius' epoch-marking *De humani corporis fabrica* and his more popular *Tabulae sex*, all of which reinforce the hoary model through striking new representations. When Vesalius is self-consciously trying to emphasize the homologies between male and female organs of generation and, ever more telling, when he is not (Figure 20.1), he is firmly in the camp of the "ancients," however much he might rail against the authority of Galen in other contexts. But the anatomical accuracy of Galen is not what is at issue here. The female reproductive system can be, and indeed on occasion was still in the late nineteenth century, "accurately" rendered in the manner of Vesalius long after the old homologies had lost their credibility. But after the late seventeenth century and the collapse of the

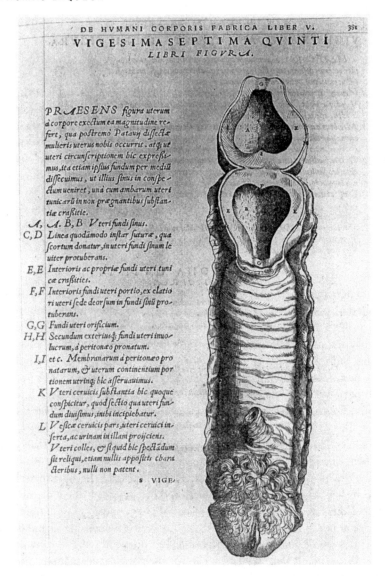

Figure 20.1 Vesalius, uterus, vagina, and external pudenda from a young woman, *De humani corporis*

Source: From *Anatomical drawings of Vesalius*.
Note: This illustration was not made to illustrate homologies with the male organ.

hierarchical model there was, in general, no longer any reason to draw the vagina and external pudenda in the same frame with the uterus and the ovaries. Bodies did not change, but the meanings of the relationship between their parts did.[9]

Seventeenth-century audiences still gave credence to a whole collection of tales, going back at least to Pliny, that illustrate the structural similarities and thus the mutability of male and female bodies. Sir Thomas Browne, in his *Enquiries into Vulgar and Common Errors* (1646), devotes an entire chapter to the question of whether "every hare is both male and female." He concludes that "as for the mutation of sexes, or transition of one into another, we cannot deny it in Hares, it being observable in Man."

[...]

Politics and the biology of sexual difference

When in the 1740s the young Princess Maria Theresa was worried because she did not immediately become pregnant after her marriage to the future Hapsburg emperor, she asked her physician what she ought to do. He is said to have replied: "Cerebrum censeo vulvam Sanctissimae Majestatis ante coitum esse titillandum. [Moreover I think the vulva of Her Most Holy Majesty is to be titillated before intercouse]." The advise seems to have worked as she bore more than a dozen children. Similarly, Albrecht von Haller, one of the giants of eighteenth-century biological science, still postulated an erection of both the external and the internal female reproductive organs during intercourse and regarded woman's orgasm as a sign that the ovum has been ejaculated from the ovary. Although he is well aware of the existence of the sperm and the egg and of their respective origins in the testes and ovaries, and has no interest in the Galenic homologies, the sexually aroused female in his account bears a remarkable resemblance to the male under similar circumstances.

[...]

The problem with which this essay began thus remains. Neither advances in reproductive biology nor anatomical discoveries seem sufficient to explain the dramatic revaluation of the female orgasm that occurred in the late eighteenth century and the even more dramatic reinterpretation of the female body in relation to that of the male. Rather, a new model of incommensurability triumphed over the old hierarchical model in the wake of new political agendas. Writers from the eighteenth century onward sought in the facts of biology a justification for cultural and political differences between the sexes that were crucial to the articulation of both feminist and antifeminist arguments. Political theorists beginning with Hobbes had argued that there is no basis in nature for any specific sort of authority – of a king over his people, of slaveholder over slave, nor, it followed, of man over woman. There seemed no reason why the universalistic claims made for human liberty and equality during the Enlightenment should exclude half of humanity. And, of course, revolution, the argument made in blood that mankind in all its social and cultural relations could be remade, engendered both a new feminism and a new fear of women. But feminism itself, and indeed the more general claims made by and for women to public life – to write, to vote, to legislate, to influence, to reform – was also predicated on difference.

Thus, women's bodies in their corporeal, scientifically accessible concreteness, in the very nature of their bones, nerves, and, most important, reproductive organs came to bear an enormous new weight of cultural meaning in the Enlightenment. Arguments about the very existence of female sexual passion, about women's special capacity to control what desires they did have, and about their moral nature generally were all part of a new enterprise seeking to discover the anatomical and physiological characteristics that distinguished men from women. As the natural body itself became the gold standard of social discourse, the bodies of women became the battleground for redefining the most ancient, the most intimate, the most fundamental of human relations: that of woman to man.

[...]

But reinterpretations of the body were more than simply ways of reestablishing hierarchy in an age when its metaphysical foundations were being rapidly effaced. Liberalism postulates a body that, if not sexless, is nevertheless undifferentiated in its desires, interests, or capacity to reason. In striking contrast to the old teleology of the body as male, liberal theory begins with a neuter body, sexed but without gender, and of no consequence to cultural discourse. The body is regarded simply as the bearer of the rational subject, which itself constitutes the person. The problem for this theory then is how to derive the real world of male dominion of women, of sexual passion and jealousy, of the sexual division of labor and cultural practices generally from an original state of genderless bodies. The dilemma, at least for theorists interested in the subordination of women, is resolved by grounding the social and cultural differentiation of the sexes in a biology of incommensurability that liberate theory itself helped bring into being. A novel construal of nature comes to serve as the foundation of otherwise indefensible social practices.

For women, of course, the problem is even more pressing. The neuter language of liberalism leaves them, as Jean Elshtain recently argues, without their own voice. But more generally the claim of equality of rights based on an essential identity of the male and female, body and spirit, robs women both of the reality of their social experience and of the ground on which to take political and cultural stands. If women are indeed simply a version of men, as the old model would have had it, then what justifies women writing, or acting in public, or making any other claims for themselves as women? Thus feminism, too – or at least historical versions of feminisms – depends upon and generates a biology of incommensurability in place of the teleologically male interpretation of bodies on the basis of which a feminist stance is impossible.[10]

Notes

1   Wisdom of Solomon 7.2 and Philo *Legum allegoriae* 2.7, cited in Peter Brown (1983) "Sexuality and Society in the Fifth Century A.D.: Augustine and Julian of Eclanum," in E. Cabba (ed.) *Tria corda: Scritti in onore di Arnaldo Momigliano*, Como, p. 56; Mrs. Jane Sharp (1671) *The Midwives Book*, pp. 43–4.

2   "There is a *jouissance* proper to her, to this 'her' which does not exist and which signifies nothing"; Jacques Lacan (1982) "God and the *Jouissance* of The Woman," in Juliet Mitchell and Jacqueline Rose (eds) *Feminine Sexuality*, New York, p. 145.

3   Regnier de Graaf, *A New Treatise Concerning the Generative Organs of Women*, translation of *De mulierum organis generation inservientibus tractatus novus* (1672) by H. D. Jocelyn and B. P. Setchell (1972) *Journal of Reproduction and Fertility*, suppl. no. 17, p. 131–5; Pierre Roussel, *System physique et moral de la femme* (1775; Paris, 1813), pp. 79–80. On Roussel who, through Pierre-Jean-Georges Cabinis, was to influence significantly the discourse on sexual politics during the French Revolution, see Paul Hoffmann, *La Femme dans la pensée des Lumières* (Paris, n.d.), pp. 142–52; Bartholomew Parr (ed.) (1819) *The London Medical Dictionary*, vol. 2, Philadelphia, pp. 88–9; *Aristotle's Masterpiece* (1803; reprint ed., New York, 1974), p. 3.

4   Jacques Moreau de la Sarthe (1803) *Histoire naturelle de la femme*, vol. 1, Paris, p. 15, which sounds the theme of the entire volume.

5   For an early and clearly presented table of embryological homologies, see Rodolf Wagner (ed.) (1853) *Handwörterbuch der Physiologie*, vol. 4, Braunschweig, s.v. "Zeugung," p. 763. Regarding skeletons, see Londa Schiebinger, "Skeletons in the Closet: The First Illustrations of the Female Skeleton in Eighteenth-Century Anatomy," in C. Gallagher and T. Laqueur (eds) (1987) *The Making of the Modern Body*, Berkeley. 1759 is an alternative date for the first representation of the female skeleton; see ibid.

6   Plato *Timaeus* 91A–C, Loeb Classical Library, R.G. Bury (ed.) (1929), Cambridge, MA pp. 248–50; Galen (1968) *On the Usefulness of the Parts of the Body*, Margaret (ed. and trans.) May, 2 vols., Ithaca, New York, 1:382 and n. 78; 2:628, 630.

7   Ibid., 2:629.

8   Ibid., 2:630–1 and, more generally, 636–8.

9   J. B. de C. M. Saunders and Charles D. O'Malley (1982) *The Anatomical Drawings of Andreas Vesalius*, New York, point out that the penis-like vagina in Figure 20.1 is simply an artifact of having to remove the organs in a great hurry. A useful table of the homologies Vesalius sought to illustrate are given in L. R. Lind (ed.) *The Epitome of Andreas Vesalius* (New York, 1949), 87. These representations became the standards for more than a century in both popular and learned tracts; see for example Alexander Read (1634) *A Description of the Body of Man*, p. 128, for an English version; and Fritz Weindler (1908) *Geschichte der gynäkologische-anatomischen Abbildung*, Dresden.

10 Jean Elshtain (1981) *Public Man, Private Women*, Princeton, NJ, chap. 3.

Chapter 21

Stephen J. Gould

MEASURING HEADS

From S. J. Gould (1981) *The Mismeasure of Man*, New York: W. W. Norton.

[...]

Masters of craniometry: Paul Broca and his school

The great circle route

IN 1861 A FIERCE DEBATE extended over several meetings of a young association still experiencing its birth pangs. Paul Broca (1824–80), professor of clinical surgery in the faculty of medicine, had founded the Anthropological Society of Paris in 1859. At a meeting of the society two years later, Louis Pierre Gratiolet read a paper that challenged Broca's most precious belief: Gratiolet dared to argue that the size of a brain bore no relationship to its degree of intelligence.

Broca rose in his own defense, arguing that "the study of the brains of human races would lose most of its interest and utility" if variation in size counted for nothing (1861, p. 141). Why had anthropologists spent so much time measuring skulls, unless their results could delineate human groups and assess their relative worth?

> Among the questions heretofore discussed within the Anthropological Society, none is equal in interest and importance to the question before us now. [...] The great importance of craniology has struck anthropologists with such force that many among us have neglected the other parts of our science in order to devote ourselves almost exclusively to the study of skulls. [...] In such data, we hoped to find some information relevant to the intellectual value of the various human races.
>
> (1861, p. 139)

[...]

Broca and his school used facts as illustrations, not as constraining documents. They began with conclusions, peered through their facts, and came back in a circle to the same conclusions. Their example repays a closer study, for unlike Morton (who manipulated data, however unconsciously), they reflected their prejudices by another, and probably more common, route: advocacy masquerading as objectivity.

Selecting characters

When the "Hottentot Venus" died in Paris, Georges Cuvier, the greatest scientist and, as Broca would later discover to his delight, the largest brain of France, remembered this African woman as he had seen her in the flesh.

> She had a way of pouting her lips exactly like what we have observed in the orang-utan. Her movements had something abrupt and fantastical about them, reminding one of those of the ape. Her lips were monstrously large [those of apes are thin and small as Cuvier apparently forgot]. Her ear was like that of many apes, being small, the tragus weak, and the external border almost obliterated behind. These are animal characters. I have never seen a human head more like an ape than that of this woman.
>
> (in Topinard, 1878, pp. 493–4)

The human body can be measured in a thousand ways. Any investigator, convinced beforehand of a group's inferiority, can select a small set of measures to illustrate its greater affinity with apes. (This procedure, of course, would work equally well for white males, though no one made the attempt. White people, for example, have thin lips – a property shared with chimpanzees – while most black Africans have thicker, consequently more "human," lips.)

Broca's cardinal bias lay in his assumption that human races could be ranked in a linear scale of mental worth. In enumerating the aims of ethnology, Broca included: "to determine the relative position of races in the human series" (in Topinard, 1878, p. 660). It did not occur to him that human variation might be ramified and random, rather than linear and hierarchical. And since he knew the order beforehand, anthropometry became a search for characters that would display the correct ranking, not a numerical exercise in raw empiricism.

Thus Broca began his search for "meaningful" characters – those that would display the established ranks. In 1862, for example, he tried the ratio of radius (lower arm bone) to humerus (upper arm bone), reasoning that a higher ratio marks a longer forearm – a character of apes. All began well: blacks yielded a ratio of 0.794, whites 0.739. But then Broca ran into trouble. An Eskimo skeleton yielded 0.703, an Australian aborigine 0.709, while the Hottentot Venus, Cuvier's near ape (her skeleton had been preserved in Paris), measured a mere 0.703. Broca now had two choices. He could either admit that, on this criterion, whites ranked lower than several dark-skinned groups, or he could abandon the criterion. Since he knew (1862a, p. 10) that Hottentots, Eskimos, and Australian aborigines ranked below most African blacks, he chose the second course: "After this, it seems difficult to me to continue to say that elongation of the forearm is a character of degradation or inferiority, because, on this account, the European occupies a place between Negroes on the one hand, and Hottentots, Australians, and eskimos on the other" (1862a, p. 11).

Later, he almost abandoned his cardinal criterion of brain size because inferior yellow people scored so well:

> A table on which races were arranged by order of their cranial capacities would not represent the degrees of their superiority or inferiority, because size represents only one element of the problem [of ranking races]. On such a table, Eskimos, Lapps, Malays, Tartars and several other peoples of the Mongolian type would surpass the most civilized people of Europe. A lowly race may therefore have a big brain.
>
> (1873, p. 38)

But Broca felt that he could salvage much of value from his crude measure of overall brain size. It may fail at the upper end because some inferior groups have big brains, but it works at the lower end because small brains belong exclusively to people of low intelligence. Broca continued:

> But this does not destroy the value of small brain size as a mark of inferiority. The table shows that West African blacks have a cranial capacity about 100 cc less than that of European races. To this figure, we may add the following: Caffirs, Nubians, Tasmanians, Hottentots, Australians. These examples are sufficient to prove that if the volume of the brain does not play a decisive role in the intellectual ranking of races, it nevertheless has a very real importance.
>
> (1873, p. 38)

An unbeatable argument. Deny it at one end where conclusions are uncongenial; affirm it by the same criterion at the other. Broca did not fudge numbers; he merely selected among them or interpreted his way around them to favored conclusions.

In choosing among measures, Broca did not just drift passively in the sway of a preconceived idea. He advocated selection among characters as a stated goal with explicit criteria. Topinard, his chief disciple, distinguished between "empirical" characters "having no apparent design," and "rational" characters "related to some physiological opinion" (1878, p. 221). How then to determine which characters are "rational"? Topinard answered: "Other characteristics are looked upon, whether rightly or wrongly, as dominant. They have an affinity in negroes to those which they exhibit in apes, and establish the transition between these and Europeans" (1878, p. 221). Broca had also considered this issue in the midst of his debate with Gratiolet, and had reached the same conclusion (1861, p. 176):

> We surmount the problem easily by choosing, for our comparison of brains, races whose intellectual inequalities are completely clear. Thus, the superiority of Europeans compared with African Negroes, American Indians, Hottentots, Australians and the Negroes of Oceania, is sufficiently certain to serve as a point of departure for the comparison of brains.

Particularly outrageous examples abound in the selection of individuals to represent groups in illustrations. Thirty years ago, when I was a child, the Hall of Man in the American Museum of Natural History still displayed the characters of human races by linear arrays running from apes to whites. Standard anatomical illustrations, until this generation, depicted a chimp, a Negro, and a white, part by part in that order – even though variation among whites and blacks is always large enough to generate a different order with other individuals: chimp, white, black.

[...]

Averting anomalies

Inevitably, since Broca amassed so much disparate and honest data, he generated numerous anomalies and apparent exceptions to his guiding generality – that size of brain records intelligence and that comfortable white males have larger brains than women, poor people, and lower races. In noting how he worked around each apparent exception, we obtain our clearest insight into Broca's methods of argument and inference. We also understand why data could never overthrow his assumptions.

[...]

Flaws in a pattern of increase through time

Of all Broca's studies, with the exception of his work on differences between men and women, none won more respect of attention than his supposed demonstration of steady increase in brain size as European civilization advanced from medieval to modern times (Broca, 1862b).

   This study merits close analysis because it probably represents the best case of hope dictating conclusion that I have ever encountered. Broca viewed himself as a liberal in the sense that he did not condemn groups to permanent inferiority based on their current status. Women's brains had degenerated through time thanks to a socially enforced underusage; they might increase again under different social conditions. Primitive races had not been sufficiently challenged, while European brains grew steadily with the march of civilization.

   Broca obtained large samples from each of three Parisian cemeteries, from the twelfth, the eighteenth, and the nineteenth centuries. Their average cranial capacities were, respectively, 1,426, 1,409, and 1,462 cc – not exactly the stuff for a firm conclusion of steady increase through time. (I have not been able to find Broca's raw data for statistical testing, but with a 3.5 percent mean difference between smallest and largest sample, it is likely that no statistically significant differences exist at all among the three samples.)

   But how did these limited data – only three sites with no information on ranges of variation at a given time and no clear pattern through time – lead Broca to his hopeful conclusion? Broca himself admitted an initial disappointment: he had expected to find intermediate values in the eighteenth-century site (1862b, p. 106). Social class, he argued, must hold the answer, for successful groups within a culture owe at least part of their status to superior wits. The twelfth-century sample came from a churchyard and must represent gentry. A common grave provided the eighteenth-century skulls. But the nineteenth-century sample was a mixture, ninety skulls from individual graves with a mean of 1,484 cc, and thirty-five from a common grave with an average of 1,403 cc. Broca claimed that if differences in social class do not explain why calculated values fail to meet expectations, then the data are unintelligible. Intelligible, to Broca, meant steadily increasing through time – the proposition that the data were meant to prove, not rest upon. Again, Broca travels in a circle:

> Without this [difference in social class], we would have to believe that the cranial capacity of Parisians has really diminished during centuries following the 12th. Now during this period [...] intellectual and social progress has been considerable, and even if we are not yet certain that the development of civilization makes the brain grow as a consequence, no one, without doubt, would want to consider this cause as capable of making the brain decrease in size.
>
> (1862b, p. 106)

But Broca's division of the nineteenth-century sample by social class also brought trouble as well as relief – for he now had two samples from common graves and the earlier one had a larger mean capacity, 1,409 for the eighteenth century vs. 1,403 for the nineteenth. But Broca was not to be defeated; he argued that the eighteenth-century common grave included a better class of people. In these prerevolutionary times, a man had to be really rich or noble to rest in a churchyard. The dregs of the poor measured 1,403 in the nineteenth century; the dregs leavened by good stock yielded about the same value one hundred years before.

Each solution brought Broca new trouble. Now that he was committed to a partition by social class within cemeteries, he had to admit that an additional seventeen skulls from the morgue's grave at the nineteenth-century site yielded a higher value than skulls of middle- and upper-class people from individual graves – 1,517 vs. 1,484 cc. How could unclaimed bodies, abandoned to the state, surpass the cream of society? Broca reasoned in a chain of surpassingly weak inference: morgues stood on river borders; they probably housed a large number of drowned people; many drowned are suicides; many suicides are insane; many insane people, like criminals, have surprisingly large brains. With a bit of imagination, nothing can be truly anomalous.

[...]

References

Broca, P. (1861) "Sur le volume et la forme du cerveau suivant les individus et suivant les races," *Bulletin Société d'Anthropologie Paris 2*, pp. 139–207, 301–321, 441–446.

—— (1862a) "Sur les proportions relatives du bras, de l'avant bras et de la clavicule chez les nègres et les européens," *Bulletin Société d'Anthropologie Paris*, vol. 3, part 2, p. 13.

—— (1862b) "Sur la capacité des crânes parisiens des diverses époques," *Bulletin Société d'Anthropologie Paris 3*, 102–116.

—— (1868) *Mémoire sur les crânes des Basques*. Paris: Masson, 79 pp.

—— (1873) "Sur les crânes de la caverne de l'Homme-Mort (Lozère)," *Revue d'Anthropologie 2*, pp. 1–53.

Topinard, P. (1878) *Anthropology*, London: Chapman and Hall, 548 pp.

Allan Sekula

THE BODY AND THE ARCHIVE

From A. Sekula (1986) "The body and the archive," *October* 39: 3–65.

[...]

On the one side we approach more closely to what is good and beautiful; on the other, vice and suffering are shut up within narrower limits; and we have to dread less the monstrosities, physical and moral, which have the power to throw perturbation into the social framework.

(Adolphe Quetelet, 1842)

THE SHEER RANGE AND VOLUME of photographic practice offers ample evidence of the paradoxical status of photography within bourgeois culture. The simultaneous threat and promise of the new medium was recognized at a very early date, even before the daguerreotype process had proliferated.

[...]

Although no "Police Act" had yet embraced photography, the 1820s and '30s had engendered a spate of governmental inquiries and legislation designed to professionalize and standardize police and penal procedures in Britain, the most important of which were the Gaols Act of 1823 and the Metropolitan Police Acts of 1829 and 1839.

[...]

Although photographic documentation of prisoners was not at all common until the 1860s, the potential for a new juridical photographic realism was widely recognized in the 1840s, in the general context of these systematic efforts to regulate the growing urban presence of the "dangerous classes," of a chronically unemployed sub-proletariat.

[...]

[A] new *instrumental* potential in photography [was recognized]: a silence that silences. The protean oral "texts" of the criminal and pauper yield to a "mute testimony" that "takes down" (that diminishes in credibility, that transcribes) and unmasks the disguises, the alibis, the excuses and multiple biographies of those who find or place themselves on the wrong side of the law. This battle between the presumed denotative univocality of the legal image and the multiplicity and presumed duplicity of the criminal voice is played out during the remainder of the nineteenth century. In the course of this battle a new object is defined – the criminal body – and, as a result, a more extensive "social body" is invented.

We are confronting, then, a double system: a system of representation capable of functioning both *honorifically* and *repressively*. This double operation is most evident in the workings of photographic portraiture. On the one hand, the photographic portrait extends, accelerates, popularizes, and degrades a traditional function. This function, which can be said to have taken its early modern form in the seventeenth century, is that of providing for the ceremonial presentation of the bourgeois *self*. Photography subverted the privileges inherent in portraiture, but without any more extensive leveling of social relationships, these privileges could be reconstructed on a new basis. That is, photography could be assigned a proper role within a new hierarchy of taste. Honorific conventions were thus able to proliferate downward. At the same time, photographic portraiture began to perform a role no painted portrait could have performed in the same thorough and rigorous fashion. This role derived, not from any honorific portrait tradition, but from the imperatives of medical and anatomical illustration. Thus photography came to establish and delimit the terrain of the *other*, to define both the *generalized look* – the typology – and the *contingent instance* of deviance and social pathology.

Michel Foucault has argued, quite crucially, that it is a mistake to describe the new regulatory sciences directed at the body in the early nineteenth century as exercises in a wholly negative, repressive power. Rather, social power operates by virtue of a positive therapeutic or reformative channeling of the body.[1] Still, we need to understand those modes of instrumental realism that do in fact operate according to a very explicit deterrent or repressive logic. These modes constitute the lower limit or "zero degree" of socially instrumental realism. Criminal identification photographs are a case in point since they are designed quite literally to facilitate the *arrest* of their referent.[2]

[...]

But first, what general connections can be charted between the honorific and repressive poles of portrait practice? To the extent that bourgeois order depends upon the systematic defense of social relations based on private property, to the extent that the legal basis of the self lies in the model of property rights, in what has been termed "possessive individualism," every proper portrait has its lurking, objectifying inverse in the files of the police. In other words, a covert Hobbesian logic links the terrain of the "National Gallery" with that of the "Police Act."[3]

In the mid-nineteenth century, the terms of this linkage between the sphere of culture and that of social regulation were specifically utilitarian. Many of the early promoters of photography struck up a Benthamite chorus, stressing the medium's promise for a social calculus of pleasure and discipline. Here was a machine for providing small doses of happiness on a mass scale, for contributing to Jeremy Bentham's famous goal: "the greatest happiness of the greatest number."[4] Thus the photographic portrait in particular was welcomed as a socially ameliorative as well as a socially repressive instrument. Jane Welsh Carlyle voiced characteristic hopes in 1859, when she described inexpensive portrait photography as a social palliative:

> Blessed be the inventor of photography. I set him even above the inventor of chloroform! It has given more positive pleasure to poor suffering humanity than anything that has been "cast up" in my time [...] – this art, by which even the poor can possess themselves of tolerable likenesses of their absent dear ones.[5]

In the United States, similar but more extensive utilitarian claims were made by the portrait photographer Marcus Aurelius Root, who was able to articulate the connection between pleasure and discipline, to argue explicitly for a moral economy of the image. Like Carlyle, he stressed the salutory effects of photography on working-class family life. Not only was photography to serve as a means of cultural enlightenment for the working classes, but family photographs sustained sentimental ties in a nation of migrants. This "primal household affection" served a socially cohesive function, Root argued – articulating a nineteenth-century familialism that would survive and become an essential ideological feature of American mass culture. Furthermore, widely distributed portraits of the great would subject everyday experience to a regular parade of moral exemplars. Root's concern for respectability and order led him to applaud the adoption of photography by the police, arguing that convicted offenders would "not find it easy to resume their criminal careers, while their faces and general aspects are familiar to so many, especially to the keen-sighted detective police."[6] The "so many" is significant here, since it implicitly enlists a wider citizenry in the vigilant work of detection. Thus Root's utilitarianism comes full circle. Beginning with cheaply affordable aesthetic pleasures and moral lessons, he ends up with the photographic extension of that exemplary utilitarian social machine, the Panopticon.

Notwithstanding the standard liberal accounts of the history of photography, the new medium did not simply inherit and "democratize" the honorific functions of bourgeois portraiture. Nor did police photography simply function repressively, although it is foolish to argue that the immediate function of police photographs was somehow more ideological or positively instrumental than negatively instrumental. But in a more general, dispersed fashion, in serving to introduce the panoptic principle into daily life, photography welded the honorific and repressive functions together. Every portrait implicitly took its place within a social and moral hierarchy. The *private* moment of sentimental individuation, the look at the frozen gaze-of-the-loved-one, was shadowed by two other more *public* looks: a look up, at one's "betters," and a look down, at one's "inferiors." Especially in the United States, photography could sustain an imaginary mobility on this vertical scale, thus provoking both ambition and fear, and interpellating, in class terms, a characteristically "petit-bourgeois" subject.

We can speak then of a generalized, inclusive *archive*, a *shadow archive* that encompasses an entire social terrain while positioning individuals within that terrain. This archive contains subordinate, territorialized archives: archives whose semantic interdependence is normally obscured by the "coherence" and "mutual exclusivity" of the social groups registered within each. The general, all-inclusive archive necessarily contains both the traces of the visible bodies of heroes, leaders, moral exemplars, celebrities, and those of the poor, the diseased, the insane, the criminal, the nonwhite, the female, and all other embodiments of the unworthy.

[...]

Notes

1   See Michel Foucault (1977) *Discipline and Punish: The Birth of the Prison*, trans. Alan Sheridan, New York, Pantheon and *The History of Sexuality, Volume I: An Introduction*, trans. Robert Hurley, New York, Pantheon, 1978.

2   Any photographs that seek to identify a *target*, such as military reconnaissance photographs, operate according to the same general logic. See my 1975 essay "The Instrumental Image: Steichen at War," in *Photography against the Grain: Essays and Photo Works, 1973–1983*, Halifax, The Press of the Nova Scotia College of Art and Design, 1984.

3   The theoretical ground for the construction of a specifically *bourgeois* subject can be found in Hobbes's *Leviathan* (1651). C. B. Macpherson has argued that Hobbes's axiomatic positing of an essentially competitive individual human "nature" was in fact quite specific to a developing market society, moreover, to a market society in which human labor power increasingly took the form of an alienable commodity. As Hobbes put it, "The *Value* or WORTH of a man, is as of all things, his Price; that is to say, so much as would be given for the use of his Power: and therefore is not absolute; but a thing dependent on the need and judgement of another" (Thomas Hobbes, *Leviathan*, Harmondsworth, Penguin, 1968, chap. 10, pp. 151–2. See Macpherson's Introduction to this edition and his *Political Theory of Possessive Individualism: Hobbes to Locke*, London, Oxford University Press, 1962).

4   Jeremy Bentham, "A Fragment on Government" (1776) in Mary P. Mack (ed.) *A Bentham Reader*, New York, Pegasus, 1969, p. 45.

5   Quoted in Helmut Gernsheim (1969) *The History of Photography: From the Camera Obscura to the Beginning of the Modern Era*, New York, McGraw-Hill, p. 239.

6   Marcus Aurelius Root, *The Camera and the Pencil*, 1864, reprint, Pawlett, Vermont, Helios, 1971, pp. 420–1.

Chapter 23

Lennard J. Davis

VISUALIZING THE DISABLED BODY
The classical nude and the fragmented torso

From L. J. Davis (1997) 'Nude Venuses, Medusa's body, and phantom limbs: disability and visuality', in D. T. Mitchell and S. L. Snyder (eds), *The Body and Physical Difference*, Ann Arbor: University of Michigan Press.

[...]

S HE HAS NO ARMS or hands, although the stump of her upper right arm extends just to her breast. Her left foot has been severed, and her face is badly scarred, with her nose torn at the tip, and her lower lip gouged out. Fortunately, her facial mutilations have been treated and are barely visible, except for minor scarring visible only up close. The big toe of her right foot has been cut off, and her torso is covered with scars, including a particularly large one between her shoulder blades, one that covers her shoulder, and one covering the tip of her breast where her left nipple was torn out.

Yet she is considered one of the most beautiful female figures in the world. When the romantic poet Heinrich Heine saw her he called her 'Notre-Dame de la Beauté.' He was referring to the Venus de Milo.

Consider too Pam Herbert, a quadriplegic with muscular dystrophy, writing her memoir by pressing her tongue on a computer keyboard, who describes herself at twenty-eight years old:

> I weigh about 130 pounds; I'm about four feet tall. It's pretty hard to get an accurate measurement on me because both of my knees are permanently bent and my spine is curved, so 4' is an estimate. I wear size two tennis shoes and strong glasses; my hair is dishwater blonde and shoulder length.
>
> (Browne *et al.* (eds) 1985, 147)

[...]

I take the liberty of bringing these two women's bodies together. Both have disabilities. The statue is considered the ideal of Western beauty and eroticism, although it is armless and disfigured. The living woman might be considered by many 'normal' people to be physically repulsive, and certainly without erotic allure. The question I wish to ask is why does the impairment of the Venus de Milo in no way prevent 'normal' people from considering her beauty, while Pam Herbert's disability becomes the focal point for horror and pity?

In asking this question, I am really raising a complex issue. On a social level, the question has to do with how people with disabilities are seen and why, by and large, they are de-eroticized. If, as I mentioned earlier, disability is a cultural phenomenon rooted in the senses, one needs to inquire how a disability occupies a field of vision, of touch, of hearing; and how that disruption or distress in the sensory field translates into psychodynamic representations. This is more a question about the nature of the subject than about the qualities of the object, more about the observer than the observed. The 'problem' of the disabled has been put at the feet of people with disabilities for too long.

Normalcy, rather than being a degree zero of existence, is more accurately a location of bio-power, as Foucault would use the term. The 'normal' person (clinging to that title) has a network of traditional ableist assumptions and social supports that empowers the gaze and interaction. The person with disabilities, until fairly recently, had only his or her own individual force or will. Classically, the encounter has been, and remains, an uneven one. Anne Finger describes it in strikingly visual terms by relating an imagined meeting between Rosa Luxemburg and Antonio Gramsci, each of whom was a person with disabilities, although Rosa is given the temporary power of the abled gaze:

> We can measure Rosa's startled reaction as she glimpses him the misshapen dwarf limping towards her in a second-hand black suit so worn that the cuffs are frayed and the fabric is turning green with age, her eye immediately drawn to this disruption in the visual field: the unconscious flinch; the realization that she is staring at him, and the too-rapid turning away of the head. And then, the moment after, the consciousness that the quick aversion of the gaze was as much of an insult as the stare, so she turns her head back but tries to make her focus general, not a sharp gape. Comrade Rosa, would you have felt a slight flicker of embarrassment? shame? revulsion? dread? of a feeling that can have no name?

In this encounter what is suppressed, at least in this moment, is the fact that Rosa Luxemburg herself is physically impaired (she walked with a limp for her whole life). The emphasis then shifts from the cultural norm to the deviation; Luxemburg, now the gazing subject, places herself in the empowered position of the norm, even if that position is not warranted.

Disability, in this and other encounters, is a disruption in the visual, auditory, or perceptual field as it relates to the power of the gaze. As such, the disruption, the rebellion of the visual, must be regulated, rationalized, contained. Why the modern binary – normal/ abnormal – must be maintained is a complex question. But we can begin by accounting for the desire to split bodies into two immutable categories: whole and incomplete, abled and disabled, normal and abnormal, functional and dysfunctional.

In the most general sense, cultures perform an act of splitting (Spaltung, to use Freud's term). These violent cleavages of consciousness are as primitive as our thought processes can be. The young infant splits the good parent from the bad parent – although the parent is the same entity. When the child is satisfied by the parent, the parent is bad. As a child grows out of the earliest phases of infancy, she learns to combine those split images into a single parent who is sometimes good and sometimes not. The residue of *Spaltung* remains in our inner life, personal and collective, to produce monsters and evil stepmothers as well as noble princes and fairy godmothers.

In this same primitive vein, culture tends to split bodies into good and bad parts. Some cultural norms are considered good and others bad. Everyone is familiar with the 'bad' body: too short or tall, too fat or thin, not masculine or feminine enough, not enough or too much hair on the head or other parts of the body, penis or breasts too small or (excepting the penis) too big. Furthermore, each individual assigns good and bad labels to body parts – good: hair, face, lips, eyes, hands; bad: sexual organs, excretory organs, underarms.

The psychological explanation may provide a reason why it is imperative for society at large to engage in *Spaltung*. The divisions whole/incomplete, able/disabled neatly cover up the frightening writing on the wall that reminds the hallucinated whole being that its wholeness is in fact a hallucination, a developmental fiction. *Spaltung* creates the absolute categories of abled and disabled, with concomitant defenses against the repressed fragmented body.

But a psychological explanation alone is finally insufficient. Historical specificity makes us understand that disability is a social process with an origin. So, why certain disabilities are labeled negatively while others have a less negative connotation is a question tied to complex social forces (some of which I have tried to lay out in earlier chapters). It is fair to say, in general, that disabilities would be most dysfunctional in postindustrial countries, where the ability to perambulate or manipulate is so concretely tied to productivity, which in itself is tied to production. The body of the average worker, as we have seen, becomes the new measure of man and woman. Michael Oliver, citing Ryan and Thomas (1980), notes:

> With the rise of the factory…[during industrialization] many more disabled people were excluded from the production process for 'The speed of factory work, the enforced discipline, the time-keeping and production norms – all these were a highly unfavourable change from the slower, more self-determined and flexible methods of work into which many handicapped people had been integrated'.
>
> (1990, 27)

Both industrial production and the concomitant standardization of the human body have had a profound impact on how we split up bodies.

We tend to group impairments into the categories either of 'disabling' (bad) or just 'limiting' (good). For example, wearing a hearing aid is seen as much more disabling than wearing glasses, although both serve to amplify a deficient sense. But loss of hearing is associated with aging in a way that nearsightedness is not. Breast removal is seen as an impairment of femininity and sexuality, whereas the removal of a foreskin is not seen as a diminution of masculinity. The coding of body parts and the importance attached to their selective function or dysfunction is part of a much larger system of signs and meanings in society, and is constructed as such.

'Splitting' may help us to understand one way in which disability is seen as part of a system in which value is attributed to body parts. The disabling of the body part or function is then part of a removal of value. The gradations of value are socially determined, but what is striking is the way that rather than being incremental or graduated, the assignment of the term 'disabled', and the consequent devaluation are total. That is, the concept of disabled seems to be an absolute rather than a gradient one. One is either disabled or not. Value is tied to the ability to earn money. If one's body is productive, it is not disabled. People with disabilities continue to earn less than 'normal' people and, even after the passage of the Americans with Disabilities Act, 69 percent of Americans with disabilities were unemployed (*New York Times*, 27 October 1994, A:22). Women and men with disabilities are seen as less attractive, less able to marry and be involved in domestic production.

The ideology of the assigning of value to the body goes back to preindustrial times. Myths of beauty and ugliness have laid the foundations for normalcy. In particular, the Venus myth is one that is dialectically linked to another. This embodiment of beauty and desire is tied to the story of the embodiment of ugliness and repulsion. So the appropriate mythological character to compare the armless Venus with is Medusa. Medusa was once a beautiful sea goddess who, because she had sexual intercourse with Poseidon at one of Athene's temples, was turned by Athene into a winged monster with glaring eyes, huge teeth, protruding tongue, brazen claws, and writhing snakes for hair. Her hideous appearance has the power to turn people into stone, and Athene eventually completes her revenge by having Perseus kill Medusa. He finds Medusa by stealing the one eye and one tooth shared by the Graiae until they agree to help him. Perseus then kills Medusa by decapitating her while looking into his brightly polished shield which neutralizes the power of her appearance: he then puts her head into a magic wallet that shields onlookers from its effects. When Athene receives the booty, she uses Medusa's head and skin to fashion her own shield.

In the Venus tradition, Medusa is a poignant double. She is the necessary counter in the dialectic of beauty and ugliness, desire and repulsion, wholeness and fragmentation. Medusa is the disabled woman to Venus's perfect body. The story is a kind of allegory of a 'normal' person's intersection with the disabled body. This intersection is marked by the power of the visual. The 'normal' person sees the disabled person and is turned to stone, in some sense, by the visual interaction. In this moment, the normal person suddenly feels self-conscious, rigid, unable to look but equally drawn to look. The visual field becomes problematic, dangerous, treacherous. The disability becomes a power derived from its otherness, its monstrosity, in the eyes of the 'normal' person. The disability must be decapitated and then contained in a variety of magic wallets. Rationality, for which Athene stands, is one of the devices for containing, controlling, and reforming the disabled body so that it no longer has the power to terrorize. And the issue of mutilation comes up as well because the disabled body is always the reminder of the whole body about to come apart at the seams. It provides a vision of, a caution about, the body as a construct held together willfully, always threatening to become its individual parts – cells, organs, limbs, perceptions – like the fragmented, shared eye and tooth that Perseus ransoms back to the Graiae.

In order to understand better how normalcy is bred into ways of viewing the body, it might be productive to think about the body as it appears in art, photography, and the other visual media. There has been a powerful tradition in Western art of representing the body in a way that serves to solidify, rather early on in history, a preferred mode of envisioning the body. This tradition, identified by Kenneth Clark, has been most clearly articulated in the 'nude'. The nude, as Clark makes clear, is not a literal depiction of the human body but rather a set of conventions about the body: 'the nude is not the subject of art, but a form of art' (1956, 5). Or, as he says, the nude is 'the body re-formed' (ibid., 3). If that is the case, then the nude is really part of the development of a set of idealized conventions about the way the body is supposed to look.

While some nudes may be male, when people talk about 'the nude' they most often mean the female nude. Lynda Nead, in a feminist correction of Clark, points out that 'more than any other subject, the female nude connotes "Art" ' (1992, 1). And in that tradition, the Venus becomes the vortex for thinking about the female body. The Venus is, rather than a subject, a masculine way of fashioning the female body, or of remaking it into a conceptual whole.

I emphasize the word 'whole', because the irony of the Venus tradition is that virtually no Venuses have been preserved intact from antiquity. Indeed, one of the reasons for the popularity of the Venus de Milo was that from the time it was discovered in 1820 until 1893 when Furtwangler's scholarship revealed otherwise, the statue was, according to Clark, 'believed to be an original of the fifth century and the only free-standing figure of a woman that had come down from the great period with the advantage of a head' (1964, 89).

The mutilation of the statues is made more ironic by the fact that their headless and armless state is usually overlooked by art historians – barely referred to at all by Clark, for example, in the entirety of his book. The art historian does not *see* the absence and so fills the absence with a presence. This compensation leads us to understand that in the discourse of the nude, one is dealing not simply with art history but with the reception of disability, the way that the 'normal' observer compensates or defends against the presence of difference.

[…]

This amnesia, this looking away from incompleteness, an averting of the attention, a sigh, is the tip of a defensive mechanism that allows the art historian still to see the statue as an object of desire. So the critic's aim is to restore the damage, bring back the limbs, through an act of imagination. This phenomenon is not unlike the experience of 'phantom limb', the paradoxical effect that amputees experience of sensing their missing limb. In the case of the art historian, the statue is seen as complete with phantom limbs and head. The art historian does not see the lack, the presence of an impairment, but rather mentally reforms the outline of the Venus so that the historian can return the damaged woman in stone to a pristine origin of wholeness. His is an act of reformation of the visual field, a sanitizing of the disruption in perception.

This is the same act of imagination, or one might say control, that bans from the nude the representation of normal biological processes. For example, there are no pregnant Venuses, there are no paintings of Venuses who are menstruating, micturating, defecating – lactating and lacrimating being the only recognized activities of idealized women. There are no old Venuses (with the exception of a Diana by Rembrandt). One might think of a pregnant Venus as a temporarily disabled woman, and as such banned from the reconstruction of the body we call 'the nude'. Clark distinguishes between prehistoric fertility goddesses, like the Willendorf Venus, images of fertility and pregnancy, and the differently ideal Grecian versions which are never pregnant. As Nead notes (1992, 19), 'Clark alludes to this image of the female body [the Willendorf Venus] as undisciplined, out of control; it is excluded from the proper concerns of art in favour of the smooth, uninterrupted line of the Cycladic [Greek] figure.' As artists and art historians shun the fluids and changes in shape that are incompatible with the process of forming the 'regular' body, the evidentiary record of mutilated Venuses must be repressed by a similar process.

A cautionary word must be said on the decapitated and armless Venuses. While it is true that male statues equally are truncated, the incompleteness of the female statues suggests another obvious point that has been repressed for so long – violence. Did all these statues lose their arms and heads by sheer accident, were the structurally fragile head and limbs more likely to deteriorate than the torso, were there random acts of vandalism, or was a particular kind of symbolic brutality committed on these stone women? Did vandals, warriors, and adolescent males amuse themselves by committing focused acts of violence, of sexual bravado and mockery on these embodiments of desire? An armless woman is a symbol of sexual allure without the ability to resist, a headless nude captures a certain kind of male fantasy of submission without the complication of the individuality and the authority granted by a face, even an idealized one. We do not know and will probably never know what happened to these statues, although the destruction of the Parthenon figures has been documented as done by occupying soldiers. The point is that the violence against the body, the acts of hacking, mutilation and so on, have to be put in the context we have been discussing. An act of violence against a female statue is constitutively different from that against a male statue – and these are acts that can be placed in a range of terrorist acts against women during war. Such acts create disabled people, and so, in a sense, these Venuses are the disabled women of art. To forget that is again to commit acts of omission of a rather damning nature.

Of course, a statue is not a person. But as representations of women, the Venus statues carry a powerful cultural signification. The reaction to such statues, both by critics and other viewers, tells much about the way in which we consider the body both as a whole and as incomplete. One point to note is that the art historian, like Clark, tends to perform a complex double act. On the one hand, the critic sees the incomplete statue as whole, imagines the phantom limbs in order to defend against incompleteness, castration, the chaotic or 'grotesque body', as Peter Stallybrass and Allon White (1987) have, using Bakhtinian terminology, called it. On the other hand (if indeed our standard is *two* hands), the critic and the artist are constantly faced with the fragmentary nature of the body, analyzing parts, facing the gaze of the missing part that must be argued into existence.

The model for the fragmentary nature of the nude is best illustrated by the famous story of Zeuxis, as told by Pliny. When Zeuxis painted his version of Aphrodite, he constructed her from the parts of five beautiful young women of his town of Kroton. His vision of the wholeness of Aphrodite was really an assemblage of unrelated parts. Likewise, the critic in regarding the whole nude must always be speaking of parts: 'their torsos have grown so long that the distance from the breasts to the division of the legs is three units instead of two, the pelvis is wide, the thighs are absurdly short' (Clark 1964, 91). The whole can only be known by the sum of its parts – even when those parts are missing. John Barrell has detailed the reactions of eighteenth-century men to the Venus dei Medici, and noted how they tended to examine every detail of the statue. Edward Wright, for example, tells observers to 'strictly examine every part' and a typical account read thus:

> One might very well insist on the beauty of the breasts. . . . They are small, distinct, and delicate to the highest degree; with an idea of softness. . . . And yet with all that softness, they have a firmness too. . . . From her breasts, her shape begins to diminish gradually down to her waist; . . . Her legs are neat and slender; the small of them is finely rounded; and her feet are little, white, and pretty.
> (Barrell 1989, 127)

Another carped:

> The head is something too little for the Body, especially for the Hips and
> Thighs: the Fingers excessively long and taper, and no match for the
> Knuckles, except for the little Finger of the Right-Hand.
>
> (ibid.)

These analyses perform a juggling act between the fragmentation of the body and its
reunification into a hallucinated erotic whole. In imagining the broken statues, the critic
must mentally replace the arms and the head, then criticize any other restoration, as does
Clark in attacking the reconstruction of the Venus of Arles: 'the sculptor Girardon ... not
only added the arms and changed the angle of the head, but smoothed down the whole
body, since the King was offended by the sight of ribs and muscles' (Clark 1964, 87). The
point here is that the attempt of the critic to keep the body in some systematic whole is
really based on a repression of the fragmentary nature of the body.

One might also want to recall that for the Greeks these statues, while certainly works
of art, were also to be venerated, since they were representations of deities. For the
Greeks, Aphrodite was not a myth; she was a goddess whose domain was desire. It somehow seems appropriate that the ritualistic or reverential attitude toward these statues,
pointed out by Walter Benjamin (1969, 223–4), indeed their very appearance in stone
(which Page Dubois sees as a cultic representation of the bones of the female spirits), has
been reproduced in the attitude of that most secular of worshippers, the art critic. For
the Venus has a double function: she is both a physical and a spiritual incarnation of desire.
In that double sense, the critic must emphasize her spiritual existence by going beyond
her physical incarnation in fallible stone, and her mutilations, to the essential body, the
body of Desire, the body of the Other.

We can put this paradox in Lacanian terms. For Lacan, the most primitive, the earliest experience of the body is actually of the fragmented body (*corps morcelé*).[1] The infant
experiences his or her body as separate parts or pieces, as 'turbulent movements' (Lacan
1977, 2). For the infant, rather than a whole, the body is an assemblage of arms, legs, surfaces. These representations/images of fragmented body parts Lacan calls *imagos* because
they are 'constituted for the "instincts" themselves':

> Among these *imagos* are some that represent the elective vectors of aggressive
> intentions, which they provide with an efficacity that might be called magical.
> These are the images of castration, mutilation, dismemberment, dislocation,
> evisceration, devouring, bursting open of the body, in short, the *imagos* that I
> have grouped together under the apparently structural term of *imagos of the
> fragmented body*.
>
> (ibid., 11)

The process that builds a self involves the enforced unifying of these fragments through
the hallucination of a whole body, 'a Gestalt, that is to say, in an exteriority' (ibid., 2), as
Lacan has pointed out. The process 'extends from a fragmented body-image to a form of
its totality ... and, lastly, to the assumption of the armour of an alienating identity' (ibid., 4).
When the child points to an image in the mirror – at that stage Lacan calls 'the mirror phase' – the child recognizes (actually misrecognizes) that unified image as his or her

self. That identification is really the donning of an identity, an 'armor' against the chaotic or fragmentary body.

In this sense, the disabled body is a direct *imago* of the repressed fragmented body. The disabled body causes a kind of hallucination of the mirror phase gone wrong. The subject looks at the disabled body and has a moment of cognitive dissonance, or should we say a moment of cognitive resonance with the earlier state of fragmentation. Rather than seeing the whole body in the mirror, the subject sees the repressed fragmented body; rather than seeing the object of desire, as controlled by the Other, the subject sees the true self of the fragmented body. For Lacan, because the child first saw its body as a 'collection of discrete part-objects, adults can never perceive their bodies in a complete fashion in later life' (Ragland-Sullivan 1987, 21). This repressed truth of self-perception revolves around a prohibited central, specular moment – of seeing the disabled body – in which the 'normal' person views the Medusa image, in which the Venus-nude cannot be sustained as a viable armor. In Lacanian terms, the *moi* is threatened with a breaking-up, literally, of its structure, is threatened with a reminder of its incompleteness. In a specular, face-to-face moment, the ego is involved in what J. B. Pontalis calls 'death work', which involves the 'fundamental process of unbinding [of the ego], of fragmentation, of breaking up, of separation, of bursting' (cited in Ragland-Sullivan 1987, 70). Thus the specular moment between the armored, unified self and its repressed double – the fragmented body – is characterized by a kind of death-work, repetition compulsion in which the unified self continuously sees itself undone – castrated, mutilated, perforated, made partial. In this context, it is worth nothing that the Venus tradition involves castration at its very origin. Aphrodite is said to have been born from the foam of Uranus's genitals which Cronus threw into the sea after castrating his father (Graves 1957, 49). The dynamic is clear. Male mutilation is mitigated by the creation of the desirable female body. The disabled body is corrected by the wholeness of the constructed body of the nude. But, as has been noted, the emphasis on wholeness never entirely erases the foundation of the Venus tradition in the idea of mutilation, fragmented bodies, decapitation, amputation.

If we follow these terms, the disabled Venus serves as an unwanted reminder that the 'real' body, the 'normal body', the observer's body, is in fact always already a 'fragmented body'. The linking together of all the disparate bodily sensations and locations is an act of will, a hallucination that always threatens to fall apart. The mutilated Venus and the disabled person, particularly the disabled person who is missing limbs or body parts, will become in fantasy visual echoes of the primal fragmented body – a signifier of castration and lack of wholeness. Missing senses, blindness, deafness, aphasia, in that sense, will point to missing bodily parts or functions. The art historian in essence dons or retains the armor of identity, needs the armor as does Perseus who must see Medusa through the polished shield. The art historian's defense is that mirror-like shield that conjures wholeness through a misrecognition linking the parts into a whole.

What this analysis tells us is that the 'disabled body' belongs to no one, just as the normal body, or even the 'phallus' belongs to no one. Even a person who is missing a limb, or is physically 'different', still has to put on, assume, the disabled body and identify with it. The disabled body, far from being the body of some small group of 'victims', is an entity from the earliest of childhood instincts, a body that is common to all humans, as Lacan would have it. The 'normal' body is actually the body we develop later. It is in effect a Gestalt – and therefore in the realm of what Lacan calls the Imaginary. The realm of the 'Real' in Lacanian terms is where the fragmented body is found because it is the body that precedes the ruse of identity and wholeness. Artists often paint this vision, and it often appears in dreams 'in the form of disjointed limbs, or of those organs represented in exosocy [...] the very same that the visionary Hieronymus Bosch has fixed for all time' (Lacan 1977, 4).

In understanding this point, we can perhaps see how the issue of disability transcends the rather narrow category to which it has been confined. Just as, I claim, we readers are all deaf, participating in a deafened moment, likewise, we all – first and foremost – have fragmented bodies. It is in tracing our tactical and self-constructing (deluding) journeys away from that originary self that we come to conceive and construct that phantom goddess of wholeness, normalcy, and unity – the nude.

One might even add that the element of repulsion and fear associated with fragmentation and disability may in fact come from the very act of repressing the primal fragmentariness of the body. As Freud wrote, 'the uncanny is in reality nothing new or foreign, but something familiar and old-established in the mind that has been estranged only [in] the process of repression' (Freud 1963, 47). The feelings of repulsion associated with the uncanny, *das Unheimlich*, the unfamiliar, are not unlike the emotions of the 'normal' when they are visualizing the disabled. The key to the idea of the uncanny is in its relation to the normal. *Heimlich* is a word associated with the home, with familiarity – and with the comfortable predictability of the home. The disabled body is seen as *unheimlich* because it is the familiar gone wrong. Disability is seen as something that does not belong at home, not to be associated with the home. Freud notes that the terror or repulsion of the uncanny is ambivalent, is found precisely in its relation to and yet deviance from the familiar. That the uncanny can be related to disability is made clear when Freud cites specifically 'dismembered limbs, a severed head, a hand cut off at the wrist' as *unheimlich* (ibid., 49). What is uncanny about dismemberment seems to be the familiarity of the body part that is then made *unheimlich* by its severing. As Freud wrote, 'the *unheimlich* is what was once *heimlich*, homelike, familiar; the prefix "un" is the token of repression' (ibid., 51).

But in this equation I think Freud is actually missing the earlier repression of the inherently fragmentary nature of the original body *imago*. The homeyness of the body, its familiarity as whole, complete, contained, is based on a dynamic act of repression. Freud is assuming that the whole body is an a priori given, as he had done with the concept of the ego. But as Lacan has shown more than adequately, the ego is a multifaceted structure to be understood in its philosophical complexity. Likewise the ground of the body, its materiality given by Freud, needs a re-analysis. The route of disability studies allows for this revisioning. In this process, the *heimisch* body becomes the *unheimlich* body, and the fragment, the disabled parts, can be seen as the originary, familiar body made unfamiliar by repression. Dominant culture has an investment in seeing the disabled, therefore, as uncanny, as something found outside the home, unfamiliar, while in fact where is the disabled body found if not at home?

[...]

We can return, again, to the Venus, neatly enclosed in its marmoreal skin and thus representing an unperforated body, despite the mutilations that have disfigured it. Most of the visual arts eschew disability and disabled images, except perhaps for the romanticized images around madness. The work of Mary Duffy, a contemporary artist without arms, provides one notable exception to this reluctance to think of Venuses without arms as the equivalent of Medusa. In the first plate of a photographic series entitled *Cutting the*

Ties that Bind, we see a standing figure draped entirely in white cloth against a dark background so that the figure beneath the drapery is not visible. In the second plate, the drapery is partially removed so that it covers mainly the thighs and legs revealing us a female body, the artist's, without arms. The figure is clearly meant to reproduce the Venus de Milo in the flesh. The third picture in the series shows the figure stepping away from the drapery with a triumphant smile. The work serves to show how the female disabled body can be reappropriated by the artist herself. Duffy writes:

> By confronting people with my naked body, with its softness, its roundness and its threat I wanted to take control, redress the balance in which media representations of disabled women [are] usually tragic, always pathetic. I wanted to hold up a mirror to all those people who had stripped me bare previously…the general public with naked stares, and more especially the medical profession.
>
> (cited in Nead 1992, 78)

The Medusa gaze is rerouted so that it comes not from the object of horror, the monstrous woman, but from the gaze of the normal observer. It is the 'normal' gaze that is seen as naked, as dangerous. And unlike Perseus slaying Medusa by holding up a mirror, it is now the 'object of horror' who holds the mirror up to the 'normal' observer.

This reappropriation of the normal gaze was further carried out by the photographer Jo Spence. Recognizing the inherent and unstated pose of normalcy imposed by the camera and by the photographic session, Spence revisioned her photography to be capable of representing the nude model as a person with disabilities. Her work, detailed in many shows and in her book *Putting Myself in the Picture: A Political, Personal, and Photographic Autobiography* (1986), partly focuses on her mastectomy. Spence links this operative and post-operative process to an understanding and participating gaze that seeks to touch, not recoil from, bodily changes. In addition to the simple fact of the partial mastectomy, Spence includes in her work photographs and texts that question assumptions about age and beauty. Her body is middle-aged, irregular, and defies the canons of ideal feminine beauty. Her work is involved with 'explaining my experience as a patient and the contradictions between ways in which the medical profession controls women's bodies and the "imaginary bodies" we inhabit as women' (Spence 1986, 156).

The visual arts have done a magnificent job of centralizing normalcy and of marginalizing different bodies. As we have seen, initially the impulse came from a move to idealize the body and make up the perfect body out of perfect sub-units. Then with the rise of hegemonic normalcy, the impulse veered from ideal to normalizing representations. Either of these paradigms pushes the ordinary body, the abnormal body, out of the picture. Photographer David Hevey has written about the paucity of images of the disabled in photographic anthologies. He concludes that 'disabled people are represented but almost exclusively as symbols of "otherness" placed within equations which take their non-integration as a natural by-product of their impairment' (Hevey 1992, 54). When he looked for any images of disabled people, he found either medical photographs in which the 'patients' appear 'passive and stiff and "done to," the images bear a bizarre resemblance to colonial pictures where "the blacks" stand frozen and curious, while "whitey" lounges confident and sure' (ibid., 53), or images like those of Diane Arbus that show the disabled as 'grotesque'. Ungrotesque, routine pictures of disabled people in advertising, 'art' photography, films and so on are hard to find. With the same regularity that bodies of color were kept out of the mainstream (and even the avant-garde) media in the years before the civil rights movement, so too are disabled bodies disqualified from representing universality.

One of the ways that visual images of the disabled have been appropriated into the modernist and postmodernist aesthetic is through the concept of the 'grotesque'. The word was used by Bakhtin to describe the aesthetic of the Middle Ages, which reveled in presenting the body in its nonidealized form. The grotesque, for Bakhtin, was associated with the common people, with a culture that periodically turned the established order upside down through the carnival and the carnivalesque. Gigantic features, scatological references, inverse political power were all hallmarks of the grotesque – an aesthetic that ultimately was displaced by humanistic notions of order, regularity, and of course power during the Renaissance.

While the term 'grotesque' has had a history of being associated with this counter-hegemonic notion of people's aesthetics and the inherent power of the masses, what the term has failed to liberate is the notion of actual bodies as grotesque. There is a thin line between the grotesque and the disabled. Hevey examines, for example, how critics have received Diane Arbus's photographs of the disabled. Susan Sontag writes that Arbus's 'work shows people who are pathetic, pitiable, as well as repulsive, but it does not arouse any compassionate feelings'. Later she adds, 'Do they see themselves, the viewer wonders, like *that?* Do they know how grotesque they are?' (Hevey 1992, 57). The grotesque, in this sense, is seen as a concept without the redeeming sense of class rebellion in Bakhtin's formulation. Here it is simply the ugly, what makes us wince, look away, feel pity – more allied with its dictionary definition of 'hideous,' 'monstrous', 'deformed', 'gnarled'. Though artists and writers may use the grotesque, they rarely write about that state from the subject position of the disabled. The grotesque, as with disability in general, is used as a metaphor for otherness, solitude, tragedy, bitterness, alterity. The grotesque is defined in this sense as a disturbance in the normal visual field, not as a set of characteristics through which a fully constituted subject views the world. One problem with terms like 'disability' and 'the grotesque' is that they disempower the object of observation. The body is seen through a set of cultural default settings arrived at by the wholesale adoption of ableist cultural values.

In no area is this set of cultural values related to the visual more compelling than in film. Film is a medium whose main goal, one might say, is the construction and reconstruction of the body. The abnormal body plays a major role in the defining of the normal body, and so one might assume that film would be concerned with the issue of disability. Martin F. Norden has recently published the most complete account to date of disability in the film industry, *The Cinema of Isolation: A History of Physical Disability in the Movies* (1994). The remarkable thing about this book is the staggering number of films that have been made about the issue of disability. When I first began to consider the issue of how the disabled body is depicted in film, I came up with my own list of twenty or so films, and I thought that I would mention the occasional way in which the disabled were included in a film industry that mainly focused on the normal body. In other words, I thought I was dealing with a parallel situation to, say, the depiction in cinema of African-Americans – a marginalized group who rarely appeared in Hollywood films until recently and, if they did, played mainly minor characters or supernumerary roles.

But the facts about the depiction of disability are quite the opposite of what I had thought. The film industry has been obsessed with the depiction of the disabled body from the earliest silent films. The blind, the deaf, the physically disabled were singled out from the very beginning of cinema. Norden finds movies about disability from as early as 1898, and the earliest one-reeler silent films of the period 1902–09 include such representative titles as *Deaf Mute Girl Reciting 'Star Spangled Banner'* (1902), *Deaf Mutes' Ball* (1907), *The Invalid's Adventure* (1907), *The Legless Runner* (1907), *The One-legged Man* (1908), *The Hunchback Brings Luck* (1908), *The Little Cripple* (1908), *A Blind Woman's Story* (1908), *The Blind Boy* (1908), *The Cripple's Marriage* (1909), *The Electrified Humpback* (1909), to name only a few. Later multi-reeler silent films routinely told the stories of the disabled. D. W. Griffith made a few disability-related films, culminating his efforts in the famous *Orphans of the Storm* (1921) in which two hapless sisters (Lilian and Dorothy Gish), one of whom is blind, try to survive on the streets of Paris. But the noteworthy fact about this film is not merely its disability-related content but that Griffith's version was the *fifth* filmic remake of the 1874 French play *Les Deux Orphelines*. With film only in its infancy, this particular disability story had been told afresh approximately once every four years from 1900 through 1921.

[…]

The point that Norden's book made clear to me is that the cinematic experience, far from including disabilities in an ancillary way, is powerfully arranged around the management and deployment of disabled and 'normal' bodies. Disabled stories, stories of people's bodies or minds going wrong, make compelling tales. But more than that, as with any obsession, there has to be an underlying reason why films are drawn obsessively to the topic of disability. In order to understand why film makers routinely incorporate disabled bodies into films, it might be relevant to ask what else routinely appears in films. The answer is more than obvious: sex and violence. While it is fashionable for liberals to decry the violent content of films, and conservatives to decry the sexual, it might be more accurate for them to think of films as vehicles for the delivery of images of the body in extreme circumstances. The inherent voyeuristic nature of film makes it a commodity that works by visualizing for viewers the body in attitudes that it is otherwise difficult to see. Few people in quotidian life see couples making love on a regular basis, but that is a routine experience to filmgoers. Likewise, most middle-class citizens rarely see dead, mutilated, bleeding bodies, but the average viewer has no shortage of such images.

So films, one could say, are a streamlined delivery system that produces dramatically these bodily images in exchange for a sum of money (as the Coca-Cola industry can be said to be a system for delivering caffeine and sugar, or as cigarettes are really timerelease delivery systems for nicotine administration). As novels were seen to be mechanisms for the cultural production of normativity, so films have to be seen in the same regard, with the addition that the phantasm of the body is particularly subject to these normativizing activities.

Films enforce the normal body but through a rather strange process. The normal body, which had been invented in the nineteenth century as a departure from the ideal body, shifted over to a new concept – the normal ideal. This normal ideal body is now the one that we see on the screen. It is the commodified body of the eroticized male and female stars. This body is not actually the norm, but it is the fantasized, hypostatized body of commodified desire. In order to generate this body and proliferate its images, films have constantly to police and to regulate the variety of bodily differences. These bodies are the modern equivalents of the nude Venuses, and to keep them viable, to encourage viewers to think on and obsess about them, the Medusa body has constantly to be shown, reshown, placed, categorized, itemized, and anatomized. In short, we cannot have Sharon Stone without Linda Hunt; we cannot have Tom Cruise without Ron Kovic; we cannot have the fantasy of the erotic femme fatale's body without having the sickened, disabled, deformed person's story testifying to the universal power of the human spirit to overcome adversity. As Norden points out when films about disabled people are made, more often than not the disabled characters get cured by the end of the film. The tension between the whole and the fragmented body, between the erotic complete body, and the uncanny incomplete body, must be constantly deployed and resolved through films.

The film *Boxing Helena* provides some interesting ways of seeing these tensions worked through. In the film, Nick (Julian Sands), a surgeon, amputates the legs of Helena (Sherilyn Fenn), the bitchy, sexualized woman with whom he is obsessed but who rejects his advances. He performs the amputation initially to save her life after a car accident but then goes on to amputate her arms as a way of keeping her and containing her – of rendering her helpless so he can take care of her.

A replica of the Venus de Milo decorates Nick's family mansion. The statue is used as a double symbol. In one aspect, it is an illustration of the former beauty of the dismembered Helena, its marmoreal glaze representing the still and ever beautiful Helena. But, it also represents idealized female beauty (in its wholeness) and is associated with Nick's mother, whose blatant sexuality was used to humiliate her son when he was young. The filmmaker wants us to see the dismemberment partly as an act of revenge against the castrating mother, whose legacy shows up in Nick's premature ejaculation syndrome.

The salient point is that when Helena's limbs are amputated, that is, [...] becomes the Venus, she becomes desexualized – merely idealized. Whereas before her dismemberment she is a fantasy of ravenous female sexuality unencumbered by the traditional female values of caring, nurturing, or sweetness, after her dismemberment, she loses her sexuality. In a typical ableist moment, she says after her amputation: 'How can I ever look at myself and think of myself as worthwhile?' Her worth in this case is her sexuality, which is lost. Her disability is actually created and owned by Nick.

In another instance of bourgeois, ableist celebration of the discursivity of sexuality, both she and Nick regain their sexual function (thus becoming undisabled) through eros. He buries his head in her lap, which of course despite all the mutilation leads us to realize that everything that is conventionally part of female sexuality is still intact – and in a moment of his fantasy she comes alive sexually, a trope that is equated with her suddenly having arms and legs. She caresses his head, walks, and whispers the answer to Freud's question, 'What do women want?' telling him how women want to be made love to. Her whispered erotic litany begins to release the bad dream of disability. But it is only he, as the owner of her body, who can fully accomplish this release, and so she begs him: 'I want to feel like a woman. Give me back what you've taken away.' The supplement that has been missing is returned like the Lacanian phallus by Nick in a very Lacanian moment. As Helena watches through a semi-opened door, Nick makes love to another woman (who in the credits is called 'fantasy woman'), and we see he is no longer sexually dysfunctional. Helena's self is reconstituted through a triangularization of desire in which her mirror imago of the whole body is re-created by viewing the desire of the

Other. The other woman represents her wholeness, and the entire issue of functionality is blurred into sexual ability.

As trendy as the director Jennifer Lynch is trying to be, she cannot separate herself from traditional views of people with disabilities. Never does the surgeon have to catheterize Helena or change her tampon; more tellingly, Helena is never allowed to be both naked and disabled – as her body was so openly revealed before her amputations. Her double-amputated body is partly held up as an object of beauty, but not of sexuality – and therefore it can never be seen naked as she had been revealed to the camera's gaze before the operations. Unlike Mary Duffy or Jo Spence, Lynch cannot allow herself to show us the naked, disabled body. This would be too great a primal-scene moment, in which the true nakedness of disability, its connection with the nakedness of the unwhole fragmented body, would be unavoidable and unable to be repressed.

The film ends with the revelation that the entire narrative has all been Nick's dream. Helena was hit by a car, but in actuality she was taken to hospital, and at the end of the film she remains physically intact. Disability is just a bad dream, as she herself had cried out when she first discovered she had had her legs amputated. She is cured.

The film returns to the whole, untarnished body because that is always seen as the norm. In general, when the body is mentioned in literature or depicted in drama and film, it is always already thought of as whole, entire, complete, and ideal. In literature, central characters of novels are imaged as normal unless specific instruction is given to alter that norm; where a disability is present, the literary work will focus on the disability as a problem. Rare indeed is a novel, play, or film that introduces a disabled character whose disability is not the central focus of the work. More often, the disability becomes part of a theme in which a 'normal' person becomes romantically involved with a person with a disability and proves that the disability is no obstacle to being attractive. At its most egregious, this theme is taken up in works such as W. Somerset Maugham's *Of Human Bondage*, in which the character's sexual life is cleared of problems only when the disability is removed. With an only slightly more educated view, films like *My Left Foot* confirm the character's inner worth when he attracts a wife at the end of the film. And Jennifer Lynch's *Boxing Helena* is simply part of this parade.

[…]

I have tried to show that the concept of disability is a crucial part of the very way we conceive of and live in our bodies. In art, photography, film, and other media in which the body is represented, the 'normal' body always exists in a dialectical play with the disabled body. Indeed, our representations of the body are really investigations of and defenses against the notion that the body is anything but a seamless whole, a complete, unfragmented entity. In addition to the terms of race, class, gender, sexual preference and so on – all of which are factors in the social construction of the body – the concept of disability adds a background of somatic concerns. But disability is more than a background. It is in some sense the basis on which the 'normal' body is constructed: disability defines the negative space the body must not occupy, it is the Manichean binary in contention with normality. But this dialectic is one that is enforced by a set of social conditions and is not natural in any sense. Only when disability is made visible as a compulsory term in a hegemonic process, only when the binary is exposed and the continuum acknowledged, only when the body is seen apart from its existence as an object of production or consumption – only then will normalcy cease being a term of enforcement in a somatic judicial system.

Note

1   The term *corps morcelé* is a bit more vivid than 'fragmented body', the now-standard translation of the term into English. *Morceler* is defined as 'to divide up into pieces'. It more actively carries the concept of chopping, cutting, or hacking. Thus the *corps morcelé* might more accurately be called 'the cut-up body'. However, I will retain the standard usage, for the sake of uniformity.

References

Barrell, John (1989) ' "The Dangerous Goddess": Masculinity, prestige, and the aesthetic in early eighteenth-century Britain', *Cultural Critique* 12, pp. 101–31.

Benjamin, Walter (1969) *Illuminations*, New York: Schocken.

Browne, S. E., Connors, D. and Stern, N. (eds) (1985) *With the Power of Each Breath: A Disabled Women's Anthology*, Pittsburgh: Cleis Press.

Clark, Kenneth (1964) *The Nude: A Study in Ideal Form*. New York: Pantheon.

Dubois, Page (1988) *Sowing the Seed: Psychoanalysis and Ancient Representations of Women*, Chicago: Chicago University Press.

Freud, Sigmund (1963) 'The uncanny', *Studies in Parapsychology*, New York: Collier.

Graves, Robert (1957) *The Greek Myths*, New York: Penguin.

Hevey, David (1992) *The Creatures Time Forgot: Photography and Disability Imagery*, London: Routledge.

Lacan, Jacques (1977) *Écrits: A Selection*, translated by Alan Sheridan, New York: Norton.

Nead, Lynda (1992) *The Female Nude: Art, Obscenity and Sexuality*, London and New York: Routledge.

Norden, Martin, F. (1994) *The Cinema of Isolation: A History of Physical Disability in the Movies*, New Brunswick: Rutgers University Press.

Oliver, Michael (1990) *The Politics of Disablement: A Sociological Approach*, New York: St Martin's Press.

Ragland-Sullivan, Elie (1987) *Jacques Lacan and the Philosophy of Psychoanalysis*, Urbana: University of Illinois Press.

Ryan, J. and Thomas, F. (1980) The Politics of Mental Handicap, Harmondsworth: Penguin.

Spence, Jo (1986) *Putting Myself in the Picture*, London: Camden Press.

Stallybrass, Peter and White, Allon (1987) *The Politics of Transgression*, Ithaca, NY: Cornell University Press.

Chapter 24

Peter Freund

BODIES, DISABILITY AND SPACES
The social model and disabling spatial organisations

From P. E. S. Freund (2001) 'Bodies, disability and spaces: the social model and disabling spatial organisations', *Disability & Society*, 16(5): 689–706.

[...]

Two disabilities

THE TERM DISABILITY CAN be used in two different senses. It can refer to a social status and a cultural category or one's bio-medical status. In disability theory, a second usage of disability emerges – a restriction on activity generated by an impairment transformed by a particular socio-cultural context into a disability. Like any label, being labelled as a 'person with a disability' has socio-political consequences ranging from exclusion (e.g. job discrimination) to the ability to claim 'special' accommodations (e.g. parking spaces for 'people with disabilities').

The first 'disability' is a dichotomous category – one either qualifies according to governmental, bio medical or activist criteria as a person with a disability or one does not. The second sense in which disability can be defined – as 'not being able to', is, of course, a sociocultural construction, but one that can seem as part of a *continuum* where one is disabled in different spheres of life and to different degrees. The focus in this essay, is on disability in the latter sense.

[...]

Definitions for both these categorisations change over time, along with rules for applying them. Political economic contexts heavily influence such constructions (Oliver, 1996). The number of individuals who are 'eligible' for such categories changes over time as well. Thus, with demographic changes (such as the 'graying' of society), more and more non-disabled people are coming to see that people with disabilities do not constitute an 'other' (Wendell, 1996, p. 18). In a sense, many individuals have 'deviant' bodies that are not easily accommodated in 'standard' spatial arrangements.

'Impairment' as a social construction (like disability) carries a negative connotation and is limited by its mostly biomedical perspective (Shakespeare, 1999). As a biomedically grounded concept, it excludes differences and variations in bodies which, while not impairments, are nonetheless 'disabling' in particular contexts (Shakespeare, 1999). Being 'very' tall or short, small or large can be disabling in a 'one size fits all' socio-material environment. In the final analysis, it is not only impairments, but also physical–mental *differences* and their relationship to socio-cultural arrangements that are at issue. By extension, thus *many* bodies, not just a few bodies, share some problems with disabling design, spatial organisation, and so on.

There is, of course, no universal discourse for defining either a disability or an impairment. Thus, what constitutes functioning (and certainly 'normal' functioning) is problematic and understandable only in reference to a particular cultural and socio-material context. There is, however, a danger in *over*-relativising definitions *within* a particular socio-cultural setting. It is possible to arrive at a tentative, however, context bound, definition of an impairment and difference as well as some insight into how various cultural norms and socio-material environments can be disabling (in the second sense of the term).

Despite the argument that one cannot, in fact, make sharp the distinctions between an impairment or a difference and a disability, nevertheless, the distinction is *analytically* useful for understanding how culture and, most significantly, socio-material environments influence functioning (however, one may wish to 'construct–deconstruct' such a concept). Such an understanding is not just relevant for 'people with disabilities', but for a constantly changing range in populations of mental and bodily physiological structures and functions (Shakespeare, 1999). If people with an impairment are not automatically or 'naturally' disabled, it is also possible that those who are *not* impaired may be *disabled* in a particular temporal–spatial context. Thus, not only 'people with disabilities' and those temporarily impaired, can benefit from enabling socio-spatial modifications that enhance functioning. An 'able'-bodied mother pushing a pram or a delivery person a hand cart, can both benefit from the same ramp that makes the built environment user-friendly for a wheelchair user. Transport accessibility, thus, is also a concern for people other than those with a disability (Gleeson, 1999). Spatial-temporal arrangements impact on virtually every 'body'. Thus, *both* 'normal' and 'deviant' bodies require particular sociomaterial contexts, if they are to 'function' (Wendell, 1996, p. 22).

The recognition that such definitions are cultural-social and to some extent political is also essential. What is significant is that not only do categories change, but so does the number of individuals over time who qualify for membership in such categories. The boundaries of categories are blurry.

[…]

The questions surrounding the relationship between impairment and disability might thus be posed in a different way, given the fluid and widespread relevance to an unspecified number of individuals in any society. What socio-material arrangements enable the widest range of mind-bodies to function (within standards and contexts of particular society)? For disability rights activists, the question can be framed asking, to what extent do the interests and material needs of those who have disability coincide with those who do not? Should 'difference' or 'universality' be emphasised (Wendell, 1996, p. 30)? If we focus on difference, do we miss common structural features of environments that disable or enable people? Of course, for political activism, in most contemporary societies, claiming difference and minority group status is very important. Claiming a minority group status gives a focus and group identity and cohesion to the battle against disabling conditions. Yet the dualism of such categories militates against universalising the acceptance and incorporation of differences into the social body.

[...]

Spatial–temporal structures are particularly important material factors in the social construction of disability. Included here is the pace of life (the social organisation of time and attendant social rhythms; Wendell, 1996). An incompatibility between socially generated rhythms and the rhythms of various bodies can be produced in workplaces, traffic systems, and other such, with disabling consequences. 'Sickening' schedules may penetrate all spheres of life, including play and leisure (Freund and McGuire, 1999).

[...]

Time–space compression is a feature of late modernity and has accelerated in 'post-modern' societies. Such a compression is fueled by political-economic tendencies inherent in contemporary capitalism (e.g. the need to extend markets and profits, increase consumption of goods, reduce cost of production, etc.; Harvey, 1996). Accordingly, speed rules transport space (as well as much of public space). Faster and larger vehicles are valorised and traffic participants (both drivers and others in traffic) are forced to accommodate their bodies to its rhythms.

[...]

Poor pedestrian signals, short traffic lights, the designs of transport platform (e.g. roadways) *materialise* an organisation of space–time that favours the 'quick' and the 'spry', and disables those who are not.

While discourses about traffic accidents tend to shift attention to those who are the most vulnerable (the 'elderly', 'people with disabilities' and children), little attention is paid to the social organisation of space and time in which such populations must move. Hoxie and Rubenstein (1994), for instance, argued that the US urban traffic signals are out of sync with the walking speed of older pedestrians. Thus, in their Los Angeles study, 27% of older pedestrians were unable to reach the opposite curb before the light changed, and one-quarter of these were stranded at least one lane away from safety. The social organisation of traffic flow in an auto-centered system favours drivers over pedestrians, bicyclists and wheelchairs. Three-quarters of the elderly pedestrians interviewed stated that fear kept them from crossing streets as often as they would like to. The implication of this for disability studies is clear.

[...]

The social organisation of space influences the relationship one has to the space one moves through and how secure one feels in it (Curtis and Jones, 1998, p. 649). For instance, in car-dominated spaces, some people with physical and mental impairments will feel excluded, marginalised and insecure, and be at greater risk of injury in public transport space. This exclusion and sense of ontological insecurity adds to the disabling features of an impairment (Curtis and Jones, 1998, p. 651). Thus, some bodies are more vulnerable and ill at ease in some spaces. In turn, how ontologically secure (or insecure) actors feel in space, may influence their sense of place and how empowered they feel. From a phenomenological perspective, one can argue that disabling features of socio-material environments produce 'a vivid but unwanted' consciousness of one's impaired body (Paterson and Hughes, 1999). Anybody that cannot comfortably use and/or 'find a home' in spaces will not only feel alienated from that space, but from his or her body as well.

Having a body as opposed to being embodied are experienced by agency in different 'balances of positionality' (for a discussion of H. Plessner's concept of positionality, see Lindemann, 1996). Different relationships may be experienced between self and body, as well as different balances of presence and absence of one's body in consciousness. Generally, when experiences and activities flow smoothly, the body is absent in 'consciousness'. When tensions occur between body, material artifacts and social material space, or when pain, fatigue and difficulties with the body occur, the body becomes present in consciousness and experienced as an object (Radley, 1996).

Social material conditions thus not only influence the body itself, but how one experiences one's body – the quality of embodiment. Ageing, for instance, may bring about impairments. These changes make previously 'friendly' spaces and temporal rhythms 'unfriendly', potentially dangerous and uncomfortable. Hence, 'enclaves', or safe spaces may become important, spaces in which people are not only physically safe, but exist in ways that affirm their bodily sense of self. The ways in which groups construct use, gain access to such places is not, as Radley (1996) emphasises, simply an ergonomic issue. It is not an ergonomic problem in the sense of mechanistic, a-social, subjectless ergonomics, but it *is* a problem of people's embodied relationship to physical artifacts and environments.

[...]

The emphasis of the biomedical model is on the 'normalisation' of impaired bodies. Such a normalisation may mean fitting an unruly, 'different' body into the Procrustean bed of social space–time. It is in this context, that the issue of 'somatic false consciousness' becomes relevant for the social model. The ability to *recognise* discomfort or pain as the result of an incompatibility between social-material arrangements, and the body depends to some degree on how one defines one's position in environments *and* the environments themselves. Zola (1982, pp. 205–6; after defining himself as a person with a disability) began to travel using a wheelchair. He observes:

> I now arrived significantly more energetic, more comfortable, more free from cramps and legs sores than in my previous decades of traveling. The conclusion I drew was inevitable. I had *always* been tired, uncomfortable, cramped and sore after a long journey. But since I had no standard to comparison, these feelings were incorporated into the cognitive reality of what traveling for me was. I did not experience the tiredness and discomfort. They were cognitively inaccessible. What I am contending is shockingly simple. The very process of successful adaptation not only involves divesting ourselves of any identification with being handicapped, but also denying the uncomfortable features of that life.
>
> (Zola, 1982, pp. 205–6)

It is not simply that the standard of comparing realities of travelling was 'cognitively' inaccessible, but *sensually* and *materially* as well. In the past, Zola's 'normalisation' led him to adapt to his spatial environment by pushing out of his psycho-somatic awareness of any experience of discomfort. The present situation was 'naturalised' and sensual experiences of alternative possibilities escaped consciousness. There were no 'body memories' of other possible spatial arrangements that Zola could draw on as a reference point prior to his accepting his status as a person with a disability. In a similar way, people become acclimatised to noise pollution and crowding, and do not consider how things might be otherwise. The experience of environments depends on one's existential–phenomenological stance to it, the organisation of materiality, as well as one's sensual experience of it (and on being able to imagine sensual alternatives, more comfortable ways of organising materiality). The problem thus for disabled people (and for many others), is to become aware of the disabling properties of their *world* through the cognitive-sensual change of consciousness (Wendell, 1996, p. 46).

Once people shift focus from their bodies and their capacities, and see such capacities linked to the organisation of the spaces they utilise, their attendant mode of being in space and how they relate to it changes. Resistance then becomes possible. Inhospitable spaces can become focal points of resistance.

References

Curtis, S. and Jones, J. R. (1998) 'Is there a place for geography in the analysis of health inequality?', *Sociology of Health and Illness*, 20(5), pp. 645–72.

Freund, P. E. S. and McGuire, M. (1999) *Health, Illness and the Social Body: A Critical Sociology*, 3rd edn, Englewood Cliffs, NJ: Prentice Hall.

Gleeson, B. (1999) *Geographies of Disability*, London: Routledge.

Harvey, D. (1996) *Justice, Nature and the Geography of Difference*, Oxford: Blackwell.

Hoxie, R. E. and Rubenstein, L. A. (1994) 'Are older pedestrians allowed enough time to cross intersections safely?', *Journal of American Geriatric Association*, 42, pp. 241–4.

Lindemann, G. (1996) 'Zeichentheoretische Überlegungen zum Verhaltnis von Korper Und Leib', in A. Barkhaus (ed.) *Identität Leiblichkeit, Normativität*, Frankfurt am Main: Suhrkamp.

Oliver, M. (1996) *Understanding Disability*, London: Macmillan.

Paterson, K. and Hughes, B. (1999) 'Disability studies and phenomenology; the carnal politics of everyday life', *Disability & Society*, 14(5), pp. 597–610.

Radley, A. (1996) 'Displays and fragments: embodiment and the configuration of social worlds', *Theory and Psychology*, 6, pp. 559–76.

Shakespeare, T. (1999) 'What is a disabled person?', in M. Jones and L. A. B. Marks (eds) *Disability, Divers-ability and Legal Change*, London: Kluwer Law International.

Wendell, S. (1996) *The Rejected Body*, London: Routledge.

Zola, I. K. (1982) *Missing Pieces: a chronicle of living with a disability*, Philadelphia, PA: Temple University Press.

Chapter 25

Georges Canguilhem

MONSTROSITY AND THE MONSTROUS

From G. Canguilhem (1998) 'La monstruosité et le monstrueux', in *La Connaissance de la Vie*, Paris: Vrin. Translated by Chris Turner.

THE EXISTENCE OF MONSTERS calls life into question so far as the power life has to teach us order is concerned. This occurs with immediate effect, no matter how longstanding our previous trust, no matter how firmly we have become used to seeing dog-roses blossom on dog-rose bushes, tadpoles change into frogs, mares suckle foals and, in general, like engender like. It takes only a dashing of that trust, a morphological disparity, an appearance of species ambiguity for a radical fear to seize hold of us. That there should be fear will be readily accepted, but why should it be radical? The answer is: because we are living beings, real effects of the laws of life and potential causes of life in our turn. A failure of life concerns us doubly, for a failure could have struck us or it could, alternatively, come about through our agency. It is only because, as human beings, we are living beings, that a morphological defect is, to our living eyes, a monster. Let us suppose that we were pure reason, that we were mere intellectual machines for recording, calculating and reporting, and hence inert and indifferent to the motives for our thinking: the monster would simply be that which is other than the same; it would be an order that is other than the most probable order.

We have to reserve the designation 'monster' for organic beings only. There are no mineral monsters. There are no mechanical monsters. What has no rule of internal cohesion, what has not, in its form and dimensions, divergences oscillating on either side of a *modulus* – which we may translate as (standard of) measure, mould or model – cannot be termed monstrous. We may say of a rock that it is enormous, but not of a mountain that it is monstrous, except in a mythical universe of discourse in which mountains may possibly give birth to mice. There would seem to be a clarification that might be ventured here regarding the relations between the enormous and the monstrous. Both refer to what lies outside the norm. The norm which the enormous defies is supposedly a mere matter of measurement. In that case, why is it only what is large that we register as enormous? No doubt because, at a certain degree of growth, quantity brings quality into question. Enormity tends towards monstrosity. This is the ambiguity of gigantism: is a giant enormous or a monster? The mythological giant is something prodigious, which is to say that 'its size ... defeats the end that forms its concept'.[1] If the human being is defined by a certain limitation of his forces, his functions, then the man who, by his size, escapes human limitations is no longer a mere man. Yet to say that he is no longer a mere man is to say that he is a man still. By contrast, smallness seems to confine the quality of the thing to the private realm, to secrecy. The quality is all the better preserved for being the less exhibited.

We must, then, include in the definition of the monster its nature as a living being. The monster is the living being of negative value. We may here borrow from Mr Eugène Dupréel some of the basic concepts of his theory of values, which is so original and so profound. What gives living beings their value or, more exactly, what makes living beings of higher value than the mode of being of their physical milieu, is their specific consistency, standing out against the vicissitudes of the material environment, a consistency that expresses itself by resistance to deformation, by the struggle for integrity of form: regeneration of mutilations in certain species, reproduction in all. Now, the monster is not simply a living being of diminished value; it is a living being whose value is that of a foil. By revealing the stability to which life had habituated us to be precarious – life had merely habituated us to it, but out of that habit we had made a law – the monster confers on species reproduction, on morphological regularity and on the success of structuration a value that is all the higher for the fact that we now grasp its contingency. It is monstrosity, not death that is the counter-value to life. Death is the permanent and unconditional threat of the organism's decomposition; it is the limitation from outside, the negation of the living by the non-living. But monstrosity is the accidental and conditional threat of incompletion or distortion in the formation of form; it is the limitation from inside, the negation of the living by the non-viable.

It is surely the confused sense of the importance of the monster for a correct and complete appreciation of the values of life that underlies the ambivalent attitude of the human mind towards it. This consists, as we have said, in fear, and even panic terror on the one hand, but also, on the other, in curiosity and even fascination. The monstrous is an instance of the marvellous in reverse, but it is, nonetheless, an instance of the marvellous. On the one hand, it is troubling: life is less sure of itself than we might have thought. On the other, it adds to life's value: since life is capable of failure, all its successes are failures avoided. The fact that its successes are not necessary, devalues those successes generally, but enhances each one in particular. When we approach the philosophy of values from the angle of negative values, we have no difficulty in saying, with Gaston Bachelard, that the true is the limit of lost illusions; and, where our present problem is concerned, we can equally well agree with Gabriel Tarde, that the normal type is the zero degree of monstrosity.

However, once consciousness has been induced to suspect life of eccentricity and to dissociate the concept of reproduction from that of repetition, what is to prevent it from regarding life as even more lively, that is to say, capable of greater freedom of action? What is to prevent it from supposing life capable not only of exceptions occasioned by cause, but of spontaneous transgressions of its own habits? In the presence of a three-legged bird, should we be more sensible of the fact that this is one leg too many or that it is only one leg more? To judge life timid or thrifty is to feel an impulse in oneself to go further than it does. And where can this impulse come from, causing, as it does, men's minds to set many-headed grylluses, perfect human beings and teratomorphic emblems alongside the monstrous products of life, as so many projects to tempt it? Does it come from the fact that life might be inscribed, in the geometric sense of the term, in the curve of a poetic élan that imagination brings to consciousness, revealing it to be infinite. Or might it be that the freaks of life could be said to incite human fantasy to imitation, thereby finally giving life back that which had been borrowed from it. But there is such a distance here between the loan and the restitution that it may seem unreasonable to accept such a virtuously rationalistic explanation. Life throws up few monsters, whereas the fantastic is a whole world.

It is at this point that the thorny question of the relations between monstrosity and the monstrous arises. They are a duality of concepts with the same etymological root. They stand in the service of two forms of normative judgement, the medical and the legal, being initially confused rather than combined in religious thought, then progressively rendered abstract and secularized.

There is no doubt that classical antiquity and the Middle Ages regarded monstrosity as an effect of the monstrous. The very term 'hybrid', in appearance so positive and descriptive, attests to this in its etymology. Interspecies animals offspring are the product of crosses that violate the rule of endogamy, of unions in which similitude is not respected. Now, from hybridization to monstrosity is a simple step. The Middle Ages retain the identification of the monstrous with the felonious, but enrich it with a reference to the diabolic. The monster is both the effect of an infringement of the rule of the sexual segregation of species and the mark of a desire to pervert the table of creatures. Monstrosity is not so much a consequence of the contingency of life as of the licentiousness of the living. Why, asks Scipion du Pleix, does Africa produce more monsters than other regions? 'Because all kinds of animals, coming together by its waters to drink, mate there ordinarily without discretion of species.'[3] Monstrosity is seen to arise for want of discretion, an ambiguous term that assumes full meaning here. Monstrosity the consequence of a carnival of the Animals — after drinking!

Where human beings are concerned, even more than in the case of animals, the occurrence of monstrosity is a signature. The question of the illicit eclipses that of the irregular; responsibility eclipses causality. [...] Zoomorphic monstrosity, if its existence is admitted, has to be held to be the consequence of a deliberate attempt to infringe the order of things — which is synonymous with their perfection — the consequence of a surrender to the dizzying fascination of the undefined, of chaos, of the anti-cosmos. The linkage of teratology with demonology in the Middle Ages appears, then, as the consequence of the dualism persisting in Christian theology. There is an abundant literature on the question. We allude to it here only insofar as it enables us to understand how the monstrous, which is initially a legal concept, was progressively constituted as a category of the imagination. What we have here, in fact, is a displacement of responsibility. The theologians, judges or philosophers who were unable to accept the possibility of direct commerce between women and incubi or succubi were ready to admit that the vision of a demoniacal apparition could produce the effect of impairing the development of a human embryo.

[...]

'The necessary complement of a monster is a child's brain', said Paul Valéry, who regarded as uniformly ridiculous the role the arts allot to painted, sung or sculpted monsters and who confessed that he had never been able to do anything but laugh at the sight of the bizarre, misshapen construction that the collections of paleontological animals offer us.[4] Valéry's statement could be taken as summing up the rationalist attitude toward the monstrous in the age of positive teratology. When monstrosity has become a biological concept, when monstrosities are divided into classes according to constant relationships, when we pride ourselves that we are able to provoke them experimentally, the monster is naturalized, the irregular brought back within the rules and the prodigious becomes a matter of prediction. It then seems natural that the scientific spirit should regard as monstrous the fact that human beings were able in the past to believe in so many monstrous animals. In the age of fable, monstrosity proclaimed the monstrous power of the imagination. In the age of experiment, the monstrous is regarded as a symptom of puerility or mental illness; it betokens feeble-mindedness or a deficiency of reason.

[…]

The scientific explanation of monstrosity and the correlative reduction in the importance of the monstrous really develops in the nineteenth century. Teratology is born at the point where comparative anatomy meets an embryology reformed by the adoption of the theory of epigenesis. Johann Friedrich Meckel the Younger explains certain simple monstrosities, particularly what were then termed 'monstrosities by default', as effects of arrested development, as had been suggested by K.-F. Wolff (*De ortu monstrorum*, 1772). Étienne Geoffroy Saint-Hilaire substitutes the notion of retardation for that of arrest. Monstrosity is the fixation of the development of one organ at a stage the others have surpassed. It is the survival of a transitory embryonic form. For an organism of a given species, today's monstrosity is the day before yesterday's normal state. And in the comparative series of species, it may happen that the monstrous form of one is, for some other, the normal form. In his *Histoire des anomalies de l'organisation* (1837), Isidore Geoffroy Saint-Hilaire, the son of Étienne, completes the domestication of monstrosities – doing so definitively on certain points – by ranking them among the anomalies, by classifying them according to the rules of natural method, by applying to them a methodical nomenclature that is still in force, but, most importantly, by naturalizing the composite monster, that in which we find united the elements, complete or incomplete, of two or more organisms. Previously, the composite monster was seen as the monster of monsters, since it was compared with the norm of a single individual. But if the composite monster is referred to the norm of two or more normal individuals, this type of monstrosity is no more monstrous than that of simple monstrosity. Isidore Geoffroy Saint-Hilaire offers some pertinent thoughts on the existence of anomalies. One of his pithy sayings sums these up: 'There are no exceptions to the laws of nature, there are exceptions to the laws of naturalists.'[5] Lastly, the comparison of the concept of anomaly with that of variety is of great interest, and it will be seen to have considerable importance towards the end of the century in the context of the theories of evolution.

Teratology, which was constituted of descriptions, definitions and classifications, was certainly a natural science by that date. But in a century barely two years older than the term and concept of *biology*, any natural history tended to become an experimental science. And in the middle of the century Camille Dareste (1822–99) founded teratogeny, the experimental study of the conditions for the artifical production of monstrosities. The medieval artist made representations of imaginary monsters. The nineteenth-century scientist sought to make real monsters. Following Marcelin Berthelot's statement that chemistry created its object, Dareste proclaimed that teratogeny must create its own. He was proud to say that he had successfully produced most of the simple monstrosities in Isidore Geoffroy Saint-Hilaire's classification on the embryo of a chicken and it was his hope that he would eventually produce hereditary varieties. Encouraged by Darwin's assessment of his experiments as 'full of promise of the future',[6] Dareste pledged to employ the resources of experimentation in the elucidation of the origin of species.[7]

Monstrosity seemed at this point to have yielded up the secret of its causes and its laws: it now seemed that the anomaly was destined to provide the explanation for normal formation. Not because the normal might be regarded merely as an attenuated form of the pathological, but because the pathological is a thwarted normal, or a normal that has run off course. Take away the obstacle to development and you obtain the norm. The transparency of monstrosity to scientific thought now severed it from any relation with the monstrous.

[...]

We would be happy to show the monstrous taking refuge, from this period on, in poetry, and might enjoy following the sulphurous trail that leads from Baudelaire to the Surrealists, by way of Rimbaud and Lautréamont. But how can we resist the temptation of finding the monstrous ensconced once again at the very heart of the scientific world, from which it had supposedly been expelled, and of catching the biologist himself red-handed in the pursuit of Surrealism? Have we not heard Dareste claim for teratology the glory of creating its object? Have we not seen Isidore Geoffroy Saint-Hilaire and Dareste connect – the former timidly, the latter self-confidently – the two questions of monstrosity and the creation of races? Might not the submission of the scientific spirit to the reality of laws merely be a ruse on the part of the Will to Power?

In 1826 at Auteuil, Étienne Geoffroy Saint-Hilaire had resumed old artificial incubation experiments first tried in Egypt, imitating the techniques used in the famous 'chicken ovens'.[8] The aim of the experiments was to bring about embryonic anomalies. In 1829, drawing a lesson from this research as it related to the question posed by Lamarck's thesis on the modifications of specific animal types, Étienne Geoffroy Saint-Hilaire wrote: 'I was trying to induce organization down some unusual paths.'[9] Doubtless this decision, inasmuch as it led to operating on birds' eggs, did not have any grandiose unconscious motivation behind it. But could we say the same of Réaumur when, after having recounted at length what he termed the *amours* of a chicken and a rabbit, he expressed his disappointment that such a bizarre union had not procured for him 'fur-covered chickens or feathered rabbits'? What shall we say on the day we learn that experiments in teratogeny have been carried out on humans? From the curious to the scabrous and from the scabrous to the monstrous, there is a straight path, if not a short one. If it is part of the code of experimentation to try out *all* possibilities in order to reveal the real, there is a danger the boundary line between the experimental and the monstrous will not be perceived when first we encounter it, for the monstrous is one of the possibilities. We should very much like to mean by this only imaginary monstrousness, but we are conscious of the ambiguity. We are well aware of the distance that lies between biologists creating their object for themselves and those who manufacture human monsters to serve as fairground attractions, such as Victor Hugo described in *L'Homme qui rit*. We must wish for such a distance to be preserved, but we cannot assert that it will be.

The ignorance of the ancients meant monsters were seen as sports of nature; the knowledge of our contemporaries makes them the sport of scientists. Let us have our sport, then, manufacturing cyclopic chickens, five-legged frogs, Siamese newts, with the future prospect, as some think, of producing not just sirens or centaurs, but perhaps a wild man of the woods. If we did not know its author, the formula to 'try to induce organization down some unusual paths' might be seen as the declaration of a diabolical scheme. If that were the case, we would once again see the monstrous functioning as the underlying cause of monstrosities, but this time genuine ones. What the Middle Ages had dreamt of would be achieved by the century of positivism that believed it was sweeping medieval dreams away.

These last sentences were in the conditional for, if it is true that the monstrous is at work, in its way, in experimental teratology, it is equally certain that it does not surpass in the quality of its effects what life obtains without it. Today's teratologist is less ambitious and more measured that Étienne Geoffroy Saint-Hilaire and Dareste. In a recent lecture, Mr Étienne Wolff pointed out that the experimental teratologist confines his intervention to perturbing a process that began without him and whose elementary initial conditions are beyond his understanding. After which he allows the living matter to do what it will; he waits and sees. In short, says Mr Wolff, 'the experimenter feels that he is merely a "properties man" '.[10] His power is strictly limited, first by the fact that the plasticity of the first embryonic stages of life is of brief duration, second by the fact that monstrosities do not contravene the blueprint of the species. Not only does the biologist today create nothing new, he actually understands why he does not. He has a better grasp of the merit of the two Geoffroy Saint-Hilaires in having seen that there are types of teratological organization governed by laws of that organization. Thus, for example, all cyclopic creatures, from fishes to human beings, are similarly organized. Nature, says Wolff on another occasion, always pulls the same strings.[11] The experimenter cannot pull more strings than nature.

We have said that life throws up few monsters, whereas the fantastic is a whole world. We can now understand why life throws up relatively few monsters. It is because organisms are capable of eccentricities of structure only for a brief moment at the onset of their development. But why did we say the fantastic is a world, if it is true that a world, a cosmos, is an order? Is is because there are types – some would even say archetypes – of the fantastic? In fact, we meant that the fantastic is capable of populating a world. The power of the imagination is inexhaustible, indefatigable. How would it be otherwise? The imagination is a function without organ. It is not one of those functions that cease to function in order to recover their functional power. It is fuelled solely by its activity. As Mr Gaston Bachelard teaches, it ceaselessly distorts and refashions old images to make new ones. One sees, in this way, that the monstrous, as an imaginary entity, is prolific in its development. Scarcity on the one hand, prodigality on the other – this is the first reason for asserting the duality of monstrosity and the monstrous.

The second reason underlies the first. Life does not transgress its laws or its structural blueprints. Its accidents are not exceptions, and there is nothing monstrous in its monstrosities. 'There are no exceptions in nature', says the teratologist in the positive age of teratology. But this positivist formula, which defines a world as a systems of laws, is unaware that it is given its concrete meaning by its relation to the meaning of a contrary maxim which science excludes, but the imagination applies. That maxim gives birth to the anti-cosmos, to the chaos of exceptions without laws. This anti-world, when seen from the standpoint of those who, after having created it, frequent it, believing anything to be exceptionally possible there – forgetting, for their part, that only laws permit of exceptions – is the imaginary, turbid, vertiginous world of the monstrous.

Notes

1   Kant, *The Critique of Judgement*, part 1 section 26, Oxford: Clarendon Press, 1988, p. 100.
2   Tarde, G. (1897) *L'Opposition universelle*, Paris: Félix Alcan, p. 25.

3   *Corps de Philosophie: La Physique ou Science des choses naturelles*, book VII, chapter 22: 'On monsters', Geneva, 1636. First published in Paris, 1607.

4   Paul Valéry, (1927) 'Au sujet d'Adonis', *Variété I*, Paris: Gallimard, p. 81.

5   *Histoire des anomalies de l'organisation* (Paris, 1837), I, p. 37.

6   Charles Darwin, (1882) *The Descent of Man and Selection in Relation to Sex*, second edn, London: John Murray, p. 608.

7   Camille Dareste, (1877) *Recherches sur la production artificielle des monstruosités*, Paris, p. 44.

8   '*Fours à poulets*'. This is a reference to the artificial incubators that had apparently been in use for many centuries in Egypt when the Fourier mission 'discovered' them in 1799. Réaumur had written on the subject in 1749 [Trans.].

9   Quoted by Dareste, *Recherches*, p. 35.

10   Lecture at the Collège philosphique, Paris, 24 January 1962.

11   E. Wolff, (1948) *La Science des monstres*, Paris: Gallimard, p. 17. See also, by the same author, the chapters on monstrosity and purpose and on the experimental production of monstrosities in *Les chemins de la vie* (Paris: Hermann, 1963).

PART FIVE

Bodies in health and disease

INTRODUCTION

Health and disease are concepts that are associated with bodies in commonsense as well as in expert discourse; the literature in this field is enormous and enormously diverse. The selections included here are designed to provide a taste for the variety of concerns, topics and approaches that engage researchers; it should be stressed once again that the scope of the selection cannot claim to represent the variety of existing work exhaustively.

The first chapter, by Emily Martin, discusses how a rapidly developing scientific discourse – that of immunology – is changing the cultural understanding of human bodies in late twentieth-century America. After summarising the features that distinguish a complex system from a mechanical or a simple one, Martin examines how the model of a complex system is applied to the body and health, and what its implications are in terms of the perception and conception of selves and their agency. On the basis of ethnographic research and interviews with a wide variety of people – including social and natural scientists, medical students, health care administrators, clergy, practitioners of alternative medicine, and a hairdresser – she demonstrates how the qualities of complex systems are translated into a rich cultural imagery characterised especially by the concepts of flexibility (or the lack of rigid and clear borders), responsiveness, integration and interaction, and ultimately complexity. These features, she argues, make the prospect of responsibility and control (over health, but not only) appear extremely problematic, not least because the interrelatedness of systems blurs and relativises the boundaries of bodily identity.

Whilst Martin's chapter focuses on changing conceptions and representations of the body and their implications for notions of personal agency and responsibility in maintaining health, the following text by Douglas Crimp explores the politics of illness representation, with a focus on AIDS. The extract included here forms part of a larger essay where Crimp examines the production of AIDS imagery and the cultural means by which artistic representations of persons with AIDS (such as photographic portraits exhibited at the New York Museum of Modern Art) are differentiated from those of photo-journalism or television. Crimp argues that, despite their different cultural contexts, these representations are often remarkably similar both in terms of their visual content and of their implied message, a message that AIDS activists see as negatively affecting crucial issues of AIDS funding, legislation, and education. The notion of 'consent', through which the two genres are distinguished by art critics, can obscure the implicitly manipulative social relationships that may underlie the production of such portraits. Crimp's emphasis is thus on the fact that, as representations, portraits of people with AIDS are the product of social relations, and are themselves productive of social relations in turn. On this basis, the extract included here focuses on a particular representation – the videotape *Danny* (1987) made by Stashu Kybartas – where the conventions of media portraits of persons with AIDS are reclaimed, through various re-investments and reversals of meaning, for the community of gay men. This is made possible, Crimp argues, by the fact that in this case 'the formulation of the relationship between artist and subject [is] not ... one of empathy or identification, but ... one of explicit sexual desire'. As well as subverting the conventional meanings and expectations surrounding persons with AIDS, the videotape demonstrates the generic salience of sexuality (and sexual politics) to social relations and their outcomes.

Nancy Scheper-Hughes' report and analysis on the global traffic in human organs takes us through a different socio-theoretical terrain, where the problematic of globalisation intersects with that of bioethics. Again, the text presented here is extracted from a much longer essay that surveys the different practices and concerns surrounding the economy of organs for transplant in a variety of national contexts ranging from Brazil to South Africa, from India to the People's Republic of China. The chapter reflects on how organ transplant technology under conditions of neoliberal economic globalism is transforming 'social relations between self and other, between individual and society, and among the "three bodies" – the existential lived body–self, the social, representational body, and the body political' (Scheper-Hughes 2000: 193). Some of the issues addressed in this chapter, despite being very complex in themselves, can be identified as typical objects of bioethical discussion and deliberation. This is the case, for example, of the human rights violations implicit in the use of executed prisoners' organs, or the grounds on which the sale of particular organs should be considered acceptable or not. The anthropological scope of the inquiry, however, allows for a contextualisation and therefore a problematisation of the classic forms of bioethical deliberation, in the light of the different meaning – or even meaninglessness – that key bioethical concepts and assumptions acquire as a function of local situations and contexts. Scheper-Hughes writes, for example:

> a critical anthropologist ... must ask: 'Just what is an organ?' Is the transplant surgeon's kidney seen as a redundancy, a 'spare part', equivalent to the Indian textile worker's kidney, seen as an 'organ of last resort'? These two 'objects' are not comparable, and neither is equivalent to the kidney seen as that precious 'gift of life' anxiously sought by the desperate transplant patient. ... Are those living under conditions of social insecurity and economic abandonment on the periphery

of the new world order really the 'owners' of their bodies? This seemingly self-evident first premise of Western bioethics would not be shared by peasants and shantytown dwellers in many parts of the Third World.

(2000: 197)

The analysis further deconstructs several rhetorical elements of the discourse of organ transplantation, with a focus on the idea of organ scarcity. It also offers an interpretation of widespread organ-stealing rumours that grants such rumours relevance and value beside and beyond the question of whether or not they always correspond to fact. Gossip, rumours and urban legends, Scheper-Hughes argues, are the only resources for resistance available to the most vulnerable citizens of the world, whose bodily integrity, security and dignity is particularly threatened by the global organ economy.

The theme of bodily integrity, security and dignity is explored from a related but rather different angle in the extract included here by Arthur Frank. Frank addresses the fear of becoming a victim of medicine – the fear of institutional colonisation – experienced by people undergoing aggressive treatment for chronic or degenerative illness; the specific example here concerns cancer and chemotherapy. This fear, Frank argues, is more complex than simple fear for one's body, and the threat involved is more complex than the threat of natural or social disasters such as epidemics, earthquakes, crime or war. What makes fear of medical colonisation 'complex' is the fact that medicine is an institution ostensibly designed to help, an institution therefore that both demands and theoretically (and often practically) deserves the patient's trust. This trust is difficult to maintain when undergoing procedures that, whilst being designed to cure, also involve side-effects that are so deeply damaging as to be comparable to torture. The patient is caught in a profound existential dilemma, since 'medicine offers real hopes, and resistance to "dying on a machine" is itself resisted by wanting what that machine might offer'. This situation of fundamental uncertainty and inner conflict is what Frank describes as 'embodied paranoia'. Despite the very different problems and contexts to which Frank and Scheper-Hughes address themselves, there are important points of contact between their two texts. The theme of paranoia echoes that of organ-stealing rumours and – without forgetting the radically different predicaments of the 'citizens' involved – a similar uncertainty underlies the two themes. In both cases, developments in high-tech medicine represent an ambiguous source of hope and opportunity (assuming here the sale rather than theft of organs), whilst concretely constituting an assault of the body's integrity, whose outcome is never guaranteed. Frank's use of the terms 'colonization' and 'post-colonial' offers another point for comparison and discussion in relation to Scheper-Hughes' text.

A further permutation on the themes of uncertainty and paranoia, the last text in this section discusses 'hypochondriasis' – or 'that disease in which there is no disease' (Kleinman 1988: 194). Through a number of clinical cases, Arthur Kleinman illustrates here the features of this clinical presentation, and the discrepancy between lay and professional meanings and experiences it entails. Doubt and uncertainty in relation to the body's health are central to hypochondriasis, as is the irony that 'the hypochondriac must maintain the social fiction of not doubting his own doubt' in order to gain the attention of physicians. The text also illustrates the collusion between medical training and the 'ironic disease', in that 'a gnawing doubt that the ultimate test has not yet been employed is part of the physicians professional scepticism as a medical detective'. The tragic aspect of the irony is that, precisely through the search for the 'ultimate test', hypochondriasis can indeed concretely affect the body with sometimes serious consequences. The extract concludes with a brief discussion of how socio-cultural factors contribute to this clinical presentation.

Chapter 26

Emily Martin

COMPLEX SYSTEMS

From E. Martin (1994) 'Complex systems', in *Flexible Bodies: Tracking Immunity in American Culture – From the Days of Polio to the Age of AIDS*, Boston: Beacon Press.

[...]

ARE PEOPLE REALLY COMING to think of their bodies as complex systems embedded in other complex systems? What is a *complex* system?[1] What are the implications of applying a systems model to the body and health for our sense of our selves and our ability to change the world?

To begin answering these questions, we need an ethnographic description of how systems models work in daily life. One thing makes such a description particularly tricky: systems models are currently being used as descriptive devices throughout the physical sciences, social sciences, and humanities, perhaps because they seem to capture best the actual nature of the world in which we live at the end of the twentieth century. My task will be to describe the main features of a complex systems model while keeping open the question of the extent to which the model "fits" the world.

[...]

Let me present some of the features that characterize a complex system, setting it apart from either a simple system or a mechanical model.

Field Concept. The notion of a field underlies and makes possible the development of models of complex systems. It implies that "reality consists not of discrete objects located in space but rather of an underlying field whose interactions *produce* both objects and space. It further implies... that there is no exterior, objective viewpoint from which to observe, for one is always already within the field, caught in and constituted through the very interactions that one is trying to describe" (Hayles 1990: xi–xii).

Regulation. In the words of one of the founders of systems theory, Ludwig von Bertalanffy, we are in the midst of the Second Industrial Revolution, which involves control engineering: machines have regulatory circuits that provide them with explicit goal-directed characteristics. "It is thus easily understandable," Bertalanffy writes, "that our present generation tries to interpret an organism as a complex regulatory mechanism while the seventeenth, eighteenth, and nineteenth centuries conceived it was a clockwork or a heat engine." He continues:

> The living organism ... is a prototype of the Heraclitean *panta rhei*, maintaining itself in a continuous flow and change of components. The structures controlling the processes within the system itself are at the same time maintained and destroyed, amalgamated and regenerated, decomposed and recomposed. Modern scientific research has shown that this "dying and becoming" in an organism is taking place at an unsuspected speed. Principles guaranteeing the maintenance of a system in a continuous flow of its components, therefore, must be deeper than the widespread principle of regulation by means of feedback mechanisms. Do we know of any theoretical concepts or models which can account for this situation? ... The starting point is the concept of *open systems*.
> (Bertalanffy 1975: 119; see also Hayles 1990: 14)

[...]

Nonlinearity.   As Katherine Hayles explains this, "With linear equations, the magnitudes of cause and effect generally correspond. Small causes give rise to small effects, large causes to large effects. Linearity connotes this kind of proportionality. Equations that demonstrate it can be mapped as straight lines or planes. Nonlinear functions, by contrast connote an often startling incongruity between cause and effect, so that a small cause can give rise to a large effect" (1990: 11). This feature is closely related to the one to which I turn next.

Sensitivity to Initial Conditions.   In models of weather systems, this is often called "the butterfly effect," after the notion that a butterfly beating its wings in Brazil today could set off tornadoes in Texas tomorrow (Kellert 1993: 12; Gleick 1987: 8). In complex systems, tiny differences in input can lead to huge differences in output; in other words, complex systems are extremely sensitive to fluctuation and change.[2]

When, during our fieldwork, people described the body as a complex system, they would often rely on some of the defining features that we have identified.

[...]

What are some of the possible or likely consequences of thinking of the body as a complex system? The first consequence might be described as the paradox of feeling responsible for everything and powerless at the same time, a kind of empowered powerlessness. Imagine a person who has learned to feel at least partially responsible for her own health, who feels that personal habits like eating and exercise are things that directly affect her health and are entirely within her control. Now imaging such a person gradually coming to believe that wider and wider circles of her existence – her family relationships, community activities, work situation – are also directly related to personal health. Once the process of linking a complex system to other complex systems begins, there is no reason, logically speaking, to stop.

[...]

If you see everything about your health connected to everything that exists but also accept the possibility of managing and controlling at least some of the factors, the enormity of the "management" task, of controlling one's body and health, becomes overwhelming. Who will manage all this? Is anyone in control? These are questions that give form to anxieties expressed in many of the interviews.

[...]

A hairdresser expresses vividly how complicated it is to manage the enormous amount of information that relates to her health:

> I still think people need to have responsibility for their own health, and yet I can see that there's just so much that I don't know. You know, so much information, so much going on that I have no way of knowing, I can understand why it becomes so complicated, and it's not simple.... Cigarettes, for instances, they're saying people shouldn't smoke cigarettes. That's a good example, but, on the other hand, I don't think that cigarettes are thing big evil enemy. I think there are probably some people that should never smoke a cigarette because they have, you know, a weakness in that area. There are people that can smoke their whole lives, and it doesn't seem to affect [them]. I don't know. I don't know. I just don't think things are that black and white.
>
> (Anita Higden)

An M.D. promulgates both the view that the systems affecting health are far too complex to be controlled by anyone and the view that people are responsible for their own health, even though they may feel guilty because they cannot control it:

> So the body does have a natural life of its own, which the yogis are very clear to state. And there are ways which we can affect [it] and ways we can't. We can't stop aging, we can't stop death, we can't stop a lot of things. And so there are things we have control over and certain phases in our development that we do. ... It's a new age perspective that's been very destructive for a lot of people with sickness' cause it creates a lot of guilt around what I did or I didn't do – that's just insane. *Life is more complex than I can control it.* ...There is far more capacity to self-regulate the physiological functions of the body than people imagined thirty or forty or fifty years ago. There's really enormous control, that can be observed, much of which has been demonstrated through biofeedback. ... So there's almost a re-owning of our own capacity to know our body, to experience it, to self-regulate it, to train it.
>
> (Peter Boswell)

Another consequence of viewing the body as a complex system is brought out vividly by William Arney in this discussion about the development of the atom bomb. In Arney's view, a sense of inexorability or relentlessness is brought about in complex systems. They are impervious to being pushed in any particular direction by any particular agent. [...] A particularly chilling example of inexorability fostered by a complex systems view was expressed by Robert Oppenheimer, as he described why he and other worked to develop the atom bomb: "When you come right down to it the reason we did this job is because it was an organic necessity. If you are a scientist you cannot stop such a thing" (quoted in Arney 1991: 113). The scientific expert in this situation is like an "agent of necessity, an executive of the inevitable. There is an irresistibility to the rationality that says it is but one's job to help something realize its potential" (Arney 1991: 113). Like Oppenheimer, individuals lose a sense of agency in the face of the systemic forces that appear to be overwhelmingly and inexorably playing themselves out.

Because complex systems can be resilient in the face of change, they are closely associated with the dampening of conflict. Thus, a third consequence of systems models applied to the body is that conflict can come to seem unthinkable. Like simple systems, complex systems can handle discord (say, illness) in one part by making adjustments in another to return to a steady state of harmony (health) (Young 1985).

[…]

But the features of a complex system that make it different from a simple system can lead to a different outcome. Because control can suddenly shift from one part of the system to another, and because small initial causes can have large effects, health and harmony are by no means guaranteed. Instead, sudden, catastrophic eruption or collapse can, and indeed eventually *will*, occur.

The last consequence of seeing everything made up of systems within systems is that humans and human purposes are no longer considered preeminent, as they typically have been in Western humanistic traditions: "The systems world may be for humans, *but it may not be*. … Systems create a certain equivalence between humans and other subsystems of the global system and lead directly to the concept of substitutability among sub-systems. There is no priority of human living over any other sub-system within the global system. The sub-system of 'living human beings' is, from a systems perspective, conceptually equivalent to the 'waste management' sub-system, for example" (Arney 1991: 57–8). This leads to a certain indifference to specifically human life, which inspires Arney to term this aspect of a systems perspective its "neutrophilic" character.

A medical student thought about how he would explain the immune system to a class if high school students. Certainly without intending any callousness, he went on to illustrate vividly Arney's point about how systems thinking encourages an indifferent attitude toward distinctions among subsystems:

> I guess I'd like to use a less military kind of approach. I think that we're part of an environment. I think AIDS is an interesting disease because it … actually causes the boundaries of the human being to be blurred between self and environment. The things that can't [usually] grow in you can grow in you. … People become culture mediums. I mean, you become a substance upon which many things can grow, can grow and flourish. If you look at it from the microorganism's point of view, they can now grow and flourish in you. You become this kind of incredible rich ground upon which to multiply. I know that's disturbing from the human being's point of view.
>
> (Allan Chase)

My argument in this chapter comes to this: in the late twentieth century, complex systems models provide a pervasive way of thinking about the world, about our bodies, about our societies, and to think in these terms may have certain significant consequences. All to often, accounts of the world from a systems perspective argue, as do David Levin and George Solomon, that a systems view of the mind–body relation will "restore the body to the larger world-order" (1990: 524) and overcome the shortcomings of mechanistic views of medicine and the body. ... Arney's theoretical statements are too full of despair, and Levin and Solomon's too full of hope, adequately to capture the complicated ways in which people struggle to comprehend their bodies, in health and diseases, as complex systems.

Notes

1   Katherine Hayles has explored what she calls the "archipelago of chaos" as it emerges in science, contemporary fiction, and poststructuralism. Her task is to describe the "broader cultural conditions that authorize the new visions of chaos," to trace how influence "spreads out through a diffuse network of everyday experiences," creating "a cultural field within which certain questions or concepts become highly charged" (1990: 3, 4).

2   In *Wonderful Life* (1989), Stephen Jay Gould stresses the role of tiny accidents early in history that affected the outcome of evolution more than the relative "fitness" of different life forms.

References

Arney, W. R. (1991) *Experts in the Age of Systems*, Albuquerque: University of New Mexico Press.

Bertalanffy, L. von (1975) *Perspectives on General System Theory: Scientific Philosophical Studies*, New York: Braziller.

Gleick, J. (1987) *Chaos Making a New Science*, New York: Penguin.

Hayles, N. K. (1990) *Chaos Bound: Orderly Disorder in Contemporary Literature and Science*, Ithaca, NY: Cornell University Press.

Kellert, S. H. (1993) *In the Wake of Chaos: Unpredictable Order in Dynamical Systems*, Chicago: University of Chicago Press.

Levin, D. M. and G. F. Solomon (1990) "The discursive formation of the body in the history of medicine." *Journal of Medicine and Philosophy* 15(5): 515–37.

Young, R. M. (1985) "Darwinism 'is' social," in *The Darwinian Heritage*, D. Kohn (ed.), Princeton, NJ: Princeton University Press.

Chapter 27

Douglas Crimp

PORTRAITS OF PEOPLE WITH AIDS

From D. Crimp (1992) "Portraits of people with AIDS," in L. Grossberg, C. Nelson, and P. Treichler (eds), *Cultural Studies*, London and New York: Routledge.

[...]

WE CAN PERHAPS AGREE that images of people with AIDS created by the media and art photographers alike are demeaning, and that they are overdetermined by a number of prejudices that precede them about the majority of the people who have AIDS – about gay men, IV drug users, people of color, poor people. Not only do journalism's (and art's) images create false stereotypes of people with AIDS, they depend upon already existing false stereotypes about the groups most significantly affected by AIDS. [...] The reaction of many of us when we see homosexuality portrayed in the media is to respond by saying, "That's not true. We're not like that" or "I'm not like that" or "we're not all like that." But what *are* we like? What portrait of a gay person, or of a people with AIDS (PWAs) would we feel comfortable with? Which one would be representative? How could it be? and why should it be? One problem of opposing a stereotype [...], is that we tacitly side with those who would distance themselves from the image portrayed, we tacitly agree that it is other. [...] To say that it is unfair to represent a gay man or a PWA as a hustler is tacitly to collaborate in the media's ready condemnation of hustlers, to pretend along with the media that prostitution is a moral failing rather than a choice based on economic and other factors limiting autonomy. [...] My interest in the videotape *Danny* (1987), made by Stashu Kybartas,[1] does not derive from its creation of a counter-type, but rather from its insistence upon a particular stereotype, one which is referred to among gay men, whether endearingly or deprecatingly, as the clone.

Without, I think, setting out deliberately or programmatically to articulate a critique of media images of PWAs, *Danny* nevertheless constitutes one of the most powerful critiques that exists to date. This is in part because it duplicates, in so many of its features, the stereotypes of PWA portraiture, but at the same time reclaims the portrait for the community from which it emerges, the community of gay men, who have thus far been the population most drastically affected by AIDS in the United States. *Danny* accomplishes this through one overriding difference: the formulation of the relationship between artist and subject not as one of empathy or identification, but as one of explicit sexual desire, a desire that simultaneously accounts for Kybartas's subjective investment in the project and celebrates Danny's own sense of gay identity and hard-won sexual freedom.

A great many of the conventions of media portraits of the PWA appear in *Danny*, but their meanings are reinvested or reversed. *Danny* begins, for example, where virtually every other television portrait ends: with the information about the death of the video's subject, here matter-of-factly announced in a rolling text before we have even seen an image. Thus, although the video ends at the second recounting of Danny's death, it does not come as a coda to tell us what has happened to the subject after the tape was made. Indeed, as we discern from the apostrophizing voice-over, the tape was made as a work of mourning, the artist's working through of his loss of a friend in the AIDS movement.

[...]

The first words uttered by Danny, in his somewhat difficult-to-understand voice, are the following: "He doesn't refer to me as his son. Instead of saying, 'My son'll be up to get it,' 'The boy'll be up to get it.' Whadaya mean the boy? It makes me feel like Tarzan and the jungle. Me boy." The statement remains somewhat opaque until we come to those fragments of dialogue in which Kybartas queries Danny further about his father. When Danny talks of his decision to return to his parents' home in Steubenville, Ohio, at the moment when he learned he'd have to begin chemotherapy for his Kaposi's sarcoma, he mentions the difficulty of telling his mother, who nevertheless accepted the fact. Kybartas asks, "Were you worried about your dad?" "Yeah," says Danny, "I was wondering how he was going to take having a gay son, and one with AIDS on top of it, but she never told him. I have to watch what I say around him, or if anything about AIDS is on television, my mom flicks it off. She doesn't want him to hear about it."

We are left to imagine Danny's home life, as his father watches his son die and never bothers to ask why. Then, in the final conversation between the two friends before the tape ends, Danny says, "What I should have done this week was to have contacted the funeral home, because I would like to feel secure knowing that I could be buried there, instead of their getting the body and saying, 'No, we can't handle that body,' and my father saying, 'Why?' 'Because he has AIDS.' That's not a time that he needs to be faced with that, not after my dying." Kybartas probes, "Why are you concerned about his reaction to that?," and Danny answers, "Trying to spare his feelings, I guess." "Why?," Kybartas persists. "I guess as much as I dislike him, I don't want to hurt him either." "Why not?," Kybartas chides, and the dialogue fades out.

It is this gruesome family scene, so typical – perhaps even stereotypical – of gay men's relations with their father, that is denied in sentimental media stories of gay men going home to die in the caring fold of the family, something they often do as a last resort when medical insurance has run out or disability benefits won't cover the rent. In the mainstream media, though, this scenario tells of the abandonment of gay men by their friends in the dark and sinful cities they inhabit, and the return to comfort and normality in some small town in the Midwest. But in Kybartas's tape it is the small hometown, a steel town near Pittsburgh, that is dark and sinister, "slowly dying," as Danny puts it, whereas the metropolis to which Danny fled to find his sexual freedom is the very opposite of dark, though it may, in conventional moralizing terms, be sinful – that, of course, is its appeal.

This reversal of mainstream media pieties about hometown USA and the biological family serves to delimit the space of the sexual for gay men, for if Danny's father has not discerned that his son is gay and dying of AIDS, it is because Danny's identity as a sexual being must be disavowed. Kybartas articulates this in the tape by saying, "I wanted you to come and live with us. We'd take care of you. We could go to the gay bars in Pittsburgh, dance, and watch the go-go boys."

Danny's image as a kid who lived for sex is complicated in the video by another subtle reversal. Manistream coverage of AIDS is padded with portentous pictures of medical procedures – IV needles being inserted, doctors listening through stethoscopes, tinkering in laboratories. Parallel imagery in *Danny* refers not to Danny's disease, but to his profession as a medical technician, showing the procedure of the carotid angiogram that he performed. But just because Danny is a full human being with a respectable profession doesn't mean he's heroicized by Kybartas. Immediately following Danny's reminiscence about his job is the "Miami Vice" sequence, in which Kybartas uses footage from that program's credits as Danny talks about shooting cocaine with shared needles back in 1981, before anyone knew the transmission risks. The result is that still another media myth is interfered with: the one that makes gay men (always presumed to be white and middle class) and IV drug users (presumed to be poor people of color) separate "risk groups."

A standard media device for constructing AIDS as a morality tale uses before-and-after images of people with AIDS. [...] In 1983, ABC's 20/20 used Kenny Ramsaur to show the effects of AIDS in one of the earliest and most lurid television newsmagazine stories on the subject, narrated by none other than Geraldo Rivera. ABC's camera first shows Ramsaur's face, horribly swollen and disfigured; then snapshots of the handsome, healthy Kenny as hedonistic homosexual appear, after which we return to the live image as the camera pans down to Kenny's arm to see him pull up his sleeve to reveal his KS lesions. Kybartas reworks this ploy in *Danny*. We see snapshots of a young and healthy hedonist in Miami as Danny talks with relish of his life, of how he would spend the day on the beach, return home and let the suntan oil sink in, and then shower. After douching in the shower, he tells us, he would shave his balls and the side of his cock, put on his tight 501s, and go out and cruise. Close-ups of Danny putting in his nipple ring are intercut with a close-up of the nipple surrounded by KS lesions, taken in Kybartas's studio in Pittsburgh during Danny's illness. And when we move from a second series of early snapshots of Danny to the video images of his face, shot after he has returned to Steubenville, it is bloated from chemotherapy. He is nevertheless still fully sexualized. Kybartas, narrating over the image of the face, laments, "Danny, when I look at all these pictures of you, I can see that the chemotherapy caused your appearance to change from week to week. One day when you walked into the studio, I thought you looked like a longshoreman who had just been in a fight.[2] [pause] The only time I saw you cry was on Christmas Eve, when your doctor told you that the chemotherapy was no longer working." This movement back and forth from the tough to the tender, from desiring to grieving in relation to the whole series of images constitutes the major text of the tape, and it may be said to encompass something of the range of gay men's sexuality as well as our present condition. The thematic is most often shown in the revelation of the KS lesions, as time and again we see stop-motion footage of Danny removing his shirt, or as still images show fragments of his chest and arms covered with lesions. But, like scars or tatoos, the lesions are always seen as marking the body as sexually attractive, a sexiness that is indicated by Kybartas in the following way: "Danny, do you remember the first night we were shooting the film at my studio? You'd taken off your shirt and we were looking at all your lesions. Later, as I was rubbing your back and you were telling me about the problems you were having with relationships and sex, something happened. It was suddenly very quiet in the studio, and my heart was beating fast. I don't know what it was … the heat, your body. The only sound was the steam hissing out of the radiator …"

After seeing *Danny*, it occurred to me that there is a deeper explanation for portrayals of PWAs, and especially of gay male PWAs, as desperately ill, as either grotesquely disfigured or as having wasted to fleshless, ethereal bodies. These are not images that are intended to overcome our fear of disease and death, as is sometimes claimed. Nor are they meant only to reinforce the status of the PWA as victim or pariah, as we often charge. Rather, they are, precisely, *phobic* images, images of the terror at imagining the person with AIDS as still sexual. […] The unwillingness to show PWAs as active, as in control of their lives, as acting up and fighting back, is the fear that they might also still be sexual.

[…]

Notes

1   *Danny*, 1987, is distributed by Video Data Bank, Chicago.
2   The sexual attractiveness of the gay clone was constructed through stylistic reference to clichéd hyper-masculine professions such as the cowboy, policeman, sailor, and, indeed, the longshoreman.

Chapter 28

Nancy Scheper-Hughes

THE GLOBAL TRAFFIC IN
HUMAN ORGANS

From N. Scheper-Hughes (2000) "The global traffic in human organs." *Current Anthropology* 41(2): 191–224.

[...]

THE URGENT NEED FOR NEW international ethical standards for human transplant surgery in light of reports of abuses against the bodies of some of the most socially disadvantaged members of society brought together in Bellagio, Italy, in September 1995 a small international group of transplant surgeons, organ procurement specialists, social scientists, and human rights activists, organized by the social historian David Rothman. This group, the Bellagio Task Force on Organ Transplantation, Bodily Integrity, and the International Traffic in Organs, of which I am a member, is examining the ethical, social, and medical effects of the commericalization of human organs and accusations of human rights abuses regarding the procurement and distribution of organs to supply a growing global market.

At the top of our agenda are allegations of the use of organs from executed prisoners in China and elsewhere in Asia and South America for commercial transactions in transplant surgery; the continuing traffic in organs in India despite new laws which make the practice illegal in most regions; and the truth, if any, behind the global rumors of body stealing, child kidnapping, and body mutilations to procure organs for transplant surgery.

[...]

This essay reports on our initial forays into alien and at times hostile and dangerous territory to explore the practice of tissue and organ harvesting and organ transplantation in the morgues, laboratories, prisons, hospitals, and discreet operating theaters where bodies, body parts, and technologies are exchanged across local, regional, and national boundaries. Virtually every site of transplant surgery is in some sense part of a global network. At the same time, the social world of transplant surgery is small and personalistic; in its upper echelons it could almost be described as a face-to-face community.

[...]

Of the many field sites in which I have found myself, none compares with the world of transplant surgery for its mythical properties, its secrecy, its impunity, and its exoticism. The organs trade is extensive, lucrative, explicitly illegal in most countries, and unethical according to every governing body of medical professional life. It is therefore covert. In some sites the organs trade links the upper strata of biomedical practice to the lowest reaches of the criminal world.

[...]

The global economy and the commodification of the body

George Soros (1998a,b) has recently analyzed some of the deficiencies of the global capitalist economy, particularly the erosion of social values and social cohesion in the face of the increasing dominance of antisocial market values. The problem is that markets are by nature indiscriminate and inclined to reduce everything – including human beings, their labor, and their reproductive capacity – to the status of commodities.

[...]

Nowhere is this more dramatically illustrated than in the current markets for human organs and tissues to supply a medical business driven by supply and demand. The rapid transfer of organ transplant technologies to countries in the East (China, Taiwan, and India) and the South (especially Argentina, Chile, and Brazil) has created a global scarcity of viable organs that has initiated a movement of sick bodies in one direction and of healthy organs – transported by commercial airlines in ordinary Styrofoam picnic coolers conveniently stored in overhead luggage compartments – often in the reverse direction, creating a kind of "kula ring" of bodies and body parts.

[...]

In General, the flow of organs follows the modern routes of capital: from South to North, from Third to First World, from poor to rich, from black and brown to white, and from female to male. Religious prohibitions in one country or region can stimulate an organs market in more secular or pluralistic neighboring areas.

[...]

Cultural notions about the dignity of the body and of sovereign states pose some barriers to the global market in body parts, but these ideas have proven fragile. In the West, theological and philosophical reservations gave way rather readily to the demands of advanced medicine and biotechnology.

[...]

No modern pope (beginning with Plus XII) has raised any moral objection to the requirements of transplant surgery. The Catholic Church decided over 30 years ago that the definition of death – unlike the definition of life – should be left up to the doctors, paving the way for the acceptance of brainstem death.

While transplant surgery has become more or less routine in the industrialized West, one can recapture some of the technology's basic strangeness by observing the effects of its expansion into new social, cultural, and economic settings. Wherever transplant surgery moves it challenges customary laws and traditional local practices bearing on the body, death, and social relations. Commonsense notions of embodiment, relations of body parts to the whole, and the treatment and disposal of the dying are consequently being reinvented throughout the world. Not only stock markets have crashed on the periphery in recent years – so have long-standing religious and cultural prohibitions.

Lawrence Cohen, who has worked in rural towns in various regions of India over the past decade, notes that in a very brief period the idea of trading a kidney for a dowry has caught on and become one strategy for poor parents desperate to arrange a comfortable marriage for an "extra" daughter. A decade ago, when townspeople first heard through newspaper reports of kidney sales occurring in the cities of Bombay and Madras, they responded with understandable alarm. Today, Cohen says, some of these same people now speak matter-of-factly about *when* it might be necessary to sell a "spare" organ.

[…]

The appearance of a new biomedical technology has reinforced a traditional practice, the dowry, that had been waning. With the emergence of new sources of capital, the dowry system is expanding, along with kidney sales, into areas where it had not traditionally been practiced.

[…]

The kidney sellers, recruited by brokers who often get half the proceeds, almost all are trapped in crippling cycles of debt. The kidney trade is another link, Cohen suggests, in a system of debt peonage reinforced by neoliberal structural adjustment. Kidney sales display some of the bizarre effects of a global capitalism that seeks to turn everything into a commodity. And though fathers and brothers talk about selling kidneys to rescue dowry-less daughters or sisters, in fact most kidney sellers are women trying to rescue a husband, whether a bad one who has prejudiced the family by his drinking and unemployment or a good one who has gotten trapped in the debt cycle. Underlying it is the logic of gender reciprocity: the husband "gives" his body in often servile and/or back-breaking labor, and the wife "gives" her body in a mutually life-saving medical procedure.

But the climate of rampant commercialism has produced rumors and allegations of organ theft in hospitals similar to those frequently encountered in Brazil.

[…]

True or false – and allegations like these are slippery because hospitals refuse to open their records to journalists or anthropologists – such stories are believed by many poor people worldwide, who therefore avoid public hospitals even for the most necessary and routine operations.

[…]

Bioethical dilemmas

While members of the Bellagio Task Force agreed on the human rights violations implicit in the use of executed prisoners' organs, they found the issue of organ sales more complex.

Those opposing the idea of sales expressed concerns about social justice and equity. Would those forced by circumstance to sell a kidney be in a roughly equivalent position to obtain dialysis or transplant surgery should their remaining kidney fail at a later date? Others noted the negative effects of organ sales on family and marital relations, gender relations, and community life. Others worried about the coarsening of medical sensibilities in the casual disregard by doctors of the primary ethical mandate to do no harm to the bodies in their care, including their donor patients.

Those favoring regulated sales argued against social science paternalism and on behalf of individual rights, bodily autonomy, and the right to sell one's organs, tissues, blood, or other body products, an argument that has gained currency in some scholarly circles.

[...]

But the social scientists and human rights activists serving on the task force remain profoundly critical of bioethical arguments based on Euro-American notions of contract and individual choice. They are mindful of the social and economic contexts that make the choice to sell a kidney in an urban slum of Calcutta or in a Brazilian *favela* anything but a free and autonomous one. Consent is problematic with the executioner – whether on death row or metaphorically at the door – looking over one's shoulder. A market price on body parts – even a fair one – exploits the desperation of the poor, turning their suffering into an opportunity, as Veena Das (n.d.) so aptly puts it. And the argument for regulation is out of touch with social and medical realities in many parts of the world, especially in Second and Third World nations. The medical institutions created to monitor organ harvesting and distribution are often dysfunctional, corrupt, or compromised by the power of organ markets and the impunity of the organ brokers.

[...]

Artificial needs and invented scarcities

The demand for human organs – and for wealthy transplant patients to purchase them – is driven by the medical discourse on scarcity. Similar to the parties in the international market in child adoption (see Scheper-Hughes 1991; Raymond 1989), those looking for transplant organs – both surgeons and their patients – are often willing to set aside questions about how the "purchased commodity" was obtained. In both instances the language of "gifts," "donations," "heroic rescues," and "saving lives" masks the extent to which ethically questionable and even illegal means are used to obtain the desired object. The specter of long transplant waiting lists – often only virtual lists with little material basis in reality – has motivated physicians, hospital administrators, government officials, and various intermediaries to employ questionable tactics for procuring organs. The results are blatant commercialism alongside "compensated gifting," doctors acting as brokers, and fierce competition between public and private hospitals for patients of means. At its worst, the scramble for organs and tissues has led to gross human rights violations in intensive care units and morgues. But the idea of organ scarcity is what Ivan Illich would call an artificially created need, [...] one that can never be satisfied, for underlying it is the unprecedented possibility of extending life indefinitely with the organs of others. I refer, with no disrespect intended to those now patiently waiting for organ transplants, to the age-old denial and refusal of death that contributes to what Ivan Illich (1976) identified as the hubris of medicine and medical technology in the face of mortality.

Meanwhile, the so-called gift of life that is extended to terminal heart, lung, and liver patients is sometimes something other than the commonsense notion of a life. The survival rates of a great many transplant patients often conceal the real living-in-death – the weeks and months of extended suffering – that precedes actual death.[1] Transplant patients today are increasingly warned that they are not exchanging a death sentence for a new life but rather exchanging one mortal, chronic disease for another. "I tell all my heart transplant patients," said a South African transplant coordinator, "that after transplant they will have a condition similar to AIDS and that in all probability they will die of an opportunistic infection resulting from the artificial suppression of their immune system." While this statement is an exaggeration, most transplant surgeons I interviewed accepted its basic premise.

[...]

The idea of organ scarcity also has historical antecedents in the long-standing "shortage" of human bodies and human body parts for autopsy, medical training, and medical experimentation (see Foucault 1975; Richardson 1989, 1996). Who and what gets defined as "waste" in any given society often has bearing on the lives of the poorest in countries with a ready surplus of unidentified, unclaimed pauper bodies, as in Brazil (see Scheper-Hughes 1992, 1996a,b; Biehl 1998), South Africa (Lerer and Matzopoulos 1996), and India. In Europe during the sixteenth, seventeenth, and eighteenth centuries, the corpses of gallows prisoners were offered to barbers and surgeons to dispose of as they wished. "Criminal" bodies were required then, just as they are now, for "scientific" and medical reasons. In Brazil as in France (Laqueur 1983) during the early phases of modernity, paupers had no autonomy at death, and their bodies could be confiscated from poorhouses and workhouses and sold to medical students and to hospitals. Because the body was considered part of the estate of the dead man and could be used to cover outstanding debts, the bodies of paupers were often left unclaimed by relatives to be used for medical research and education. Indeed, medical claims to "surplus" bodies have a long history. To this day many rural people in Northeast Brazil fear medicine and the state, imagining that almost anything can be done to them either before or at the hour of their deaths. Those fears – once specific to the rural and shantytown poor – have spread today to working class Brazilians, who are united in their opposition to Brazil's universal donation law, fearing that it will be used against them to serve the needs of more affluent citizens. Such fears, we have learned, are not entirely groundless.

[...]

Bio-piracy: the State and its subcitizens

It is important to note the timing and the geopolitical mapping of these organ-theft rumors. While blood-stealing (see Dundes 1991) and body-snatching rumors have appeared in various historical periods, the current generation of rumors arose and spread in the 1980s within specific political contexts. They followed the recent history of military regimes, police states, civil wars, and "dirty wars" in which abductions, disappearances, mutilations, and deaths in detention and under strange circumstances were commonplace. During the military regimes of the 1970s and 1980s in Brazil, Argentina, and Chile, the state launched a series of violent attacks on certain classes of "subcitizens" – subversives, Jewish intellectuals, journalists, university students, labor leaders, and writers and other social critics – whose bodies, in addition to being subjected to the usual tortures, were mined for their reproductive capacities and sometimes even for their organs to serve the needs of "supercitizens," especially elite military families.

[...]

Similar allegations of body tampering and organ theft against doctors working in hospitals and morgues in South Africa during the late apartheid years surfaced during the hearings of the South African Truth and Reconciliation Commission.

[...]

The body- and organ-stealing rumors of the 1980s and 1990s were at the very least metaphorically true, operating by means of symbolic substitutions. They spoke to the onto-logical insecurity of poor people to whom almost anything could be done, reflecting every-day threats to bodily security, urban violence, police terror, social anarchy, theft, loss and fragmentation. Recently, new variants of the organ-stealing rumor, originating in the impov-erished periphery of the global economic order, have migrated to the industrialized North, where they circulate among affluent people through e-mail chain letters despite the efforts of an organized U.S. government disinformation campaign to kill them (see USIA 1994).

[...]

The transplant community's narrative concerning the absurdity of the organ-stealing rumors offers a remarkably resilient defense against having to respond seriously to allegations of medical abuses in organ harvesting.

For example, a transplantation website (TransWeb) posts the "Top Ten Myths About Donation and Transplantation" with authoritative refutations of each. The "myth" that "rich and famous people get moved to the top of the waiting list while regular people have to wait a long time for a transplant" is refuted with the following blanket statement: "The organ allocation system is blind to wealth or social status." But our preliminary research indicates that this, like some other transplant myths, has some basis in contemporary transplant practices.

[...]

Even the most preposterous of the organ-stealing rumors, which the TransWeb authors say has never been documented anywhere – "I heard about this guy who woke up the next morning in a bathtub full of ice. His kidneys were stolen for sale on the black market" – finds some basis in lawsuits and criminal proceedings, some still unresolved or pending.

Conclusion

Under what social conditions can organ harvesting and distribution for transplant surgery be fair, equitable, just, and ethical? Organ transplantation depends on a social contract and social trust, the grounds for which must be explicit. Minimally, this requires national laws and international guidelines outlining and protecting the rights of organ donors, living and dead, as well as organ recipients. Additionally, organ transplantation requires a reasonably fair and equitable health care system.

It also requires a reasonably democratic state in which basic human rights are guaranteed. Organ transplantation, even in elite medical centers by the most conscientious of physicians, that occurs in the context of an authoritarian or police state can lead to gross abuses. Similarly, where vestiges of debt peonage persist and where class, race, and caste ideologies cause certain kinds of bodies — whether women, common criminals, paupers, or street children — to be treated as "waste," these sentiments will corrupt medical practices concerning brain death, organ harvesting, and distribution.

Under conditions such as these the most vulnerable citizens will fight back with the only resources they have — gossip, rumors, urban legends, and resistance to modern laws. In this way, they act and react to the state of emergency that exists for them in this time of economic and democratic readjustments. They express their consciousness of social exclusions and articulate their own ethical and political categories in the face of the "consuming" demands which value their bodies most when they can be claimed by the state as repositories of spare parts. While for transplant specialists an organ is just a "thing," a commodity better used than wasted, to a great many people an organ is something else — a lively, animate, and spiritualized part of the self which most would still like to take with them when they die.

Note

1   The suffering of transplant patients caused by the blend of clinical and "experimental" liver transplant procedures has led one noted bioethicist (M. Rorty, personal communication) to stipulate an exception in *her* own living will: All "usable" organs – *minus her liver* – are to be donated to medical science. Likewise, Das (n.d.) refers to "the tension between the therapeutic and the experimental" in liver transplant surgeries performed in parts of India.

References

Biehl, João (1998) "A morte de sonhadora: Iluminismo, A. Guerra Mucker e o campo do inconsciente no sul do brasil, século XIX," in *Psicanálise e colonização*. Edited by Edson Souza. Porto Alegre: Artes e Ofícios.

Das, Veena (n.d.) "The practice of organ transplants: Networks, documents, translations," in *Cultures of Biomedicine*, Margaret Lock *et al.* (ed.), Cambridge: Cambridge University Press. In press.

Dundes, Alan (ed.) (1991) *The Blood Libel Legend*, Madison: University of Wisconsin Press.

Foucault, Michel (1975) *The Birth of the Clinic*, New York: Vintage Books.

Illich, Ivan (1976) *Medical Nemesis*, New York: Pantheon.

Laqueur, Thomas (1983) "Bodies, death, and pauper funerals," *Representations* 191, pp. 109–31.

Lerer, Leonard and Richard Matzopoulos (1996) *A Profile of Violence and Injury: Mortality in the Cape Town Métropole*, Tygerberg: South African Medical Research Council.

Raymond, Janice (1989) "Children for organ export?" *Reproductive and Genetic Engineering* 2, pp. 237–45.

Richardson, Ruth (1989) *Death, Dissection, and the Destitute*, London: Penguin.

—— (1996) "Fearful symmetry: Corpses for anatomy, organs for transplantation," in *Organ Transplantation: Meanings and Realities*, Stuart Younger, Renée Fox, and Laurence O'Connell (eds), Madison: University of Wisconsin Press, pp. 66–100.

Scheper-Hughes, Nancy (1991) "Theft of life," *Transaction: Society* 27(6), pp: 57–62.

—— (1992) *Death Without Weeping: The Violence of Everyday Life in Brazil*, Berkeley: University of California Press.

—— (1996a) "Theft of life: Globalization of organ-stealing rumors," *Anthropology Today* 12(3): pp. 3–11.

—— (1996b) "Small wars and invisible genocides," *Social Science and Medicine* 43, pp. 889–900.

Soros, George (1998a) "Toward a global open society," *Atlantic Monthly*, pp. 20–32.

—— (1998b) *The Crisis of Global Capitalism: Open Society Endangered*, New York: Public Affairs.

USIA (1994) "The child organ trafficking rumor: A modern urban legend," Report submitted to the UN Special Rapporteur on the Sale of Children.

Chapter 29

Arthur Frank

THE SELF UNMADE
Embodied paranoia

From A. Frank (1995) "The self unmade: embodied paranoia," extract from *The Wounded Storyteller: Body, Illness, and Ethics*, Chicago/London: University of Chicago Press.

ILLNESS HAS ALWAYS THREATENED the intactness of mind and body, but in postmodern times this threat takes the particular form I have called *embodied paranoia*.[1] The clearest epigram for embodied paranoia is the phrase heard often at public symposia on euthanasia: "I don't want to die on a machine." In post-modern times people fear for their bodies not only from natural threats such as storms or disease and from social threats such as crime or war. People are also threatened by institutions ostensibly designed to help them.

Becoming a victim of medicine is a recurring theme in illness stories. The incompetence of individual physicians is sometimes an issue, but more often physicians are understood as fronting a bureaucratic administrative system that colonizes the body by making it into its "case." People feel victimized when decisions about them are made by strangers.[2] The sick role is no longer understood as a release from normal obligations; instead it becomes a vulnerability to extended institutional colonization.

I use the term embodied *paranoia* to suggest the internal conflicts that attend this fear of colonization; what is involved is more complex than simple fear for one's body. Even war and crime are "natural" threats in the sense that they are intended to harm and fear of them is natural. Fearing institutions that are designed to help is not natural. This fear is *reflectively* paranoid in its self-doubt about whether it ought to be afraid or has a right to be afraid. The inner conflicts of this reflective paranoia are evident in the troubling analogy between torture and medical treatment.

Some of my deepest, even haunted, discussions with other members of the remission society have been attempts to sort out whether chemotherapy is a form of torture. We know that in most "objective" respects the two situations differ, and we seek only to make sense of our own memories and fears, not to appropriate the far greater suffering of torture victims. But chemotherapy fits with disturbing ease into Elaine Scarry's definition of torture as "unmaking the world."[3] The realization that obsessed me during chemotherapy was how easily every strength I thought I had could be reduced to weakness. I was unmade as my mind sought to hold onto the promise that this treatment was curing me, while my body deteriorated: my intactness, my integrity as a body-self, disintegrated.

"I never thought of myself as ill with cancer," says Marcia in her story. "I was never sick before or after the mastectomy. ... Not true of chemo; chemo was hell. Chemo was not therapeutic; it produced illness. I hated it. I cried every time I had it and did not trust it at all. I felt so vulnerable."[4] The voice heard here is someone undergoing a kind of torture. In chemotherapy, Marcia's body becomes what Scarry calls "the agent of [her] agony."[5] Her body is, in the treatment, "made to be the enemy." Physicians believe chemotherapy will cure Marcia; she does not. As Scarry writes of torture, "the body belongs to a person other than the person whose body is used to confirm [the belief]." Yet people in chemotherapy also believe that they are being *cared* for. Or they believe they ought to believe this, or they have given up believing but still confront others who insist that their treatment is care. The self is unmade in the opposition of the mind's message of care and the body's message of pain.

Chemotherapy is hardly the only occasion for comparing medical treatment to torture. Intensive care residents observed by Zussman describe their work as torture and feel tortured themselves by what they believe their work requires.[6] Zussman, Klass, and Quill all report the "cheechee" story as standard medical black humor that illustrates physicians' attempts to neutralize the grim realities of their work.[7] The point of the "joke" is to make its telling as grotesque as possible; without those flourishes, the basic plot describes two or more explorers captured by savages. The first explorer is offered a choice of death or cheechee. Not knowing what the latter means, he chooses it and is horribly tortured to death. The second explorer is given the same choice and chooses death. The chief is puzzled at his decision. "All right," he says, "but first, a little cheechee."

Surrendering one's body to the medical world of "limited liability" is frightening: cheechee does happen. The fear of cheechee is complicated, and conflicted, because the high-tech medical world remains the perpetual source of the hope that keeps restitution stories going.[8] Marcia lives to tell her story, although even years later she does not give much credit to chemotherapy. High-tech medicine offers real hopes, and resistance to "dying on a machine" is itself resisted by wanting what that machine might offer.

[...]

Embodied paranoia is not knowing what to fear most, and then feeling guilty about this very uncertainty. The patient knows full well that most of those inflicting the torture are sincerely trying to help; thus he cannot hate them, but neither can he offer them the gratitude that the intensity of their efforts seems to demand. Max Lerner reports being mildly reprimanded by his student-physician son for his ambivalent gratitude toward the physicians who administered his chemotherapy. Lerner takes the point but retains his ambivalence: "I wish however that those who came up with Adriamycin and Cytoxan for my advanced large-cell lymphoma might have hit upon a less bruising mixture," he writes.[9]

The other source of Lerner's ambivalence is that, in chemotherapy, medicine appropriates his healing to itself. Lerner's healing is *his* story, and he wants it back: "We don't know how much of the healing was due to the chemical, how much ... to the patient who was fighting not only the tumor but, to a degree, the doctors and even the chemotherapies addressed to the tumors." Lerner's embodied paranoia is not fear of medicine, yet his reflection on his need to fight his doctors shows a profound resistance.

[...]

Disease and treatment happen to a body-self that is already substantially unmade by a combination of embodied paranoia and post-colonial skepticism. [...] Postmodern times place the embodied self in a *perpetual* condition of multiply threatened intactness. Disease is all too effective as a journalistic metaphor for social problems – crime, poverty, drug use, inflation – because disease metaphors tap the intuitive connection between internal threats to the body and external threats. Embodied paranoia reflects a blurring of internal and external: everything has potential to threaten.

When illness happens, the disease carries a metonymic overload that compounds suffering. The disease is fully real in itself; the tip of the iceberg is still real ice. *And* the disease is a part standing for a larger whole, the external threats. Some of these threats, like fear of "cheechee," are related to the disease, while other fears of being made a victim have no necessary relation but are summoned up nonetheless. The losses brought by the disease open up extensive fears that one's intactness has always been more imaginary than the self has wanted to believe.

Notes

1 Frank, Arthur W. (1992) "Cyberpunk bodies and postmodern times," *Studies in Symbolic Interaction* 13, pp. 39–50.

2 Providers confirm the legitimacy of this paranoia; see Dubler, N. and Nimmons, D. (1992) *Ethics on Call*, New York: Harmony Books.

3 Scarry, E. (1985) *The Body in Pain: The Making and Unmaking of the World*, Oxford and New York: Oxford University Press. In particular my discussions with Susan DiGiacomo have shaped my thoughts about torture. I consider the analogy in an earlier article, "The rhetoric of self-change: illness experience as narrative," The Sociological Quarterly 34, no. 1 (1993): pp. 39–52.

4 Kahane, D. H. (1990) *No Less a Woman*, New York: Simon & Schuster, p. 122.

5 Scarry, E. (1985) *The Body in Pain*, p. 47.

6 Zussman, R. (1992) *Intensive Care: Medical Ethics and the Medical Profession*, Chicago: University of Chicago Press, pp.109–15.

7 Ibid., III; Klass, Perri (1988) *A Not Entirely Benign Procedure*, New York: Signet, pp. 240–1; Quill, T. E. (1993) *Death and Dignity: Making Choices and Taking Charge*, New York: W. W. Norton, pp. 57–80.

8 At the end of support group meetings when all sorts of resentments against medicine have been expressed, organizers have told me that their largest attendance turns out to hear physicians who might promise some new treatment.

9 Lerner, M. (1990) *Wrestling with the Angel*, New York: Norton, p. 56.

Chapter 30

Arthur Kleinman

HYPOCHONDRIASIS
The ironic disease

From Geertz, C. (1986) "Making experiences, authorizing selves," in V. W. Turner and E. M. Brunes (eds), *The Anthropology of Experience*, Urbana: University of *Illinois* Press.

> It is the copying that originates.
> (Clifford Geertz 1986, p. 380)

[…]

HYPOCHONDRIASIS CREATES A REVERSAL of the archetypal medical relationship in which the patient complains of illness and the physician diagnoses disease. Rather, in hypochondriasis the patient complains of disease ("I fear that I have cancer of the throat"; "I'm convinced I'm dying of heart disease"; "I know, I just know I've got an autoimmune disease"), and the doctor can confirm only illness.

The patient, in the classic textbook description of hypochondriasis, is not supposed to doubt his fear of having a disease in which his doctors do not believe. But in reality, few hypochondriacal patients are psychotic in this way.[1] Thus, they have some degree of insight into the gap between what they believe to be wrong and what the practitioner believes is not wrong; the hypochondriac's persistent fear is based not on the certainty of a delusion but on the profound uncertainty of persistent doubt. He can't convince himself or be convinced by the physician that disease is *not* present. This is why hypochondriasis leads to so many futile tests of biological functioning: the hypochondriac knows that no test in complete or precise enough in its ability to define disease at it earliest, most minimal stage and thus to offer absolute certainty that he is free of disease. It is ironic that hypochondriacs, faced with medical disbelief, are forced to act as if they lacked irony.[2] The sufferer of hypochondriasis may be an extremely humorous person in his day-to-day world, but in the physician's office he is stolid, self-righteous, and unable to laugh at himself. If he acted with an ironic smile in the medical encounter, he could not portray his problem as a serious one. Rather, both he and the practitioner would dissolve in laughter over the patent absurdity of their conflict. Thus, the hypochondriac must maintain the social fiction of not doubting his own doubt, when perhaps the most disturbing part of the experience of hypochondriasis is the patient's intractable doubt that his belief is correct. Of course, there are certain patients with this condition who do seem genuinely to lack a sense of irony about their complaints – who, as it were, take the body overly seriously, humorlessly, and with dread.

The patient often claims that his illness behavior is unique, which is why he feels it fails to fit into established biomedical categories, but in fact it is all too apparent to the clinician that the hypochondriacal behavior is a remarkable copy of the language and experience of every other patient with the problem he has seen. The patient's intuition that the illness is unique and the doctor's counter-intuition that the disease is a copy of textbook examples is a conflict not limited to hypochondriasis: many doctor–patient relationships in the care of the chronically ill reproduce this central tension. The contradiction creates predictable problems in communication within the therapeutic relationship. In fact, the perceptions of both patients and practitioners are correct. The conflict arises because they are talking about two distinctive modes of experiencing reality. Patient's behavior superficially replicates what they share with others who harbor the same pathology. However, patients' behavior also expresses the distinctive meanings in their lives that come to shape the experience of illness as most decidedly theirs and not someone else's. The essence of effective care for the chronically ill is reintegration of what is unique and what is a copy into holistic care.[3]

The treatment of hypochondriasis includes persuading patients that instead of having the disease they fear they have, they are suffering from a psychiatric disorder.[4] Hypochondriasis can be an edifying irony for the practitioner. He knows that it is not, as the official (DSM-III) diagnostic criteria of the American Psychiatric Association claim it to be, a disease entity. Rather, it is a symptom found in a wide assortment of psychiatric conditions, running from schizophrenia and depression to anxiety and personality disorders. The biomedical practitioner also knows that he contributes to the problem, inasmuch as he has been trained to act as if he can never be entirely sure there isn't a hidden biological lesion responsible for the patient's symptoms. A gnawing doubt that the ultimate test has not yet been employed is part of the physician's professional skepticism as a medical detective. Hence, the hypochondriac's doubt has an exact complement in that of the practitioner, who knows at heart that, in spite of trying to convince the hypochondriac to the contrary, he can never be completely certain himself that the patient doesn't have a disease. Clinical work is a matter of probabilities, as is biology, unlike physics (Mayr 1982). The physician is never 100 percent sure. Usually 90 or 95 percent is good enough, but there is always room for doubt. The hypochondriacal patient elicits the physician's doubt and makes him decidedly uncomfortable. Perhaps this is one of the reasons why physicians often find such patients irksome.

The following cases exemplify my points. The case descriptions include only those aspects of the four patients' lives that demonstrate what is ironic in illness meanings.

The hidden disorder

Arnie Springer is a thirty-eight-year-old unmarried systems analyst for a small computer company. For fourteen months Arnie has been visiting physicians because of fear that he has cancer of the bowel. During that period, he has consulted his primary care physician more than twenty times. That physician eventually referred Arnie to a gastroenterologist who performed upper and lower gastrointestinal X-ray studies, along with gastroscopy, sigmoidoscopy, and enteroscopy (that is, direct visualization with fiber-optic scopes of the entire large bowel, rectum, and stomach). On his own, Arnie Springer has visited two other gastroenterologists who have repeated these examinations and given him a CT-scan (computerized axial tomography, an even more precise type of X-ray examination) of the gastrointestinal tract. Arnie was referred to me by a surgeon whom he had consulted to discuss whether laparotomy (surgical exploration of the abdomen) might detect a cancerous growth.

Arnie Springer and his primary care physician have reached an impasse.

> He is basically a nice guy, and I'm sure he is a competent doctor – at least I think he is – but he just won't believe me that I could have an intestinal cancer. There is after all a lot of the small intestine that isn't well visualized by endoscopic or X-ray techniques. How can he be sure I don't have cancer? Not when you take the different layers of the bowel into account, and if the tumor were a real small one. Well, tell me, short of taking out the entire intestine and examining it under the microscope – actually an electron microscope might be necessary if we were to discover a tumor in its earliest phase – well short of that, how can he or you or the other doctors be sure, I mean 100 percent certain, I don't have cancer?

When his physicians challenge Arnie's approach to disease and talk about probabilities, they may be on firm scientific footing, but as far as Arnie is concerned they have lost their case.

> You see, supposing it is 99.9 percent sure that a certain test can disprove cancer, there would still be that tiny bit of uncertainty, wouldn't there? Just that little bit, and that would be all it would take to have the disease. And, of course, there is no test anywhere as accurate as that as far as the intestine in concerned.

Arnie is also well prepared for the other medical ploy, the one that suggests the problem is a question not of cancer but of anxiety. He made that clear to me at our first meeting.

> I know you are a psychiatrist, Dr. Kleinman. But, you see, my problem is not psychiatric but medical. I have lots of gastrointestinal symptoms, and I'm worried I may have cancer, cancer of the intestine. The studies have been normal, so far that is. Anyway, my, I mean the last doctor I saw, Dr. Lewis, a surgeon, recommended I see a psychiatrist, because he – like my regular physician and the other specialists I have visited – thinks my concern is, well, unreasonable. I mean they feel I am obsessed by this fear that I may have cancer. Now that's the problem. I know I'm anxious about this, but wouldn't you be if you felt like I do that there was the possibility of a cancer – potentially treatable if caught early – but you couldn't convince your doctors?

Arnie Springer does not have a delusion about intestinal cancer.

> I'm not entirely sure it's there. In fact, often I think it can't be there with all these negative tests. But then I began to get my doubts. The more you go into

this thing, the more doubts you have. I'm a Ph.D. in applied physics and a systems analyst. Now when I read the medical literature on the detection of cancer, I'm appalled, I mean really appalled. There are so many possibilities for false negatives [tests that give a misleadingly normal result by failing to detect existing pathology]. The science is really not all that good. And this probability thing is, well, for a physicist, deeply problematic. I mean, in physics we work with laws. Biomedicine doesn't have any real laws. Now probability is good enough if you're estimating the frequency of a problem, its prevalence in a group, perhaps. But probability is really unacceptable, at least to me it is, when you want absolute confidence about an individual, i.e., me.

Indeed, Arnie Springer occasionally can laugh at his intense preoccupation with intestinal cancer.

It really is absurd. What the hell am I doing challenging the expert's diagnoses and worrying so much about what everyone else feels is a figment of my imagination? I mean, it's laughable, it really is. Or it would be if I weren't spending so much time and money, my own money, on this thing.

I know it's an obsession. I really do doubt my own worry. I can look on at what I'm doing and think to myself, "This guy is mad." But the symptoms are real enough, though probably nonspecific. And the worry is there; I can't get rid of it. Sometimes – I can tell you this but could never tell my doctors or they would throw me out of the office – I am amazed at how upset I get and how seriously they take my worry. Other times I feel like I have to convince them or they won't believe me. What an absurd position to be in. I doubt them when they tell me, "There is nothing to worry about, you are OK," and I doubt them when they tell me there may be something the matter and they need to do more tests. After all, the exposure to X-rays is dangerous; even the scopes can perforate your colon. After I get through convincing them to do something, then I worry that I may be creating problems by what I convince them to do. I really know there is a good reason I'm here talking to you.

Arnie Springer has been hypochondriacal for a long time. Ten years ago persistent headaches led him to believe he had a brain tumor. After three years he came to accept his physician's diagnosis of chronic tension headaches. After that, he developed a fear that he had skin cancer. Inasmuch as he has many nevae (moles), Arnie went through repeated skin biopsies to rule out melanoma – all of them were normal – and even consulted a plastic surgeon about the possibility of extensive skin grafting. He recalls being fearful even as a child that he might be suffering a "hidden disorder."

That's the thing, Dr. Kleinman, the feeling I have is that this thing is hidden and we have got to find it. It's lurking there in the dark. It's a scary feeling, kind of like when you were a kid and afraid of the dark at the top of the stairs. I'm a systems analyst, you know, and I am always trying to organize things, make them better ordered. I guess you could say I don't like disorder, not even professionally.

The metaphor of the hidden disorder is pervasive in his complaints. "I feel a vague, cramping, queasy sensation, like pressure in my small intestine, you know the part of the bowel that's hidden, can't be seen too well by the GI [gastrointestinal] specialist, that part could have a hidden growth, a cancer." And almost always it is associated with the idea of cancer as a hidden killer.

> You see, if we don't find it – I mean, if it stays hidden, then grows and metastasizes – silently, you know – it could kill you, I mean me. … You see, Dr. Kleinman, I can't accept that in a world as scientifically sophisticated as ours we can't be sure there isn't a hidden killer. With all the technology we've got, I want to know, and I want control over this possibility.

The utterly serious worrier

Wolf Segal is a forty-one-year-old unemployed businessman with a strong conviction that he has a a serious heart disease. He has visited emergency rooms of local hospitals more than ten times in the past eighteen months. Each time he complains of chest pain, numbness in his hands, shortness of breath, rapid breathing, and palpitations. He feels as if he is going to die.[5]

"They think I'm a nut, I'm sure they do. I can sense they are laughing behind my back, but I'm utterly serious about his problem. Each time I feel I am dying."

Wolf Segal is worried about many things. He worries about finding a job at a level suitable for his skills. He also worries about the pressure he has put on his wife, a bank officer, to support them both. He worries about his parents, who are getting old; his investments, which have not been doing well recently; and his tennis game, which has never done well. But most of all, Wolf ("Just call me Wolf; I'm actually just a sheep in wolf's clothing, but call me Wolf") worries about his body: "It's deteriorating. Age is part of it; not enough exercise. I like eating too much. Cholesterol: that's what gave my father his heart problem, and mine is the upper limit of normal." Wolf used to worry about hyperventilation – a long-term problem – asthma (he doesn't have it, but his grandfather did and his brother does), and diabetes ("It runs on my mother's side of the family"). He even worries about anxiety: "I'm an utterly serious worrier, the original worrier. Until you see me, you don't know what worrying is about." But for eighteen months his chief worry has been his heart: "They tell me I'm normal, completely normal. What nonsense! If I were normal, would I have the chest pain, the palpitations, or the numbness in my hands? They think I'm normal. Me! I know I'm not."

Wolf has been going to the same internist for almost ten years. He is the same physician who treats Wolf's father and mother.

> Now Harry, that's my doc, he has a problem with me. He says that I am too serious about this heart condition. That I should relax, not worry so much, step away from it and it would go away. "Wolfy" (he's known me a long time), he says, "don't worry about it. There's no problem with your heart. It's with your nerves. Relax. Take your wife out to dinner. Have a good time." You'd think he didn't know me. When I have a problem, I worry. This is a problem, so I'm worried. Is he tellin' me this isn't a problem?

It is an odd experience speaking to Wolf Segal. You begin to think you are about to break out in laughter. It's as if he were a caricature of a hypochondriac, an ethnic one, to boot. But you realize after a while that Wolf, at least while he is in the office, is utterly serious.[6] He has no sense of humor about his fear of disease. About other things Wolf has, to say the least, a mischievous twinkle in his eye. He likes repartee, and he spices his remarks with a jaundiced earthiness that is endearing. But with respect to his symptoms he is an enormous bore. He goes on and on, often repeating himself several times, totally preoccupied.

I suggested to Wolf Segal that his problem was psychophysiological, a mixture of hyper-ventilation and panic and their physiological concomitants, and I suggested that treatment of his anxiety disorder and the personality characteristics that contributed to it could reduce the intensity of or actually remove his hypochondriasis. He acted as if he were stunned:

> Doc, you mean I've seen you three times and *you* think there is nothing to worry about, too? The worrying is a personality problem or an anxiety disorder? I grant you I'm a worrier, anxiety neurotic if you like, but a hypochondriac? Me? Wolf Segal, who would give his right arm to be rid of these attacks of pain? A stoic, not a hypochondriac! If it sounds to you like amplification – is that the word you used? – I can assure you that's not what if feels like. I'm worried about a real problem in my body. Psychological problems I've got no time for. I wouldn't bother to worry about them. Maybe I emphasize the symptoms here so that you will know what it is like, what I am going through – torture. That's what it feels like. Not many people could stand what I go through. The heart, it's the problem. The other worries, they are something else. Put them aside, I've come to you with the real problem, my heart disease, and you treat me like Harry does. You don't believe. That hurts. Let me tell you about the symptoms I had after lunch today – and I didn't go to the emergency room, either. ...

The single-minded interpreter

Gladys "Di" Isfahandiarian is a forty-nine-year-old unmarried Armenian-American interpreter for a large international organization in Washington, D.C. She was born in the Soviet Union and is fluent in seven languages: Armenian, English, Turkish, Persian, French Italian, and Russian. She gives a history of more than fifteen years of chest discomfort: pres-sure, tenderness, dull and sharp pains, but mostly a feeling of "discomfort" – a term she expresses in all seven of her languages. "The terms are more or less similar – a vague, unset-tling, apprehensive feeling in my chest, around the heart, it seems." For most of the fifteen years she has experienced these symptoms, Di has visited doctors for what she fears is heart and lung disease.

> Probably it is both. It runs it the Isfahandiarian family. I am also a smoker, so there it is. ... It is astonishing, almost unbelievable, but in all those years not one of the doctors could find anything wrong. I have undergone very many tests. Sometimes one shows a small abnormality, but in the end nothing. It is a terrible experience to go through all these years of illness and be left with, what? How shall I say it? Stripped of your identity. In limbo, you might say. I am neither well nor ill. My illness has no name. Oh! I have been told it is "stress-related," "psychosomatic,"

"hypochondriacal" – in other words, in my imagination. That is nonsense! If it were in my mind, would I feel it in my chest? Ridiculous! So why am I visiting a psychiatrist, and not the first either? To see if "psychological factors play a role and can be treated," says Dr. Tahardi. Well, what better way can I spend my time but speaking to a psychiatrist? Excuse the irritability, but much as I am delighted to meet you, and for certain will learn from speaking to a professor, my problem is in my chest, not my mind.

Di is a charming, cosmopolitan, well-traveled professional woman. But she begins or ends each of her well-turned statements about herself with either a description of her symptoms or a review of her fears of the consequences of her condition.

Probably I will die. They will say I lived too soon for medical science to define the nature of the pathology. "Isfahandiarian disease" they will call it perhaps, inasmuch as I seem to be an original. But that is only too foolish. My family is filled with people with the same problem. And they tell me in the old country this is a common problem. If I don't die from it – and there is no evidence I am that sick – I will be incapacitated. Already it takes up so much of my time, interfering with all sorts of activities. Even my interpreting is hampered.

Don't tell me about stress, doctor. And please don't speak about depression and anxiety. These are not the problems, I can assure you. The problem is here, right here, in the center of my chest – the heart and lungs are injured. Why do you need to know about my personal history? What possible relationship could it have to heart and lung disease?

I am thinking of willing my body to science. Perhaps only then will it be determined what is wrong with the cells, the tissue. But what tragedy! For when they discover the disease, I will be dead. Too late for me.

During the course of our several meetings, I found it extremely difficult to turn the conversation toward Di's feelings or personal life. I did learn eventually that her "heart and lung disease" is worsened by her tempestuous relationship with her long-term boyfriend, Nikki Kashli, who seems always on the point of marrying her, only to break off and beg for more time to "think about it."

What could he be thinking about? For eight years? Yes, yes. Nikki could be a reason my disease is worse. You are right. Look at what he is doing to my heart, and the lungs as well. He is a scoundrel! In *The Magic Mountain* one of Thomas Mann's characters says that passion is disease, or something like that. But I don't believe it is the cause, only one of many reasons my disease worsens.

In the last of our three meetings, Di complimented me: "I am pleased to see that you now ask me how my disease makes me feel? So you know now that you are dealing with a person with real disease. You must write this to my doctors. You can help me convince them that I am heart and lung patient!" In that same session, Di told me:

You are trying to interpret my illness one way, and me another. I feel there is a problem in translation, and here I am, the expert. I am talking about physical sensations – discomfort, pressure, a vague feeling of, of discomfort – you are talking of metaphors and double entendres. This is not a semantic disease; it is a disease in my body. Can the mind be in the body? I don't believe it. But then again, passion is in the heart we say, and if passion is a physical state, perhaps it worsens the disease already there. You are making me confused. The problem is simpler than you think. It is a heart and lung disorder.

The memorializer of death

Phillips Bingman is a fifty-year-old professor of the humanities in a large West Coast university. He is a tall, extremely thin man with close-cropped gray hair, wire-rim glasses, and prominent black eyebrows; his large face is made to look even larger by the thin bowties he wears. For the six years following the death of his wife from leukemia, Professor Bingman has been, in his own words, "obsessed with the radical realization that I am dying." He believes that his disorder is

an imbalance, a fundamental imbalance in hormonal secretions. That is the problem. I have had thyroid disease for many years. Only one of the doctors I have visited could detect it. It seems to be transient, and extremely mild. For all I know it could be just an acceleration of the aging process. But my energy is running down. It can feel the life force petering out.[7]

Professor Bingman is the first to add, however: "The disease is not what bothers me. We all must die. And I feel myself confronting death. I know I am moving inexorably toward the grave. Every day I think of death, and it is a terrible burden. A cold hand has hold of me and won't let go. I feel death in my skin and in my bones." Phillips Bingman does not meet the criteria for depression or any other psychiatric disorder. But somehow hypochondriasis as fear of disease does not capture his turn concern, which is less about the disease he believes he has than about death.

I am a memorializer of death. Like the Chinese literati of ancient times who wrote memorials to the emperor on various problems affecting the Confucian state, I hear myself memorializing death. I see it coming in so many different ways. I feel its slow, steady movement within. I am not delusional or hallucinating. I am just extremely sensitive to a process that I'm sure affects us all. I wish to hold it in place or delay its progress. I am, I am the first to admit, frightened of dying. I saw my wife die. It shocked me. Then I began to sense it in me. When I visit doctors, what can I say? Help me, please, I am dying and I am terribly fearful of dying? Perhaps I should say I see too clearly what everyone else disguises. But in my case the disease may be aging too rapidly, death coming on prematurely.

There are so many ironies. I know the literature, the great works on death. I read and reread them: Plato, Cicero, Marcus Aurelius, the early church father, Shakespeare even modern authors. What good does it do? It certainly doesn't relieve my fear; it may worsen things. I also know it is a weakness, a moral weakness, a spiritual sickness, to be obsessed with death.

But I seem to have identified the physical sensations that are those internal transformations through which we come to die. *Identified* is wrong. I should say learned to perceive and am now unable to cease observing. I feel like a naturalist watching a garden enter winter. I feel Petrarch's "freeze in summer," but it isn't love or lust but death, quite simply death, that I feel. I don't know what kind of help you give for this sort of thing. Fear of the physical experience of dying – premature, precocious fear. But it has taken over. I am no longer an historian looking at death from the outside; I am the history itself of a death.

Interpretation

It is possible – and, for the physician trained to do it, very easy – to write up a patient's case history or, as in the preceding cases, to select and arrange quotations from a transcript in order to demonstrate the classical signs and symptoms of a particular disease. And I am convinced that the same filter the doctor employs to write the case account is present in his professional mode of listening and inquiring about a patient's problems. From that welter of troubles, the classic disease is fashioned like a sculpture – in this case, a reproduction. Were I to describe these cases in their rich complexity, the differences between them would become more apparent. The trick for the master clinician is first to diagnose and treat the disease, so that the patient receives appropriate biomedical treatment, but then to regard it as an artifact of his diagnostic training in the symbolic forms of biomedicine. Technological intervention may ameliorate or even cure the disease but not the illness. To treat illness, the healer must dare to meet the patient in the messy, confusing, always special context of lived experience.

Disease is a psychobiological process of copying: it duplicates signs, symptoms, and behaviors. The paradox in human disorder is that out of such universal processes comes something specific to a culture and unique to a person. Surely, Arnie Springer, Wolf Segal, Di Isfahandiarian, and Phillips Bingman share nosophobia and other attributes of hypochondriasis. Yet that very fear of disease is elaborated into the "hidden killer," "utterly serious worries," "Isfahandiarian disease," and "the history itself of a death." In much the same way, each person in the context of shared culture creates an original identity out of similar patterns of dress, etiquette, food, aesthetic preference, and (in this instance) disease. Illness meanings, I submit, illumine the manner in which the transformation of the individual out of the group, the particular out of the general, occurs. Those meanings are both created by *and* create the transforming dialectic that makes Wolf Segal who he is and Di Isfahandiarian who she is.

Arnie Springer's illness experience is redolent of the mainline American cultural themes challenged by cancer: the secular engineering view of the world, the expectation of precise control over the physical environment and the body, the unwillingness to grant that life is inherently risky, the fear of hidden killers in our cells (and in our streets). Phillips Bingman also seems to locate a fearsome Western cultural image: after muscular and lithe youth and the robustness of early middle age pass, we move down the long slope of decline at the bottom of which death awaits us. Aging has become a disease in the contemporary West; Professor Bingman's exquisite yet morbid sensibility is as much as creation of that cultural transformation of normality into abnormality as of personal processes. Wolf's and Di's expressions are more ethnic, and thereby replicate more particular, less generalizable idioms and metaphors. Nonetheless, the process of creating originality out of copying is the same.

The physician and family care givers are situated in the gap between copy and original. There is a great danger when they recognize only the copy. Medical journals and lectures are filled with comments such as "the hypochondriacal patient is … ," "all nosophobic patients are … ," and so forth. But even with what little I have done to sketch personal detail, Arnie Springer, Wolf Segal, Gladys Isfahandiarian, and Phillips Bingman can be appreciated as an odd lot to put under a single rubric. Their irrepressible humanity continues to break through as a celebration of remarkable differences: not just in who they are but in how they live their chronic illness: No diagnostic rubric should be authorized to describe those individuals and their illness experiences one-dimensionally, in a look-alike caricature that is carried over into treating them as if they were the same. The purpose of a diagnostic system, after all, is to guide treatment of disease through a recognition of patterns. It is not meant to be a prefect representation of types of individuals or a guide to caring for their life problems. It is also the case that the copy should not be denied, the diagnosis jettisoned, lest the disease go untreated. There are similarities in the fears of hypochondriacal patients that can be treated if the fears are properly diagnosed and if the care givers are educated in what to do. But to provide humane care, healers must not lose sight of what is unique to each patient.

The ultimate irony in hypochondriasis is that it reminds us of a tension between the nature of life problems and the professional and family systems that respond to them. Mastery of the craft of healing – whether by the doctor or by the patient's spouse – like mastery of any other craft, begins with the memorization of rules, copying copies. That is the stage of the novice. What the master practitioner (and the accomplished family member) has learned is how to improvise from those copies, how to move beyond stereotyping and caricaturing, with all the dangers implicit in such routinization, toward healing, which is a fundamentally humanizing art.

Treating hypochondriasis is notoriously difficult. It is easy to see how practitioners and family members can joke about patients in order to relieve their own sense of inadequacy and failure. Not just the patient's disease, but the practitioner's and family member's response, is a copy. That copy of the therapeutic relationship often is demeaning and rejecting. Even the best of intentions may contribute to a worsening in the patient's condition: excessive concern can encourage a trajectory of help seeking with unneccessary hospitalizations, costly tests, dangerous treatments, and frustration on all sides. What can I recommend?

I have found that maintaining one's own sense of irony is a barrier to feelings of therapeutic helplessness and rage. Working with hypochondriacal patients and their families explicitly to increase their awareness of the multiple ironies we have reviewed can be a means of reducing the more disabling consequences of this chronic condition. I urge that hypochondriasis be treated as a language of distress and that care givers be taught to work within that language to use the same metaphors patients use. An approach to the language of hypochondriasis could be a useful complement to psychotherapeutic explorations of the life tensions and intimate pressures that intensify patients' fear of disease and their doubt of their own and their doctors' judgments. The systematic exploration of the meanings of hypochondriacal illness can become the basis of a therapy that also focuses on the ironical position of the protagonists as actors and onlookers simultaneously. Such therapy is still a long and difficult and uncertain passage. Many cases just barely manage to pull through, in large part because they are periodically revivified by a sense of the ironic.

Notes

1   There is an uncommon form of hypochondriasis in which the patient lacks insight and his nosophobia has all the characteristics of a delusion (a fixed false belief that is not shared by others), namely, monosymptomatic hypochondriacal psychosis. The remarkable thing about this disorder is that the psychosis is limited to this single aspect of experience.

2   "Simulated ignorance" is the original ancient Greek meaning of *irony*.

3   Perhaps no other word in recent years has been more abused than *holistic*, which gained popularity as a gloss for psychosocially attentive as well as biomedically competent care but has been transformed tendentiously into a commercialized slogan for selling a brand name of medical care. I use *holistic* in its earlier sense.

4   Patients who begin with somatic hypochondriasis are increasingly being transformed into psychological hypochondriacs. In my experience, this is a dangerous and undesirable change, because there are so few benchmarks in psychiatry, unlike the rest of medicine, to disconfirm a patient's (or a psychiatrist's) concern that a certain disease process is present.

5   These symptoms are all consistent with panic attacks, a form of anxiety disorder. Previously this was called hyperventilation syndrome; now panic disorder is known to be one of the causes of hyperventilation.

6   I thought Woody Allen's performance in the movie *Hannah and Her Sisters* was reminiscent of Wolf Segal, but not quite as funny.

7   The likelihood is that Bingman never had thyroid disease, but he did have one or two abnormal results in the dozen or so thyroid tests he has undergone. This is consistent with the probability of random laboratory error. I do know from his current internist that there is no laboratory evidence of active thyroid disease or clinical reason to suspect its presence.

References

Geertz, C. (1986) "Making experiences, authorizing selves," in V. W. Turner and E. M. Brunes (eds) *The Anthropology of Experience*, Urbana: University of Illinois Press, pp. 373–80.

Mayr, R. (1982) *The Growth of Biological Thought, Diversity, Evolution and Inheritance*, Cambridge, MA: Harvard University Press.

PART SIX

Bodies and technologies

INTRODUCTION

IN HIS ANALYSIS OF what he calls biosociality,[1] Paul Rabinow predicts that the identities of 'race', gender, class and age 'will be joined by a vast array of new ones, which will cross-cut, partially supersede and eventually redefine the older categories in ways that are well worth monitoring' (Rabinow 1992: 245). The texts in this section begin to do precisely this: they consider the extent to which bio- and information technologies begin to unravel the established identities that, from the eighteenth to mid-twentieth centuries, were 'embedded in the organically marked bodies of woman, the colonized or enslaved, and the worker' (Haraway 1991: 210). In doing so, they illustrate the relevance of technology to how we think about the substance and boundaries of the human body, and raise questions as to the relations between nature, culture, body, mind, technology, science – and so on. As N. Katherine Hayles neatly summarises it:

> On the one side, the dream of freely flowing information strains to escape scarcity, restricted physical space, class, gender, embodiment, time, and mortality. On the other, the claims of corporate profit, stratified social structures, physical confinement, female dependence on powerful males, and marked and failing bodies reassert their inevitability.
>
> (Hayles 2002: 236)

The section begins with Carlos Novas and Nikolas Rose's claim that contemporary developments in biotechnology, and in particular the so-called 'geneticization of identity', do not bring *any* inevitabilities with them. Contra arguments which assume that genetics reduces individuals to 'merely' an expression of their genetic complement, Novas and Rose insist that advances in the life sciences, biomedicine, and biotechnology have contributed to the *creation* of new subjects. In this respect they illustrate the point (raised in the Introduction to this Reader) that information is not simply a metaphor that describes 'life', but a set of practices that organise ways of living. For example, the creation of the person 'genetically at risk', Novas and Rose suggest, does not engender passivity and fatalism in the face of biological and medical determinism. Instead, it demands a considerable degree of activity – and ethical responsibility – on the part of that person, as well as on the part of the communities of obligation and identity in which they are situated. Genetic information reaches out, and those who are touched by it are required to address, negotiate, and calculate all aspects of their lives, from their relationship to their work, to questions relating to marriage, child-bearing, financial affairs, and so on. Although, in this respect, the geneticisation of identity might be said to be closely bound up with the norms of enterprising and responsible personhood that govern individuals in advanced liberal societies, Novas and Rose also argue that it is distinguished by the establishment of new and direct relations between body and self. The new molecular genetics, for these authors, is part of a wider reshaping of personhood along somatic lines.

The second extract in this section also considers how biomedical, biotechnical bodies are constructed, this time in relation to immune system discourses. Although Donna Haraway uses the term 'constructed', she does not mean to suggest that 'scientific bodies' are solely ideological or discursive. On the contrary, she understands bodies as objects of knowledge to be 'material–semiotic generative nodes'; embodied entities which are active and effective, but not in the sense of a self-identical presence or instrumental *agent*. Instead, the boundaries of material–semiotic actors materialise *through* historically specific social interaction. Indeed, it is because Haraway insists on the specificities of the histories of her objects – as well as an awareness of how they are cross-cut by 'race', gender, and the New World Order[2] – that her texts spill over not only with scientific narratives, but with narratives of 'myth, self-reflection, biography, culture' (Michael 2000: 34). For her, the immune system is

> a historically specific terrain, where global and local politics; Nobel Prize-winning research; heteroglossic cultural productions, from popular dietary practices, feminist science fiction, religious imagery, and children's games, to photographic techniques and military strategic theory; clinical medical practice; venture capital investment strategies; world-changing developments in business and technology; and the deepest personal and collective experiences of embodiment, vulnerability, power, and mortality interact with an intensity matched perhaps only in the biopolitics of sex and reproduction.
>
> (Haraway 1991: 205)

In the extract that we have included here, Haraway considers the ways in which immune system discourses, outlined in popular and technical languages in scientific culture in the United States during the 1980s, construct the postmodern, biomedical, biotechnical body. This is a body best described not in terms of a rationalist paradigm, but rather in relation to contemporary communication systems.

To understand the body as a communication system is to displace any notion of normalised functions in favour of 'a highly mobile field of strategic differences'. The postmodern, biomedical, biotechnical body does not refer, in other words, to a bounded and discrete natural entity which is the bearer of properties and which enters into relations with other bounded entities but, rather, to *shared codes or languages* that enable strategic connections to be established across a range of spheres (cultural, natural, artificial, technical and/or textual) and in a variety of different registers. This, Haraway argues, is the cyborg: a 'text, machine, body, and metaphor – all theorized and engaged in practice in terms of communications'. In place of militaristic and rationalist discourses, which privilege disembodied instrumentalism, the bodies constituted in immune system discourses are organised by a dispersed and fluid network. 'Defence', in this instance, is not about protection against something foreign which threatens to overtake a central controller. It is, rather, 'a subtle play of same and different, maintenance and dissolution'. This is one example of how the immune system can be understood as an 'icon for principal systems of symbolic and material "difference" in late capitalism' (Haraway 1991: 204). For just as the 'hierarchical, localized, organic body' is destabilised in biomedical discourses in the mid-twentieth century, so 'the question of "differences" has destabilized humanist discourses of liberation based on a politics of identity and substantive unity' (Haraway 1991: 211). Terms such as 'organism' and 'individual' are everywhere denaturalised and replaced by permeable assemblages – and they are so not only in the 'loose ravings of a cultural critic or feminist historian of science', as Haraway humurously characterises herself!, but also in the most unlikely of places, in Richard Dawkins' *The Extended Phenotype* for instance, where even here previously stable unities are rendered ontologically contingent.

The cyborg is a shifting and heterogeneous creature which, fittingly, embodies a politics grounded not in authentic identities but in inter-textual and inter-material entities. However for Haraway, this figure is (potentially) liberatory only insofar as it is ungendered and in this it represents a departure from many mainstream images of the human/machine interface. As Claudia Springer illustrates in the third extract in this section, such images are more usually characterised by heightened physicality and exaggerated gender and sexuality. Eroticised images of technology precede the cyborg, and can be identified in early modernist representations of trains, cars, pistons and turbines. Films such as Fritz Lang's *Metropolis* capture something of both the allure and threat of technology, an ambivalence which is framed and expressed in specifically feminised and, in the more recent *Alien* trilogy, maternal forms. Unlike robots and machines, cyborgs often seek to incorporate rather than exclude human beings, with the act of incorporation itself often resembling a sexual act (consider William Gibson's description of 'jacking in' to cyberspace). While this certainly opens the door to a variety of non-traditional sexual representations (such as solitary and/or voyeuristic sex, or sexual experiences which are not intended to culminate in heterosexual sex), Springer also shows how, in their simultaneous disparagement and fascination for the human body, cyborg imagery continues the tradition of ambivalence towards the body that characterises Western cultural and philosophical thought.

Like Springer, both Paul Gilroy and Catherine Waldby address themselves to the different ways in which bodies and technologies are seen and, moreover, how they *organise* ways of seeing. In this polemical extract, Gilroy focuses on the role that different scientific disciplines – natural history, biology, physiology – have played in establishing 'race', and in stitching together metaphysics and technology. Against the assumption that 'race' *pre-exists* its figuration through technologies (technologies which subsequently appear to confirm it), Gilroy suggests that seeing 'race' is always mediated by technical and social processes. This given, he asks his reader to consider whether, and in what ways, eighteenth-century perceptual regimes of 'race' have been superseded by microscopic, and now molecular, visions. Where does the change in scale – and the related shift away from blood, skin and bone as the referents of identities – leave racial difference?

As Gilroy notes, ontologies of 'race' are anything but natural. The question as to what *is* natural however, runs obliquely through nearly every text cited on bodies and technologies. Catherine Waldby begins to address it in her analysis of the Visible Human Project (VHP), in the context of her discussion of the term 'cybernatural', which she understands to refer to the convergence of life and information. This term, as she underscores, like many others which are used to denote 'nature' and 'the natural', is not intended to signify what nature 'really' is, or how it has 'really' changed, but is rather one of the latest examples in a long line of various *positings* of the natural. Different conceptions of nature situate bodies differently, and render them amenable to instrumentalisation in a range of often startling ways. The VHP dramatically exemplifies this: not simply a case of sophisticated animation techniques, it is produced through the visual processing of actual corpses. In the shift from biomass to information, the bodies in the VHP appear to have been rendered 'immortal', delivered from the entropy, degradation and loss associated with temporality of matter. They do not run down or out. They are available to be carved up and studied by medical students and others again and again.

The VHP illustrates Adrian Mackenzie's claim (as discussed in the above Introduction) that contemporary bio- and information technologies are characterised by the interlacing of living and non-living processes (and, as Waldby's analysis suggests, by the *creation* of new living and non-living forms). The final extract in this section is also concerned with this point, from a very different perspective. In Margaret Lock's analysis of brain-death, it is not digital cadavers which are at stake, but 'living cadavers', as the victims of major brain injuries were once called. Although only a relatively simple piece of technology – the artificial ventilator – is required to sustain the victim of major brain trauma, this assemblage of living and non-living entities raises the most complex of issues. These issues are not reducible to the technology but are rather bound up in a variety of cultural and technical practices, social values, and political interests, which shape our understandings of the relations between physical bodies, life, and death. Demands for organ donation and the status of the foetus are just two of the examples that Lock raises in this piece. If her analysis installs a measure of discomfort, it is perhaps because it returns us to the contested, and ostensibly intractable, relations between body and mind which continue to haunt so many accounts of bodies and technologies.

NOTES

1   In place of sociobiological understandings of culture, which proceed on the basis of the metaphor of nature, in biosociality, Rabinow argues, '[n]ature will be known and remade through technique and will finally become artificial, just as culture becomes natural' (Rabinow 1992: 241–2). For a good summary of conceptions of the relations between nature, culture, and artifice, see the introduction to Franklin *et al.* (2000).

2   The New World Order emerges from the marriage of technoscience and transnational capital. Although it colonises everything, Haraway argues, it is yet available to be unravelled and diffracted.

REFERENCES

Franklin, S., Lury, C. and Stacey, J. (2000) *Global Culture, Global Nature*, London: Sage.

Haraway, D. (1991) *Simians, Cyborgs, and Women: The Reinvention of Nature*, London: Free Association Books.

Hayles, N. K. (2002) 'Escape and constraint: three fictions dream of moving from energy to information', in B. Clarke and L. D. Henderson (eds), *Representation in Science and Technology, Art, and Literature*, Standford, California: Stanford University Press.

Michael, M. (2000) *Reconnecting Culture, Technology and Nature: From Society to Heterogeniety*, London and New York: Routledge.

Rabinow, P. (1992) 'Artificiality and enlightenment: from sociobiology to biosociality', in J. Crary and S. Kwinter (eds), *Incorporations*, New York: Zone.

Chapter 31

Carlos Novas and Nikolas Rose

GENETIC RISK AND THE BIRTH OF
THE SOMATIC INDIVIDUAL

From C. Novas and N. Rose (2000) 'Genetic risk and the birth of the somatic individual', *Economy and Society*, 29: 485–513.

[…]

THE RISE OF THE PERSON genetically at risk is one aspect of a wider change in the vision of life itself – a new 'molecular optics'. Life is now imagined, investigated, explained, and intervened upon at a molecular level – in terms of the molecular structure of bodily components, the molecular processes of life functions, and the molecular properties of pharmaceutical products. Of course, geneticists still gather information on family histories. But increasingly this gross level of data is only a stepping-stone in the attempt to construct linkage maps which can then be the basis of DNA sequencing and gene hunting which will identify the exact chromosomal location and sequence of the mutated gene in question.[1] We can see the molecular optic at work when heredity is visualized in terms of the sequences of bases on the human genome and when illnesses or susceptibilities are identified in terms of mutations at particular locations on a specific chromosome. For example, one condition involving fronto-temporal Dementia and Parkinsonism is known as FTDP-17 because it is linked to a number of mutations in a specific a region of chromosome 17. Increased susceptibility to breast cancer has been linked to the mutations known as BRCA1 and BRCA2 on chromosome 13. Researchers have tried to link variations in personality such as novelty seeking, or psychiatric disorders such as manic depression, with the synthesis or non-synthesis of particular proteins or the characteristics of particular neuronal transmitters or neural receptor sites – chromosome 11 being a particular favourite.[2] As the body becomes the subject of a molecular gaze, life is recast as a series of processes that can be accounted for and potentially re-engineered at the molecular level.

Most generally we will suggest that the birth of the individual 'genetically at risk' has to be understood as one dimension of a wider mutation in personhood that we tern 'somatic individuality' – in which new and direct relations are established between body and self. New biomedical languages of description and judgement – high blood pressure, abnormal heart rhythm, raised blood cholesterol and the like – have moved from the esoteric discourse of science to the lay expertise of citizens. Genetic ideas of personhood are already beginning to infuse the languages of somatic individualization, inscribing an indelible genetic truth into the heart of corporeal existence [cf. Kenen 1994]. Like earlier languages – that of intelligence, or that of 'hormones' – these genetic languages render visible to others and to oneself aspects of human individuality that go beyond 'experience', not only making sense of it in new ways, but actually reorganizing it in a new way and according to new values about who we are, what we must do, and what we can hope for.

New genetic languages and techniques thus come into an association with all the other shifts that are assembling somatic individuality, with the norms of enterprising, self-actualizing, responsible personhood that characterize 'advanced liberal' societies, and with the ethics of health and illness that play such a key role in their production and organization.

[…]

Somatic individuality

A number of authors have suggested that we are witnessing a whole-scale geneticization of identity with the consequent reduction of the human subject to a mere expression of their genetic complement (Dreyfuss and Nelkin 1992; Lippman 1991, 1992). While these authors accept that genes play a role in all sorts of illnesses, in interaction with one another and with social, biographical psychological and environmental factors, they claim that 'geneticization' is a determinism which asserts that genes 'cause' disorders. They argue that these genetic narratives of health and disease orient the ways in which prob-lems are defined, viewed and managed within society. They suggest that this legitimates funding and support for the projects of the gene mappers, and hence defines more and more problems of health and disease as 'genetic disorders'. Geneticization is seen as an individualizing tactic that redirects scarce resources away from social solutions to social problems, and represents a threat to doctrines such as equal opportunities, as well as to ideas to free will, intentionality and responsibility. 'The individual affixed with a genetic label can be isolated from the context in which s/he became sick … The individual, not society, is seen to require change; social problems improperly become individual patholo-gies' (Lippman 1992: 1472–3). Hence the application of genetic knowledge in diagnosis, assessment and treatment is associated – wittingly or unwittingly – with strategies for the subjection and control of individuals and groups.

These arguments make some significant points, but taken as a whole we find them misleading.

The geneticization argument implies that to ascribe genetic identity to individuals or groups is to objectify them, hence denying something essential to human subjectivity. But to make human individuality the object of positive knowledge is not 'subjection' in the sense of domination and the suppression of freedom – it is the *creation* of subjects that is at stake here. Today, as at the birth of clinical medicine, the sick person bears their illness within their corporeality and vitality – it is the body itself that has become ill. But this somaticization of illness did not, in fact, mandate the eternal passivity of the patient. In fact, clinical medicine, increasingly over the last half of the twentieth century, constituted the patient as an 'active' subject – one who must play their part in the game of cure

(Armstrong 1984; Arney and Bergen 1984). While not denying that illness was inscribed in the body, medical practice required the patient to offer up their voice in the diagnostic process in order to permit the disease itself to be identified, to commit themselves to the practice of the cure as part of a therapeutic alliance, and to conduct themselves prudently prior to illness, in the light of information about risks to health. The same is true of the role of contemporary medical genetics in the fabrication of the person genetically at risk. The patient is to become skilled, prudent and active, an ally of the doctor, a proto-professional – and to take their own share of their responsibility for getting themselves better. Patients at genetic risk and their families are not passive elements in the practice of cure. The studies carried out by Paul Rabinow (1999) as well as Vololona Rabeharisoa and Michel Callon (1998) have shown that such persons – the ill patients themselves, those 'asymptomatically ill' and their families – are increasingly demanding control over the practices linked to their own health, seeking multiple forms of expert and non-expert advice in devising their life strategies, and asking of medics that they act as the servants and not the masters of this process.[3] These persons defined by genetic disease have an investment in scientists fulfilling their promises and discovering the basis of, and the cure or treatment for, genetic conditions. Medicine, including medical genetics, notwithstanding its resolutely somatic understanding of the mechanisms of disease, has been one of the key sites for the fabrication of the contemporary self – free yet responsible, enterprising, prudent, encouraging the conduct of life in a calculative manner by acts of choice with an eye to the future and to increasing self well-being and that of the family.

Critics also tend to suggest that the new medical genetics leads to a focus upon the individual as an isolate. We disagree. Within such practices, individuals are subjectified through their location in a matrix of networks. [...] The illness or condition becomes a 'family' matter. The 'cause' of the patient's problem might be a family member in a previous generation; the diagnosis in one person has all kinds of implications not only for themselves but also for their relatives. New connections are traced in terms of the genetic threads that connected one person with another. Genetic identity is revealed and established only within a web of genetic connectedness, which is overlaid upon a web of family bonds and family memories, with their burden of mutual obligations and caring commitments, and with all the ethical dilemmas they entail. In becoming part of a genetic network, the subject genetically at risk may re-think their relation to their current family – lovers, potential and actual spouses, children, grandchildren and so forth – in terms of these issues of risk and inheritance. They may reshape their form of life – lifestyle, diet, leisure activities, alcohol, smoking – in these terms, which also reshapes their relations with those with whom they interact. They are brought into relation with novel networks of interaction – those not of 'society', but of 'community' – groups, associations, communities of those similarly at risk; groups of patients at particular hospitals or clinics; participants in trials of new therapies; subjects of documentaries and dramas on radio, television and the movies.

Further, the mutations in personhood associated with the new life sciences and bio-medical technologies of life are multiple and not simply genetic. For example, new reproductive technologies have split apart categories that were previously coterminous – birth mother, psychological mother, familial father, sperm donor, egg donor and so forth – thus transforming the relations of kinship that used to play such a fundamental role in the rhetorics and practices of identity formation (Franklin 1997; Strathern 1992, 1999). Developments in psychopharmacology have transformed the ways in which individuals are understood, as the very features that seemed to constitute their individuals are understood, as the very features that seemed to constitute their individuality – such as personality or mood – now appear to be amenable to transformation by the use of specially engineered drugs such as Prozac (Fraser 2000; Slater 1999). New visions of personhood are coming to the fore associated with the growing interest and sophistica-tion in brain-imaging techniques, which localize the features of the personality, affects, cognition and the like in particular regions of the brain (Beaulieu 2000; Dumit forth-coming). Practices of subjectification that operate in genetic terms – in terms of genetic forms of reasoning, explanation, prediction and treatment of human individuals, families or groups – find their place within this wider array of ways of thinking about and acting upon human individuality in 'bodily' terms. Or, to put it more positively, recent devel-opments in the life sciences, biomedicine and biotechnology are associated with a general 'somaticization' of personhood in an array of practices and styles of thought, from tech-niques of bodily modification to the rise of corporealism in social and feminist theory and philosophy. This is what we mean when we speak of 'somatic individuality'.

In any event, we suggest, the geneticization of identity has to be located in a more complex field of identity practices. Advanced liberal democracies are traversed by multi-ple practices of identification and identity claims – in terms of nationality, culture, sexu-ality, religion, dietary choice, lifestyle preference and much more. Only some of these ascriptions of, and claims about, identity are biological or biomedical. Indeed, biomed-ical identity practices and identity claims, including those that operate in terms of genet-ics, find their place among a bewildering array of other identity claims and identificatory practices, sometimes taken up, by subjects or by others, in a rewriting of identity in bio-logical terms, sometimes vehemently contested. If anything, identities are plural and multiple: one is identified as a gay man within some practices, as a Muslim within others, as a carrier for sickle cell disease within others. Even when regulatory practices utilize biological conceptions of personhood, genetic identity is rarely hegemonic. In insurance, as we shall see, genetic information is considered alongside other non-genetic aspects of personhood – medical history, habits such as smoking, risks associated with lifestyle choices and so forth. In the courtroom, a range of biological evidence is now entering, including that from brain scans, in the determination of aspects of personhood such as capacity to stand trial or responsibility – but courts have proved remarkably resistant to arguments that responsibility or intentionality at law should be re-conceptualized in terms of evidence from genetics (Rose 2000). Ideas about biological, biomedical and genetic identity will certainly infuse, interact, combine and contest with other identity claims; we doubt that they will supplant them.

[…]

Notes

1   Nancy Wexler's work on genetic linkages in a community of Venezuelan families with a very high incidence of Huntington's Disease, which led to the location of its genetic basis to the short arm of chromosome 4, is an exemplar here – best described by Alice Wexler (1996).

2   Novelty seeking was linked to variations in the D4DR site on the short arm of chromosome 11; bipolar affective disorder was linked to specific DNA markers on

chromosome 11 in the Old Order Amish, although the correlation later proved to be false – for a popular account, see Ridley (1999).

3   For further examples, see the website of the Genetic Alliance which 'fosters a dynamic coalition of consumers and professionals to promote the interests of children, adults and families living with genetic conditions. For twelve years the Alliance has brought together support groups, consumers and health care professionals, creating partnership solutions to common concerns about access and availability of quality genetics services. Currently numbering 287 support groups and 214 consumers and professional members, the Alliance was founded in 1986 – propelled by the energy of the self help and support group movements' (http://www.geneticalliance.org/allianceinfo.html).

References

Armstrong, D. (1984) 'The patient's view', *Social Science and Medicine*, 18: 737–44.

Arney, W. R. and Bergen, B. J. (1984) *Medicine and the Management of Living: Taming the Last Great Beast*, Chicago: University of Chicago Press.

Beaulieu, A. (2000) 'The space inside the skull: digital representation, brain and mapping and cognitive neuroscience in the decade of the brain', PhD dissertation, University of Amsterdam.

Dreyfuss, R. C. and Nelkin, D. (1992) 'The jurisprudence of genetics', *Vanderbilt Law Review* 45(2): 313–48.

Dumit, J. (forthcoming) *Whose Brain is This? PET Scans and Personhood in Biomedical America*, Princeton, NJ: Princeton University Press.

Fraser, M. (2000) 'The nature of Prozac', forthcoming.

Kenen, R. (1994) 'The Human Genome Project: creator of the potentially sick, potentially vulnerable and potentially stigmatized?', in I. Robinson (ed.) *Life and Death under High Technology Medicine*, Manchester: Manchester University Press.

Lippman, A. (1991) 'Prenatal genetic testing and screening: constructing needs and reinforcing inequities', *American Journal of Law and Medicine* 17(1–2): 15–50.

Lippman, A. (1992) 'Led (astray) by genetic maps: the cartography of the human genome and health care', *Social Science and Medicine* 35(12): 1469–76.

Rabeharisoa, V. and Callon, M. (1998) 'L'implication des malades dans les activités de recherche soutenues par l'Association Française contre les myopathies', *Sciences sociales et santé* 16(3): 41–65.

Rabinow, P. (1999) *French DNA: Trouble in Purgatory*, Chicago IL: University of Chicago Press.

Ridley, M. (1999) *Genome: The Autobiography of the Species in 23 Chapters*, London: Fourth Estate.

Rose, N. (2000) 'The biology of culpability: pathological identity and crime control in a biological culture', *Theoretical Criminology* 4(1): 5–43.

Slater, I. (1999) *Prozac Diary*, London: Hamish Hamilton.

Strathern, M. (1992) *After Nature: English Kinship in the Late Twentieth Century*, Cambridge and New York: Cambridge University Press.

Strathern, M. (1999) *Property, Substance and Effect*, London: Athlone.

Wexler, A. (1996) *Mapping Fate: A Memoir of Family, Risk and Genetic Research*, Berkeley, CA: University of California Press.

Chapter 32

Donna J. Haraway

THE BIOPOLITICS OF POSTMODERN BODIES
Constitutions of self in immune system discourse

From D. Haraway (1991) *Simians, Cyborgs, and Women: The Reinvention of Nature,* London: Free Association Books.

[...]

FROM THE MID-TWENTIETH CENTURY, biomedical discourses have been progressively organized around a very different set of technologies and practices, which have destabilized the symbolic privilege of the hierarchical, localized, organic body. Concurrently – and out of some of the same historical, matrices of decolonization, multinational capitalism, world-wide high-tech militarization, and the emergence of new collective political actors in local and global politics from among those persons previously consigned to labour in silence – the question of 'differences' has destabilized humanist discourses of liberation based on a politics of identity and substantive unity. Feminist theory as a self-conscious discursive practice has been generated in this post-Second World War period characterized by the translation of Western scientific and political languages of nature from those based on work, localization, and the marked body to those based on codes, dispersal and networking, and the fragmented postmodern subject. An account of the biomedical, biotechnical body must start from the multiple molecular interfacings of genetic, nervous, endocrine, and immune systems. Biology is about recognition and misrecognition, coding errors, the body's reading practices (for example, frameshift mutations), and billion-dollar projects to sequence the human genome to be published and stored in a national genetic 'library'. The body is conceived as a strategic system, highly militarized in key arenas of imagery and practice. Sex, sexuality, and reproduction are theorized in terms of local investment strategies; the body ceases to be a stable spatial map of normalized functions and instead emerges as a highly mobile field of strategic differences. The biomedical–biotechnical body is a semiotic system, a complex meaning-producing field, for which the discourse of immunology, that is, the central biomedical discourse on recognition/misrecognition, has become a high-stakes practice in many senses.

In relation to objects like biotic components and codes, one must think, not in terms of laws of growth and essential properties, but rather in terms of strategies of design, boundary constraints, rates of flows, system logics, and costs of lowering constraints. Sexual reproduction becomes one possible strategy among many, with costs and benefits theorized as a function of the system environment. Disease is a subspecies of information malfunction or communications pathology; disease is a process of misrecognition or transgression of the boundaries of a strategic assemblage called self. Ideologies of sexual reproduction can no longer easily call upon the notions of unproblematic sex and sex role as organic aspects in 'healthy' natural objects like organisms and families. Likewise for race, ideologies of human diversity have to be developed in terms of frequencies of parameters and fields of power-charged differences, not essences and natural origins or homes. Race and sex, like individuals, are artefacts sustained or undermined by the dis- cursive nexus of knowledge and power. Any object or person can be reasonably thought of in terms of disassembly and reassembly; no 'natural' architectures constrain system design. Design is none the less highly constrained. What counts as a 'unit', a one, is highly problematic, not a permanent given. Individuality is a strategic defence problem.

One should expect control strategies to concentrate on boundary conditions and inter- faces, on rates of flow across boundaries, not on the integrity of natural objects. [...] Human beings, like any other component or subsystem, must be localized in a system architecture whose basic modes of operation are probabilistic. No objects, spaces, or bodies are sacred in themselves; any component can be interfaced with any other if the proper standard, the proper code, can be constructed for processing signals in a common language. In particular, there is no ground for ontologically opposing the organic, the technical, and the textual. [...] Bodies have become cyborgs – cybernetic organisms – compounds of hybrid techno-organic embodiment and textuality (Haraway 1985, 1991: 149–81). The cyborg is text, machine, body and metaphor – all theorized and engaged in practice in terms of communications.

[...]

The one and the many: selves, individuals, units and subjects

What is constituted as an individual within postmodern biotechnical, biomedical discourse? There is no easy answer to this question, for even the most reliable Western indi- viduated bodies, the mice and men of a well-equipped laboratory, neither stop nor start at the skin, which is itself something of a teeming jungle threatening illicit fusions, especially from the perspective of a scanning electron microscope. The multi-billion-dollar project to sequence 'the human genome' in a definitive genetic library might be seen as one prac- tical answer to the construction of 'man' as 'subject' of science. The genome project is a kind of technology of postmodern humanism, defining 'the' genome by reading and writ- ing it. The technology required for this particular kind of literacy is suggested by the adver- tisement for MacroGene Workstation. The ad ties the mythical, organic, technical and textual together in its graphic invocation of the 'missing link' crawling from the water on to the land, while the text reads, 'In the LKB MacroGene Workstation [for sequencing nucleic acids], there are no "missing links." The monster *Ichthyostega* crawling out of the deep in one of earth's great transitions is a perfect figure for late twentieth-century bodily and technical metamorphoses. An act of canonization to make the theorists of the human- ities pause, the standard reference work called the human genome would be the means through which human diversity and its pathologies could be tamed in the exhaustive code kept by a national or international genetic bureau of standards. Costs of storage of the giant dictionary will probably exceed costs of its production, but this is a mundane matter to any librarian (Kanigel 1987; Roberts 1987a,b,c). Access to this standard for 'man' will be a matter of international financial, patent and similar struggles. The Peoples of the Book will finally have a standard genesis story. In the beginning was the copy.

The Human Genome Project might define postmodern species being (*pace* the philosophers), but what of *individual* being? Richard Dawkins raised this knotty problem in *The Extended Phenotype*. He noted that in 1912, Julian Huxley defined individuality in biological terms as 'literally indivisibility – the quality of being sufficiently heterogeneous in form to be rendered non-functional if cut in half' (Dawkins 1982: 250). That seems a promising start. In Huxley's terms, surely you or I would count as an individual, while many worms would not. The individuality of worms was not achieved even at the height of bourgeois liberalism, so no cause to worry there. But Huxley's definition does not answer *which function* is at issue. Nothing answers that in the abstract; it depends on what is to be done. You or I (whatever problematic address these pronouns have) might be an individual for some purposes, but not for others. This is a normal ontological state for cyborgs and women, if not for Aristotelians and men. Function is about action. Here is where Dawkins has a radical solution, as he proposes a view of individuality that is strategic at every level of meaning. There are many kinds of individuals for Dawkins, but one kind has primacy. 'The whole purpose of our search for a "unit of selection" is to discover a suitable actor to play the leading role in our metaphors of purpose' (1982: 91). The 'metaphors of purpose' come down to a single bottom line: replication. 'A successful replicator is one that succeeds in lasting, in the form of copies, for a very long time measured in generations, and succeeds in propogating many copies of itself' (1982: 87–8).

The replicator fragment whose individuality finally matters most, in the constructed time of evolutionary theory, is not particularly 'unitary'. For all that it serves, for Dawkins, as the 'unit' of natural selection, the replicator's boundaries are not fixed and its inner reaches remain mutable. But still, these units must be a bit smaller than a 'single' gene coding for a protein. Units are only good enough to sustain the technology of copying. Like the replicons' borders, the boundaries of other strategic assemblages are not fixed either – it all has to do with the broad net cast by strategies of replication in a world where self and other are very much at stake.

> The integrated multi-cellular organism is a phenomenon which has emerged as a result of natural selection on primitively selfish replicators. It has paid replicators to behave gregariously [so much for 'harmony', in the short run]. The phenotypic power by which they ensure their survival is in principle extended and unbounded. In practice the organism has arisen as a partially bounded local concentration, a shared knot of replicator power.
>
> (Dawkins 1982: 264)

'In principle extended and unbounded' – this is a remarkable statement of interconnectedness, but of a very particular kind, one that leads to theorizing the living world as one vast arms race. '[P]henotypes that extend outside the body do not have to be inanimate artefacts: they themselves can be built of living tissue … I shall show that it is logically sensible to regard parasite genes as having phenotypic expression in host bodies *and behaviour*'

(1982: 210, emphasis mine). But the being who serves as another's phenotype is itself populated by propagules with their own replicative ends. '[A]n animal will not necessarily submit passively to being manipulated, and an evolutionary 'arms race' is expected to develop' (1982: 39). This is an arms race that must take account of the stage of the development of the means of bodily production and the costs of maintaining it:

> The many-celled body is a machine for the production of single-celled propagules. Large bodies, like elephants, are best seen as heavy plant and machinery, a temporary resource drain, invested so as to improve later propagule production. In a sense the germ-line would 'like' to reduce capital investment in heavy machinery …
>
> (Dawkins 1982: 254)

Large capital is indeed a drain; small is beautiful. But you and I have required large capital investments, in more than genetic terms. Perhaps we should keep an eye on the germline, especially since 'we' – the non-germline components of adult mammals (unless you identify with your haploid gametes and their contents, and some do) – cannot be copy units. 'We' can only aim for a defended self, not copy fidelity, the property of other sorts of units. Within 'us' is the most threatening other – the propagules, whose phenotype we, temporarily, are.

What does all this have to do with the discourse of immunology as a map of systems of 'difference' in late capitalism? Let me attempt to convey the flavour of representations of the curious bodily object called the human immune system, culled from textbooks and research reports published in 1980s. The IS is composed of about 10 to the 12th cells, two orders of magnitude more cells than the nervous system has. These cells are regenerated throughout life from pluripotent stem cells that themselves remain undifferentiated. From embryonic life through adulthood, the immune system is sited in several relatively amorphous tissues and organs, including the thymus, bone marrow, spleen, and lymph nodes; but a large fraction of its cells are in the blood and lymph circulatory systems and in body fluids and spaces. There are two major cell lineages to the system. The first is the *lymphocytes*, which include the several types of T cells (helper, suppressor, killer, and variations of all these) and the B cells (each type of which can produce only one sort of the vast array of potential circulating antibodies). T and B cells have particular specificities capable of recognizing almost any molecular array of the right size that can ever exist, no matter how clever industrial chemistry gets. This specificity is enabled by a baroque somatic mutation mechanism, clonal selection, and a polygenic receptor or maker system. The second immune cell lineage is the *mononuclear phagocyte system*, including the multi-talented macrophages, which, in addition to their other recognition skills and connections, also appear to share receptors and some hormonal peptide products with neural cells. Besides the cellular compartment, the immune system comprises a vast array of circulating acellular products, such as antibodies, lymphokines, and complement components. These molecules mediate communication among components of the immune system, but also between the immune system and the nervous and endocrine systems, thus linking the body's multiple control and co-ordination sites and functions. The genetics of the immune system cells, with their high rates of somatic mutation and gene product splicings and rearrangings to make finished surface receptors and antibodies, makes a mockery of the notion of a constant genome even within 'one' body.

The hierarchical body of old has given way to a network-body of truly amazing complexity and specificity. The immune system is everywhere and nowhere. Its specificities are indefinite if not infinite, and they arise randomly; yet these extraordinary variations are the critical means of maintaining individual bodily coherence.

[...]

Dawkins (1976, 1982) has been among the most radical disrupters of cyborg biological holism, and in that sense he is most deeply informed by a postmodern consciousness, in which the logic of the permeability among the textual, the technic, and the biotic and of the deep theorization of all possible texts and bodies as strategic assemblages has made the notions of 'organism' or 'individual' extremely problematic. He ignores the mythic, but it pervades his texts. 'Organism' and 'individual' have not disappeared; rather, they have been fully denaturalized. That is, they are ontologically contingent constructs from the point of view of the biologist, not just in the loose ravings of a cultural critic or feminist historian of science.

[...]

References

Dawkins, Richard (1976) *The Selfish Gene*, Oxford: Oxford University Press.
———— (1982) *The Extended Phenotype: The Gene as the Unit of Selection*, Oxford: Oxford University Press.
Haraway, Donna J. (1985) 'Manifesto for cyborgs: science, technology, and socialist feminism in the 1980s', *Socialist Review* 80: 65–108.
———— (1991) *Simians, Cyborgs, and Women: The Reinvention of Nature*, London: Free Association Books.
Kanigel, Robert (1986) 'Where mind and body meet', *Mosaic* 17(2): 52–60.
———— (1987) 'The genome project', *New York Times Sunday Magazine* 13 December, pp. 44, 98–101, 106.
Roberts, Leslie (1987a) 'Who owns the human genome?', *Science* 237: 358–61.
———— (1987b) 'Human genome: questions of cost', *Science* 237: 1411–12.
———— (1987c) 'New sequencers take on the genome', *Science* 238: 271–3.

Chapter 33

Claudia Springer

THE PLEASURE OF THE INTERFACE

From C. Springer (1991) 'The pleasure of the interface', *Screen* 32: 3.

[...]

THE LANGUAGE AND IMAGERY of technological bodies exist across a variety of diverse texts. Scientists who are currently designing ways to integrate human consciousness with computers (as opposed to creating Artificial Intelligence) describe a future in which human bodies will be obsolete, replaced by computers that retain human intelligence on software. *Omni* magazine postulates a 'postbiological era'. The *Whole Earth Review* publishes a forum titled 'Is the body obsolete?'. Jean-François Lyotard asks, 'Can thought go on without a body?'[1] Popular culture has appropriated the scientific project; but instead of effacing the human body, these texts intensify corporeality in their representation of cyborgs. A mostly technological system is represented as its opposite: a muscular human body with robotic parts that heighten physicality and sexuality. In other words, these contemporary texts represent a future where human bodies are on the verge of becoming obsolete but sexuality nevertheless prevails.

[...]

Cyborgs [...] belong to the information age, where, as D'Alessandro writes, 'huge, thrusting machines have been replaced with the circuitry maze of the microship, the minimal curve of aerodynamic design'.[2] Indeed, machines have been replaced by systems, and the microelectronic circuitry of computers bears little resemblance to the thrusting pistons and grinding gears that characterized industrial machinery. D'Alessandro asks: 'What is sensual, erotic, or exciting about electronic tech?' She answers by suggesting that cybernetics makes possible the thrill of control over information and, for the corporate executives who own the technology, control over the consumer classes. What popular culture's cyborg imagery suggests is that electronic technology also makes possible the thrill of escape from the confines of the body and from the boundaries that have separated organic from inorganic matter.

While robots represent the acclaim and fear evoked by industrial age machines for their ability to function independently of humans, cyborgs incorporate rather than exclude humans, and in so doing erase the distinctions previously assumed to distinguish humanity from technology. Transgressed boundaries, in fact, define the cyborg, making it the consummate postmodern concept. When humans interface with computer technology in popular culture texts, the process consists of more than just adding external robotic prostheses to their bodies. It involves transforming the self into something entirely new, combining technological with human identity. Although human subjectivity is not lost in the process, it is significantly altered.

[...]

One of many examples is provided by the comic book *Cyberpunk*[3] whose protagonist, Topo, mentally enters the 'Playing Field' — a consensual hallucination where all the world's data exists in three-dimensional abstraction (called cyberspace in the cyberpunk novels of William Gibson) — saying 'it's the most beautiful thing in the human universe. If I could leave my meat behind and just live here. If I could just be pure consciousness I could be happy.' While in the Playing Field he meets Neon Rose, a plant/woman with a rose for a head and two thorny tendrils for arms (and like Topo, only present through hallucination). Even her name inscribes the collapse of boundaries between organic plant life and a technological construct. He engages her in a contest of wills, represented as their bodies entwined around each other while he narrates: 'In here, you're what you will. Time and space at our command. No limits, except how good your software is. No restraints.' Topo's spoken desire — to leave his meat behind and become pure consciousness, which is in fact what he has done — is contradicted by the imagery: his body — his meat — wrapped around another body.

The word 'meat' is widely used to refer to the human body in cyberpunk texts. Cyberpunk, a movement in science fiction dating from the early 1980s, combines an aggressive punk sensibility rooted in urban street culture with a highly technological future where distinctions between technology and humanity have dissolved. In this context, 'meat' typically carries a negative connotation along with its conventional association with the penis. It is an insult to be called meat in these texts, and to be meat is to be vulnerable. And yet despite its aversion to meat, *Cyberpunk* visually depicts Topo's body after he has abandoned it to float through the Playing Field's ever-changing topography. His body, however, only seems to be inside the Playing Field because of an illusion, and he is capable of transforming it in any way he desires. As he sees Neon Rose approach, he transforms himself into mechanical parts shaped like his own human body, but more formidable. He has lost his flesh and become steel. Only his face remains unchanged, and it is protected by a helmet. Topo's new powerful body, a product of his fantasy, inscribes the conventional signifiers of masculinity: he is angular with broad shoulder and chest; and, most importantly, he is hard. It is no accident that he adopts this appearance in order to greet Neon Rose, who is coded in stereotypical feminine fashion as a sinewy plant who throws her tendrils like lassos to wrap them around him. In case the reader is still in doubt about Neon Rose's gender, *Cyberpunk* shows here as a human woman after Topo defeats her in their mock battle.

This example from *Cyberpunk* indicates that while popular culture texts enthusiastically explore boundary breakdowns between humans and computers, gender boundaries are treated less flexibly.

Cyberbodies, in fact, tend to appear masculine or feminine to an exaggerated degree. We find giant pumped-up pectoral muscles on the males and enormous breasts on the females; or, in the case of Neon Rose, cliched flower imagery meant to represent female consciousness adrift in the computer matrix. Cyborg imagery has not so far realized the ungendered ideal theorized by Donna Haraway.[4] Haraway praises the cyborg as a potentially liberatory concept, one that could release women from their inequality under patriarchy by making genders obsolete. When gender difference ceases to be an issue, she explains, then equality becomes possible. Janet Bergstrom points out that exaggerated genders dominate in science fiction because where the basic fact of identity as a human is suspect and subject to transformation into its opposite, the representation of sexual identity carries a potentially heightened significance, because it can be used as the primary marker of difference in a world otherwise beyond our norms.[5]

[...]

Nowhere is the confusion of boundaries between humanity and electronic technology more apparent than in films involving cyborg imagery: here cyborgs are often indistinguishable from humans. The Terminator (The Terminator (James Cameron, 1984)), for example, can be recognized as nonhuman only by dogs, not by humans. Even when cyborgs in films look different from humans, they are often represented as fundamentally human. In Robocop (Paul Verhoeven, 1987). Robocop is created by fusing electronic technology and robotic prostheses with the face of a policeman, Alex J. Murphy, after he has died from multiple gunshot wounds. He clearly looks technological, while at the same time he retains a human shape. His most recognizably human feature is his face, with its flesh still intact, while the rest of his body is entirely constructed of metal and electronic circuitry. The film shows that despite his creators, attempts to fashion him into a purely mechanical tool, his humanity keeps surfacing. He seeks information about Murphy, his human precursor; and increasingly identifies with him, particularly since he retains memories of the attack that killed Murphy. At the end of the film, Robocop identifies himself, when asked for his name, as Murphy. In the sequel, Robocop II (Irvin Kershner, 1990), Robocop's basic humanity is further confirmed when he is continually stirred by memories of Murphy's wife and young son, and takes to watching them from the street outside their new home. Robocop's inability to act on his human desires constitutes the tragic theme of the film, which takes for granted that Robocop is basically human.

If there is a single feature that consistently separates cyborgs from humans in these films, it is the cyborg's greater capacity for violence, combined with enormous physical prowess. Instead of representing cyborgs as intellectual wizards whose bodies have withered away and been replaced by computer terminals, popular culture gives us muscular hulks distinguished by their superior fighting skills. To some extent the phenomenon of the rampaging cyborg in films suggests a residual fear of technology of the sort that found similar expression in older films like Metropolis. Electronic technology's incredible capabilities can certainly evoke fear and awe, which can be translated in fictional representation into massive bodies that overpower human characters.

But fear of the computer's abilities does not entirely explain why cyborgs are consistently associated with violence. Significantly, musclebound cyborgs in films are informed by a tradition of muscular comic-book superheroes; and, like the superheroes, their erotic appeal lies in the promise of power they embody. Their heightened physicality culminates not in sexual climax but in acts of violence. Violence substitutes for sexual release. Steve Neale has theorized that violence displaces male sexuality in films in response to a cultural taboo against a homoerotic gaze.[6] Certain narrative films continue to be made for a presumed male audience, and homophobia exerts a strong influence on cinematic techniques. For example, closeup shots that caress the male body on screen might encourage a homoerotic response from the male spectator. But, as Neale explains, the spectacle of a passive and desirable male body is typically undermined by the narrative, which intervenes to make him the object or the perpetrator of violence, thereby justifying the camera's objectification of his body.

[...]

Neither alive nor dead, the cyborg in popular culture is constituted by paradoxes: its contradictions are its essence, and its vision of a discordant future is in fact a projection of our own conflictual present. What is really being debated in the discourses surrounding a cyborg future are contemporary disputes concerning gender and sexuality, with the future providing a clean slate, or a blank screen, onto which we can project our fascination and fears. While some texts cling to traditional gender roles and circumscribed sexual relations, others experiment with alternatives. It is perhaps ironic, though, that a debate over gender and sexuality finds expression in the context of the cyborg, an entity that makes sexuality, gender, even humankind itself, anachronistic. Foucault's statement that 'man is an invention of recent date. And one perhaps nearing its end' prefigures the consequences of a cyborg future.[7] But, as Foucault also argues, it is precisely during a time of discursive crisis, when categories previously taken for granted become subject to dispute, that new concepts emerge. Late twentieth-century debates over sexuality and gender roles have thus contributed to producing the concept of the cyborg. And, depending on one's stake in the outcome, one can look to the cyborg to provide either liberation or annihilation.

Notes

1   (1989) 'Interview with Hans Moravec', *Omni* 11(11): 88; (1989) 'Is the body obsolete? A forum', *Whole Earth Review* no. 63: 34–55; Jean-François Lyotard (1988–9) 'Can thought, go on without a body?', *Discourse* 11(11): 74–87.

2   K.C. D'Alessandro (July 1988) 'Technophilia: Cyberpunk Cinema', a paper presented at the society for Cinema Studies Conference, Bozeman, Montana.

3   Scott Rockwell (1989) *Cyberpunk*, book one, vol. 1, no. 1. Wheeling, West Virgina: Innovative Corporation.

4   Donna Haraway (1985) 'A manifesto for cyborgs: science, technology, and socialist feminism in the 1980s'. *Socialist Review* 80: 65–107; reprinted in Elizabeth Weed (ed.) *Coming to Terms: Feminism, Theory, and Practice* (New York: Routledge, 1989).

5   Janet Bergstrom (1886) 'Androids and androgyn', *Camera Obscura*, no. 15, p. 89.

6   Steve Neale (1983) 'Masculinity as spectacle: reflections on men and mainstream cinema', *Screen* 24(6): 2–16.

7   Michel Foucalt (1973) *The Order of Things: An Archaeology of the Human Sciences*, New York: Vintage Books, p. 387.

Chapter 34

Paul Gilroy

RACE ENDS HERE

From P. Gilroy (1998) 'Race ends here', *Ethnic and Racial Studies,* 21(5): 838–47.

[…]

THIS BRIEF AND HIGHLY POLEMICAL presentation might have been more appropriately entitled 'Now you see it, now you don't'. It seeks to question how we see 'race', how the signs and symbols of racial difference become apparent to our senses. It does not admit the integrity of any avowedly natural perceptual scheme. It does not concede the idea of a way of seeing race that remains unmediated by technical and social processes, for there is no raw perception dwelling in the body. The human sensorium has had to be educated. When it comes to the visualization of 'race' a great deal of fine tuning has been required. Underpinning my argument is a desire to link the historical and critical study of raciologies and 'racial' metaphysics to the new histories of visuality and perception that are being produced, to connect it with some timely critiques of absolute identity and their associated genealogies of subjectivity and, above all, to link it to an understanding of the technoscientific means that have fostered and mediated particular relations with our race-coded selves in the modern past. […]

The history of racism is a narrative in which the congruency of micro- and macrocosm has been disrupted at the point of their analogical intersection: the human body. Biology was only one of many possible ways of addressing this relationship with ourselves. Though it preceded the distinctive quality of sociality we distinguish as modern, the order of active differentiation that gets called 'race' may be modernity's most pernicious signature. It articulated reason and unreason. It knitted together science and superstition. Raciology required that enlightenment and myth be intertwined. Indeed, 'race' and nationality supplied the logic and mechanism of their interconnections. The specious ontologies of 'race' are anything but spontaneous and natural. They should be awarded no immunity from prosecution amidst the reveries of reflexivity and the comfortable forms of inertia induced by capitulation to the lazy essentialisms from which post-modern sages inform us we cannot escape. To cut a long story short. We could begin again by asking what that trope 'race' lodged in the body might mean in the age defined by globalization and digital technologies on the one hand and molecular biology on the other?

Today, we have been productively estranged from the anatomical scale defined at the end of the eighteenth century when natural history gave way initially to biology. We are more sceptical than ever about the status of visible differences in relation to the unseen. On what scale is human sameness, human diversity now to be calibrated? Can a different sense of scale and scaling combine with a new sense of illumination to form a counterweight to the appeal of absolute particularity celebrated under the sign of 'race'? Can a sense of the arbitrariness of scale help to answer the seductions of self and kind projected on to the surface of the body but stubbornly repudiated inside it by the proliferation of invisible differences that produce catastrophic consequences where people are not what they seem to be? In the instability of scale that characterizes our episteme, how is racialized and racializing identity to be imagined when we know that it has already been imaged? Is there still a place for 'race' when human life and human difference are contemplated on a restlessly sliding scale?

The modern idea of race operated within the strictest of perceptual limits. The shift from natural history to biology prompted changes in the modes and meanings of the visual and the visible. When it appeared to make sense of life and nature biology promoted specific modes of communication and representation that, on the basis of particular technologies, both created and marked out a novel relationship between text and image. Life, fractured along raciological lines, was visualized, imaged in novel and striking ways. Race was intrinsic to this change. Later, the consolidation of physiology as a distinct branch of medical knowledge would be accompanied by a refinement in the technical and instrumental basis of bio-representation. Here, too, 'race' was a primary object of knowledge and power.

For simplicity's sake, let's call that distinctive ratio, the scale of comparative or Euclidean anatomy. The idea of 'race' leaked out of the lofty confines where what Foucault calls the 'chemical gaze' was most fully developed. But it always worked best in the setting provided by those distinctive ways of looking, enumerating, measuring, dissecting and evaluating. More than this, the idea of 'race' defined and consolidated typologies that could not be dissociated from their very specific representational technology and its perceptual and cognitive regimes. The truths of race were produced 'performatively' from the hat that biological science provided, like so many startled rabbits in front of a noisy, eager, imperial crowd. 'Race' became an important means to link metaphysics and technology; it made sense readily within these unprecedented historical conditions.

Our situation is different. The call of racial being has been weakened by a different technological and communicative revolution, by the idea that the body is nothing more than an incidental moment in the transmission of code and information, by its openness to the new imaging technologies, and by the loss of mortality as a horizon against which life is to be lived. Blackness can now signify vital prestige rather than abjection in a global info-tainment telesector, where the residues of slave societies and the parochial traces of American racial conflict must yield to different imperatives deriving from the planetarization of profit and the cultivation of new markets far from the memory of bondage. They had Sartje Baartman, we have a *pas de deux* between the super-human, godly Michael Jordan and Bugs Bunny, the *reductio ad absurdum* of hybridized African trixter tale-telling. Can we agree that the eighteenth-century perceptual regimes that gave us 'race' have been superseded along with their epistemological and metaphysical pretensions?

The story of how the one-to-one scale of comparative anatomy and its world of natural light were recontextualized by the advent of the microscopic and the artificial has been addressed by several historians and need not be outlined in detail here. Rather, I would like to leapfrog over the exemplary image of the cinematographically minded physician Robert Lincoln Watkins peering at tainted blood through his 'micro-motoscope' and turn instead towards the more recent situation in which the microscopic has given way to the molecular. This development means that much of the contemporary discourse producing 'races' and racial consciousness can be identified as an anachronistic and even vestigial phenomenon. Where screens rather than lenses and mirrors mediate the pursuit of bodily truths, 'race' might best be approached as an after-image – a lingering symptom of looking too intently or too casually into the damaging glare emanating from colonial conflicts at home and abroad.

On the journey away from modernity's inaugural catastrophes in the new world, raciological ways of organizing and classifying the world have retained that special baggage of perspectival inclinations, perceptual habits and scalar assumptions. Their anthropologies depended and still depend upon observations that cannot be wholly disassociated from the technological means that have both fostered and mediated them. This was where the anatomical scale was first broken. Optical microscopes transformed what could be seen but the new technologies of seeing on ever smaller and smaller scales moved the threshold of visibility and has contributed to an enhanced sense of the power of the unseen and the unseeable. The eugenic ravings of Francis Crick, the Nobel prize winning co-discoverer of DNA, demonstrate exactly how the fateful change of scale involved in the founding of molecular biology and the redefinition of life in terms of information, messages and code was recognized as having cataclysmic moral and political consequences. Rubble from the broken palace of bio-politics provided the foundations for what might now be called 'nanopolitics'.

Let me be blunt: scientific and biological, historical and cultural, rational and irrational, skin, bone and even blood are no longer primary referents of racial discourse. If the modern episteme was constituted through processes that forsook the integrity of the whole body and moved inside the skin to enumerate organs and describe their functional relationship to an organic totality, the situation today is different. The same 'inward' direction has been maintained and the momentum increased in ways that compound the difficulties involved in separating inside from outside. The aspiration to perceive and explain through recourse to the power of the minute, the microscopic and now the molecular, has been consolidated. In a space beyond and below that of comparative anatomy, the whole integral body and its obvious, functional components no longer delimit the scale upon which assessments of the unity and variation of the species are to be made. The naked eye was long ago recognized as insufficient to the lowly tasks of evaluation and description demanded by the condition of everyday extremity and the eugenic answers to its manifold problems. More than merely technological change makes what was hitherto invisible not only visible but decisive.

Nuclear magnetic resonance spectroscopy (NMR/MRI), positron emission tomography (PET) and several other parallel innovations in multidimensional body imaging have remade the relationship between the seeable and the unseen. By imaging the body in new ways, they impact upon the ways that embodied humanity is imagined and upon the status of bio-racial differences that vanish at these levels of resolution. Whether it is the IBM logo being spelled out in individual atoms of xenon or the non-specific dream of gaining control over the big world 'by fiddling with the nanoscale entities of which it is composed', the movement is always in one direction: downwards and inwards. Our question should be this: where do these changes leave racial difference, particularly where it cannot readily be correlated with simple genetic variation?

Michel Foucault, whose early work explored useful historical precedents for the contemporary shift towards this nanoscale is an inspiring but frustrating guide to these problems. From my standpoint, he seems to have been insufficiently attuned to the significance of protracted struggles over the unity of mankind that attended the emergence of biopolitics and appears to have been disinterested in the meaning of specifically raciological differences in the context of anthropology's presentation of the species as a unified object of knowledge and power. To put it simply, though he identified man as both the pivot and the product of the new relationship between words and things, he moved too swiftly towards a sense of modern humanity unified in its immiserating passage from sanguinuity to sexuality. He, too, failed to appreciate how the fervent belief that Africans and their new world descendants were less than human, might have affected this transformation and its epistemic correlates. Perhaps he was not haunted, as I think we still should be, by the famous image of an orangutan carrying off a Negro girl that comprised the frontispiece of Linnaeus' *A Genuine and Universal System of Natural History*. The central, inescapable problem presented in that picture is the suggested kinship between these sub- and anti-human species rather than the fact that their conflictual interrelation is figured through the idea of rape. The picture's historic setting and the interpretative puzzle presents point to the unresolved issue of how 'race' interrelates with sex, gender and sexuality; something that is further than ever from being settled and which focuses a new and urgent agenda for future work. The picture and its relation to that foundational text raise other uncomfortable matters: the characteristics of the new, post-Vesalian semiotics of the body and the relationship between text and image in the performative constitution of 'races' were not one in which words were simply, automatically or consistently able to dominate images – icons – that went far beyond any merely illustrative function.

The extensive debate as to whether Negroes should be accorded membership of the family of mankind (a group whose particularity was inaugurated, proved, produced and celebrated by the transformed relationship between words and things that crystallized at the end of the eighteenth century) was more central to the formation and reproduction of the modern episteme than Foucault appreciated. I raise this, not to pillory him, nor to reopen discussion of how that process has been reconstructed by historians of science, but rather because his study of that fateful change is an important resource in our own situation where similar processes are observable.

One intermediate example may help to make the argument about scale less abstract. Let me propose that the dismal order of power and differentiation -- defined by its intention to make the mute body disclose the truth of its racial identities – can be apprehended through the critical notion of 'epidermalization' bequeathed to us by Frantz Fanon. That idea was born from a philosopher-psychologist's phenomenological ambitions and their distinctive way of seeing, as well as understanding, the importance of sight. It refers to a historically specific system for making bodies meaningful by endowing in them qualities of 'colour'. But the term has a wider applicability than its recent colonial origins would suggest. Emmanuel Chukwudi Eze and Christian M. Neugebauer have reminded us recently that Kant's *Physische Geographie* said more than his contemporary celebrants like to admit about the qualities of Negro skin and the practical problems it presented when pain had to be inflicted with a split bamboo cane. Like Hegel's better known opinions on the Negro and the limitations he placed upon the African's capacity for historical action, these sentiments can be thought of as exemplifying epidermal thinking in its emergent form.

In an era where colonial power had made epidermalizing into a dominant principle of political power, Dr. Fanon used the idea of indexing the estrangement from authentic human being in the body and being in the world that colonial social relations had wrought. Epidermalized power violated the human body in its symmetrical, intersubjective, social humanity, in its species being, in its fragile relationship to other fragile bodies and in its connection to the redemptive potential inherent in its own wholesome or perhaps its suffering corporeality, our being towards death. Fanon's notion supplies an interesting footnote to the whole history of racial sciences and the exclusive notions of colour-coded humanity that they specified. We need to find its contemporary analogs not where he looked, on the surface of the body, but deep within it. Their pursuit may yet yield the anti-toxins capable of silencing raciology forever.

Chapter 35

Catherine Waldby

IATROGENESIS
The Visible Human Project and the reproduction of life

From C. Waldby (1999) 'IatroGenesis: the Visible Human Project and the reproduction of life', *Australian Feminist Studies*, 14(29).

[...]

T HE VISIBLE HUMAN PROJECT (VHP)[1] is one of the more spectacular instances of a particular technical/epistemic moment – a moment succinctly described by Haraway as the 'translation of the world into a problem of coding'[2] – which is well in train in fin-de-millennium culture. Like its 'sister' project, the Human Genome Project, the VHP is driven by a desire to render human bodies as compendia of data, information archives which can be stored, retrieved and rewritten in digital and/or genetic modes. Unlike the tedious productions of the Human Genome Project (endless strings of nucleotide sequence – TGCCTGGACTT…) the VHP is a dramatic and compelling visual object, a three-dimensional, photorealistic anatomical image of an entire body which can be rotated, dissected, animated and worked from the multiple points of view afforded by computer vision (see Figure 35.1). [...] This anatomical spectacle is not simply clever animation but rather is produced through the visual processing of actual corpses. The two bodies imaged so far, one male and one female, were first frozen and then very finely sliced into oblivion. The VHP produces its volumetric spectacle by 'restacking' planner images of the corpse produced by photographing successive one millimetre slices made through the frozen body (see Figure 35.2). Each photograph registers a small move through the body's mass and each forms a computer file, which can be reformulated into an uncanny icon of the three-dimensional body, using volumetric software.

[...]

Digital Eden and cybernatural life

To pose the data figures imaged in the VHP as 'Adam' and 'Eve' is to specify a particular imaginary matrix of relations between the project's scientists, the nature of the screen and

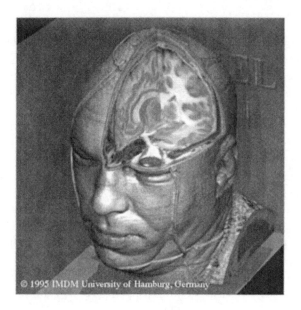

Figure 35.1 Volume rendering of head. Visible Human Male

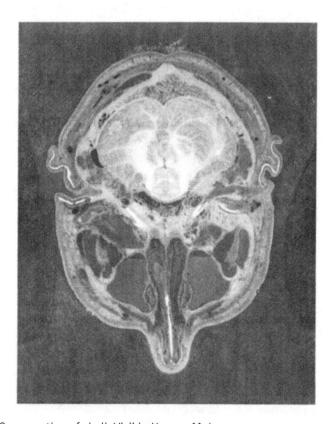

Figure 35.2 Cross-section of skull. Visible Human Male

the status of the figures themselves. If in actual space the bodies used by the project were particular beings with individual names and lives, their 'relocation' to the other, virtual side of screen interface is understood to have transformed them into a new and exemplary form of being, normative entities which can stand for all other bodies. Moreover, if in actual space the bodies imaged were corpses, their digital icons are miraculously alive. It is clear that for the project the figures can lay claim to a form of vitality. At the most practical level this claim is unsurprising. After all, the point of the project is to create figures which act *as if* they are alive, to use the particular simulational qualities of virtual space to imitate living processes. Great energy is currently being put into the animation of the figures, and into their endowment with haptic resistance, differential tissue quality and density, pulsation and tremor, so that virtual surgery will provide feedback to the hand of the proto-surgeon. Dr Spitzer, the Director of the Centre for Human Simulation, where the original processing of the bodies was performed, explains the name of the Centre in the following terms:

SPITZER: What we want to happen here, we want this data stuff to react, to act human.

INTERVIEWER: You mean alive? Act alive?

SPITZER: Yeah sure [referring to surgical simulation using the VHP data]. When you [enter a person's aorta with a needle] as soon as your needle gets up near his aorta you can feel his aorta pulsing ... So you think he's alive. Now of course he's not alive ... [but] now for all practical purposes, for that little tiny application, I don't think I have to do any more to convince you that he is human.[3]

Spitzer clearly equates the force of animation with the force of life. In posing the figures as vital, able to support and demonstrate physiological processes and motility, the VHP partakes of long tradition of anatomical iconography. Vesalius' osteological and myological figures is the *Fabrica*[4] are depicted in moments of exemplary action, walking, bending and posing, and subsequent anatomical texts have habitually placed their anatomical figures in various kinds of motion.[5] This tradition arises in part as a way to demonstrate relations between anatomical structure and physiological function, but it is also thrown up to deal with the central paradox of anatomical knowledge, a science of life which owes a problematic debt to death. Anatomical practice produces knowledge of living bodies through the analysis of dead bodies, generating its models of living tissue and vital physiology from the study of the corpse. This dependence on the corpse is profoundly disavowed by the biomedical imaginary, at the same time as it exercises far reaching effects on the medical idea of life. The spectacular animation of its anatomical figures is one of a complex range of strategies which seek to minimise the difference between living and dead bodies, and to efface the analytic violence involved in all modes of anatomical preparation.

Technical practices of animation are routinely posed as analogues for the processes of life but the attribution of vitality to the VHP figures takes a specific energy from the elaboration of virtual space as vital space currently underway in multiple sites of technoculture and the cybersciences. If the figures can be nicknamed 'Adam' and 'Eve' this locates the space of the screen, a space projected out of the play of data, as a vital 'world', a new Eden for the technical production of artificial life. The apparent self-enclosure of computed space, its ability to model and manipulate complex partial geometries, to make and unmake visual objects, to set out complexity within strictly confined parameters, all of these qualities lend themselves to the conceptualisation of the screen as the outer surface of a micro-world, to borrow Paul Edwards' term. He writes:

> Computer simulations are ... by nature partial, internally consistent but externally incomplete; this is the significance of the term "micro-world". Every micro-world has a unique ontological and epistemological structure, simpler than that of the world it represents. Computer programs are thus intellectually useful and emotionally appealing for the same reason: they create worlds without irrelevant or unwanted complexity.[6]
>
> (Edwards 1990)

The space of the screen is in this sense a space of autonomous production, a medium in which worlds can be invented, modified and destroyed. To pose computed space as a prelapsarian Eden is to specify such a world, a bio-graphic space where forms of post-natural vivacity can be authorised. This conceit is not only a function of the visually imaginative qualities of virtual space but also arises out of a more specific conflation of living process with data process, of life with information.

Here I want to borrow Sean Cubitt's term 'the cybernatural' to designate this convergence between the force of life and the force of information. The cybernatural is, in his typology, one form of postnatural life, a rubric for a number of ways of thinking about 'what comes after the natural'. The 'natural' is acknowledged here as the most problematic of categories, a limit which is constantly placed and replaced, trying to secure the distinction between what is considered the organic, the given, the locus of animate but unconscious matter, and what counts as the human, the cultural, artifice. The content of the 'natural' is understood to be always tendentious, constantly pressed into service to some end as a self-reproducing limit, resource or truth. 'The natural is something which has constantly to be posited: either as the source or goal of the human, or as the other of the human which serves to define the human as species.'[7] At the same time the category of the natural is, according to Cubitt, increasingly open to speculation about what he terms the 'postnatural', that is to speculation about the possibility of forms of vitality which do not find their support in the organic processes of matter which is understood to be the domain of the 'natural', but rather in the arena of the artificial. The cybernatural designates any practice which uses the space of the virtual screen as a space of 'second nature' through a conflation of information with vitality.

Given the persistent traffic between ideas of the organic and the artificial within the rhetoric of 'nature', Cubitt's temporalisation of this relation seems questionable. Canguilhem's[8] history of mechanistic theories of the organism suggest that there is no positing of the natural within the history of European Science that is not always/already technologically enframed. As Haraway puts it, the history of nature is one of 'relentless artifactualism'.[9] On this account the cybernatural is not a new configuration of nature but rather the most recent rereading of the natural, a 'positing of the natural' to bring it into line with new forms of animation and new economies of representation made possible by virtual space.

[...]

Resurrection and reproduction

The deployment of Genesis rhetoric in the VHP [...] summons up a cybernatural space, one which depends on a similar play and implosion of distinctions as those found in A-Life. Its resort to Genesis is nevertheless modified in particular ways, a rewriting motivated by the fact that it must negotiate a much more complex creation story than that found in A-Life. 'Adam' and 'Eve' in the VHP are not posed as creations *ex nihilo*. Rather they appear as re-creations, re-animations which have given new life to the lifeless, to figures in whom life has been extinguished. The journalistic and scientific rhetoric generated around the VHP is full of references to and metaphors for the resurrection of the figures. This rhetoric clearly indicates a desire that the figures should be understood as a re-animation of vitality, a rebirth into some new form of life on the far side of the screen. So, for example, Wirthlin's hypertext article on the Visible Woman concludes, 'The anonymous woman who donated her body to science to be scanned, sliced and digitised, will be reborn many times in the name of science.'[10] Science's article about the project states:

> Meet the Visible Human. In the real world he was a 39 year old prisoner who was executed by lethal injection in Texas. But now in the virtual world he was been resurrected ... to star in the National Library of Medicine's gruesomely fascinating effort to create a comprehensive digital atlas of the human body.[11]
>
> (Waldorp 1995)

The detour of Genesis rhetoric through a narrative which properly belongs in the New Testament, or, on an abject reading, to Shelley's *Frankenstein*, is motivated by the necessity for the VHP to simultaneously acknowledge and deny a complex debt to the bodies used in the imaging process. Anatomy [...] must always negotiate the problem of its debt to death and the corpse, a negotiation assisted by the Cartesian dualism which is foundational to the practice of scientific anatomy. If, for medicine in general and anatomy in particular, complex subjectivity can be partitioned into immaterial mind and mechanical body, the significance of death for an understanding of the body can be minimised. If the body is mechanism, death occurs when the mechanism fails or runs down. Death can be reduced to a matter of technical difference in *state*, matter which is either animate or inanimate, an idea of death which necessarily conditions the medical idea of life.

> The body's so-called life is modelled according to the workings of an inanimate machine. The [dead, anatomized] body can constitute the place of life only because life itself has been fundamentally conceived according to the life-less ... Dissection of the corpse can provide a method of studying the living body only because the latter is itself a sort of animated corpse.[12]

It is within the terms of this conceit that a power of animation, the technical motivation of traces, can count as a power or re-animation, the 'bestowing of life upon lifeless matter'. To cast the image-figures in the VHP as kinds of resurrection is to claim both that they are forms of the 'original' bodies and to cancel out the effects of death on those bodies.

At its strongest the rhetoric of resurrection poses the images as *transubstantiations*, entities created by the perfect substitution of data for flesh. Here the VHP betrays the same valuation of form over matter so clearly articulated in A-Life research. If the materiality of flesh, its density, recalcitrance, palpability and opacity were to be considered as a positive value, the process of production of the VHP figures could only be evaluated as a violent procedure, one which annihilates bodily substance in favour of the production of navigable spectacle. If materiality is subordinated to form, this process of production reads quite differently. On a form/matter distinction, the only significance of matter for anatomy is its yielding of form to the gaze, whereas the palpability of matter is simply an obstacle to the eye, an inert and incidental biomass. On this logic the cryosectioning and photographing of the corpse constitutes a technique for the temporal and visual 'arrest' of the iconic form of the body. Frozen soon after death, the form of the body is preserved at the moment before organic decomposition sets in, and the process of cryosectioning substitutes a technical decomposition driven by the logic of photographic optics. This technical decomposition acts to effectively remove the body's iconic form from organic time, rendering it up to the camera to be 'arrested' in digital photospace, at the same time as its biomass is reduced, in a reversal of Genesis, to dust.[13]

[...]

Notes

1   The Visible Human Project is an initiative of the National Library of Medicine, in Bethesda, Maryland, USA. Details and extensive image archives of the project may be found at http://www.nlm.nih.gov.

2   Haraway, Donna (1991) *Simians, Cyborgs and Women: the Reinvention of Nature*, New York: Routledge, p. 164.

3   Personal communication, Dr Victor Spitzer (1950).

4   Saunders, M. and O'Malley, C. (eds) *The Illustrations from the Works of Andreas Vesalius of Brussels*, Cleveland: World Publishing.

5   This habit of vitality in anatomical images is so well established that the work of John Bell, an eighteenth-century anatomist whose depictions are clearly corpses, looks shocking and violent. See Roberts, K. 'The contexts of anatomical illustration', in Cazort, Kornell and Roberts (eds) *The Ingenious Machine of Nature*, pp. 71–102.

6   Edwards, Paul (1990) 'The army and the micro-word: computers and the politics of gender identity', *Signs*, 16 (1), p. 109.

7   Cubitt, Sean, 'Supernatural futures: theses on digital aesthetics' in G. Robertson, M. Mash, L. Tickner, J. Bird, B. Curtis and T. Putnam (eds) (1996) *Future Natural: Nature, Science, Culture*, London and New York: Routledge, p. 238.

8   Canguilhem, Georges, 'Machine and organism', in J. Crary and S. Kwinter (eds) (1992) *Incorporations* (Zone Books) New York, pp. 44–69.

9   Haraway, Donna (1991) *Simians, Cyborgs and Women: the Reinvention of Nature*, New York: Routledge, p. 295.

10   Wirthlin, 'The visible woman', p. 2, http://www.sqi.com/winter_96/vis_woman.html.1996.

11   Waldorp (1995) 'The visible man steps out', *Science* 269, p. 1358.

12   Drew Leder, (1990) *The Absent Body*, Chicago: University of Chicago Press, p. 143.

13   The slices planed from the frozen corpse are desiccated by the freezing procedure, and literally disintegrate into something like sawdust.

Chapter 36

Margaret Lock

TWICE DEAD
Organ transplants and the reinvention of death

From M. Lock (2002) *Twice Dead: Organ Transplants and the Reinvention of Death*, Berkeley: University of California Press.

From a letter to the *Journal of the American Medical Association*:

This reader ... was stunned by Dr. Liptak's statement about the "disconcerting" aspects of disconnecting children from ventilators: "They shudder and gasp and twitch and inevitably lead you to believe that you have made a mistake and should not have disconnected them." Disconcerting indeed! ...

Readers of the *Journal* should understand clearly that patients who have been competently diagnosed to be brain dead neither shudder, nor gasp, nor twitch when ventilatory support is disconnected. The absence of such responses is, in fact, part of the process of certification of brain death.

It would be reassuring were Dr. Liptak to explain to us that his description was simply literary license ... If Dr. Liptak's "brain-dead" patients are indeed responding to disconnection of the ventilator in the manner described, then it is chillingly clear that they are not, in fact, brain dead.

(Poulton 1986: 2028)

Gregory Liptak responded:

Patients who are brain dead often have unusual spontaneous movements when they are disconnected from their ventilators. Numerous authors have described these disconcerting phenomena.

Patients who fulfill all the criteria for death, including deep unresponsive coma, may experience any of the following: goose bumps, shivering, extensor movements of the arms, rapid flexion of the elbows, elevation of the arms above the bed, crossing of the hands, reaching of the hands towards the neck, forced exhalation, and thoracic respiratory-like movements. These complex sequential movements are felt to be release phenomena from the spinal cord including the upper cervical cord and do *not* mean that the patient is no longer brain dead.

(Liptak 1986: 2028)

[...]

A "LIVING CADAVER," AS THE BRAIN-DEAD were first called, is created by an accident and sustained by medical technology. Major injury to the brain must occur, whether caused by an automobile or motorcycle crash, a drowning, smoke inhalation, a major blow to the head, a "cerebral accident" (stroke) in which the brain suddenly floods with blood, or some act of violence, such as a gunshot wound. Most victims of severe head trauma are kept alive by a relatively simple piece of technology – the artificial ventilator. Solid organ transplants,[1] which depend on the procurement of organs from brain-dead patients, could not have been institutionalized without the existence of the ventilator and other life-support technologies. But this coincidence of new technologies and living bodies, some with irreversibly damaged brains, could not alone mean that organs could then be procured from these new entities: a new death had to be legally recognized before commodification of the brain-dead could come about.

[...]

With the assistance of technology we can postpone the physical death of patients whose entire brains are traumatized beyond hope of recovery. If the patient is not to become an organ donor, then usually the process is prolonged only briefly, while brain death is confirmed.[2] When a brain-dead patient is to become an organ donor, then biological dying is postponed for a much longer period, specifically so that the body may be commodified. Here resides a new, technologically manipulated death. To go one step further and equate an irreversible loss of consciousness alone with human death would constitute a radically new departure, one that should not be countenanced without extensive *public* debate. If patients with cerebral death are to become organ donors, then we would be practicing active euthanasia by killing the "person" while preserving the living body as best we can.

Brain-dead patients will, we know for certain, "die" as soon as they are removed from the ventilator. We take comfort from this knowledge when proclaiming them dead even though they look alive. But patients in cerebral death are rarely on ventilators and can usually breathe without assistance. All they need is assistance with feeding – as do a great number of patients who are obviously fully alive. To think of them as dead is entirely counterintuitive, and their condition raises a set of urgent, obdurate problems that we have conveniently ducked. What exactly do we mean by consciousness? Is it located entirely in the brain? Can we determine its irreversibility with certainty? If so, will we be able to reach consensus that an irreversible loss of consciousness alone is the death of a person? Will we then be comfortable having the death of the person routinely count as legal death, so that the physical end can be hastened? Which doctors will be willing to take organs for donation from individuals who may be breathing unaided, even when they have previously given their consent? What should be our response to members of society who do not support cerebral death: do we override their sentiments? What if we find that they are in the majority? How will the economics of long-term care for permanently comatose patients affect these decisions? And how will the so-called shortage of organs for transplant affect our course of action? [...]

Confusion in the Clinic

[...]

What is the relationship between the soul (or mind, or vital essence) and the body? More specifically, when do individuals or persons – as opposed to bodies – die? And how does individual death relate to the moment or process in which the vital essence "leaves" the physical body and ceases to exist? What relationship is there among death as a familial and social event, death of the person, and physical death? Is one form of death given priority over others? And what moral status is assigned to each of these deaths?

Clearly, the condition of "living cadavers" causes confusion, particularly so because we insist categorically that they must be dead if their organs are to be removed; no one considers the possibility, even remotely, of institutionalizing vivisection, although we refer to "vital" organs being removed from the "body." The contradictions created by living cadavers leave room for the production of imaginative discourse. Conceptual maneuvers must be mobilized, whether to enable or to prohibit organ procurement. In the United States and Canada, the dominant discourse has enabled the diagnosis of irreversible loss of consciousness to count as equivalent to the death of the person, thus permitting the utilitarian procurement of organs. In Japan, on the other hand, recognition of brain death was blocked because the dominant discourse in that country insists that an irreversible loss of consciousness is neither biological death nor the death of the person. Recognition of brain death in Japan has come about after years of professional and political rhetorical manipulation, and even now is recognized only conditionally.

[...]

Born of a brain-dead mother

The following case study was reported in the *Journal of the American Medical Association* in August 1983:

On Jan. 25, 1983, a previously healthy 27-year-old woman presented to her local hospital at 22 weeks' gestation with a five-day history of worsening headaches followed by several hours of vomiting and disorientation. Results of physical examination were consistent with a 22-week gestation and were otherwise unremarkable; normal vital signs and no focal neurological deficits were noted. Results of a lumbar puncture were normal except for a slightly elevated opening pressure of 20 cm of water. ... Four hours after presentation, the patient had a generalized seizure and a respiratory arrest.

After cardiopulmonary resuscitation, ventilatory support was continued in the intensive care unit, where examination revealed no response to painful stimuli, fixed and dilated pupils, papilledema, and absent doll's eye movements. A computed tomographic scan of the head showed marked dilation of

the lateral and third ventricles with a mass obstructing the fourth ventricle ...
The electroencephalogram was again isoelectric[3] two days later. There was no
change in the patient's condition, and a diagnosis of brain death was made at
that time, using the Harvard criteria. During this period the fetal heart rate
pattern remained normal. In accordance with the strongly expressed wishes
of the father, a decision was made to provide cardiorespiratory support to the
mother in an attempt to maintain the fetus in utero until it reached a viable
gestational age.

(Field et al. 1988: 816)

A massive technological onslaught was undertaken with this patient that continued until
the thirty-first week of gestation. The fetal heart rate was monitored at every nursing
shift, and serial sonograms were performed. In addition to constant monitoring, feeding,
and nursing care, the living cadaver was treated for hypotension, temperature fluctuations, diabetes insipidus, hypothyroidism, and cortisol deficiency. On the twenty-eighth
day a major infection took hold, but it was eventually controlled with antibiotics. On
the fifty-eighth day a staphylococcus infection developed. While this was being treated,
repeated sonograms showed no growth of the fetus over the previous two weeks. A
decision was made to deliver the fetus by cesarean section on the sixty-third day of
hospitalization. A male infant weighing 1,440 grams (just over 3 pounds) was delivered.
The ventilator was turned off, and the heart of the mother stopped beating shortly
thereafter. The infant was taken to the neonatal intensive care unit, and at three weeks
of age was transferred to a hospital near his home. At eighteen months of age he was
doing well.

As part of the ethical discussion that followed the presentation of this case, the
authors note:

> A long tradition of fetal rescue exists in Western society. Asklepios was "cut
> out alive from the womb of his dead mother by Apollo." During the reign of
> King Numa Pompilius of Rome in the seventh century B.C., the Lex Regia was
> established, mandating the abdominal delivery of a term fetus in the event of
> the death of its mother. Six hundred years later, during the time of the Roman
> emperors, this became known as Lex Cesarea, the origination of the term
> cesarean delivery. ...Current available technology has made postmortem
> somatic support of a mother possible to effect the "rescue" of her very pre-
> mature fetus. Could the existence of this technology lead to the requirement
> that it be applied in all cases of maternal death?

(Field et al. 1988: 821)

There is no mention in this ethical discussion of how the nurses and other involved ICU
attendants felt about caring intensively for sixty-three days for a brain-dead body and its
fetus. Nor is there any discussion about whether the father visited his wife during this
time. The chronic ambiguity created by keeping a living cadaver suspended in a hybrid
state for over two months is suppressed in favor of a discussion about how the feat was
accomplished and whether it should be routinized because the technology is available.
In the United States, as contrasted with Japan, the social repercussions of this case go
unremarked.

Notes

1   "Solid organ" refers to the internal organs, including the heart, liver, kidney, and lungs, that have clearly defined anatomical boundaries.
2   This is not the case in Japan, where the ventilator is routinely kept in place even after a diagnosis of brain death.
3   That is, the EEG tracing was flat.

References

Field, David R., Elena A. Gates, Robert K. Creasy, Albert R. Jonsen, and Russell K. Laros Jr. (1988) "Maternal brain death during pregnancy: medical and ethical issues," *Journal of the American Medical Association,* 260 (6): 816–22.

Liptak, Gregory (1986) "In Reply," *Journal of the American Medical Association,* 255 (April 18): 2028.

Poulton, Thomas J. (1986) "Spontaneous movements in brain-dead patients," *Journal of the American Medical Association,* 255 (April 18): 2028.

PART SEVEN

Bodies in consumer culture

INTRODUCTION

The texts in this section begin to address some of the key characteristics of the body in consumer culture, focusing in particular on the relation *between* bodies and consumer objects, as well as on the notion of the body *as* an object. This tension between bodies and/as objects serves in its turn to draw attention to how, as bodies are opened up to consumer choice (or at least are perceived to be opened up in this way), the boundaries of the 'natural' and the 'cultural' can be, and indeed often are, redefined. The role of choice, and relatedly of responsibility and style, is thus crucial to any understanding of the body in consumer culture.

The section begins with an article that addresses the ascension of consumer culture in the nineteenth century. By the end of that century, the commodity not only dominated a new industrial economy, but was also an integral part of a new system for representing social values. In the extract from *Imperial Leather* that we have chosen here, Anne McClintock shows how profoundly implicated in the imperial project those values were. Soap in particular, she argues, captured the spirit of the era, with soap sales flourishing not only because of the gap that existed in the domestic market but also because soap 'could persuasively mediate the Victorian poetics of racial hygiene and imperial progress' (McClintock 1995: 209):

> the cult of domesticity and the new imperialism found in soap an exemplary mediating form. The emergent middle class values – monogamy ('clean' sex, which has value), industrial capital ('clean' money, which has value), Christianity ('being washed in the blood of the lamb'), class control ('cleansing the great unwashed') and the imperial civilizing mission ('washing and clothing the savage') – could all be marvelously embodied in a single household commodity.
> (McClintock 1995: 208)

While the dissemination of scientific racism had previously been limited to those with the means and education to read journals, travel writings and novels, 'commodity racism' was able to travel fast and widely on the back of the consumer spectacle. Advertising took that message into the intimate space of the home, subverting the distinction between the public and the private spheres as it went. Thus, in each of her examples, McClintock shows how the purification – or metamorphosis, or evolution – of the domestic body that was evident in advertising for soap was also paralleled by some kind of (hope for the) transformation of the body politic. 'More than merely a *symbol* of imperial progress', McClintock writes, 'the domestic commodity becomes the *agent* of history itself' (McClintock 1995: 220).

The Victorian era, buoyed up by imperial capital, was characterised by 'an uproar not only of things', McClintock writes, 'but of signs' (McClintock 1995: 208). It is this – the proliferating production, exchange, and consumptions of signs and symbols – that particularly interests Jean Baudrillard, established theorist of postmodern and consumer culture. First published in 1976, Baudrillard's *The Consumer Society* is striking in its anticipation of many of the themes that have since been developed in the field of consumption studies, including those that touch on the body. In this extract, Baudrillard focuses on the implications of the *homology* between bodies and objects, which he suggests specifically characterises the body in consumer culture. For even if the body is considered to be the finest and most precious of consumer objects, Baudrillard argues, it is no less an object for that – an object of salvation indeed, one which has taken over many of the functions of the soul. The sin of omission for example, neglecting one's bodily devotions, inspires a 'latent terrorism' (directed particularly at women). Blackmail, repression, persecution may follow. Beauty (evacuated of meaning) and the erotic (a sexual foil) function primarily as sign-value: the reappropriation of the body in consumer culture is no less alienated than the exploitation of the body as labour power. In short, for Baudrillard, the narcissistic investment in the body is precisely that: an *investment*. Like the management of an inheritance, it is expected to yield a return, in the form of social status. It is for these reasons that Baudrillard also suggests that the 'cult of the body' should not necessarily be opposed to the 'cult of the soul' (whose demise began in the eighteenth century), but can instead be deemed its successor. No more material than the soul, the body in consumer culture is an idea, an abstraction, equivalent to any other functional object.

It is precisely functionality that characterises the aesthetics of the body in the fitness centres in Italy that Roberta Sassatelli analyses. Interestingly, while gender differences continue to shape how these centres or clubs and gyms are used, Sassatelli notes that this particular fitness aesthetic overcomes traditional gender distinctions insofar as it combines features associated both with masculinity (such as strength) and femininity (suppleness, for example). Above all however, a fit body is defined as an energetic body, where energy is not only an instrument that the subject can exploit in daily life, but also an indicator of their (self-)worth. Sassatelli underscores therefore, that although the commercial success of fitness centres (like other technologies for the improvement and transformation of the body) is often situated in the context of 'the postmodern paradigm of absolute plasticity which has been associated with commercial culture', the construction of a 'fit' body is also a project bound by heavy, sometimes moral, burdens. As is often the case in consumer culture, she argues, social phenomena that promise to emancipate the subject also serve to discipline him or her. With consumer choice, comes individual responsibility. Nevertheless, caring for the body cannot be understood to be a purely personal affair. For while the 'modern gym no longer offers the physical education propounded by the nation states of the nineteenth century' (Sassatelli 2000: 399), training is still a highly organised and productive time. What is *produced* is not solely 'fitness', but also, importantly, 'a special notion of what is natural, what is right for the body and the self' (Sassatelli 2000: 409). Herein lies the focus of the extract that we have chosen to include in this section. In it, Sassatelli explores precisely where the limits of the 'natural' are understood to lie in the gym, not only in terms of the body, but also in terms of the transformations that are wrought upon it.

If the participants in Sassatelli's research are constrained in their bodily activities by some notion of the 'natural', Oliviero Toscani, the Italian photographer behind many of Benetton's advertising campaigns, seems to recognise no such boundaries. In this extract, Celia Lury explores some of the implications of Toscani's vision of 'race'. First, she begins by noting the striking way that Benetton exploits racially coded models (see the discussion of Susan Willis's claim, in the Introduction to this book, that consumer culture is overwhelmingly white). 'Race', in Benetton's world, is undoubtedly real. It is not however, Lury argues, given in nature, if nature is understood to be that which is immutable, or fixed for all time. On the contrary, the stylistic effect of Toscani's photographs is to shift the locus of 'race' away from a fixed biological essence to *colour*, 'not any particular colour but colour as such, colour as the medium of difference'. With this shift, Toscani also 'liberates' a series of other boundaries. For if it is colour that counts, then it makes *no difference* whether the object of colour is skin or cloth, animal or human. Just as Baudrillard argues that the fashion model's body in consumer culture is not so much a body as an abstract shape, so Lury suggests, not entirely dissimilarly, that 'race' is part of a forum of signs, 'constituted in the arbitrary relations between signifier and signified'. The neutral backgrounds which frequently characterise Benetton adverts point in addition to an effacement of *context*, of scale, and of perspective. It is this erasure – of things and the relations between them that 'bind' as it were (whether they be natural or cultural) – that enables 'race' (and indeed sex) to be reworked as *cultural essentialism*, by which Lury means that 'race' becomes a matter of personal style, a choice, much like the colour of one's clothes is a choice. 'Race', in short, is 'enterprised up'.

In making this claim, Lury is drawing on the work of the anthropologist Marilyn Strathern. For Strathern, as indicated in the extract here, something is 'enterprised up' when the natural dimension of a product is culturally enhanced during the course of the marketing process. The marketed apple, for example, is both the 'natural' apple and a bit more. Importantly, this difference between the 'natural' and the 'cultural' is conflated: they become one. And so again, as is often the case in discussions of the body in consumer culture, the issue concerns the changing 'nature' of the relation between nature and culture, and the implications of those changes. In this extract, Strathern considers some of those implications in relation to the new reproductive technologies. These technologies, she argues, take kinship and kinship relations out of the sphere of the given and re-position them as a matter of choice. Biology is now 'under control' (or at least so it appears) – and, as such, can no longer be understood to be 'nature'. But what then, Strathern asks, does the child born of these technologies embody? Not a set of social relations about which one can do very little, she answers, but rather the choices of the parents. And in so concluding, Strathern shows us a glimpse of a world which is presently full of 'persons embodying the choices of others', but which perhaps one day will be 'able to reproduce the choices without the bother of putting them into bodies'.

REFERENCES

McClintock, A. (1995) 'Soft-soaping empire: commodity racism and imperial advertising', *Imperial Leather: Race, Gender and Sexuality in the Colonial Conquest*, London and New York: Routledge.

Sassatelli, R. (2000) 'The commercialization of discipline: keep-fit culture and its values', *Journal of Modern Italian Studies*, 5, 3: 396–411.

Chapter 37

Anne McClintock

SOFT-SOAPING EMPIRE
Commodity racism and imperial advertising

From A. McClintock (1995) *Imperial Leather: Race, Gender and Sexuality in the Colonial Conquest*, London: Routledge.

> Soap is Civilization.
> (Unilever Company Slogan)
>
> Doc: My, it's so clean.
> Grumpy: There's dirty work afoot.
> (Snow White and the Seven Dwarfs)

[...]

Soap and commodity spectacle

BEFORE THE LATE NINETEENTH CENTURY, clothes and bedding washing was done in most households only once or twice a year in great, communal binges, usually in public at streams or rivers.[1] As for body washing, not much had changed since the days when Queen Elizabeth I was distinguished by the frequency with which she washed: "regularly every month whether she needed it or not."[2] By the 1890s, however, soap sales had soared, Victorians were consuming 26,000 tons of soap a year, and advertising had emerged as the central cultural form of commodity capitalism.[3]

Before 1851, advertising scarcely existed. As a commercial form, it was generally regarded as a confession of weakness, a rather shabby last resort. Most advertising was limited to small newspaper advertisements, cheap handbills and posters. After midcentury, however, soap manufacturers began to pioneer the use of pictorial advertising as a central part of business policy.

The initial impetus for soap advertising came from the realm of empire. With the burgeoning of imperial cotton on the slave plantations came the surplus of cheap cotton goods, alongside the growing buying power of a middle class that could afford for the first time to consume such goods in large quantities. Similarly, the sources for cheap palm oil, coconut oil and cottonseed oil flourished in the imperial plantations of West Africa, Malay, Ceylon, Fiji and New Guinea. As rapid changes in the technology of soapmaking took place in Britain after midcentury, the prospect dawned of a large domestic market for soft body soaps, which had previously been a luxury that only the upper class could afford.

Economic competition with the United States and Germany created the need for a more aggressive promotion of British products and led to the first real innovations in advertising. In 1884, the year of the Berlin Conference, the first wrapped soap was sold under a brand name. This small event signified a major transformation in capitalism, as imperial competition gave rise to the creation of monopolies. Henceforth, items formerly indistinguishable from each other (soap sold simply as soap) would be marketed by their corporate signature (Pears, Monkey Brand, etc). Soap became one of the first commodities to register the historic shift from myriad small businesses to the great imperial monopolies. In the 1870s, hundreds of small soap companies plied the new trade in hygiene, but by the end of the century, the trade was monopolized by ten large companies.

In order to manage the great soap show, an aggressively entrepreneurial breed of advertisers emerged, dedicated to gracing each homely product with a radiant halo of imperial glamour and racial potency. The advertising agent, like the bureaucrat, played a vital role in the imperial expansion of foreign trade. Advertisers billed themselves as "empire builders" and flattered themselves with "the responsibility of the historic imperial mission." Said one: "Commerce even more than sentiment binds the ocean sundered portions of empire together. Anyone who increases these commercial interests strengthens the whole fabric of the empire."[4] Soap was credited not only with bringing moral and economic salvation to Britain's "great unwashed" but also with magically embodying the spiritual ingredient of the imperial mission itself.

In an ad for Pears, for example, a black and implicitly racialized coalsweeper holds in his hands a glowing, occult object. Luminous with its own inner radiance, the simple soap bar glows like a fetish, pulsating magically with spiritual enlightenment and imperial grandeur, promising to warm the hands and hearts of working people across the globe.[5] Pears, in particular, became intimately associated with a purified nature magically cleansed of polluting industry (tumbling kittens, faithful dogs, children festooned with flowers) and a purified working class magically cleansed of polluting labor (smiling servants in crisp white aprons, rosy-cheeked match girls and scrubbed scullions).[6]

Nonetheless, the Victorian obsession with cotton and cleanliness was not simply a mechanical reflex of economic surplus. If imperialism garnered a bounty of cheap cotton and soap oils from coerced colonial labor, the middle class Victorian fascination with clean, white bodies and clean, white clothing stemmed not only from the rampant profiteering of the imperial economy but also from the realms of ritual and fetish.

Soap did not flourish when imperial ebullience was at its peak. It emerged commercially during an era of impending crisis and social calamity, serving to preserve, through fetish ritual, the uncertain boundaries of class, gender and race identity in a social order felt to be threatened by the fetid effluvia of the slums, the belching smoke of industry, social agitation, economic upheaval, imperial competition and anticolonial resistance. Soap offered the promise of spiritual salvation and regeneration through commodity consumption, a regime of domestic hygiene that could restore the threatened potency of the imperial body politic and the race.

[...]

Empire of the home: racializing domesticity

The soap

Four fetishes recur ritualistically in soap advertising: soap itself, white clothing (especially aprons), mirrors and monkeys. A typical Pears' advertisement figures a black child and a white child together in a bathroom. The Victorian bathroom is the innermost sanctuary of domestic hygiene and by extension the private temple of public regeneration. The sacrament of soap offers a reformation allegory whereby the purification of the domestic body becomes a metaphor for the regeneration of the body politic. In this particular ad, a black boy sits in the bath, gazing wide-eyed into the water as if into a foreign element. A white boy, clothed in a white apron – the familiar fetish of domestic purity – bends benevolently over his "lesser" brother, bestowing upon him the precious talisman of racial progress. The magical fetish of soap promises that the commodity can regenerate the Family of Man by washing from the skin the very stigma of racial and class degeneration.

Soap advertising offers an allegory of imperial progress as spectacle. In this ad, the imperial topos that I call panoptical time (progress consumed as a spectacle from a point of privileged invisibility) enters the domain of the commodity. In the second frame of the ad, the black child is out of the bath and the white boy shows him his startled visage in the mirror. The black boy's body has become magically white, but his face – for Victorians the seat of rational individuality and self-consciousness – remains stubbornly black. The white child is thereby figured as the agent of history and the male heir to progress, reflecting his lesser brother in the European mirror of self-consciousness. In the Victorian mirror, the black child witnesses his predetermined destiny of imperial metamorphosis but remains a passive racial hybrid, part black, part white, brought to the brink of civilization by the twin commodity fetishes of soap and mirror. The advertisement discloses a crucial element of late Victorian commodity culture: the metaphoric transformation of imperial *time* into consumer *space* – imperial progress consumed at a glance as domestic spectacle.

The monkey

The metamorphosis of imperial time into domestic space is captured most vividly by the advertising campaign for Monkey Brand Soap. During the 1880s, the urban landscape of Victorian Britain teemed with the fetish monkeys of this soap. The monkey with its frying pan and bar of soap perched everywhere, on grimy hoardings and buses, on walls and shop fronts, promoting the soap that promised magically to do away with domestic labor: "No dust, no dirt, no labor." Monkey Brand Soap promised not only to regenerate the race but also to magically erase the unseemly spectacle of women's manual labor.

In an exemplary ad, the fetish soap-monkey sits cross-legged on a doorstep, the threshold boundary between private domesticity and public commerce – the embodiment of anachronistic space (Figure 37.1). Dressed like an organ grinder's minion in a gentleman's ragged suit, white shirt and tie, but with improbably human hands and feet, the monkey extends a frying pan to catch the surplus cash of passersby. On the doormat before him, a great bar of soap is displayed, accompanied by a placard that reads: "My Own Work." In every respect the soap-monkey is a hybrid: not entirely ape, not entirely human; part street beggar, part gentleman; part artist, part advertiser. The creature

Figure 37.1 Anachronistic space: the threshold of domesticity and market

inhabits the ambivalent border of jungle and city, private and public, the domestic and the commercial, and offers as its handiwork a fetish that is both art and commodity.

Monkeys inhabit Western discourse on the borders of social limit, marking the place of a contradiction in social value. As Donna Haraway has argued: "the primate body, as part of the body of nature, may be read as a map of power."[7] Primatology, Haraway insists, "is a Western discourse ... a political order that works by the negotiation of boundaries achieved through ordering differences."[8] In Victorian iconography, the ritual recurrence of the monkey figure is eloquent of a crisis in value and hence anxiety at possible boundary breakdown. The primate body became a symbolic space for reordering and policing boundaries between humans and nature, women and men, family and politics, empire and metropolis.

Simian imperialism is also centrally concerned with the problem of representing *social change*. By projecting history (rather than fate, or God's will) onto the theater of nature, primatology made nature the alibi of political violence and placed in the hands of "rational science" the authority to sanction and legitimize social change. Here, "the scene of origins," Haraway argues, "is not the cradle of civilization, but the cradle of culture ... the origin of sociality itself, especially in the densely meaning-laden icon of the family."[9] Primatology emerges as a theater for negotiating the perilous boundaries between the family (as natural and female) and power (as political and male).

The appearance of monkeys in soap advertising signals a dilemma: *how to represent domesticity without representing women at work*. The Victorian middle-class house was structured round the fundamental contradiction between women's paid and unpaid domestic work. As women were driven from paid work in mines, factories, shops and trades to private, unpaid work in the home, domestic work became economically undervalued and the middle-class definition of femininity figured the "proper" woman as one who did not work for profit. At the same time, a *cordon sanitaire* of racial degeneration was thrown around those women who did work publicly and visibly for money. What could not be incorporated into the industrial formation (women's domestic economic value) was displaced onto the invented domain of the primitive, and thereby disciplined and contained.

Monkeys, in particular, were deployed to legitimize social boundaries as edicts of nature. Fetishes straddling nature and culture, monkeys were seen as allied with the dangerous classes: the "apelike" wandering poor, the hungry Irish, Jews, prostitutes, impoverished black people, the ragged working class, criminals, the insane and female miners and servants, who were collectively seen to inhabit the threshold of racial degeneration. When Charles Kingsley visited Ireland, for example, he lamented: "I am haunted by the human chimpanzees I saw along that hundred miles of horrible country. ... But to see white chimpanzees in dreadful; if they were black, one would not feel it so much, but their skins, except where tanned by exposure, are as white as ours."[10]

In the Monkey Brand advertisement, the monkey's signature of labor ("My Own Work") signals a double disavowal. Soap is masculinized, figured as a male product, while the (mostly female) labor of the workers in the huge, unhealthy soap factories is disavowed. At the same time, the labor of social transformation in the daily scrubbing and scouring of the sinks, pans and dishes, labyrinthine floors and corridors of Victorian domestic space vanishes – refigured as anachronistic space, primitive and bestial. Female servants disappear and in their place crouches a phantasmic male hybrid. Thus, domesticity – seen as the sphere most separate from the marketplace and the masculine hurly-burly of empire – takes shape around the invented ideas of the primitive and the commodity fetish.

In Victorian culture, the monkey was an icon of metamorphosis, perfectly serving soap's liminal role in mediating the transformations of nature (dirt, waste and disorder) into culture (cleanliness, rationality and industry). Like all fetishes, the monkey is a contradictory image, embodying the hope of imperial progress through commerce while at the same time rendering visible deepening Victorian fears of urban militancy and colonial misrule. The soap-monkey became the emblem of industrial progress and imperial evolution, embodying the double promise that nature could be redeemed by consumer capital and that consumer capital could be guaranteed by natural law. At the same time, however, the soap-monkey was eloquent of the degree to which fetishism structures industrial rationality.

The mirror

In most Monkey Brand advertisements, the monkey holds a frying pan, which is also a mirror. In a similar Brook's Soap ad, a classical female beauty with bare white arms stands draped in white, her skin and clothes epitomizing the exhibition value of sexual purity and domestic leisure, while from the cornucopia she holds flows a grotesque effluvium of hobgoblin angels. Each hybrid fetish embodies the doubled Victorian image of woman as "angel in the drawing room, monkey in the bedroom," as well as the racial iconography of evolutionary progress from ape to angel. Historical time, again, is captured as domestic spectacle, eerily reflected in the frying pan/mirror fetish.

[…]

Notes

1. Davidoff Leonore and Hall Catherine (1992) *Family Fortunes: Men and Women of the English Middle Class,* London: Routledge.

2. Lindsey David T. A. and Bamber Geoffrey C. (1965) *Soap-Making. Past and Present, 1876–1976,* Nottingham: Gerard Brothers Ltd, p. 34.

3. Lindsey and Bamber, *Soap-Making,* p. 38. Just how deeply the relation between soap and advertising became embedded in popular memory is expressed in words such as "soft-soap" and "soap opera." For histories of advertising, see also Elliott Blanche B. (1962) *A History of English Advertising,* London: Business Publications Ltd); and Nevett, T. R. (1982) *Advertising in Britain. A History,* London: Heinemann.

4. Quoted in Diana and Hindley Geoffrey (1972) *Advertising in Victorian England, 1837–1901,* London: Wayland, p. 117.

5. Dempsey Mike (ed.) (1978) *Bubbles: Early Advertising Art from A. & Pears Ltd,* London: Fontana.

6. Bradley Laurel "From Eden to Empire: John Everett Millais' Cherry Ripe," *Victorian Studies* 34(2) (Winter 1991) pp. 179–203. See also, Michael Dempsey, *Bubbles.*

7. Haraway Donna (1989) *Primate Visions: Gender, Race, and Nature in the World of Modern Science,* London: Routledge, p. 10.

8. Haraway, *Primate Visions,* p. 10.

9. Haraway, *Primate Visions,* pp. 10–11.

10. Charles Kingsley, Letter to his wife, 4 July 1860, in *Charles Kingsley: His Letters and Memories of His Life,* Francis E. Kingsley (ed.) (1877) London: Henry S. King and Co, p. 107. See also Richard Kearney (ed.) (1985) *The Irish Mind,* Dublin: Wolfhound Press; Curtis, L. P. Jr., (1968) *Anglo-Saxons and Celts: A Study of Anti-Irish Prejudice in Victorian England,* Bridgeport: Conference on British Studies of University of Bridgeport and Deane Seamus (1985) "Civilians and Barbarians," *Ireland's Field Day,* London: Hutchinson, pp. 33–42.

Chapter 38

Jean Baudrillard

THE FINEST CONSUMER OBJECT
The body

From J. Baudrillard (1998) 'The finest consumer object: the body', in *The Consumer Society: Myths and Structures*, London: Sage.

IN THE CONSUMER PACKAGE, there is one object finer, more precious and more dazzling than any other – and even more laden with connotations than the automobile, in spite of the fact that that encapsulates them all. That object is the BODY. Its 'rediscovery', in a spirit of physical and sexual liberation, after a millennial age of puritanism; its omnipresence (specifically the omnipresence of the female body, a fact we shall have to try to explain) in advertising, fashion and mass culture; the hygienic, dietetic, therapeutic cult which surrounds it, the obsession with youth, elegance, virility/femininity, treatments and regimes, and the sacrificial practices attaching to it all bear witness to the fact that the body has today become an *object of salvation*. It has literally taken over that moral and ideological function from the soul.

Unremitting propaganda reminds us that, in the words of the old hymn, we have only one body and it has to be saved. For centuries, there was a relentless effort to convince people they had no bodies (though they were never really convinced); today, there is a relentless effort to *convince them of their bodies*. There is something strange about this. Is not the body the most obvious of things? It seems not. The body is a *cultural* fact. Now, in any culture whatsoever, the mode of organization of the relation to the body reflects the mode of organization of the relation to things and of social relations. In a capitalist society, the general status of private property applies also to the body, to the way we operate socially with it and the mental representation we have of it. In the traditional order – in the case of the peasant, for example – there was no narcissistic investment or spectacular perception of his body, but an instrumental/magical vision, induced by the labour process and the relation to nature.

What we want to show is that the current structures of production/consumption induce in the subject a dual practice, linked to a split (but profoundly interdependent) representation of his/her own body: the representation of the body as **capital** and as **fetish** (or consumer object). In both cases, it is important that, far from the body being denied or left out of account, there is deliberate *investment in* it (in the two senses, economic and psychical, of the term).

The secret keys to your body

A fine example of this managed reappropriation of the body is provided by *Elle*, in an article entitled 'The secret keys to your body which unlock the door to complex-free living'.

'Your body is both your outer limit and your sixth sense,' the article begins, and it assumes a serious air by recounting the psycho-genesis of the appropriation of the body and its image: 'At around six months, you began to perceive, as yet very obscurely, that you had a distinct body.' After an allusion to the mirror-stage ('psychologists call this ...') and a timid allusion to erogenous zones ('Freud says that ...'), it comes to the central point: 'Are you at ease in your body?' Right away, in comes Brigitte Bardot (BB): she 'is at ease in her body'. 'Everything about her is beautiful: her neck, her back, particularly the small of the back ... BB's secret? She really inhabits her body. She is like a little animal who precisely fills up her dress.' (Does she inhabit her body or her dress? Which of these, the body or the dress, is her second home? This is precisely the point: she wears her body like a dress, and this makes 'inhabiting' a fashion effect, a 'package' effect, and relates it to a ludic principle which is further reinforced by the 'little animal' reference.) If, in the past, it was 'the soul which clothed the body', today it is the skin which clothes it, though not the skin as irruption of nudity (and, hence, of desire), but as prestige garment and second home, as sign and as fashion reference (and therefore substitutable for the dress without change of meaning, as can be seen in the current exploitation of nudity in the theatre and elsewhere, where, in spite of the false sexual pathos, it appears as one more term in the fashion paradigm).

[...]

If you don't make your bodily devotions, if you sin by omission, you will be punished. Everything that ails you comes from being culpably irresponsible towards yourself (your own salvation). Quite apart from the atmosphere of singular moral terrorism which infuses this *carte du tendre* (and which equates with puritan terrorism, except that in this case it is no longer God punishing you, but your own body – a suddenly maleficent, repressive agency which takes its revenge if you are not gentle with it), one can see how this discourse, under the guise of reconciling everyone with their own body, does in fact reintroduce, between the subject and the objectivized body as threatening double, the same relations which are those of social life, the same determinations which are those of social relations: blackmail, repression, persecution syndrome, conjugal neurosis (the same women who read this will read a few pages further on that if they are not affectionate to their husbands, they will bear the responsibility for the failure of their marriages). Apart, then, from this latent terrorism, directed in *Elle* more particularly at women, what is interesting is the suggestion that one should revert back into one's own body and invest it narcissistically 'from the inside', not in any sense to get to know it in depth, but, by a wholly fetishistic and spectacular logic, to form it into a smoother, more perfect, more functional object for the outside world. This narcissistic relation – it is a *managed* narcissism, operating on the body as in colonized virgin 'territory', 'affectionately' [*tendrement*] exploring the body like a deposit to be mined in order to extract from it the visible signs of happiness, health, beauty, and the animality which triumphs in the marketplace of fashion – finds its mystical expression in the readers' confessions which follow: 'I was discovering my body. I could feel it in all its purity.' And, even better: 'It was as though I was being hugged by my body. I began to love it. And, loving it, I wanted to care for it with the same affection I felt for my children.' What is significant is this regressive involution of affectivity into the body-as-child, the body-as-trinket – inexhaustible metaphor of a penis cherished, cradled and … castrated. In this sense, the body, become the finest object of solicitude, monopolizes for itself all so-called normal affectivity (towards other real persons), without, however, taking on a value of its own, since, in this process of affective rerouting [détournement], any other object can, by the same fetishistic logic, play this role. The body is simply the finest of these psychically possessed, manipulated and consumed objects.

But the main thing is that this narcissistic reinvestment, orchestrated as a mystique of liberation and accomplishment, is in fact always simultaneously an investment of an efficient, competitive, economic type. The body 'reappropriated' in this way is reappropriated first to meet 'capitalist' objectives: in other words, where it is invested, it is invested in order to produce a yield. The body is not reappropriated for the autonomous ends of the subject, but in terms of a *normative* principle of enjoyment and hedonistic profitability, in terms of an enforced instrumentality that is indexed to the code and the norms of a society of production and managed consumption. In other words, one manages one's body; one handles it as one might handle an inheritance; one manipulates it as one of the many *signifiers of social status*. The woman who said she 'wanted to care for it with the same affection [she] felt for [her] children' immediately adds: 'I began to visit beauticians … The people who saw me after that crisis found me happier, better looking.' 'Recuperated' as an instrument of enjoyment and an indicator of prestige, the body is then subjected to a *labour of investment* (solicitude, obsession) which, once the myth of liberation that acts as cover is peeled away, doubtless represents a more profoundly alienated labour than the exploitation of the body as labour power.

Functional beauty

In this long process of sacralization of the body as exponential value, of the *functional* body – that is to say, the body which is no longer 'flesh' as in the religious conception, or labour power as in industrial logic, but is taken up again in its materiality (or its 'visible' ideality) as narcissistic cult object or element of social ritual and tactics – beauty and eroticism are two major leitmotivs.

They are inseparable and the two together institute this *new ethics of the relation to the body*. Though valid for both men and women, they are, nevertheless, differentiated into feminine and masculine poles. The two opposing models – the basic elements of which are largely interchangeable – might be termed **phryneism** and **athleticism**. Still, the feminine model has a kind of priority: it is this model which, to some extent, functions as the template of this new ethics. And it is not by chance that it is in *Elle* that we find the type of material we have analysed above.

For women, beauty has become an absolute, religious imperative. Being beautiful is no longer an effect of nature or a supplement to moral qualities. It is **the** basic, imperative quality of those who take the same care of their faces and figures as they do of their souls. It is a sign, at the level of the body, that one is a member of the elect, just as success is such a sign in business. And, indeed, in their respective magazines, beauty and success are accorded *the same mystical foundation*: for women, it is *sensitivity*, exploring and evoking 'from the inside' all the parts of the body; for the entrepreneur, it is the adequate *intuition* of all the possibilities of the market. A sign of election and salvation: the Protestant ethic is not far away here. And it is true that beauty is such an absolute imperative only because it is a form of capital.

Let us take this same logic a little further. The ethics of beauty, which is the very ethics of fashion, may be defined as the reduction of all concrete values – the 'use-values' of the body (energetic, gestural, sexual) – to a single functional 'exchange-value', which itself alone, in its abstraction, encapsulates the *idea* of the glorious, fulfilled body, the *idea* of desire and pleasure [*jouissance*], and of course thereby also denies and forgets them in their reality and in the end simply peters out into an exchange of signs. For beauty is nothing more than sign material being exchanged. It *functions* as sign-value. That is why we can say that the beauty imperative is one of the modalities of the functional imperative, this being valid for objects as much as it is for women (and men), the beautician every woman has become being the counterpart of the designer and stylist in the business sphere.

Moreover, if we look at the dominant principles of industrial aesthetics (functionalism), we can see that they apply generally to the charter for beauty: BB feeling 'at ease in her body' or 'precisely fill[ing] up her dress' is part of this same pattern of the 'harmonious marriage of function and form'.

Functional eroticism

Alongside beauty, as we have just defined it, sexuality everywhere orientates the 'rediscovery' and *consumption* of the body today. The beauty imperative, which is an imperative of turning the body to advantage by way of narcissistic reinvestment, involves *the erotic as sexual foil*. We have clearly to distinguish the erotic as a generalized dimension of exchange in our societies from sexuality properly so called. We have to distinguish the erotic body – substrate of the exchanged signs of desire – from the body as site of fantasy and abode of desire. In the drive/body, the fantasy/body, the individual structure of desire predominates. In the 'eroticized' body, it is the social function of exchange which predominates. In this sense, the erotic imperative – which, like courtesy or so many other social rituals, is mediated by an instrumental code of signs – is merely (like the aesthetic imperative in beauty) a variant or metaphor of the functional imperative.

The *Elle* woman is 'hot' with that same heat, that same warmth one finds in modern furniture: it is an 'atmosphere' heat. It no longer comes from intimacy and sensuality, but from calculated sexual signification. Sensuality is heat. This sexuality, for its part, is *hot and cold*, like the play of warm and cold colours in a 'functional' interior. It has the same 'whiteness' as the enveloping forms of 'stylized', 'dressed-up' modern objects. But it is also not a 'frigidity', as has been suggested, since frigidity still implies a sexual resonance of violation. The fashion model is not frigid: she is an *abstraction*.

The fashion model's body is no longer an object of desire, but a functional object, a forum of signs in which fashion and the erotic are mingled. It is no longer a synthesis of gestures, even if fashion photography puts all its artistry into *re-creating* gesture and naturalness by a process of simulation. It is no longer, strictly speaking, a body, but a *shape*.

This is where all modern censors are misled (or are content to be misled): the fact is that in advertising and fashion naked bodies (both women's and men's) refuse the status of flesh, of sex, of finality of desire, instrumentalizing rather the fragmented parts of the body in a gigantic process of *sublimation*, of denying the body in its very evocation.

Just as the erotic is never in desire but in signs, so the functional beauty of the fashion models is never in their expressions but in their 'figures'. Irregularity or ugliness would bring out a meaning again: they are excluded. For beauty here is wholly in abstraction, in emptiness, in ecstatic absence and transparency. This disembodiment is ultimately encapsulated in the *gaze*. These fascinating/fascinated, sunken eyes, this objectless gaze – both oversignification of desire and total absence of desire – are beautiful in their empty erection, in the exaltation of their censorship. That is their functionality. Medusa eyes, eyes themselves turned to stone, pure signs. Thus, all along the unveiled, exalted body, in these spectacular eyes, eyes ringed by fashion, not by pleasure, it is the very meaning of the body, the truth of the body which vanishes in a hypnotic process. It is to this extent that the body – particularly the female body and, most particularly, the body of that absolute model, the fashion mannequin – constitutes itself as an object that is the equivalent to the other sexless and functional objects purveyed in advertising.

Pleasure principle and productive force

Conversely, the least of objects, implicitly cathected on the pattern of the female body/object, is fetishized in this same way. Hence the generalized imbuing of the whole field of 'consumption' by eroticism. This is not *a* fashion in the lighter sense of the term; it is the specific, rigorous logic of *fashion*. Bodies and objects form a network of homogeneous signs which may, on the basis of the abstraction we have just discussed, exchange their significations (this is, properly speaking, their 'exchange-value') and 'show each other off [*se faire valoir*] mutually'.

This *homology between bodies and objects* takes us into the deep mechanisms of managed consumption. If the 'rediscovery of the body' is always the rediscovery of the body/object in the generalized context of other objects, one can see how easy, logical and necessary a transition there is from the functional appropriation of the body to the appropriation of goods and objects in shopping. And we know, indeed, to what extent the modern eroticism and aesthetics of the body are steeped in an environment teeming with products, gadgets and accessories in an atmosphere of total sophistication. From hygiene to make-up (not forgetting suntans, exercise and the many 'liberations' of fashion), the rediscovery of the body takes place initially through objects. It even seems that the only drive that is really liberated is the *drive to buy*.

[...]

This is where all the psycho-functionality analysed above assumes its full economic and ideological meaning. The body sells products. Beauty sells products. Eroticism sells products. And this is not the least of the reasons which, in the last instance, orientate the entire historical process of the 'liberation of the body'. It is the same with the body as it is with labour power. It *has to be* 'liberated, emancipated' to be able to be exploited rationally for productivist ends. Just as freedom to dispose of oneself and personal interest – the formal principles of the individual freedom of the worker – have to operate for labour power to be able to transform itself into the demand for wages and exchange-value, so the individual has to rediscover his body and invest it narcissistically – *the formal principle of pleasure* – for the force of desire to be able to transform itself into a demand for rationally manipulable objects/signs. *The individual has to take himself as object, as the finest of objects, as the most precious exchange material, for an economic process of profit generation to be established at the level of the deconstructed body, of deconstructed sexuality.*

Modern strategy of the body

[…]

A long desacralization and secularization in favour of the body has run through the whole of the Western era: the values of the body have been subversive values, sources of the most acute ideological contradiction. But how do matters stand today when these values are largely uncontested and have gained acceptance as a new ethic (there is much to be said on this subject: we are now, rather, in a phase in which the puritan and hedonist ideologies are concertinaed, their themes intermingling at every level)? We can see that the body today, apparently triumphant, instead of still constituting a living, contradictory force, a force for 'demystification', has quite simply taken over from the soul as mythic instance, as dogma and as salvational scheme. Its 'discovery', which for many centuries represented a critique of the sacred, a call for greater freedom, truth and emancipation – in short a battling for humanity, against God – today occurs as an act of *resacralization*. The cult of the body no longer stands in contradiction to the cult of the soul: it is the successor to that cult and heir to its ideological function. As Norman O. Brown says in *Life against Death:* 'We must not be misled by the flat antinomy of the sacred and the secular, and interpret as "secularization" what is only a metamorphosis of the sacred.'[1]

The material evidence of the 'liberated' body (though, as we have seen, liberated as sign/object and censored in its subversive truth as desire, not only in athletic activity and hygiene, but also in eroticism) must not be allowed to deceive us here: it merely expresses the supplanting of an outdated ideology – that of the soul, which is inadequate for a developed productivist system and incapable now of ensuring ideological integration – by a more functional modern ideology which, in all essentials, preserves the individualistic value system and the social structures connected with it. And it even reinforces these, establishing them on an almost permanent basis, since it substitutes for the transcendence of the soul the total immanence, the spontaneous self-evidence of the body. Now, that self-evidence is false evidence. The body as instituted by modern mythology is no more material than the soul. Like the soul, it is an *idea*, or, rather – since the term 'idea' does not mean much – it is a hypostasized part-object, a double privileged and invested as such. It has become, as the soul was in its time, the privileged substrate of objectivization – *the guiding myth of an ethic of consumption*. We can see how intimately the body is involved in the goals of production as (economic) support, as principle of the managed (psychological) integration of the individual, and as (political) strategy of social control.

[…]

Note

1   Brown, Norman, O. *Life Against Death: The Psychoanalytic Meaning of History,* Middletown, CT: Wesleyan University Press.

Chapter 39

Roberta Sassatelli

THE COMMERCIALIZATION OF DISCIPLINE
Keep-fit culture and its values

From R. Sassatelli (2000) 'The commercialization of discipline: keep-fit culture and its values', translated by Anne Collins, *Journal of Modern Italian Studies*, 5(3): 396–411.

[...]

Natural plasticity

DESPITE THE EMPHASIS ON PHYSICAL efficiency and individual choice, despite its proclaimed pluralistic attitude to body shape, the legitimation of the gym is bound to a strong normative vision. First of all, the ideal of fitness calls into play the idea of 'nature' and is based on specific notion of how the body can be transformed in a 'natural' way.

Although apparently a foregone conclusion, it should be noted that the body you get to know in the gym is not characterized by absolute plasticity. The body's plasticity is bound to the effective capacity of individuals to complete a training programme. Only training in the gym appears able to call into play the body's intrinsic plastic capacity. Training represents not only the instrument, but also the limit of the body's plasticity. Whenever they got the chance, the trainers I have seen in action would repeat that only exercise effectively helps improve physical defects and specified the extent to which the body could be transformed. For example, during a step lesson, we learn that it is 'useless to follow impossible diets': 'if you were born ... with a large bottom, the most you can do is exercise to prevent cellulitis!'

Clients also perceive the existence of specific limits to the body's plasticity. Among regular clients, many say they are not searching for 'anything excessive'. Working out, they claim, 'is not magic', it should be taken as 'something which in any case improves you and makes you feel better'. Regular attendance at a gym seems to teach clients to reclassify their own ideals of the body in line with the achievement limits of fitness training. A good example is Loretta, a 20-year-old sales assistant. Loretta claims she started going to the gym 'to model her body to perfection' and, at the same time, she recognizes that her ideal body is an illusion: 'I would like to have a figure like Anna Falchi, you think that by doing a few things you'll get there, like dieting, exercising and using creams, but it's virtually impossible if you don't have the right build. For me it's difficult to reach my goal because of my frame, wide hips and thick ankles'. Yet Loretta is satisfied with the gym, not because it has given her that 'impossible' body which still attracts her, but because by training she has obtained a better body: 'you make the most of what you've got: you and your energy'.

All this is crucial because there are many other commercially available ways of transforming your body. New transformation techniques, from plastic surgery to hormone therapy, are among the many possibilities open to individuals. In fact, in our culture a body plasticity beyond fitness exists and is, so to speak, legitimized by mediation of the market. Even for fitness enthusiasts, absolute plasticity is a potent utopia which induces discomfort and curiosity at the same time. Fitness participants are thereby forever engaged in defining the 'right' boundaries for body plasticity and they appear to do so on the basis of what they have learnt in the gym. This may be why, during interviews, clients were so quick and keen to emphasize that the changes obtained by training are very specific. Mentioning the possible alternatives to the gym, for example, all the clients interviewed immediately indicated some other way of 'exercising', from 'country walks', to 'swimming', 'cycling', 'tennis' and 'jogging'; some mentioned 'massage', 'hydromassage' or 'creams', but only when repeatedly solicited did they discuss more invasive techniques which, however, they adamantly rejected.

In a way which may give rise to contradictions and is based on an unstable equilibrium, gyms draw clients towards the idea that the body, though plastic, has a plasticity limit defined by each person's ability to work on his or her own body. The people I interviewed were very critical of commercially widespread 'invasive' techniques like plastic surgery. Plastic surgery, most of them claimed, changes your body directly, but in an 'unnatural' way, without making it work, without exploiting its intrinsic capacity, and this is why it clashes with fitness. Even a young woman worried about her appearance like Loretta says that she 'doesn't trust' the scalpel: 'I wouldn't like to change like that ... it's against the nature of ageing, like removing flesh, having a face lift. Old age affects everyone, and you are as you are. I can't understand it! It's against nature! Dieting or working out is always natural, even make-up can help, but that is something that leaves you free to return to how you were before. With surgery you can't'.

[...]

Working out is always deemed the natural option, even when compared with other less intrusive and more mundane interventions on the body.

[...]

All these products [beauty treatments, make-up, clothes], though appreciated, are generally seen as 'superficial': they are 'external', compared to exercising which 'actively' exploits the body's 'internal' capabilities, and do not produce 'true' transformations. It is in this sense that Sandro [a decorator] sets the artificial nature of clothes, mainly construed as false and misleading, against the naturalness of working out: 'clothes are fake', they are 'something which makes you look different'. Clothes, but also make-up and beauty treatments, albeit with different nuances, do not belong intimately to the subject, to his/her 'feeling', but only to the dimension of self-presentation.

The naturalness of the changes wrought in the gym is twofold, cognitive and normative. First, the appeal to nature embodies a claim of truth about the body. By the same token, plasticity beyond the confines allowed by fitness is deemed unnatural since it is objectively incompatible with what is known about the body. Thus, in launching *Fitness Magazine*, the first widely circulated Italian periodical entirely devoted to fitness, the editorial office insists on the fact that fitness exercise mixes and merges nature and science. Most fitness publications normally contain a few pages devoted to anatomy and physiology. There are manuals that liken exercising to 'natural' medicine, and reject 'repressive' treatment that only 'tends to eliminate the symptoms of disease'. Clients also find training in the gym 'natural' in that it fits in with the body 'as it really is'. An enthusiast like Alessia, a 30-year-old post office worker, explains for example that 'you must' make your body 'act directly', 'not control it with drugs or other things', especially because in the end no other way works. With surgery, she added, 'you can have everything pulled up as much as you like, but it will still sag again: then you're worse off than before!'; 'massage machines ... are no use whatsoever', if anything 'they are really bad for you': they have made some people 'feel ill and throw up'; with massage 'you feel good there and then ... but afterwards your body doesn't really feel better, you haven't got rid of your nerves and you may even find it harder to go upstairs than you did before'; with make-up 'you look better', but your skin 'isn't oxygenated'. It is because the gym exploits the body's 'true' characteristics that it can produce a 'true' transformation. Techniques which clash with exercising may be admissible, but are destined to fail; they don't give people what they want because their bodies either rebel or are not even affected.

Absolute plasticity is also perceived as morally problematic. Training in the gym is not only rational, exact and effective, it is also right, correct and virtuous. This is discussed by Callan Pickney, an American trainer who has made a fortune all over the world and whose manuals are widely circulated in Italy too. She writes that physical exercise becomes part of our lives when and because 'nature needs a push' and that only we can 'take our lives in our hands', 'stop complaining' and 'get to work-out'. In other words, recourse to the notion of nature also underlies a moral justification. Elisa, a young student who doesn't want to appear 'vain', helps us to understand this point. 'Improving your external appearance', she explains, 'is not vanity' if it is the fruit of physical activity, if it is achieved 'by natural means, being careful what you do with your body'.

Elisa's words echo the majority of clients: exercise is natural since it engages the body's intrinsic capacity for changes. Training, they claim, changes the body by means of its own strength, it is a 'work-out on your own body by your own body.' The importance of this claim emerges on rereading the clients' stories. Even from the brief extracts given above, it is evident that clients consider the fact of using the body's energy for the purposes of changing it to be something which puts fitness in pride of place among the commercially available means of body intervention. This is combined with a moral emphasis which goes well beyond the body to involve the subject. Just as the docile instrumentality of the fit body alludes to a better, stronger individual, more in control of him/herself, so too the naturalness of fitness alludes to authenticity and willingness to endure fatigue for self-improvement. The effort required to improve the body makes it not only more useful to the subject, but also avoids the subject being 'unnatural'. It ensures, so to speak, that the transformations are legitimately acquired.

[...]

Fitness, choice and subjectivity

Straddling commercial culture and physical discipline, fitness, gyms occupy a highly significant cultural space. The practices and discourses of body control, health mainte- nance and the promotion of physical efficiency may serve the need of western nations to regulate an ageing population, but they are increasingly delivered by the private market of goods and services. More and more often, care for the body takes place within com- mercial facilities like fitness gyms and by practices carried out by individuals exercising free choice on the market and on themselves. A critical assessment of the keep-fit culture starting from this Italian study must start with commercial culture.

Even though it would be simplistic to say that clients are drawn to the gym by a rational choice, it is nonetheless important to recall tnat as commercial institutions, gyms cannot to without the notion of choice. For their very social legitimacy, today's gyms seem to need to depict those who frequent them as clients, consumers, that is, subjects able to decide their preferences autonomously. Voluntary attendance at a gym is therefore accom- panied by a strong emphasis on the individual. Yet unlike what is broadly claimed by both critics and supporters of commercial culture, individualism is expressed, at least in the Italian gyms I investigated, not in total freedom, but within the confines of responsibility and self-control. In turn, this seems to break away from the postmodern paradigm of absolute plasticity which has been associated with commercial culture and which sees indi- viduals intent on transforming their bodies, solely concerned with pleasing others and indiscriminately greedy for everything which will serve the purpose (Bordo 1993). Instead, today's gym seems to be an expression of another, perhaps older commercial culture – certainly a less permissive and indulgent one. Fitness enthusiasts are not simply invited to choose the body they prefer, but to work diligently and, as it were, with hum- ble determination, towards their own goals, in short to choose to discipline themselves. Likewise, as we have seen, clients tend to justify their preference for gyms in relation to the twofold desire to use their bodies to the full and not to be unnatural.

[...]

Fitness embodies the notion of choice and that special form of body – self dualism typ- ical of modern disciplinary techniques for which better self-control is obtained not through mortification of the flesh, but by controlled stimulation of its capabilities. For men and women alike, an athletic, toned, docile body has become an important sign of virtue and character (Gillick 1984; Glassner 1989; Rader 1991; White *et al*. 1995). The body is seen as the only area over which subjects think they can keep control in an uncontrollable world, or the starting place to demonstrate their superiority in times of hard social competition.

[...]

Abstract as the ideal of fitness may be, its characteristics stress certain key values: the instrumentality of the body, the naturalness of fitness in enhancing that instrumentality and the authenticity of the subject who acquires a better body by his/her own efforts. Gyms unfurl and govern individualism. Although attendance is voluntary, clients do not rely only on their own free choice to enhance the training and the resultant transforma- tions. On the contrary, they appeal to the idea that by working out with weights, step and exercise bicycles they can discover their own body and its naturalness, thereby becoming better, stronger selves.

References

Bordo, S. (1993) *Unbearable Weight. Feminism, Western Culture and the Body*, Berkeley: University of California Press.

Gillick, M. (1984) 'Health promotion, jogging and the pursuit of the moral life', *Journal of Health Politics, Policy and the Law*, 9(3): 369–87.

Glassner, B. (1989) 'Fitness and thex postmodern self', *Journal of Health Behaviour*, 30: 180–91.

Rader, B. J. (1991) 'The quest for self-sufficiency and the new strenuosity', *Journal of Sport History*, 18(2): 255–66.

White, P., Young, K. and Gillett, J. (1995) 'Bodywork as a moral imperative. Some critical notes on health and fitness', *Loisir et Société*, 18(1): 159–81.

Chapter 40

Celia Lury

THE UNITED COLORS OF DIVERSITY
Essential and inessential culture

From C. Lury (2000) 'The United Colors of diversity: essential and inessential culture', in S. Franklin, C. Lury and J. Stacey (eds), *Global Nature, Global Culture*, London: Sage.

[...]

Difference

[...]

BENETTON'S ADVERTISING IS DISTINCTIVE – at least in the UK – for its use of explicitly racially coded models: in general, advertising continues to be remarkably white. In what ways, though, do Benetton's photographic images represent diversity? How do these pictures mediate the relations between the specific and the universal, the cultural and the natural? As Back and Quaade observe, the dominant theme of Benetton's campaign is 'the accentuation of difference coupled with a simple statement of transcendence and global unity' (1993: 68). Applying the work of Stuart Hall, Back and Quaade further argue that this accentuation of difference is generated within a grammer of race:

> [T]he overpowering reference point in their imagery is that *race* is *real*: racial archetypes provide the vehicle for their message, and racial common sense is overbearingly *present* in the 'United Colors' myth, such that the reality of race is legitimated in Benetton's discourse.
>
> (1993: 79, original emphasis)

However, while the legitimation of race in Benetton's campaigns seems beyond dispute, I want to suggest that the novel productivity of these images is missed if it is argued that racial difference is *naturalized* here, if by that is meant that race is presented as an unchanging and eternal biological essence. 'Race', in this imagery, is not a matter of skin colour, of physical characteristics as the expression of a biological or natural essence, but rather of style, of the colour of skin, of colour itself as the medium of what might be called a second nature or, more provocatively, a *cultural essentialism*.

As noted above, 'The idea that's being sold is mainly colour and *joie de vivre* and can be recognized as such' (Mattei, n.d.: 4). So, for example, in Benetton promotional campaigns, young people are colour-coded: they are juxtaposed together to bring out colour contrasts as in Benetton outlets, in which stacks of jumpers are folded and piled up so as to seem as if they are paint colour charts. The overall effect of colour – not any particular colour but colour as such, colour as the medium of difference – is enhanced through the graduations in tone, the suggested compatibility of hues and contrasts in tints created by the endless repositioning of one shade against another. In the creation of this effect, the distinction between cloth and skin is eschewed. In a promotional illustration for tights, for example, the viewer is confronted by a series of legs in profile, each slightly different in shape ('different races and sizes'), completely encased in multi-coloured tights. Here, skin colour is not simply made invisible but displaced and reworked as a stylized act of choice: what colour is your skin going to be today? (The same choice was promoted by Crayola in the production of 'My World Colors', a box of sixteen crayons, supposedly representing the diversity of skin, hair and eye colours, from sepia to raw peach, of the peoples of a colouring-book world.) Similarly, in the publicity images adopted by Benetton of white and black faces daubed with brightly coloured sun-protection creams, the colour of skin is made up/out to be artificial. Race is not not 'real' here, but it is no longer founded in biology but in culture, that is, in culture as a second nature (despite or, rather, precisely because of the play on the white western depiction of 'primitive' tribes through the trope of face-painting).

In yet another example, two eyes, of different colours, look out from a black face. The face is shot in such close-up that only the area surrounding the eyes is visible; the skin appears stretched to the edges of the image such that the contours of the face are flattened: its features and outline are hard to make out. Across this canvas is written, in white capitals, FABRICA, a word which, while taken from the Italian *fabbrica* (factory), also draws on the idea of Andy Warhol's New York City Factory of the 1960s. It resonates with the association of fabrication for English speakers: skin is once again represented as cloth. The promotional slogan 'United Colors of Benetton' is attached, as always, to the side of the image, as if it were a label. This is, in Marilyn Strathern's phrase, nature 'enterprised up' (1992): the natural, innate property and the artificial, cultural enhancement become one. Perusing Benetton's fashion catalogues, the viewer's gaze is drawn from shade to shade, obeying the textual laws of writing rather than the realist ones of verisimilitude, depth and figure. Biology is no longer a referent for race; rather, race is created in the colours constituted in the arbitrary relations between signifier and signified.

In fashion, what Walter Benjamin (1970) termed the phantasmagoria of commodities has always pressed close to the skin; clothing is quite literally at the borderline between subject and object, the cultural and the natural. Traversing this borderline is Benetton's problematic; indeed, it is the concern of a number of other fashion companies as well. For example, Moschino produced t-shirts with the slogan 'La nature c'est mieux que la couture'; while a brochure claims,

In regards to prints we have chosen only nature themes taken photographically from scientific texts in an effort not to alter even in the slightest way the God-given details. It is a sign of respect for God that we enthusiastically have begun to show, and indeed, to stress, not only the conceptual and symbolic value of nature, but also to emphasize the incredible variety of shapes, designs, and arabesques … images that nature has always possessed.

(Moschino promotional leaflet)

What distinguishes Benetton's iconography, however, is that it is explicitly concerned with a second nature, a nature that is a matter of choice.

The naturalness of choice

The representation of race as a choice (and of choice as a compulsory act) is central to Benetton's entire brand image and marketing strategy. This position is clearly elaborated in the fourth edition of *Colors*, a promotional magazine published by Benetton, the editor-in-chief of which was Toscani (although it is largely put together by the editor; in this case, Tibor Kalman). Here, the natural basis of race is both literally and figuratively decon-structed: photographic images of discrete parts of the bodies of people of different races – ears, noses, eyes, hair and blood – are juxtaposed, and the biological differences between different races are described and found to be either non-existent or unimpor-tant. But this does not mean that race is done away with; rather, nature is enterprised up and skin colour, hair type and eye shape are represented as nothing more nor less than artifice, or the art of choice. Culture ('a few simple procedures') is represented as a natural extension of this artifice. There is, for example, a feature on,

> How to change your race. You mean you're not a round-eyed, blond haired, white skinned, perky nosed god or goddess? No problem. All you have to do is to undergo a few simple procedures.
>
> (*Colors* no. 4, spring/summer 1993)

Information, costings and advice on cosmetic surgery, make-up and hairstyling are pro-vided, and there are photographic illustrations showing how a model, who is 'half black and half native American' can be made up/out to look realistically 'black', 'white' or 'oriental'. There are computer-generated images of a 'black' Queen Elizabeth II (Figure 40.1), a 'black' Arnold Schwarzenegger, a 'white' Spike Lee, an 'oriental' Pope John Paul II and a 'white' Michael Jackson.

[…]

'[C]olour and *joie de vivre*. … You like it because it reminds you of childhood, of well-defined, coloured pictures. Let us say that it is that type of style, more like printed paper, not necessarily real but neither totally unreal' (Mattei, n.d.: 4). In this not totally unreal reality, the aesthetic equivalence of cloth and skin as colours displaces not only the natural foundation of race, but also that of sex. This sidestepping is aided by the youthfulness of the models, one of the few constants in Benetton's universe of diver-sity, and a more general function of fashion itself. Of this function, Roland Barthes writes,

> Structurally, the junior is presented as the complex degree of the *feminine/ masculine*: it tends towards androgyny; but what is more remarkable in this

Figure 40.1 A 'black' Queen Elizabeth II provokes the viewer to consider the likelihood of black rule in the UK

new term is that it effaces sex to the advantage of age; this is, it seems, a profound process of fashion: it is age which is important not sex.

(1985: 258)

At the same time that sex is displaced, however, just as with race, this categorial difference is also reworked and made newly productive. In the images which feature couples of both sexes many show individuals of visibly contrasting races. The *frisson* of a 'mixed-race', heterosexual coupling reintroduces sex as a voluntaristic category of social being. Fashion critics Evans and Thornton suggest that this tendency – submerging sexual difference to enable it to resurface as stylistic effect – was more generally visible in fashion imagery in the mid-1980s. They write,

Much of the excitement of fashion imagery of this period, especially, ... in those magazines aimed at both sexes, was achieved by the deployment of sexual difference as a pure signifier, detached from biological difference. In such images the play of clothing signifiers presented gender as just one term among many. However the *frisson* of excitement that accompanied these manipulations only existed because sexual difference waited in the wings, always ready to re-emerge as a 'naturalized' polarity – man or woman, precisely because sexual difference was construed as old-fashioned, it could be recycled in postmodern fashion.

(1989: 64)

In later Benetton campaigns, the stylistic equivalence of skin and cloth as achieved in the photographic imagery of the fashion shots was extended to invert a whole series of natural relations and hierarchies. It lies behind the challenge to the biological basis of mothering in both the image of a black woman breast-feeding a white child, and in that of two women, one white, one black, holding an oriental child. It dissolves and reconstructs the natural distinction between animals and humans in the use of starkly black and starkly white animals – a white wolf 'kissing' a black sheep, a black horse mounting a white horse – as models, counterparts to the young people of different races in other images, and in the use of images of different breeds of chicken to illustrate the different styles of contemporary fashion designers. In the latter case, cloth and skin – or rather feathers – are represented as stylistically equivalent. Jean Paul Gaultier's designer style, for example, is represented by a Naked Neck chicken from Hungary: 'Modern yet nostalgic. Deliberate yet improvisational. Gaultier plays with constrasts in a peekaboo sable dress and thigh-high furry boots. The result is serious fun' (*Colors* no. 2, spring/summer 1992).

The erasure of context in these pictures through the use of neutral colour backgrounds to the pages' ends is characteristic of Benetton iconography. This technique makes it difficult not only to contextualise the subjects of the photograph but also to identify their size, and the resulting effacement of scale and perspective reinforces the tendency for culture to displace nature, and for difference to be defined as a matter of choice. Toscani comments,

> I studied at the Zurich School of Applied Arts. They taught us the new photographic objectivity in the best Bauhaus tradition.
>   ... The white backgrounds of my photographs, the way the subjects all face the camera, the direct message, the strict objectivity – all that comes from Zurich.
>
> (1995: 20)

Through the consistent 'objectivity' of such stylistic devices, the context is represented as environment: the background is reduced to its capacity to act as a function of the subject, no more than a foil to give the subject its definition. In all these examples, then, the flattening of perspective and the playful juxtaposition of colour inverts and displaces the relations between figure and context, subject and object, culture and nature.

[...]

References

Back, Les and Quaade, Vibeke (1993) 'Dream utopias, nightmare realities: imaging race and culture within the world of Benetton advertising', *Third Text* 22, pp. 65–80.

Barthes, Roland (1985) *The Fashion System* (trans. Matthew Ward and Richard Howard), London: Cape.

Benjamin, Walter (1970) *Illuminations* (trans. Harry Zotin), London: Fontana.

Evans, Caroline and Thornton, Minna (1989) *Women and Fashion: a New Look*, London: Quartet.

Mattei, Francesca (n.d.) 'A matter of style', *News: United Colors of Benetton*, pp. 4–5.

Strathern, Marilyn (1992) *Reproducing the Future: Anthropology, Kinship and the New Reproductive Technologies*, Manchester: Manchester University Press.

Toscani, Oliviero (1995) 'Taboos for sale', interview with Michel Guerrin, *Guardian Weekly*, 26 March, p. 20.

Chapter 41

Marilyn Strathern

ENTERPRISING KINSHIP
Consumer choice and the new reproductive technologies

From M. Strathern (1992) *Reproducing the Future,* Essays on anthropology. Kinship and the new reproductive technologies, Manchester: Manchester University Press.

THERE IS, WE ARE told, an argument 'for letting the future shape of the family evolve experimentally. No doubt people should be discouraged from taking high risks ... And it goes without saying that new forms of family life must only be tried voluntarily. But subject to these qualifications, we *prefer a society* predisposed in favour of "experiments in living" to one in which they are stifled' (Glover *et al.* 1989: 63, my emphasis).

Thus the Glover Report on Reproductive Technologies to the European Commission. The committee was asked to consider ethical and other social issues raised by the techniques that (as they put it) 'extend our reproductive options' (1989: 13). By reproductive option they mean primarily fertility, although their concern extends from artificial insemination, *in vitro* fertilisation and 'maternal surrogacy' to future implications of gene therapy and embryo research. They suggest that these new techniques will enable us to influence the kinds of people who are born. Indeed, the techniques are bracketed together under the opening observation that perhaps our time will be seen as 'the era when we became able to take control of our own biology, and in particular to take control of our own reproductive process' (1989: 13).

But what are we supposedly taking control of? What is being reproduced? In many cultures of the world, a child is thought to embody the relationship between its parents and the relationships its parents have with other kin. The child is thus regarded as a social being, and what is reproduced is a set of social relations. At the least, the child reproduces parents' relational capacities in its own future capacity to make relations itself, as often indicated for instance in marriage rules. Yet the future that the Glover Report holds out to us, with its benign language of voluntarism and preference, is rather different. What is apparently at stake is the fate of human tissue, and what these techniques will reproduce is parental *choice*. The child will embody the desire of its parents to have a child.

Consequently, conflict of interest is expressed as a matter of who wants what. Hence the brief discussion of donor anonymity turns on what the donating man 'wants' and whether or not the social parents will 'want' their family complicated by a relationship with the biological father (1989: 24). Again, the question of surrogacy contracts turns on the couple 'wanting' the child to be healthy, 'wanting' to end the relationship with the surrogate mother (1989: 69), and so on. In the language of desire, the question of rights turns on the right to fulfil what one wants, and in a much larger way that is the justification for the enabling technologies. They help persons fulfil themselves.

This has for long been a significant if unremarkable cultural motivation, in both Britain and Europe, for having families. The point is that the kind of people on whose opinions the Glover Report drew now see themselves in a world that is developing technologies specifically enabling of this desire. That potency can eclipse or summate the diversity of factors that lead to children being born. Hence the equation between reproduction and fertility: What is 'extended' is the choice to have children.

[...]

Extending the choice

[...]

Perhaps there is nothing remarkable about all this, except for one thing. Until now, it has been part of most of the indigenous cultural repertories in Europe to see the domain of kinship, and what is called its biological base in procreation, as an area of relationships that provided a given baseline to human existence. Kin relations, like genetic make-up, were something one could not do anything about. More powerfully, when these relations were thought of as belonging to the domain of 'nature', nature also came to stand for everything that was immutable, that was intrinsic to persons or things, and as those essential qualities without which they would not be what they were. It is not just that kin relations were regarded as constructed out of natural materials, but that the connection between kinship and the natural facts of life symbolised immutability in social relations.

By now my point must be obvious. What do we do with the idea that a child embodies its parents' wishes, that families will find whatever form their members desire, that kinship might no longer be something one cannot do anything about? How will this all work as an analogy for other relationship? If till now kinship has been a symbol for everything that cannot be changed about social affairs, if biology has been a symbol for the given parameters of human existence, what will it mean for the way we construe any of our relationships with one another to think of parenting as the implementing of an option and genetic make-up as an outcome of cultural preference? How shall we think about what is inevitable and not really open to change in relationships, a question that bears on the perception of people's obligations and responsibilities towards one another.

Parents as customers of parenting services? Biology under control? Customers respond to a market, not to 'society'; biology under control is no longer 'nature'. Shall we find ourselves bereft of analogies – shall we no longer be able to 'see' nature, or 'see' society for that matter? For if kinship and procreation have been understood as belonging to a domain of nature, if nature has in turn symbolised what we have taken as inevitable constraints on the conduct of social life, then society by contrast has been thought about as human enterprise working on these givens, and thus a realm of endeavour carved *out of* the natural world. If the givens of our existence vanish, by what shall we measure enterprise? But I go ahead of myself. Let me remain with the fact that we now live in a world where alongside whatever other thoughts one had about parent – child relations must come the thought that the child ought to exist by choice. In this world the idea of choice is already embedded in a matrix of other analogies.

This matrix is the Enterprise Culture. As the report to the European Commission indicates, it is a culture more widespread than its particular manifestations in Britain. Nevertheless, it is useful to draw on Keat's (1990) account of the British version.

The value given to preference and choice in decision-making over the new reproductive technologies (NRT) already reveals the workings of analogy on analogy. Those who seek assistance, we are told, are better thought of not as the disabled seeking alleviation or the sick seeking remedy – analogies that also come to mind – but as customers seeking services. The new technology, meanwhile, enables persons to achieve desires that they could not achieve unaided. However, a further enablement is required to take advantage of the services. (cf. Pfeffer 1987): money is literally enabling of the enabling devices. We can think of these services not just as human enterprise being exerted on behalf of those who wish to be enterprising, but as a business that caters to those who will make a business out of being a family.

Yet there is something about the market analogy that is less than benign. It tends to collapse all other analogies into itself, the effect being rather like that of money itself which, in differentiating everything makes itself the only source of difference.

[...]

Choice has become the privileged vantage from which to measure all action.

[...]

Consumers and producers live alike by one another's choices. In fact, we could say that producers turn out the embodied choices of their customers, and consumers choose among the embodied choices of those who provide the services. One glimpses a world full of persons embodying the choices of others. Perhaps one day we shall find some way of being able to reproduce the choices without the bother of putting them into bodies.

The absurdity offers the real glimpse of a situation where choice might cease to be enablement. In fact we could have made that connection long ago. If we are to look for what is 'rigid' about the Enterprise Culture, for what stifles enterprise, for the new givens of our existence, it lies in the hidden prescription that we *ought* to act by choice. This is not sophistry; it is a point of political concern.

Prescribing the choice

Not everyone has been tunnel-visioned about the NRT. Notable exceptions are found in the works of feminist scholars, and many of my observations simply remake observations already made (for a recent review, see Franklin and McNeill 1988). There is the question of prescriptive fertility, for instance, that accompanies what one could call prescriptive consumerism, namely the idea that if you have the opportunity to enhance yourself you should take it. Feminists are aware of pressures put on persons to appear to be fulfilled in certain ways. For, in the Enterprise Culture, one's choices must always be self-enhancing, the catch being that the self and its enhancement will only be recognised if it takes specific forms (Rose 1991).

Thus Pfeffer (1987) asks why, in the late twentieth century, personhood has become equated with the capacity to reproduce, almost to the point of the difference between the fertile and infertile becoming analogous to that between the donors and recipients of charity. New techniques of 'fertilisation' do not remedy fertility as such, but childlessness; they enable a potential parent to have access to the fertility of others. A new divide between have and have-not is implied, insofar as technology has already opened up to personal choice the 'decision' to have children. The enterprising self, as Keat says, is not just one who is able to choose between alternative ways, but one who implements that choice through consumption (self-enhancement) and for whom there is, in a sense, no choice *not* to consume. Satisfaction is not in this rhetoric the absence of desire, but the meeting of desire. To imagine an absence of desire, would be an affront to the means that exist to satisfy it.

The sense that one has no choice not to consume is a version of the feeling that one has no choice not to make a choice. Choice is imagined as the only source of difference: this is the collapsing effect of the market analogy. Like the Warnock Report (1985) before it, the Glover Report goes out of its way to comment on commercialisation in transactions involving gametes. One can think of reasons why commerce is discouraged. Yet the point is surely that the market analogy has already done its work: we think so freely of the providing and purchasing of goods and services that transactions in gametes is already a thought-of act of commerce. All that rearguard action to protect the idea of the family from the idea of financial exploitation, to reconceive such transactions as altruistic or acts of love or as real gifts between persons, are after the event – these ideas have no other ideas to fall back on. If kinship is to be an enterprise like anything else, then where are the relationships that will enable us to think of gamete donation as a gift? Glover *et al.* say that in 'families and between friends, gifts are more common than sales' (1989: 88). But gifts pass between friends and kin precisely to indicate the non-transactable part of their relationship. With whatever nuance of taste or sentiment, one gives to express a solidarity or celebrate a relationship that once in place has no choice about it. If the idea of a gift sounds hollow or off-key in reference to gamete transfer, it is because the Enterprise Culture provides many more and readier ways of thinking about a calculating self.

Enterprising culture

Prescriptive consumerism dictates that there is no choice but to always exercise choice; its other side is prescriptive marketing. Culture is being enterprised-up.

I was once – naively – appalled meeting a colleague (from another profession admittedly) who cheerfully announced being on the way to the library in order to 'scholar-up' a paper, to add the references that would make it look scholarly. Naively, because I had imagined scholarship was in the nature of the product. Now in exercising their choices, consumers are concerned both with product identity and with product identification. The exercise of choice that defines the active citizen is market choice, not just because of the kinds of rules of the game associated with free bargaining or an equation between enterprising selves and business enterprises, but because the market deals in things which have been marketed. That is, they are designed for selling, made to specifications that anticipate consumer wants, presenting back to the consumer 'choice' in the form of a range of products out of which 'choice' can visibly be made. To choose repsonsibly, our active citizen must know what is being offered, much of this knowledge being filtered through appearance: things must look what they are supposed to be. Apples must look like apples. One might say they have to be appled-up; varieties are selected for marketing which have the most apple-like qualities. Qualities essential to the realisation of choice become displaced, as it were, from the product onto what is presented for the consumer's discrimination.

Marketed products are quality-enhanced. Quality is not there to be discovered: those attributes which define things are made explicit, even superadded, in the course of the marketing process. Marketing does much of the selection for you, and consumer activism is generally in the area of greater determination over what the producer claims to present. So one selects for quality where quality means both an innate characteristic (firmness, taste) and an enhanced version (unblemished flesh, shiny skin). The term 'quality' has always had this ambiguity. But the marketing of products forces an interesting collapse of its two senses. The natural, innate property and the artificial, cultural enhancement become one. To select an apple for its appleness is to discriminate between those which conform more and those which conform less to cultural expectations about what the natural apple should be. Glover *et al.* raise the question of whether handicapped people and those born with physical blemish can have a totally fulfilled life.

There is a little more at stake here than one might think. This is not a new essentialism but a collapse of the difference between the essential and superadded. The market*ed* apple is 'the apple and a bit more', that is, a fruit that will attract the consumer for its appleness. What is collapsed is the difference between what is taken for granted in the nature of the product and what is perceived to be the result of extra human effort.

Although in referring to apples I have, so to speak, natured-up my example, the same point can be made with respect to manufactured articles, for whether utilitarian or luxury their qualities are enhanced by the efforts of advertiser and marketer. Indeed, they are not 'marketable' without 'extra' attention being drawn to their 'inherent' characteristics. It is of some further significance that what we take as the domain that stands for what is natural, inherent and so forth in human affairs is not immune from an elision of a similar kind.

Among various models for human affairs that have held sway over the last 200 years has been a distinction between the taken-for-granted in human relationships and the culturally constructed, between the natural individual and the society that socialises the individual into its own mould. This is one of many such binarisms that has moulded the development of social science and is arguably where our model of enterprise comes from – its natural parents, if you like. In this model, human beings are enterprising creatures who 'construct' and made what they will 'out of' the givens of existence and environmental constraints. We would thus contrast enterprise, that is, culture or society in the twentieth-century sense, endless variety testifying to an endless ingenuity, with other factors that appear given, immutable, universal, of which biological reproduction, like sexual difference, has till now been a prime example.

[...]

To enterprise (vb.) kinship is to touch on an area of central significance to the English – and no doubt British and European too – idea of what enterprise is all about. It collapses the idea of culture as human enterprise working against or out of nature. One will no longer think one can do nothing about the sex of one's children, about birth abnormalities and about the characteristics they will inherit, any more than one will be able to regard one's own endowment as a matter of fate. One's fate will be to put up with the results of other persons' enterprises.

There is a footnote here about the fate of a subject such as anthropology, insofar as anthropology has prided itself on its own enterprise in uncovering other people's cultures as enterprises. It uncovers what people take for granted and shows them for the cultural artifacts they are, revealing other people's naturalisms as cultural constructs. Bit of a facer, then, to find onself in a culture which is becoming cultured-up, that is, where it is not substantive products or values that are marketed but the activity of producing value itself – where what a culture values of itself is its own enterprise.

[...]

References

Franklin, S. and McNeill, M. (1988), 'Review essay: recent literature and current feminist debates on reproductive technologies', *Feminist Studies*, 14: 545–60.

Glover, J. *et al.* (1989), *Fertility and the Family*. The Glover Report on Reproductive Technologies to the European Commission, Fourth Estate, London.

Keat, R. (1990), 'Starship Britian or universal enterprise', in R. Keat and N. Abercrombie (eds), *Enterprise Culture*, London: Routledge.

Pfeffer, N. (1987), 'Artificial insemination, in-vitro fertilization and the stigma of infertility', in M. Stanworth (ed.), *Reproductive Technologies*, Oxford: Polity Press.

Rose, N. (1991), 'Governing the enterprising self', in P. Heelas and P. Morris (eds), *The Values of the Enterprise Culture – The Moral Debate*, London: Unwin Hyman.

Warnock, M. (1985), *A Question of Life: The Warnock Report on Human Fertilisation and Embryology [1984]*, Oxford: Basil Blackwell.

PART EIGHT

Body ethics

INTRODUCTION

The first text in this section is from Peter Brown's *The Body and Society: Men, Women and Sexual Renunciation in Early Christianity*, one of the rare secondary sources that Michel Foucault acknowledged as an inspiration for his own work on ethics. Here Brown draws a direct contrast between the conception and perception of the body in late antiquity, and in Christianity. A body/soul dualism pervades both models, but Brown characterises this dualism in antiquity as 'benevolent', in the sense that an ethical life demanded something like a relation of mutual adjustment and compromise between the two terms. The body had an authority of its own to which 'it was only prudent to listen at times'. Accordingly, it was 'there to be administered, not to be changed'. The Christian approach, by contrast, reflects an ethics predicated on the mastery over bodily impulses, a radicalisation of resistance to passions. Underlying this difference between pagan and Christian attitudes are different assumptions as to the 'horizons of the possible' for the body itself: the Christian supposed a potentially infinite malleability of the material body through faith as interaction with the divine. This infinite malleability was implicit in the ascetic feats of biblical characters and in Christ himself, both incarnated and resurrected. Brown underscores how the changeability of the human body, specifically through renunciation of all sexual activity, was the key to seeing (and making) social arrangements and relations similarly open to fundamental transformation.

The text by Orlan illustrates one sense in which Foucault's ethics as 'aesthetics of existence', with the body as its primary object or vehicle, can be understood. Orlan considers her own body as the 'primary material' for her creative work as an artist. Her early installations and performance pieces involved the use (and/or the occurrence) of bodily fluids such as sperm, menstrual blood and vomit. It was in the context of a medical emergency, however, that Orlan first used surgery as performance art, turning 'the situation back on itself, by considering life as a recuperable aesthetic phenomenon' (Orlan 1995: 7). The description of her subsequent difficulties in finding surgeons willing to perform surgery as art illustrates the difficulty in overcoming the gulf between ethics and aesthetics in modern, post-Kantian society (cf. discussion of Foucault's ethics in our Introduction). Plastic surgery is, of course, increasingly performed for aesthetic reasons – and this blurring of medical and aesthetic rationality, in the eyes of many, is what makes the practice ethically controversial. Even so, plastic surgery is ordinarily performed strictly to produce aesthetic 'improvement', on the implicit or explicit understanding that such improvement is desirable from the point of view of the patient's psychological well being or health. Ethical controversy becomes much more intense when patients ask for amputations or other interventions that do not obey the logic of 'improvement', as in cases of body dysmorphic disorder for example. On one level, Orlan's artistic projects involving surgery subvert the banalisation of aesthetics whereby 'aesthetics' is taken to signify correspondence to socially dominant canons of beauty ('I am the first artist ... to divert plastic surgery from its aim of improvement and rejuvenation'). Orlan here reclaims aesthetics for the purposes of experiment and resistance that may specifically be associated with a deliberate practice of freedom. On another level, these projects may be read as a commentary on the reality of suffering – which, Orlan specifies, she does *not* masochistically enjoy – and on the possibility of reinterpreting a situation of suffering in terms of an aesthetic project for the constitution of one's self as a different subject.

A denunciation of 'improvement' as a cultural imperative is implicitly present in the extract by Zygmunt Bauman, in the form of a reference to the modernist utopia that forbids contemporary individuals from confronting the reality of death without hypocrisy or self-deception. Death, Bauman writes, 'blatantly defies the power of reason: reason's power is to be a guide to good choice but death is not a matter of choice. Death is the scandal of reason' (1992: 1). This premise offers the key for a particular interpretation of the logic of 'healthism', or the socially sustained individual effort to prevent disease through the management of lifestyle choices. Among medical sociologists it is not uncommon to interpret healthism as involving a re-moralisation of health issues, in the sense that individuals are regarded as having a responsibility towards maintaining their own bodies in good health, and that being unwell can carry the connotation of having misbehaved (Crawford 1977, 1980; Fiztgerald 1994). Bauman's reading, by contrast, invites us to consider the healthist 'expedient' from the perspective of its ethical poverty or weakness, as a mode of life lacking in the moral courage to come to terms with the fact of mortality. The reason for interpreting healthism as a failure of ethics rather than as the exercise of an ethical responsibility (although Bauman himself does not use these terms) is that ultimately the pursuit of health, even when optimal, does not free us from the prospect of death, or make us stronger in relation to it. On the contrary, the avoidance of death becomes life's fundamental meaning, usurping all potential others, and we live as if constantly under death's 'surveillance'.

Arthur Frank's text invites us to reflect on how the body is implicated in the exercise of ethical responsibility, and how responsibility is implicated, folded into, the body. In so doing it touches on some of the points raised also by Bauman – such as the search for optimal levels of control over our bodies, or how the recognition of mortality complicates how we relate to the body and its needs. Central to this is the conceptualisation of bodies as being 'more than mere corporeality'. Bodies – including their physiology – are constantly interpreted by the self in relation to the self and to others, and individuals have some degree of choice in relation to such interpretations. Frank thus uses the expression 'body-selves' to indicate that different ideal types of body also represent 'ideal types of ethical *choices*'. The relationship between body and self, however, is reciprocal rather than unilateral: '[s]elves act in ways that choose their bodies, but bodies also create the selves who act'. Although we do not understand much of this second process, Frank argues that the fact of illness constitutes a particular predisposition towards embodying an ethics of witnessing that implies opening to, and being for, the other. In the final part of this text, Frank also relates the fact of illness to the affective and creative dimension of desire; as a zero-point of desire, illness can constitute the occasion for problematising desire anew, and renegotiating the values and aspirations hitherto taken for granted. This exploration of desire involves not only ethical questions but also aesthetic ones, since it concerns the necessity, for the ill person, of finding ways of falling back in love with themselves.

In apparent contrast to this, Scarry writes that 'pain comes unsharably into our midst as at once that which cannot be denied and that which cannot be confirmed'. Far from constituting the condition of possibility for an ethical form of communication, pain here is considered from the perspective of its negative relation to language: 'pain does not simply resist language but actively destroys it'. Correspondingly, language can belie and invert the reality of pain. This is evident in the situation of torture, where the language/pain polarity is mapped onto that of torturer/tortured. Scarry argues that the verbal aspect (the interrogation) is as essential to the reality of torture as the physical one (of inflicting pain), because it is specifically through their interaction that the victim of torture is defeated. For 'the person in great pain experiences his own body as the agent of his agony', and the verbal aspect of torture, by demanding and obtaining a confession, colludes to produce the illusion that the victim is the agent of their own destruction through a form of self-betrayal: in this way, not only the victim's body but their self and their world are lost to them. Despite the apparent contradiction, Scarry's argument is not incompatible with the vision of an ethics rooted in the experience of pain or illness put forward by Frank (see earlier, and also our discussion in the Introduction). For, precisely insofar as pain is unsharable, the readiness to *commune* with someone else's pain, the acceptance of its reality, is necessarily a highly subjective, free, and therefore *ethical* act – an act, that is, that no external facticity compels or requires us to perform. In the light of the same unsharability, it is also understandable how the first-hand experience of pain or illness may be at once the source of a heightened capacity for such ethical acts, and the source of an ethical responsibility not to deny the reality of pain – to witness it, in fact.

REFERENCES

Bauman, Z. (1992) 'Survival as a social construct', *Theory, Culture and Society* 9: 1–36.

Crawford, R. (1977) 'You are dangerous to your health: the ideology and politics of victim-blaming', *International Journal of Health Services* 7: 663–80.

Crawford, R. (1980) 'Healthism and the medicalisation of everyday life', *International Journal of Health Services* 10: 365–88.

Fitzgerald, F. T. (1994) 'The tyranny of health', *New England Journal of Medicine* 331: 196–8.

Orlan (1995) 'I do not want to look like ... ', *Women's Art Magazine* 64: 5–10.

Chapter 42

Peter Brown

'CLAY CUNNINGLY COMPOUNDED'

From P. Brown (1988) *The Body and Society: Men, Women and Sexual Renunciation in Early Christianity*, Columbia University Press.

IT IS IMPOSSIBLE TO sum up in so short a survey, and from such documents, the moral tone of a society as extensive, as diverse, and as little known to us in its day-to-day life as was the Roman Empire at its height. We are dealing with a society among whose upper classes areas of extreme rigidity coexisted with areas which immediately strike a modern reader as marked by a graciousness, a tolerance, and a matter-of-factness that vanished in medieval Byzantium and in the Catholic West. This peculiar juxtapostion of severity and tolerance made sense to thinking pagans in terms of an image of the human person based on what may best be called a "benevolent dualism." The soul met the body as the inferior "other" to the self. The body was as different from the soul, and as intractable, as were women, slaves, and the opaque and restless populace of the cities. Not even the gods could change that fact.

> What says Zeus? "Epictetus, had it been possible, I should have made this paltry body, this small estate of thine, free and unhampered. But, as it is – let it not escape thee – this body is not thine own, but is only clay cunningly compounded."[1]

It was a clay on which age, disease, and death fastened inexorably. At the end of so much long pain, it was best for the soul to go away – perhaps to the stars – "clean of a body," the diseased flesh melted at last from the mind.[2]

Yet the soul had been sent down from heaven for a time to act as an administrator to the murmurous and fertile province of the body. A wise man's relation to his body was one of benevolent concern. Its government demanded a refined *sprezzatura*. The body's observed physical needs could not be overruled in a tyrannical manner by "overmeticulous and rigid control."[3] The soul must learn to exercise gentle violence on the body, much as the husband groomed his young bride, "entering into its feelings, being knit to it by good will."[4]

An unaffected symbiosis of body and soul was the aim both of medicine and of philosophical exhortation. The body must not be permitted to force its needs upon the tranquil mind: it was to be kept well-tuned according to its own, intrinsic laws. The mind, in turn, must constantly refine itself, lest, through weakness and uncertainty, it come to participate in the lability of the flesh.[5] A man unduly preoccupied with his body was an undignified sight. To spend one's time "in much exercise, in much eating, drinking, much evacuating the bowels and much copulating" was, quite simply, "a mark of lack of refinement."[6] From a well-born Greek, no judgment could have been more crushing. But the ostentatious ascetic was equally distasteful. A young man might opt not to have love affairs before marriage: "but do not make yourself offensive or censorious to those who so indulge, and do not make frequent mentions of the fact that you yourself do not indulge."[7]

The body had its rightful place in a great chain of being that linked man both to the gods and to the beasts. It had risen toward the soul, like the highest crest of a dancing wave, from the mighty ocean of an eternal Nature. Even the dull earth, which both gave and reclaimed the body, was not neutral: it could be addressed as divine, a majestic presence forever stirring with new life.[8] The men we meet in the literature of the second century still belonged to the rustling universe of late classical polytheism. They knew that they had been knit, by the cunning of the gods, to the animal world. They felt pulsing in their own bodies the same fiery spirit that covered the hills every year with newborn lambs and that ripened the crops, in seasonal love-play, as the spring winds embraced the fertile ears.[9] Above them, the same fire glowed in the twinkling stars.[10] Their bodies, and their sexual drives, shared directly in the unshakable perpetuity of an immense universe, through which the gods played exuberantly.[11]

A thing of the natural world, the body was expected to speak of its own needs in an ancient, authoritative voice. It was only prudent to listen at times. The tolerance that was extended to the body in late classical times was based on a sense that the antithesis to the animal world, the city, was so strong that, once made, the claims of the city were inexorable. The family and the city determined the degree to which the results of the body's connection with the natural world was acceptable in organized society. The mere fact of physical birth, for instance, did not make a Roman child a person. Its father must lift it from the floor. If not, the little bundle of ensouled matter, as much a fetus as if it were still in its mother's womb, must wait for others to collect it from a place outside the father's house. The fetus could be aborted in the womb; and it might yet die, if no one picked it up and made it part of their own family, when left out in a public place to be claimed by passers-by.[12]

Young men found themselves in an analogous, if less perilous, situation. Nature made their bodies different from those of children long before they were useful to the city. The boy's first ejaculation was celebrated by his family at the feast of the Liberalia, on March 17.[13] For a few years, he was free to "sprout rank growth."[14] The unsteadying heats of adolescence (or, on another account, the lingering damp humors that were betrayed in a boy's wavering voice) must be burned off a little before the young man could take on the hard-baked role of a civic dignitary.[15] This was the time of the *ludus*.

> Nature itself developes a young man's desire. If these desires break out in such a way that they disrupt no one's life and undermine no household [by adultery], they are generally regarded as unproblematic: we tolerate them.[16]

The call of the city would come soon enough; only "soft" men – among them, the great erotic poets of Augustan Rome![17] – were slow to answer the summons of duty, by abandoning the life of the lover:

> Finally, when he has hearkened to pleasure ... let him, at last, recall himself
> to action, to the business of the household, to the forum, to the service of the
> state.[18]

Even Marcus Aurelius, a paragon of public sobriety, had "given way to amatory passions"
for a requisite, short time.[19] Though a man of great austerity, he by no means considered
himself to be bound to perpetual sexual abstinence. Rather than remarrying, he spent his
old age with a concubine, the daughter of an estate-manager of his former wife, so as not
to burden his children with a stepmother.[20]

The young woman was often treated in a similar, matter-of-fact manner. Too labile
a creature to be allowed the periods of sexual freedom granted to young men, and toler-
ated even in husbands, her family must guard her carefully. But the physical integrity of
her body had not yet become the charged symbol that we now associate with
Mediterranean Christian societies.[21] The girl's loss of her virginity was, simply, a bad
omen for her future conduct. A girl who had already enjoyed furtive love affairs might do
the same when married. She was not a "well brought up" girl.[22] From a second-century
author, no harsher judgment was necessary.

The effect of such benevolent dualism was to make late classical attitudes toward the
body seem deeply alien to later, Christian eyes, and hence to modern observers of the
ancient world. In the pagan world of second century AD, a marked degree of tolerance
was accorded to men, both on the matter of homosexuality and in their love affairs before
and outside marriage. But to emphasize this fact alone is to trivialize the meaning of the
changes that occurred in later centuries. It is not sufficient to talk of the rise of
Christianity in the Roman world simply in terms of a shift from a less to a more repressive society. What was at stake was a subtle change in the perception of the body itself.
The men and women of later centuries were not only hedged around with a different and
more exacting set of prohibitions. They had also come to see their own bodies in a
different light.

Seen through the lens of the fully elaborated Christianity of the early middle ages,
the body image of second-century persons seemed strangely blurred. A diffused sensuality flickered through it. Sexual desire lacked the distinctive flavor that it soon acquired in
Christian circles. No one need for sensual gratification was brought into sharper focus
than any other. None was considered peculiarly deeply rooted, or exceptionally revealing
of human frailty. Nor was any one desire singled out as uniquely worthy of reprobation.
Sexual desire itself was unproblematic: it was a predictable response to physical beauty;
its satisfaction was accepted as an occasion that brought intense physical pleasure. The city
could be safely left to judge the further consequences of having yielded to the sweet
delight of "the things of Venus." That men might wish to caress and penetrate other beautiful men caused the Greeks, at least, little surprise.[23] What was judged harshly was the
fact that the pursuit of pleasure might lead some men to wish to play the female role, by
offering themselves to be penetrated by their lovers: such behavior was puzzling to the
doctors and shocking to most people.[24] No free man should allow himself to be so weakened by desire as to allow himself to step out of the ferociously maintained hierarchy that
placed all free men, in all their dealings, above women and slaves.[25]

What might appear at first sight as tolerance reveals, in fact, the comprehensiveness of the codes adopted by the elites. They lay across the whole body of the public man. As well they might. Wealthy, perpetually in the public gaze, exercising the power of life and limb over others, and close to figures who could exercise such power over themselves, the civic notables found anger, irrational cruelty, the exuberant and menacing physicality of the greedy eater, and the erratic savagery of the tippler subjects far more worthy of concern than was the soft passion of desire. It was to those passions that moralists devoted their most serious attention.

Where second-century pagans differed most profoundly from the views that had already begun to circulate in Christian circles was in their estimate of the horizons of the possible for the body itself. Potentially formless and eternal matter, the body was barely held together, for a short lifetime, by the vivid soul of the well-born man. Its solid matter could change as little as the crystalline marble of a sharply cut and exquisitely polished statue might blossom magically in its depths, into a more refined and malleable substance. Like society, the body was there to be administered, not to be changed. Others had begun to disagree with this view. Writing at the end of the second century, Clement of Alexandria, a Christian who knew his pagan authors well, summed up with admirable clarity and fairness the essence of the expectations of the body that we have described. Pagan philosophers, he knew, subscribed to an austere image of the person:

> The human ideal of continence, I mean that which is set forth by the Greek philosophers, teaches one to resist passion, so as not to be made subservient to it, and to train the instincts to pursue rational goals.

But Christians, he added, went further: "our ideal is not to experience desire at all."

Moses had stood on Sinai for 40 days, a man transfigured by the close presence of God. The needs of the body were stilled in him for all that time.[26] Through the Incarnation of Christ, the Highest God had reached down to make even the body capable of transformation. In admitting this possibility, Clement implied that the stable environment posited by pagan thought, an intractable body and a social order adjusted to its unchanging needs, might burst from its ancient bounds. Sexual renunciation might lead the Christian to transform the body and, in transforming the body, to break with the discreet discipline of the ancient city.

Clement was a moderate among Christians. He stood closer to Plutarch, Musonius Rufus, and the doctors of his age than he did to many of his fellow-believers. In little groups scattered throughout the eastern Mediterranean, other Christians had seized upon the body. They had set it up as a palpable blazon of the end of the "present age." They believed that the universe itself had shattered with the rising of Christ from the grave. By renouncing all sexual activity the human body could join in Christ's victory: it could turn back the inexorable. The body could wrench itself free from the grip of the animal world. By refusing to act upon the youthful stirrings of desire, Christians could bring marriage and childbirth to an end. With marriage at an end, the huge fabric of organized society would crumble like a sandcastle, touched by the "ocean-flood of the Messiah."[27]

These were the views of exact contemporaries of Galen and Marcus Aurelius. Their implications could hardly have been more appalling to the pagan elites of Rome and the Aegean, and more calculated to upset the average married householder in any Mediterranean or Near Eastern community. In the century that followed the death of

Jesus of Nazareth, the issue of sexual renunciation came to be eleborated in Christian circles as a drastic alternative to the moral and social order that seemed so secure, so prepared to expatiate upon its fundamental values in treatises, in works of medicine and on the warm stones of so many monuments in so many little cities.

Notes

1   Epictetus, *Discourses* 1.1.11, Oldfather, ed. *Epictetus*, 1:8–10.
2   *Studia Pontica* 3, J. G. C. Anderson, F. Cumont and H. Grégoire, eds, inscription no. 86, p. 102; compare Aretaeus, *Cause and Symptoms of Acute Diseases* 2.4, pp. 272–3.
3   Plutarch, *de san. tuenda* 17.131B, p. 260.
4   Plutarch, *Praecept. Conjug.* 33.142E, p. 323.
5   Well seen by Foucault, *Souci de Soi*, pp. 72–3 and 157–8, *Care of the Self*, pp. 56–7 and 133–4.
6   Epictetus, *Enchiridion* 41, Oldfather, p. 527.
7   Ibid. 33.8, p. 519.
8   *Corpus Inscriptionum Latinarum* 6.4, fasc. 2. 35887, C. Huelsen (ed.), 3681 – all the more poignant as the tomb is that of a thirteen-year-old virgin girl. For the background, see Sabine G. MacCormack, "Roma, Constantinopolis, the Emperor and his Genius," pp. 133–4.
9   Ephraim the Syrian, *de Paradiso* 9.10–13 and 10.5–8, R. Lavenant, trans. *Éphrem de Nisibe: Hymnes sur le Paradis*, Sources chrétiennes 137:125–6; 137–8 is an exceptionally beautiful rendering of this theme.
10   Cicero, *de natura deorum* 2.10.28.
11   Lane Fox, *Pagoans and Christians*, pp. 41–6, 110–33 is an impressive evocation of this mentality.
12   Veyne, "L'Empire romain," *Vie privée*, pp. 23–7, *Private Life*, pp. 9–14; W. V. Harris, "The Roman Father's Power of Life and Death," in R. S. Bagnall and W. V. Harris (eds) *Studies in Roman Law in Memory of A. Arthur Schiller*.
13   Rousselle, *Porneia*, p. 79.
14   Augustine, *Confessions* 2.1.1, describing himself at the age of sixteen.
15   Quintilian, *Institutio oratoria* 11.3.28.
16   Cicero, *Pro Caelio* 28, from the translation of Lyne, *Latin Love Poets*, pp. 1–2.
17   Jasper Griffin, "Augustan Poetry and the Life of Luxury;" Lyne, *Latin Love Poets*, pp. 65–81; Paul Veyne, *L'Élégie érotique romaine*, pp. 170–83.
18   Cicero, *Pro Caelio* 42.
19   Marcus Aurelius, *Meditations* 1.17.6.
20   Marcus Aurelius, *Scriptores Historiae Augustae* 29.10.
21   G. Sissa, "Une virginité sans hymen: le corps féminin en Grèce ancienne," p. 1132, and *Le corps virginal*, pp. 97–143 and 189–98.
22   Soranus, *Gynaecia* 1.8.33.4, Ilberg, p. 22; Temkin, p. 31 – on the precocious sexual desires of "ill-bred" girls.
23   Ramsay MacMullen, "Roman Attitudes to Greek Love," would wish to contrast Greek and Roman attitudes; but see T. Wade Richardson, "Homosexuality in the *Satyricon*."
24   P. H. Schrijvers, *Eine medizinische Erklärung der männlichen Homosexualität aus der Antike*, p. 7 – the desires of the active partner were "medically of no interest."
25   Paul Veyne, "Amour et famille," pp. 50–5 and "L'homosexualité à Rome," pp. 26–33, now translated in P. Ariès and A. Béjin (eds) *Western Sexuality: Practice and Precept in Past Times*, pp. 26–35; Rousselle, "Gestes et signes de la famille," pp. 257–61 now offers important nuances.

26   Clement, *Stromateis* 3.7.57, in Henry Chadwick, trans., *Alexandrian Christianity*, p. 66.
27   *Acts of Judas Thomas* 31, A. F. J. Klijn, trans. *The Acts of Judas Thomas*, Supplements to Novum Testamentum 5:80.

References

Acts of [*Judas*] *Thomas* (1962) Trans. with commentary, A. F. J. Klijn. Supplements to Novum Testamentum 5, Leiden: Brill.

Anderson, J. G. C., Cumont F. and Grégoire, H. (eds) (1910) *Studia Pontica*. Brussels: H. Lamartin.

Clement of Alexandria (1954) *Stromata* III and VIII, in H. Chadwick, trans. *Alexandrian Christianity*, Philadelphia: Westminster Press.

Ephraim the Syrian (1968). *De Paradiso*. Trans. R. Lavenant. *Éphrem de Nisibe: Hymnes sur le Paradis*. Sources chrétiennes 137, Paris: Éditions du Cerf.

Epictetus. (1965) *Enchiridion*, in W. A. Oldfather (ed.) and trans. *Epictetus*. Loeb Classical Library. Cambridge: Harvard University Press.

Foucault, Michel (1985) *Le Souci de Soi*. Paris: Gallimard, 1984. English translation: R. Hurley, trans. *the Care of the Self*, New York: Pantheon.

Griffin, Jasper (1976) "Augustan Poetry and the Life of Luxury." *Journal of Roman Studies* 66: 87–105.

Harris, W. V. (1986) "The Roman Father's Power of Life and Death," in R. S. Bagnall and W. V. Harris (eds) *Studies in Roman Law in Memory of A. Arthur Schiller*, Leiden: Brill pp. 81–95.

Huelsen, C. (ed.) (1992) *Corpus Inscriptionum Latinarum*, Berlin: Reimer.

Isidore of Pelusium. Letters. *PG* 78.177–1646.

Klijn, A. F. J. (1962) "The 'Single One' in the Gospel of Thomas." *Journal of Biblical Literature* 81: 271–8.

Lane Fox, Robin (1987) *Pagans and Christians*, New York: Knopf.

Lyne, R. O. A. M. (1980) *The Latin Love Poets*. Oxford: Clarendon Press.

MacCormack, Sabine G. (1975) "Roma, Constantinopolis, the Emperor and his Genius." *Classical Quarterly* n.s. 25: 131–50.

MacMullen, Ramsay (1982) "Roman Attitudes to Greek Love." *Historia* 31: 484–502.

Pelagius. *Ad Demetriadem*. *PL* 30.16–487.

—— *Expositio in epistolam ad Romanos*. *PL Supp*. 1.1112–81.

Plutarch (1971) *De Sanitate tuenda*, in F. C. Babbitt (ed.) *Plutarch's Moralia*. Loeb Classical Library. Cambridge: Harvard University Press.

Plutarch. *Praecepta conjugalia*, in Babbitt (ed.) *Plutarch's Moralia*, vol. 2.

Quintilian (1969–79) *Institutio Oratoria*, in H. E. Butler (ed.) *Quintilian*, 4 vols, Loeb Classical Library, Cambridge: Harvard University Press.

Richardson, T. Wade (1984) "Homosexuality in the *Satyricon*," *Classica et Medievalia* 35: 105–27.

Rousselle, Aline (1986) "Gestes et signes de la famille dans l'Empire romain," in André Burguière, *et al.* (eds) *Histoire de la famille*, vol. 1, pp. 231–69, Paris: Armand Colin.

Schrijvers, P. H. (1985) *Eine medizinische Erklärung der männlichen Homosexualität aus der Antike*, Amsterdam: Grüner Verlag.

Sissa, Giulia (1984) "Une virginité sans hymen: le corps féminin en Grèce ancienne." *Annales É.S.C.* 39: 1119–39.

—— (1987) *Le corps virginal*, Paris: J. Vrin.

Soranus (1956) *Gynaecia*. (ed.) J. Illberg. Leipzig: Teubner, 1927. English translation: O.Temkin, *Soranus' Gynaecology*, Baltimore: Johns Hopkins University Press.

Veyne, P. (1978) "La famille et l'amour sous le Haut-empire romain," *Annales É.S.C.* 33: 35–63.

Veyne, P. (1982) "L'homosexualité à Rome," *Communications* 35: 25–33. Translated in P. Ariès and A. Béjin (eds) q.v. *Western Sexuality: Practice and Precept in Past Times*, pp. 26–35.

Veyne, P. (1983) *L'Élégie érotique romaine*, Paris: Editions du Seuil.

Veyne, P. (1985) "L'Empire romain," in Veyne (ed.) *Histoire de la Vie Privée*. Vol. 1, *De l'Empire romain à l'an mil* Paris: Le Seuil. pp. 19–224. English translation: A.Goldhammer, trans. *A History of Private Life*. Vol. 1, *From Pagan Rome to Byzantium* Cambridge: Harvard University Press, 1987, pp. 16–233.

Chapter 43

Orlan on becoming-Orlan

'I DO NOT WANT TO LOOK LIKE ...'

From Orlan (1995) 'I do not want to look like ...', *Women's Art Magazine,* 64: 5–10.

The skin is deceptive ... in life one only has one's skin ... there is an error in human relations because one is never what one has ... I have an angel's skin, but I am a jackal ... a crocodile's skin but I am a puppy, a black skin but I am white, a woman's skin but I am a man; I never have the skin of what I am. There is no exception to the rule because I am never what I have ...

WHEN I READ THIS TEXT I thought about how, in our era, we are beginning to have the means of reducing this distance, specifically by surgery ... It is now possible therefore to bring the internal image closer to the external image.

[...]

My work can be considered as the classical work of a classical self-portrait even though it is initially developed on a computer. But what is the reaction when it becomes a matter of inscribing this portrait in the flesh in a permanent fashion? ... I want to talk of a 'carnal art', amongst other things, as a way of differentiating my work from body art, to which it is nevertheless related.

My work and ideas as incarnated in my flesh. They ask questions about the status of the body in our society and its future in coming generations in terms of new technologies and the genetic manipulation which will not be long in coming.

My body has become a place of public debate, asking a question which is crucial to our era.

At the beginning of this performance, I devised my self-portrait using a computer to combine and make a hybrid of representations of goddesses from Greek mythology. I chose them not for the canons of beauty they are supposed to represent (seen from afar), but rather on account of the stories associated with them. [...] After having mixed my image with these other images I reworked the whole as any painter might, until a final portrait emerged and it was possible to come to a halt and to sign it.

[...]

Once I had created a computer-generated image, I asked various surgeons to make me look as similar as possible to it. Initially it was extremely difficult to find a surgeon. Only after many refusals did I find a very careful one who started by gradual stages, allowing me to understand what it was I was undertaking and helping me evaluate what is possible to achieve in an operating theatre: what its limits are and what mine are, to know how I and my body would react, thereby learning to manage better the overall operation.

Each operation was constructed like a rite of passage.

As a plastic artist I wanted to intervene in the cold and stereotyped image of plastic surgery, to alter it with other forms, to challenge it. I transformed the decor, the surgeons and my team were dressed in costumes by top designers, myself and young stylists (Paco Rabanne, Franck Sorbier, Issey Miyaké, Lan Vu, an American stylist and his team).

Each operation has its own particular style, from the carnivalesque (this is not a pejorative word for me, the word carnival originally means *Carne Vaut*, Flesh Values) to High Tech style, by way of the Baroque, etc …

For I believe that there are as many pressures on the bodies of women as there are on the physical body of works of art.

Our epoch hates flesh.

Works of art are only accepted within certain networks and in certain galleries because of their moulds and compulsory ways of speech: the parodical, grotesque and ironic styles are an irritation, often scorned for being in bad taste.

During surgery I read texts as long as possible, even while my face is being operated on. In the most recent operations this produced an image of a cadaver under autopsy which keeps on speaking, as if its words were detached from its body …

Each operation-performance has been constructed around a philosophical, psychoanalytic or literary text (Eugénie Lemoine Luccioni, Michel Serres, Hindu Sanskrit texts, Alphonse Allais, Antonin Artaud, Elizabeth Betuel Fiebig, Raphael Cuir …)

The operating theatre becomes my art studio in which I am conscious of producing images, making films, videos, photographs, drawings with my blood, and objects to be exhibited later. These works are variously autonomous attempts to make inscriptions in matter. They are based on the same ideas that lead to the development of the performances, so that the quality of their materiality reveals the essence of the ideas. It is therefore less a question of repeating the passage to the act and the violence of the act, than identifying the elements in the construction of an idea free of the taboo-act; like any artist, I start from a position, a social project and/or an artistic problematic, with the challenge of finding a plastic solution to be realised.

I am on my ninth operation-performance. The first six were done in Europe with two French surgeons, Doctor Kamel Chérif Zahar and Doctor Bernard Cornette from Saint-Cyr, together with a Belgian surgeon, Doctor Pierrequin.

The seventh operation was the most extensive, and the eighth, and ninth, performed by a feminist surgeon, Doctor Marjorie Cramer, in New York.

The seventh operation-performance, of the 21st November 1993, was based on the concept of omnipresence. It was transmitted live by satellite to Gallery Sandra Gering in New York, to the Centre Georges Pompidou, to the Centre Mac-Luhan in Toronto, to the Banff multimedia centre and to ten other places with which we had interactive contact. Specialists around the world were therefore able to watch the operation, and what is more, they were able to ask questions which I answered live.

Amongst other things it was a matter of de-sacrilising the surgical act and making a transparent, public event of a private act.

In the gallery the photographic installation was based on two ideas: to show that which is usually kept secret and to establish a comparison between the self-portrait done by the computer-machine and the self-portrait done by the body-machine.

During the last three operations we used the largest implants possible for my anatomy, plus two other implants usually used to emphasise cheek bones, on the temples on either side of my forehead, creating two bumps.

The next operation will probably take place in Japan, to give me a very large nose, the biggest nose technically possible in relation to my anatomy and deontologically acceptable to a surgeon from that country. This operation will not take place for another three or four years, perhaps even more, for it will take time to find the necessary technical and financial infrastructures to develop the overall project. But above all, the greatest danger I am taking is that this extremely radical and shocking performance will obscure the plastic art work which results from it. My current aim is also to produce and exhibit works from earlier operations, making clear the process whereby this performance is created and debating the questions which it raises with the widest possible public.

My work is not intended to be against plastic surgery, but rather against the norms of beauty and the dictates of the dominant ideology which is becoming more and more deeply embedded in female … as well as masculine … flesh.

Plastic surgery is one of the areas in which man's power can be most powerfully asserted on women's bodies. I was not able to obtain from male surgeons what I was able to achieve with a female surgeon, for I believe they wanted to keep me 'cute'.

[…]

I am the first artist to use surgery as a medium and to divert plastic surgery from its aim of improvement and rejuvenation.

'I am another': I am at the most extreme point of this confrontation.

Like the Australian artist Stelarc, I believe that the body is obsolete. It can no longer deal with the situation. We mutate at the speed of cockroaches, and yet we are cockroaches with their memories on computer, piloting airplanes and driving cars which we have developed even though our bodies are not made for their speeds and even though everything is going faster and faster.

We are at the junction of a world for which we are no longer mentally or physically prepared.

Psychoanalysis and religion agree that: 'The body must not be attacked', one must accept oneself. These are primitive, ancestral and anachronistic ideas: we believe that the sky is going to fall on our head if we meddle with the body!

And yet many damaged faces have been reconstructed and many people have had organ transplants; and how many more noses have been remade or shortened, not so much for physical problems as for psychological ones?

Are we still convinced that we should bend to the determinations of nature? This lottery of arbitrarily distributed genes …

My work is a fight against, the innate, the inexorable, the programmed, nature, DNA (which is our direct rival as artists of representation) and God! One can therefore say that my work is blasphemous. It is an attempt to move the bars of the cage, a radical and uncomfortable attempt. It is only an attempt.

[...]

A few words on pain. I am trying to make this work the least masochistic possible, but there is a price to be paid for the anaesthetic injections are not at all pleasurable! (I prefer to be drinking champagne or a good wine with my friends rather than being operated on!) And yet, everybody experiences this, it's like going to the dentist, you grimace for a few seconds ... There are of course several injections and so several grimaces ... But as I have not paid my tribute to nature by experiencing the pains of childbirth, I consider myself happy. After the operations it is more or less uncomfortable and more or less painful, and so I take analgesics like everyone else.

As my French artist friend Ben Vautier would say: 'Art is a dirty job, but someone has to do it.'

In fact, it is my public, above all, which suffers when it looks at the images, and I myself when I look at the video clips. I compare myself to a high level sportsperson: there is the training, the moment of the performance where one has to go beyond ones limits, which cannot be done without effort and pain, and then there is recuperation. Like a sportsperson who crosses the Atlantic solo we often do crazy things without necessarily being crazy.

'I have given my body to art', for after my death it will not be given to science, but rather to a museum to be mummified: it will be the main part of a video installation. When the operations are finished, I will employ an advertising agency to find me a first and second name and an artist name, then I will get a lawyer to appeal to the Public Prosecutor to accept my new identities with my new face. This is a performance inscribed within the social fabric, a performance which goes as far as the law ... as far as a complete change of identity. In any case, if it proves to be impossible the attempt and the lawyer's appeal will be a part of the work.

[...]

Chapter 44

Zygmunt Bauman

SURVIVAL AS A SOCIAL CONSTRUCT

From Z. Bauman (1992) 'Survival as a social construct', *Theory, Culture and Society*, 9, pp. 1–36.

[...]

MODERN PRIVATIZATION OF DEATH comes together with the privatization of life. Both are to be filled with sense and purpose by those who live and die. There are many devices that help life to be lived with a purpose, or to be lived as a series or a succession of purposes. The most important of the devices are supplied by instrumental reason. There are no devices (there can be no specifically *modern* devices) to anticipate death as a meaningful event. Our own death cannot be thought of as instrumental. It invalidates the discourse of instrumentality as it spells the termination of purposeful action. This is where its horror resides in the modern world of instrumental rationality: the world where deeds are lived as means to ends and justify themselves by the ends which they serve as means. There is no way in which this horror could be argued away. It can be only barred from consciousness, tabooed as a topic, heaved out away from current concerns; or, in the typically modern way, split into small-scale worries, each one separately removable – so that the fearful finality and irremediability of the original worry can be never scanned in its totality.

The latter expedient strives to conceal the fact that death, as the ultimate end of life, cannot be resisted. The truth that death cannot be escaped is not denied – it cannot be denied; but it could be held out of the agenda, elbowed out by another truth: that each *particular* case of death (most importantly, death which threatens the particular person, me, at the particular moment, now) can be resisted, postponed or avoided altogether. Death as such is inevitable; but each concrete instance of death is contingent. Death is omnipotent and invincible; but none of the specific cases of death is.

All deaths have causes, each death has a cause, each particular death has its particular cause. Corpses are cut open, explored, scanned, tested. The cause is found: blood clot, kidney failure, haemorrhage, heart arrest, lung collapse. We do not hear of people dying of mortality. They die only of individual causes; *because* there was an individual cause. No postmortem stops before the individual causes have been revealed. There are so many causes of death; given enough time, one can name them all. If I defeat, escape or cheat twenty among them, twenty less will be left to defeat me. One does not die; one dies of a *disease* or of *murder*. I can do nothing to defy mortality. But I can do quite a lot to avoid a blood clot or a lung cancer. I can stop eating eggs, refrain from smoking, do physical exercises, keep my weight down; I can do so many other things. And while doing all these right things and forcing myself to abstain from the wrong ones, I have no time left to ruminate that the effectiveness of each thing I am doing, however foolproof it could be made, does not in the least detract from the uselessness of them all taken together. The cause of instrumental rationality celebrates more triumphant battles – and in the din of festivities the news of the lost war is inaudible.

[...]

The doctors who stand between me and my death do not fight mortality either; but they do fight, gallantly and skilfully, each and any of its particular cases. They fight *mortal diseases*. Quite often they win. Each victory is an occasion for rejoicing: once more, *death has been avoided*. Sometimes they lose the battle. And then, in Helmut Thielicke's (1983: 44) words, the death of a patient – *this* patient, *here* and *now* – is 'felt to be a personal defeat. Doctors are like attorneys who lose cases and are thus forced to face up to the limit of their own powers. No wonder that they conceal their faces and turn aside.' A lost court case does not put in question the importance and the competence of lawyers; at worst, it may cast shadow on the skills of a particular barrister. A death that has not been prevented does not undermine the authority of the medical profession. At worst it may stain the reputation of an individual doctor. But the condemnation of the individual practitioner only reinforces the authority of the art: the doctor's fault was not to use the tools and the procedures he *could use*. He is guilty precisely because the profession as a whole is capable of doing what he did not do, though should have done. Or in case a learned council resolves that the suspicion of neglect has been ill founded, as the proper tools and procedures are not available *at the moment* – the cause of hiding the lost war against mortality behind loudly hailed victorious frays and skirmishes with cholesterols, infections and tumours receives another powerful boost. The means have not been invented *yet;* the equipment has not been developed, the vaccine has not been discovered, the technique has not been tested. But they will, given time and money. Conquest of no disease is *in principle* impossible. Did you say that another disease will threaten life once this one here and now has been conquered? Well, we will cross that bridge when we come to it. Let us concentrate on the task at hand, on this trouble here and now. This we *can* do; and this we will go on doing.

From a hangman, death has been turned into a prison guard. The horror of mortality has been sliced into thin rashers of fearful, yet curable (or potentially curable) afflictions; they can be now fit neatly into every nook and cranny of life. Death does not come now at the end of life: it is there from the start, in a position of constant surveillance, never relaxing its vigil. Death is watching when we work, when we eat, when we love, when we rest. Through its many deputies, death presides over life. Fighting death is meaningless. But fighting the *causes* of dying turns into the meaning of life.

Reference

Thielicke, Herbert (1983) *Living with Death*, Grand Rapids: Eydermans.

Chapter 45

Arthur Frank

THE BODY'S PROBLEMS WITH ILLNESS

From A. Frank (1995) *The Wounded Storyteller*, Chicago and London: University of Chicago Press.

DURING ILLNESS, PEOPLE WHO HAVE always *been* bodies have distinctive problems *continuing* to be bodies, particularly continuing to be the same sorts of bodies they have been. The body's problems during illness are not new; being a body always involves certain problems. Illness requires new and more self-conscious solutions to these general problems. One way or another, everyone has been resolving – if never finally "solving" – these problems throughout her life.

Each body problem is a problem of *action:* to act, a body-self must achieve some working resolution to each problem. The ways that a body-self responds to each problem are presented as a continuum or range of possible responses; thus four problems yield four continua. I emphasize that each range of possible actions, while it looks on paper like a dichotomy, is in reality a continuum of responses.

The problem of control

Everyone must ask in any situation, Can I reliably predict how my body will function; can I *control* its functioning?

People define themselves in terms of their body's varying capacity for control. So long as these capacities are predictable, control as an action problem does not require self-conscious monitoring. But disease itself is a loss of predictability, and it causes further losses: incontinence, shortness of breath or memory, tremors and seizures, and all the other "failures" of the sick body. Some ill people adapt to these contingencies easily; others experience a crisis of control. Illness is about learning to live with lost control.

The question of control suggests that the body is lived along a continuum from the *predictability* that may reach its highest expression in ballet and gymnastics to *contingency* at the other end. Contingency is the body's condition of being subject to forces that cannot be controlled. The infantile body is contingent: burping, spitting, and defecating according to its own internal needs and rhythms. Society expects nothing more, and infants are afforded some period to acquire control. When adult bodies lose control, they are expected to attempt to regain it if possible, and if not then at least to conceal the loss as effectively as possible.

A man described to me the social problems he experienced when he lost bladder control following surgery for prostate cancer. He was expected to conceal the contingency of his bladder; stains and smells are stigmatizing. But he also found that sales people in home-care stores were unwilling to discuss incontinence products with him, in part, it seemed to him, because he was male (incontinence is, demographically, more a female problem) and perhaps also because he was younger than social stereotypes of incontinence allowed.

[…]

A body's place on the continuum of control depends not only on the physiological possibility of predictability or contingency, but also on how the person chooses to interpret this physiology. The flesh cannot be denied, but bodies are more than mere corporeality. As body-selves, people interpret their bodies and make choices: the person can either seek perfected levels of predictability, at whatever cost, or can accept varying degrees of contingency. Most people do both, and strategies vary as to what is sought to be controlled, where, and how.

How any individual responds to lost predictability is woven into the dense fabric of how the other action problems of the body are managed, since the same illness provokes crises in these other dimensions as well.

Body-relatedness[1]

Is my body the flesh that "I," the cognitive, ethereal I, only happen to inhabit, or is whatever "I" am only to be found as my body? Do I *have* a body, or *am* I a body?[2]

A friend of mine had an inflammation of lymph nodes under his arms. Physicians did not find any disease (and the years proved them correct), but they advised him to check the swelling daily for any change, tenderness, or other symptom. He told me what he disliked was "having to be embodied," which I understood to mean having to attend to his body on a daily and intimate basis, taking this body seriously as having implications for who he was. He preferred, apparently, to get his body dressed as soon as possible and then regard "it" as disappeared within his clothes. He didn't like to eat, and liquids were consumed for the pleasure of that consumption, not in recognition of the body's needs. He represents the *dissociated* end of the continuum.

I myself tend toward the opposite end, choosing to live in a body that I am compulsively *associated* with. I believe I am what I eat. I do *tai chi* exercises in order to become more aware of my body's balance and tensions. I once saw enlargements of a slide of my recently drawn blood. I think about that blood: the red cells sometimes bonding together, the white cells eating bacteria, and even the odd cancer cells, whose presence is perfectly normal. I know who I am as much in that blood as in this writing or any other activity.

But bodies are not simply associated with or dissociated from. Here as elsewhere, the continuum is not really linear; in this case the quality of association changes.

As long as the body is healthy and mortality is beyond the horizon of consciousness, associating the self with the body comes easily. The recognition of mortality complicates this association. Legend has it that Gautama who later became the Buddha left his palace and became an ascetic after seeing bodies that exemplified suffering, decay, and death. Until then he had been sheltered from such sights, and his association with his body was based on the illusion that bodies brought only gratification. When he learned what troubles the body is prone to, he dissociated himself from his body through asceticism.

The Buddha's later enlightenment included his renunciation of asceticism and ability to move back into his body. By then the quality of association changed for him. His body association was no longer either tacit or hedonistic but became a moral choice to accept his lot as a body prone to suffering. Some body association is simply naïve to suffering; another level of association accepts its mortality. In the really real, the continuum of body-relatedness is not linear but spirals.

[...]

Other-relatedness

What is my relationship, as a body, to other persons who are also bodies? How does our shared corporeality affect who we are, not only to each other, but more specifically *for* each other? Other-relatedness as an action problem is concerned with how the shared condition of being bodies becomes a basis of empathic relations among living beings. Albert Schweitzer expressed this concern in his phrase, the "brotherhood of those who bear the mark of pain."

In 1921, following both his first medical missionary expedition to Africa and a period of severe illness resulting from his internment as an enemy alien during World War I, Schweitzer wrote what became one of his most famous passages:

> Whoever among us has learned through personal
> experience what pain and anxiety really are must help
> to ensure that those out there who are in physical
> need obtain the same help that once came to him.
> He no longer belongs to himself alone; he has
> become the brother of all who suffer. It is this
> "brotherhood of those who bear the mark of pain"
> that demands humane medical services ... [3]

My term for the body's sense of this "brotherhood" is the *dyadic* body. Illness presents a particular opening to becoming a dyadic body, because the ill person is immersed in a suffering that is both wholly individual – my pain is mine alone – but also shared: the ill person sees others around her, before and after her, who have gone through this same illness and suffered their own wholly particular pains. She sees others who are pained by her pain.

At the opposite end of the other-relatedness continuum is the *monadic* body, understanding itself as existentially separate and alone. A 1991 film, *The Doctor*, shows William Hurt as a surgeon who has just been told he has cancer. His wife receives the news with a "we" statement about their ability as a couple to cope with whatever comes. He corrects her, saying that *he* alone has cancer. Many, like this character, choose the monadic body when faced with illness. That the character is a surgeon is an interesting comment on cultural perceptions of where medicine places bodies on the continuum from monadic to dyadic.

Medicine encourages monadic bodies in many ways. Hospitals treat patients in close enough proximity to each other to obviate any meaningful privacy, but at just enough distance to eliminate any meaningful contact. Some friendships are formed in waiting rooms and between roommates, but in my observations of cancer centers, most contact among patients is minimal and transitory. Patients relate individually to medical staff, not collectively among themselves, and this pattern of relating seems to result from how medical spaces are designed and how movement within them is orchestrated. Modernist administrative systems not only prefer the monadic body, but the disease model that grounds medical practice has little ability to admit any other concept of the body.[4]

The monadic body of medicine articulates well with modernist society's emphasis on individual achievement in education or in the marketplace. The dyadic body thus represents an ethical *choice* to place oneself in a different relationship to others. This choice is to be a body *for* other bodies. Living for others means placing one's self and body within the "community of pain," to render Schweitzer's phrase contemporary.

Thus my continua are not only not linear, as the shifting nature of body association demonstrates; they are also ideal types of ethical *choices*. The choice to live as a dyadic body points toward an ethics of the body. Dyadic bodies exist *for* each other: they exist for the task of discovering what it means to live for other bodies.

[...]

Desire

What do I *want*, and how is this desire expressed *for* my body, *with* my body, and *through* my body?

My usage of desire has its conceptual roots in the psychoanalytic theory of Jacques Lacan.[5] Lacan places desire in a triad with need and demand. The need is fully corporeal and can be satisfied at that level. The baby needs milk or a dry diaper. The expression of the need is the demand, but the demand differs from the need itself: the baby's cry is not the same as its hunger or wetness. The demand's difference from the need enlarges the context: the demand asks for more than the need it seeks to express.

Desire is this quality of *more*. When the child asks for one more of whatever at bedtime – one more story, one more drink, one more hug – that displacement of each "more" by another expresses the desire in the demand. The parents' frustration is that when they fulfill the demand, the child remains unhappy. Desire, Lacan teaches, cannot be filled: there is always more.

[...]

Yet some bodies, particularly ill bodies, do cease desiring. The body's problem of desire generates a continuum between bodies that have come to *lack* desire and those that remain *productive* of desire. Illness often precipitates a condition of lacking desire. Stewart Alsop, dying of leukemia, writes of his approaching birthday that perhaps being sixty "is a good time to bow out."[6]

Malcolm Diamond, writing about his reaction to the diagnosis of multiple myeloma, expresses questions that – so far as I can tell – virtually every person facing such a disease asks: "Why buy shoes? Why have dental work done?"[7] The plot of his story centers on desire: the narrative tension is whether lost desire will be regained. The initial loss of desire is expressed in indifference to such mundane acts as keeping up one's footwear and teeth. Diamond's story ends, happily, with him in a remission that is stable enough for him to want to buy shoes; he has made a transition from diagnostic shock to living with cancer. This plot of desire lost and regained informs all lives at various points, but illness demands reflection on cycles of when desire is lacking and when the body produces desire.

Just as illness almost invariably plunges the body into lacking desire, illness can instigate new reflections on how to be a body producing desire. Anatole Broyard describes critical illness as "like a great permission."[8] Part of what becomes permitted is the exploration of desires. Broyard writes that he began taking tap-dancing lessons after his diagnosis with prostate cancer. These lessons, besides probably being something he always wanted to do, were part of his self-conscious attempt "to develop a style" to meet his illness: "I think that only by insisting on your style can you keep from falling out of love with yourself as the illness attempts to diminish or disfigure you."

[…]

Broyard concludes that "it may not be dying we fear so much, but the diminished self." What diminishes the self is no longer desiring for itself. Falling out of love with yourself means ceasing to consider yourself desirable to yourself: the ill person fears he is no longer worth clean teeth and new shoes.

As desire becomes reflective, an opening exists to assume enhanced responsibility for what is desired. Although desire is always for more than the immediate object – Diamond's shoes or Broyard's tap-dancing are self-consciously metonymic of a desire that will always exceed its tokens – the immediate objects remain ethical choices. For the dyadic body, productive desire leads to what Schweitzer called service.[9] Schweitzer's community of pain expresses a productive desire grounded in the ethical choice to be a body for other bodies.

[…]

The emphasis on choice is a reminder that the body is, ultimately, a moral problem, perhaps *the* moral problem a person has to address. Yet choice is also a deceptive word, because the body-self is created in reciprocal processes. Selves act in ways that choose their bodies, but bodies also create the selves who act. We can observe more of the first process than of the second; how bodies create selves is scarcely understood at all.

Notes

1   In earlier writing I called this problem "self-relatedness." "Self-relatedness" juxtaposes more neatly to the next problem of "other-relatedness," but what I am discussing under this topic is relation to one's self as a body, hence body-relatedness.

2   For a useful review of the positions taken on this question by classical and early Christian writers, see Synnott, *The Body Social*.

3   Originally written in Schweitzer's *On the Edge of the Primeval Forest*. Quoted by Schweitzer in *Out of My Life and Thought: An Autobiography*, trans. Antje Bultmann Lemke (1933; New York: Henry Holt, 1990), 195.

4   For a sociological perspective on the disease model, see Elliot G. Mishler (1981) "Viewpoint: Critical Perspectives on the Biomedical Model," in Elliot G. Mishler *et al.* (eds) *Social Contexts of Health, Illness, and Patient Care*, Cambridge: Cambridge University Press, pp. 1–23. Larry Dossey, MD, has been most provocative in his criticisms of medicine's inability to think beyond the monadic body; see his *Meaning and Medicine*, New York: Bantam, 1991 and *Healing Words: The Power of Prayer and the Practice of Medicine*, New York: HarperCollins, 1993. For the conclusions he suggests about how much bodies have to do with each other, Dossey would be regarded as a "fringe" figure by many.

5   Jacques Lacan (1978) *Écrits: A Selection*, trans. Alan Sheridan, New York: Norton, 1977 and *The Four Fundamental Concepts of Psychoanalysis*, ed. Jacques-Alain Miller, trans. Alan Sheridan, New York: Norton.

6   Stewart Alsop (1973) *Stay of Execution: A Sort of Memoir*. Philadelphia: Lippincott, 288.

7   Malcolm Diamond (1994) "Coping with cancer: a funny thing happened on my way to retirement," *The Princeton Alumni Weekly*, April 6: 13–16.

8   Anatole Broyard (1992) *Intoxicated by My Illness: And Other Writings on Life and Death*, comp. and ed. Alexandra Broyard, New York: Clarkson N. Potter, 23.

9   For contemporary statements of the centrality of service to medicine, see Robert Coles, *The Call of Stories*, and David Hilfiker (1994) *Not All of Us Are Saints: A Doctor's Journey with the Poor*, New York: Hill and Wang.

Chapter 46

Elaine Scarry

THE BODY IN PAIN

The making and unmaking of the world

From E. Scarry (1985) *The Body in Pain: The Making and Unmaking of the World*, Oxford and New York: Oxford University Press.

WHEN ONE SPEAKS ABOUT "one's own physical pain" and about "another person's physical pain," one might almost appear to be speaking about two wholly distinct orders of events. For the person whose pain it is, it is "effortlessly" grasped (i.e. even with the most heroic effort it cannot *not* be grasped); while for the person outside the sufferer's body, what is "effortless" is *not* grasping it (it is easy to remain wholly unaware of its existence; even with effort, one may remain in doubt about its existence or may retain the astonishing freedom of denying its existence; and, finally, if with the best effort of sustained attention one successfully apprehends it, the aversiveness of the "it" one apprehends will only be a shadowy fraction of the actual "it"). So, for the person in pain, so incontestably and unnegotiably present is it that "having pain" may come to be thought of as the most vibrant example of what it is to "have certainty," while for the other person it is so elusive that "hearing about pain" may exist as the primary model of what it is "to have doubt." Thus pain comes unsharably into our midst as at once that which cannot be denied and that which cannot be confirmed.

Whatever pain achieves, it achieves in part through its unsharability, and it ensures this unsharability through its resistance to language. "English," writes Virginia Woolf, "which can express the thoughts of Hamlet and the tragedy of Lear has no words for the shiver or the headache. ... The merest schoolgirl when she falls in love has Shakespeare or Keats to speak her mind for her, but let a sufferer try to describe a pain in his head to a doctor and language at once runs dry."[1] True of the headache, Woolf's account is of course more radically true of the severe and prolonged pain that may accompany cancer or burns or phantom limb or stroke, as well as of the severe and prolonged pain that may occur unaccompanied by any nameable disease. Physical pain does not simply resist language but actively destroys it, bringing about an immediate reversion to a state anterior to language, to the sounds and cries a human being makes before language is learned.

[...]

Torture, then, consists of a primary physical act, the infliction of pain, and a primary verbal act, the interrogation. The verbal act, in turn, consists of two parts, "the question" and "the answer," each with conventional connotations that wholly falsify it. "The question" is mistakenly understood to be "the motive"; "the answer" is mistakenly understood to be "the betrayal." The first mistake credits the torturer, providing him with a justification, his cruelty with an explanation. The second discredits the prisoner, making him rather than the torturer, his voice rather than his pain, the cause of his loss of self and world. These two misinterpretations are obviously neither accidental nor unrelated. The one is an absolution of responsibility; the other is a conferring of responsibility; the two together turn the moral reality of torture upside down. Almost anyone looking at the *physical* act of torture would be immediately appalled and repulsed by the torturers. It is difficult to think of a human situation in which the lines of moral responsibility are more starkly or simply drawn, in which there is a more compelling reason to ally one's sympathies with the one person and to repel the claims of the other. Yet as soon as the focus of attention shifts to the *verbal* aspect of torture, those lines have begun to waver and change their shape in the direction of accommodating and crediting the torturers. This inversion, this interruption and redirecting of a basic moral reflex, is indicative of the kind of interactions occurring between body and voice in torture and suggests why the infliction of acute physical pain is inevitably accompanied by the interrogation.

However near the prisoner the torturer stands, the distance between their physical realities is colossal, for the prisoner is in overwhelming physical pain while the torturer is utterly without pain; he is free of any pain originating in his own body; he is also free of the pain originating in the agonized body so near him. He is so without any human recognition of or identification with the pain that he is not only able to bear its presence but able to bring it continually into the present, inflict it, sustain it, minute after minute, hour after hour. Although the distance separating the two is probably the greatest distance that can separate two human beings, it is an invisible distance since the physical realities it lies between are each invisible. The prisoner experiences an annihilating negation so hugely felt throughout his own body that it overflows into the spaces before his eyes and in his ears and mouth; yet one which is unfelt, unsensed by anybody else. The torturer experiences the absence of this annihilating negation. These physical realities, an annihilating negation and an absence of negation, are therefore translated into verbal realities in order to make the invisible distance visible, in order to make what is taking place in terms of pain take place in terms of power, in order to shift what is occurring exclusively in the mode of sentience into the mode of self-extension and world. The torturer's questions – asked, shouted, insisted upon, pleaded for – objectify the fact that he has a world, announce in their feigned urgency the critical importance of that world, a world whose asserted magnitude is confirmed by the cruelty it is able to motivate and justify. Part of what makes his world so huge is its continual juxtaposition with the small and shredded world objectified in the prisoner's answers, answers that articulate and comment on the disintegration of all objects to which he might have been bonded in loyalty or love or good sense or long familiarity. It is only the prisoner's steadily shrinking ground that wins for the torturer his swelling sense of territory. The question and the answer are a prolonged comparative display, an unfurling of world maps.

[…]

There is a second equally crucial and equally cruel bond between physical pain and interrogation that further explains their inevitable appearance together. Just as the interrogation, like the pain, is a way of wounding, so the pain, like the interrogation, is a vehicle of self-betrayal. Torture systematically prevents the prisoner from being the agent of anything and simultaneously pretends that he is the agent of some things. Despite the fact that in reality he has been deprived of all control over, and therefore all responsibility for, his world, his words, and his body, he is to understand his confession as it will be understood by others, as an act of self-betrayal. In forcing him to confess or, as often happens, to sign an unread confession, the torturers are producing a mime in which the one annihilated shifts to being the agent of his own annihilation. But this mime, though itself a lie, mimes something real and already present in the physical pain; it is a visible counterpart to an invisible but intensely felt aspect of pain. Regardless of the setting in which he suffers (home, hospital, or torture room), and regardless of the cause of his suffering (disease, burns, torture, or malfunctioning of the pain network itself), the person in great pain experiences his own body as the agent of his agony. The ceaseless, self-announcing signal of the body in pain, at once so empty and undifferentiated and so full of blaring adversity, contains not only the feeling "my body hurts" but the feeling "my body hurts me." This part of the pain, like almost all others, is usually invisible to anyone outside the boundaries of the sufferer's body, though it sometimes becomes visible when a young child or an animal in the first moments of acute distress takes maddening flight, fleeing from its own body as though it were a part of the environment that could be left behind. If self-hatred, self-alienation, and self-betrayal (as well as the hatred of, alienation from, and betrayal of all that is contained in the self – friends, family, ideas, ideology) were translated out of the psychological realm where it has content and is accessible to language into the unspeakable and contentless realm of physical sensation it would be intense pain.

[...]

Every act of civilization is an act of transcending the body in a way consonant with the body's needs: in building a wall, to return to an old friend, one overcomes the body, projects oneself out beyond the body's boundaries but in a way that expresses and fulfills the body's need for stable temperatures. Higher moments of civilization, more elaborate forms of self-extension, occur at a greater distance from the body: the telephone or the airplane is a more emphatic instance of overcoming the limitation of the human body than is the cart. Yet even as here when most exhilaratingly defiant of the body, civilization always has embedded within it a profound allegiance to the body, for it is only by paying attention that it can free attention. Torture is a condensation of the act of "overcoming" the body present in benign forms of power. Although the torturer dominates the prisoner both in physical acts and verbal acts, ultimate domination requires that the prisoner's ground become increasingly physical and the torturer's increasingly verbal, that the prisoner become a colossal body with no voice and the torturer a colossal voice (a voice composed of two voices) with no body, that eventually the prisoner experience himself exclusively in terms of sentience and the torturer exclusively in terms of self-extension. All those ways in which the torturer dramatizes his opposition to and distance from the prisoner are ways of dramatizing his distance from the body. The most radical act of distancing resides in his disclaiming of the other's hurt. Within the strategies of power based on denial there is, as in affirmative and civilized forms of power, a hierarchy of achievement, successive intensifications based on increasing distance from, increasingly great transcendence of, the body: a regime's refusal to recognize the rights of the normal and healthy is its cart; its refusal to recognize and care for those in agony is its airplane.

Note

1   Woolf, V. (1967) 'On being ill', in *Collected Essays*, vol. 4, New York: Harcourt.

Guide to further reading

W E HAVE GATHERED HERE a series of suggestions for further reading on the questions and themes addressed in this Reader. We have structured our selection into sections that match the Parts of the Reader itself, although many texts could have been listed under a number of different headings. Whilst we have aimed to include a variety of conceptual perspectives and of historical, empirical and cross-cultural examples, it should be stressed that the selection is not comprehensive – nor could it be, in the light of the rapid expansion of literature on each of the problem-areas we have focused on in this volume. We have deliberately not included works by major figures in the history of philosophy who have addressed the body; we have also excluded vast areas of scholarship that do not correspond directly to the main themes addressed in this volume (such as the body and art, the body and space, sense and sensation). Otherwise we hope that the reader will find the following annotated references helpful in structuring further study.

General introduction and what is a body?

Ahmed, S. and Stacey, J. (2001) *Thinking Through Skin*, London and New York: Routledge. This edited collection explores skin as a site of inscription, a boundary and a point of connection. Contributions are informed by psychoanalytic, phenomenological, postcolonial and feminist approaches to lived and imagined embodiment.

Ansell-Pearson, K. (1997) *Viroid Life: Perspectives on Nietzsche and the Transhuman Condition*, London: Routledge. Also by the same author (1999) *Germinal Life: The Difference and Repetition of Deleuze*, London: Routledge. These two 'companion' books explore ethology, biology, ethics, literature and cyborgs.

Artaud, A. (1999) 'An affective athleticism', in A. Artaud, *Collected Works*, Vol. 4, London: John Calder. A comparative discussion of actors and athletes where actors are presented has having 'a kind of affective musculature matching the bodily localisation of our feelings'.

Barker, F. (1984) *The Tremulous Private Body: Essays on Subjection*, London: Methuen. A short and elegant book which draws on post-structuralist theory to explore changes in representations of the body in the seventeenth century. Barker addresses not only the separation of the body from the soul, but also the perceived distinction between the 'absent' and the 'positive' body.

Bartky, S. L. (1988) 'Foucault, femininity, and the modernization of patriarchal power', in I. Diamond and L. Quinby (eds) *Feminism and Foucault: Reflections on Resistance*, Boston: Northeastern University Press. In an analysis of femininity informed by Foucault's conception of docile bodies, Bartky explores body-size, body gestures and the body as ornamented surface.

Benthall, J. and Polhemus, T. (eds) (1975) *The Body as a Medium of Expression*, London: Allen Lane. This book looks at the expressive and symbolic resources of the body. Here, the body is a complex of mechanisms, shapes, meanings and symbols.

Berthelot, J. M. (1986) 'Sociological discourse and the body', *Theory, Culture and Society* 3: 155–64. What is the body, and what is a sociology of the body? This text addresses these questions from a number of different dimensions.

Birke, L. (1999) *Feminism and the Biological Body*, Edinburgh: Edinburgh University Press. Birke explores the relation between feminism and biology, arguing that it would be a mistake for feminist theory to entirely 'lose' the biological body.

Blacking, J. (ed.) (1977) *The Anthropology of the Body*, London/New York/San Francisco: Academic Press. Contributions from nine social anthropologists who focus on the relation between body and society and the symbolic/cultural dimension of bodies. At the time of its publication, the volume aimed to contrast the tendency for the anthropological study of the body to be identified with the approaches of physical anthropology and socio-biology.

Body Image (2003–) a recently launched journal dedicated to body image and human physical appearance. 'Body image' is a multifaceted concept that refers to persons' perceptions and attitudes about their own body, particularly but not only concerning physical appearance.

Braidotti, R. (1994) *Nomadic Subjects: Embodiment and Sexual Difference in Contemporary Feminist Theory*, New York: Columbia University Press. Braidotti traverses a range of subjects – including philosophy, bioethics, monsters – in the course of explicating her understanding of embodied 'nomadic subjectivity'.

Budgeon, S. (2003) 'Identity as embodied event', *Body and Society* 9, 1: 35–55. A study of the relation between body and self, particularly as it is understood to be increasingly open to choice. Budgeon claims that the accent on representation in analyses of bodies reinstalls the mind/body split. Through an empirical exploration of young women's experiences of embodiment, she focuses instead on the body as event, and on what a body can *do*.

Butler, J. (1998) 'Sex and gender in Simone de Beauvoir's *Second Sex*', in E. Fallaize (ed.) *Simone de Beauvoir: A Critical Reader*, London and New York: Routledge. This piece offers an accessible point of entry into Judith Butler's work. In it, she argues that if the relation between sex and gender is an arbitrary one, if one is not born but rather becomes a woman, then this 'becoming' will be informed by a complex array of power relations which will themselves be productive of differences between women.

Cheah, P. (1996) 'Mattering', *Diacritics* 26, 1: 108–39. This is a lengthy and difficult text, but it offers a thorough and incisive critique of Butler's conception of materiality in *Bodies That Matter*. The final part of the article adopts a Derridean approach to the problems raised by the relations between matter and ontology.

Csordas, T. J. (ed.) (1990) *Embodiment and Experience: The Existential Ground of Culture and Self*, Cambridge: Cambridge University Press. A collection of essays exploring embodiment as the existential condition of cultural life, including contributions on the expression of emotion, the experience of pain, ritual healing, dietary customs and political violence.

Cunningham-Burley, S. and Backett-Milburn, K. (eds) *Exploring the Body*, Basingstoke: Palgrave. This book includes a wide variety of sociological essays, with subjects on the body ranging from homeopathy, scars, and death to bodies and leisure.

Fraser, M. (2002) 'What is the matter of feminist criticism?', *Economy and Society* 31, 4: 606–25. This article explores recent debates about matter, ontology and substance in feminist theory.

Grosz, E. (1995) *Space, Time and Perversion: Essays on the Politics of Bodies*, New York and London: Routledge. In this book, Grosz investigates the work of a wide range of theorists and draws on philosophy, feminism, cultural analysis and queer theory in order to develop her own innovative conception of bodies and body politics.

Hassard, J. and Holliday R. (eds) (2001) *Contested Bodies*, London: Routledge. This book explores the lack of consensus around what bodies are or how they are constituted, through a number of diverse contributions. Themes that run through the work include the place of the body in theory, the notion of labour in the production of bodies and the transformative potential of bodies on spaces.

Jacobus, M., Fox Keller, E., and Shuttleworth, S. (1990) *Body/Politics: Women and the Discourses of Science*, New York and London: Routledge. This classic text which explores the feminine body at the intersection of literary, social, and scientific discourses. Includes Susan Bordo's 'Reading the Slender Body' and Paula A. Teicher's 'Feminism, Medicine, and the Meaning of Childbirth'.

Kroker, A. and Kroker, M. (eds) (1988) *Body Invaders: Sexuality and the Postmodern Condition*, Basingstoke: Macmillan. This text is a good illustration of postmodern work on the postmodern body/the body in postmodernity. The pieces engage with the work of, among others, Bataille, Foucault, Baudrillard, and Kristeva and cover topics such as sex and eroticism, fashion, reproduction, and bodily decay.

Lash, S. (1995) 'Genealogy and the body: Foucault/Deleuze/Nietzsche', in M. Featherstone, M. Hepworth and B. S. Turner (eds) *The Body: Social Process and Cultural Theory*, London: Sage. Excellent introduction to the points of comparison and contrast between Michel Foucault, Gilles Deleuze and Friedrich Neitzsche through the prism of genealogy (and particularly the concept of agency).

MacNaghten, P. and Urry, J. (2000) 'Bodies of Nature', Special issue of *Theory, Culture and Society* 6, 2–3. This special issue considers the embodied nature of people's experiences in and of the physical world. It focuses in particular on the ways in which the body is implicated in social practices that are involved in being in nature, the countryside, the outdoors, etc.

Moss, D. (1978) 'Brain, body and world: perspectives on body image', in R. S. Valle and M. King (eds) *Existential Phenomenological Alternatives for Psychology*, New York: Oxford University Press. This chapter introduces the phenomenological use of 'body image' in psychology.

Schilder, P. (1950) *The Image and Appearance of the Human Body: Studies in the Constructive Energies of the Psyche*, New York: International Universities Press. A classic phenomenological text discussing our mental image of our body and how we come to experience it as a unique entity.

Schwartz, H. (1992) 'Torque: The New Kinaesthetic of the Twentieth Century', in J. Crary and S. Kwinter (eds) *Incorporations*, London and New York: Zone. This brilliant roller coaster of an essay explores bodies of motion and movement from dance through to handwriting, the zip and the escalator.

Simondon, G. (1992) 'The genesis of the individual', in J. Crary and S. Kwinter (ed.) *Incorporations*, New York: Zone. An introduction to Simondon's classic work on individuation. Rather than taking the individual as a given, Simondon argues for an understanding of the individual which begins from processes of individuation.

Spelman, E. (1990) Section IV in 'Gender and race: The Ampersand Problem in Feminist Thought,' in *Inessential Woman*, London: The Women's Press. In this short section Spelman clearly outlines the implications of somatophobia in feminist thinking.

Turner, B. S. and Wainwright, S. P. (2003) 'Corps de ballet: the case of the injured ballet dancer', *Body and Society* 25, 4: 268–88. Through an empirical study of classical ballet dancers, the authors formulate a phenomenological understanding of the experiences of embodiment, and offer a critique of the social constructionist notion of the body as text.

Vinge, L. (1975) *The Five Senses: Studies in a Literary Tradition*, Lund: Liber Laromedel. A historical study that refers to literary traditions to explore how the senses came to be divided and enumerated as sight, hearing, smell, taste and touch.

Welton, D. (1999) *The Body: Classic and Contemporary Readings*, Oxford: Blackwell. This book provides an accessible introduction to some of the key philosophical theorists on the body. Each section includes a 'primary' text, and two 'secondary' texts (although note that those secondary texts are often important pieces in their own right). Includes sections on Merleau-Ponty, Foucault, Kristeva, and Irigaray among others.

Wiess, G. (1999) *Body Images: Embodiment as Intercorporeality*, New York and London: Routledge. Chapters one and two offer a critical analysis of Merleau-Ponty's work on the body and body image. Chapter three focuses on the constitutive role of imagination and fantasy in the construction of individual and cultural body images.

Williams, S. J. and Bendelow, G. (1998) *The Lived Body: Sociological Themes, Embodied Issues*. London and New York: Routledge. This book begins by exploring how the mind/body dualism is constituted in classical and contemporary social thought. It re-reads this literature in a 'new, more corporeal, light', as well as investigating specifically anti-Cartesian traditions. It also seeks to develop the notion of embodiment, particularly in relation to an embodied sociology.

Zaner, R. M. (1981) *The Context of Self: A Phenomenological Inquiry Using Medicine as a Clue*, Athens, OH: Ohio University Press. This book has been described as 'the best introduction to the twentieth-century development of phenomenological studies of the body'.

Bodies and social (dis)order

Agamben, G. (1998) *Homo Sacer: Sovereign Power and Bare Life*, Stanford, CA: Stanford University Press. A critical development of Foucault's theses concerning biopower, this text examines the relation between politics and 'bare' life. Contains an extensive and original discussion of the Holocaust, and proposes the camp as a paradigm of political rationality in Western modernity.

Benbow, H. M. (2003) 'Ways in, ways out: theorizing the Kantian body', *Body and Society*, 9: 57–72. An analysis of the Kantian body where the motif of bodily fluids, and their transgression of corporeal boundaries, is considered within the context of an emerging consumer economy, and the changes being wrought on the 'body politic' in the Enlightenment and Romantic periods.

Bloch, M. (1973) *The Royal Touch: Sacred Monarchy and Scrofula in England and France*. London: Routledge & Kegan Paul. One of the first studies to discuss the metaphysical and symbolic qualities attributed to the body of kings, by one of the key historians of the *Annales* school.

Bremmer, J. and Roodenburg, H. (eds) (1992) *A Cultural History of Gesture*, Ithaca, MA:
Cornell University Press. A rich collection of essays that survey the language and
conventions of gesture across time and cultures in Europe, correlating different
practices with different aspects and types of social order.

Dudink, S. (2001) 'Cuts and bruises and democratic contestation: male bodies, history and
politics', *European Journal of Cultural Studies*, 4: 153–70. This article argues that the
neoclassical model of the male body had a special place in late eighteenth-century political culture; against this background, it explores the meanings of visual representations
of mutilated male bodies, linking their significance to the emergence of modern
democratic political life.

Dudley, E. and Novak, M. (eds) (1972) *The Wild Man Within: An Image in Western Thought from
the Renaissance to Romanticism*. Pittsburgh, PA: University of Pittsburgh Press. 'The book
focuses on the importance of wildness and wildman during the period of Western
experience which came to hold up ideals of culture and civilization as its finest accom-
plishments. [During this period] the savage became something to come to terms with,
to be discovered beneath clothes and possibly below the skin. In the mirror of the wildman the historical nature of civilized flesh and blood was reflected' (Duden, in Feher,
Naddaff and Tazi (eds) (1989), vol. 3).

Dunning, E. and Rojek, C. (eds) (1992) *Sport and Leisure in the Civilizing Process*, London:
Macmillan. A collection of essays on sport and leisure from a figurational perspective
employing the concepts and framework of Norbert Elias.

Elias, N. and Dunning, E. (1986) *The Quest for Excitement: Sport and Leisure in the Civilizing
Process*, Oxford: Blackwell. A collection of essays – some of which were originally published by Elias in German journals – where the basic argument Elias set forth in *The
Civilizing Process* is applied to the field of sport. Discusses sport as a 'mimetic' activity
providing 'a social enclave where excitement can be enjoyed without its socially and
personally dangerous implications'. Contains discussions of sports and violence. A good
example of the intersection between the historical sociology of the emotions, of the
body and of state formation.

Feher, M. with R. Naddaff and N. Tazi (eds) (1989) *Fragments for a History of the Human Body*,
Part Three, New York: Zone. Of the three volumes that comprise this excellent collection, this one is conceptually organised around 'the uses of certain organs and bodily substances as metaphors for or models of the functioning of human society' and around the
attribution of 'several remarkable characteristics ... to certain bodies because of the status of the individuals they incarnate'(Feher in Part One, p. 15). In particular, see essays by
Le Goff on the political use of body metaphors in the Middle Ages; by Sissa on the symbolic significance of semen and virginity; by Duverger and by de Heusch on the meaning
of sacrifice; by Dupont on the im/mortality of emperor's bodies in the context of
Ancient Rome; and the excellent iconographic collection of body 'maps' by Kidel and
Rowe-Leete.

Figlio, K. M. (1976) 'The metaphor of organization: an historiographical perspective on the
biomedical sciences of the early nineteenth century', *History of Science*, 14: 17–53.
Figlio explores the social origin of the metaphor of organisation, and its 'naturalisation'
through biomedical science.

Freund, P. E. S. (1998) 'Social performances and their discontents: the dramaturgical aspects
of biopsychosocial stress', in G. Bendelow and S. Williams (eds) *Emotions In Social Life –
Critical Themes and Contemporary Issues*, London: Routledge. A piece that illustrates well
the mutual relevance of the sociology of emotions, the sociology of the body and the
microsociology of the interaction order.

Hargreaves, J. (1986) *Sport, Power and Culture*, Oxford: Polity. A systematic analysis of the links between sport and power in Britian, starting with the development of popular sports during the Industrial Revolution. See particularly the chapter entitled 'Schooling the body'.

Kantorowicz, E. (1997) *The King's Two Bodies*, Princeton: Princeton University Press. A seminal study of sacral kingship in medieval Christendom (originally published in 1957) illustrating and discussing the notion that the king had two bodies, a mortal 'body natural' and an immortal 'body politic'.

Marcovich, A. (1982) 'Concerning the continuity between the image of society and the image of the human body: an examination of the work of the English physician J. C. Lettsom 1746–1815', in P. Wright and A. Treacher (eds) *The Problem of Medical Knowledge*, Edinburgh: Edinburgh University Press. A historical illustration and discussion of the metaphorical relationship between the individual body and the body politic.

Scott, G. R. (2004) *The History of Corporal Punishment: A Survey of Flagellation in Its Historical, Anthropological and Sociological Aspects*, Kegan Paul: London. A study of flagellation in its penal, religious, educational and erotic aspects. The study discusses the various forms of flagellation used throughout the ages on soldiers and sailors, thieves and prostitutes, schoolboys and schoolgirls, slaves and servants.

Spierenburg, P. (1995) 'The body and the state: early modern Europe', in N. Morris and D. Rothman (eds) *The Oxford History of the Prison*, Oxford, NY: Oxford University Press. See also, by the same author (1984) *The Spectacle of Suffering. Execution and the Evolution of Repression: From a Pre-Industrial Metropolis to the European Experience*, Cambridge: Cambridge University Press. These texts discuss the changing place of the body in questions of punishment in Western society.

Turner, B. S. (2003) 'Social fluids: metaphors and meanings of society', *Body and Society*, 9: 1–10. An analysis of different bodily metaphors for social and political relations with a focus on bodily fluids and 'leaking bodies' as metaphors of disorder. Contemporary examples are considered in the light of the concept of 'liquid modernity'.

Weiss, M. (2001) 'The body of the nation: terrorism and the embodiment of nationalism in contemporary Israel', *Anthropological Quarterly*, 75: 37–62. A study of the non-discursive management of concrete bodies and practices of body identification following terrorist attacks in Israel, based on interviews and observations conducted at the Israeli National Institute of Forensic Medicine supplemented by narrative analysis of media texts.

Bodies and identities

Banks, I. (2000) *Hair Matters: Beauty, Power and Black Women's Consciousness*, New York: New York University Press. This book explores how black women's talk about their hair is informed by race, gender and sexuality.

Davis, K. (2003) 'Surgical passing: or why Michael Jackson's nose makes "us" uneasy', *Body and Society* 4, 1: 73–92. A recent article by Kathy Davis, whose early work on cosmetic surgery has been influential (see *Reshaping the Female Body: The Dilemma of Cosmetic Surgery* (1995)). Here, she examines the normative, ethical and political issues raised by 'ethnic cosmetic surgery' and considers how this might differ from other kinds of cosmetic surgeries.

Dyer, R. (1982) 'Don't Look Now', *Screen* 23, 3–4: 61–73. Dyer investigates the implications for sexuality and gender – how they are reaffirmed or destabilised – by the male pin-up and, in particular, by particular bodily poses and positions.

Evans, M. and Lee, E. (eds) (2002) *Real Bodies: A Sociological Introduction*, Basingstoke: Palgrave. This edited collection, which is aimed at undergraduates, addresses the 'real' – that is,

the 'lived' – body as it is experienced in and across a range of identities. Includes
chapters on masculinity, 'race', sexuality, disability, age, as well as the child's body, the
pregnant body, and the dressed body.

Fanon, F. (1986 [1952]) *Black Skin, White Masks*, Translated by Charles Lam Markmann,
London: Pluto Press. A key text in theoretical debates about 'race' and colonialism.
Fanon explores how colonial institutions constructed ideas about 'blackness', the
'negro' and the 'native', among others.

Fanon, F. (1970) 'Algeria unveiled', in *A Dying Colonialism*, New York: Grove Press. This essay
focuses on the relations between the body, dress, and cultural identity both as sites of
play and contestation in the Algerian war of independence.

Featherstone, M. (ed.) (1999) *Body and Society* 5, 2–3. This special issue on Body Modification
includes pieces on surgery, tattoos, self-mutilation, gymnastics, marking, and 'modern
primitivism'. Also includes interviews with Orlan, and with Stelarc.

Featherstone, M. and Wernicke, A. (eds) (1995) *Images of Aging: Cultural Representations of Later
Life*, London and New York: Routledge. Although many of the texts in this book are relevant to the aging body, see in particular Bryan Turner's chapter, 'Aging and identity: some
reflections on the somatization of the self'. Here, Turner argues that sociology has
neglected to analyse the aging process because it has not developed an adequate sociology
of the body.

Gilman, S. (1991) *The Jew's Body*, New York: Routledge. This book focuses on images of the
body in discourses about Jews.

Greer, G. (1999) 'Body', in *The Whole Woman*, London and New York: Doubleday. Here
Greer revisits some of the key themes of the now classic text of the Anglo-American
feminist movement, *The Female Eunuch* (1971) London: Flamingo.

Kanneh, K. (1995) 'Feminism and the Colonial Body', in B. Ashcroft, G. Griffiths and
H. Tiffin (eds) *The Post-Colonial Studies Reader*, London and New York: Routledge. This
is a striking piece on feminism, female circumcision and the 'battle' for the bodies of
'Third World women'.

Keywood, K. (2000) 'My body and other stories: anorexia nervosa and the legal politics of
embodiment', *Social and Legal Studies* 9, 4: 495–514. Keywood investigates the construction of anorexic identities in law, particularly in relation to medical positivism and dual-
istic conceptions of the body and mind. She also considers possible modes of resisting
these legal understandings of anorexia.

Lingis, A. (1994) *Foreign Bodies*, London and New York: Routledge. This book compares *theories* of power, pleasure and pain, and libidinal identity to a variety of *practices* of the body
(including body building) from different cultures (e.g. Japan).

Meyer, R. (1991) 'Rock Hudson's Body', in D. Fuss (ed.) *Inside/Out*, London and New York:
Routledge. Meyer explores the different ways in which the film star Rock Hudson's
body 'filled the frame' over the course of his life, and across his various identities.

Negrin, L. (2002) 'Cosmetic surgery and the eclipse of identity', *Body and Society* 8, 4: 21–42.
In this article, Negrin offers a critical appraisal of the 'rehabilitation' of cosmetic surgery, especially in the light of the power relations that it leaves unchallenged. The
author also addresses the status of the body as matter.

Piper, A. (1992) 'Passing for White, passing for Black', in J. Frueh, C. L. Langer and A. Raven
(eds) *New Feminist Criticism: Art, Identity, Action*, New York: Icon Editions. Piper explores
some of the different ways in which 'black' and 'white' are identified (and where they
are perceived to be located in the body) in the context of her own experiences of passing.

Pitts, V. (2003) *In the Flesh: The Cultural Politics of Body Modification*, New York and Basingstoke,
England: Palgrave Macmillan. Based on interviews and textual analysis, this book

explores the rise of the body modification movement in the 1990s from the perspective of its pioneers – cyberpunks, radical queers, leatherdykes and modern primitives.

Probyn, E. (2000) 'Bodies that eat', in *Carnal Appetites: Food Sex Identities*, London and New York: Routledge. 'Do we eat what we are, or are we what we eat?' This question opens Probyn's exploration of the relation between eating and identity in relation to the body.

Schultze, L. (1990) 'On the Muscle', in J. Gaines and C. Herzog (eds) *Fabrications*, London: Routledge. Schultze explores how the deliberately muscular woman disturbs dominant notions of sex, gender and sexuality. She situates the bodybuilding woman in relation to the body in consumer culture, Bakhtin's notion of the 'grotesque', and in relation to class.

Scott, S. and Morgan, D. (eds) (1993) *Body Matters: Essays on the Sociology of the Body*, London and Washington: Falmer Press. This edited collection explores the embodiment of social actors both in relation to the problems of everyday life and in relation to sociological theorising. Essays cover a range of topics, including marital sex problems, women bodybuilders, masculinity, prostitution and infancy.

Slater, D. (1998) 'Trading sexpics on IRC: embodiment and authenticity on the internet', *Body and Society* 4, 4: 90–117. Based on an ethnographic study of one CMC setting (sexpics trading in an Internet Relay Chat), Slater explores the relation between identity and physical embodiment on the internet.

Vitellone, N. (2002) 'Condoms and the making of sexual differences in AIDS heterosexual culture', *Body and Society* 8, 3: 71–94. Through an analysis of the condom in AIDS research findings on safer heterosexual practice, Vitellone shows how the object of the condom contributes to the production of heterosexual masculine self-identity.

Weekes, D. (1997) 'Shades of blackness: young Black female constructions of beauty', in H. S. Mirza (ed.) *Black British Feminism: A Reader*, London and New York: Routledge. In her analysis of the ways that young black women aspire to, reject, and/or police outward physical features, Weekes shows how the recourse to essentialist discourses often affords strategic empowerment (for some).

Wittig, M. (1973) *The Lesbian Body*, Boston: Beacon Press. This is a classic text, and difficult one. In it, Wittig describes lesbian love in anatomical detail, and in doing so challenges the boundaries of both bodies and language.

Zita, J. N. (1992) 'Male Lesbians and the Postmodernist Body', *Hypatia* 7, 4: 106–27. Here Zita explores the criteria for lesbian identity attribution through the case study of 'male lesbians'. In doing so, she reveals the limitations of the constructed/essential dyad.

Normal bodies (or not)

Bowker, N. and Tuffin, K. (2002) 'Disability discourses for online identities', *Disability and Society*, 17: 327–44. An empirical study that examines the management of disability disclosure in the social context of online interaction, where impairment is invisible.

Cooter, R. (1984) *The Cultural Meaning of Popular Science. Phrenology and the Organization of Consent in Nineteenth-Century Britain*, Cambridge, NY: Cambridge University Press. This study of the popularity of phrenology in the second quarter of the nineteenth century concentrates on the social and ideological functions of science during the consolidation of urban industrial society. The book challenges attempts to establish neat demarcations between scientific ideas and their philosophical, theological and social contexts.

De Swaan, A. (1990) *The Management of Normality: Critical Essays in Health and Welfare*, New York and London: Routledge. A critical analysis from a broadly Eliasian perspective of the individual and collective effort to achieve and maintain normality. Part One examines medicalisation and affect management within hospital settings. Part Three includes a critical discussion of agoraphobia.

Dutton, K. R. (1995) *The Perfectible Body: the Western Ideal of Physical Development*, London: Cassell. A study of the 'symbolic language of muscularity' in the Western tradition of depicting human or superhuman perfection in terms of a male, muscular body. This study has been criticised by some reviewers for limiting the analysis to one gender.

Elson, J. (2003) 'Hormonal hierarchy: hysterectomy and stratified stigma', *Gender and Society*, 17: 750–70. An empirical study illustrating the great symbolic value placed by women on ovaries (or parts of ovaries) as the source of female normality.

Fee, E. (1979) 'Nineteenth-century craniology: the study of the female skull', *Bullettin of the History of Medicine* 53: 415–33. A study illustrating the historical construction of bodily norms to uphold gender differentiation.

Furth, C. (1993) 'Androgynous males and deficient females: biology and gender boundaries in sixteenth and seventeenth century China', in H. Abelove, M. A. Barale and D. M. Halperin (eds) *The Lesbian and Gay Reader*, London and New York: Routledge. Furth explores definitions of the anomalous, and attempts to explain it, through an investigation of men changing into women and vice versa during the Ming era.

Gilman, S. (1999) *Making the Body Beautiful: A Cultural History of Aesthetic Surgery*, Princeton New Jersey: Princeton University Press. Gilman explores meanings associated with 'aesthetic surgery', and especially the relations between bodies, doctors and patients from the nineteenth century to the present. With particular emphasis on the nose, the author shows how the expectations associated with aesthetic surgery are bound up with the history of racial science.

Hacking, I. (1986) 'Making up people', in T. C. Heller, D. E. Wellbery and M. Sosna (eds) *Reconstructing Individualism: Autonomy, Individuality and the Self in Western Thought*, Stanford, CA: Stanford University Press. Also in M. Biagioli (ed.) *The Science Studies Reader*, New York/London: Routledge. An accessible analysis of the realism of constructionism in the spirit of Michel Foucault, with reference to various categories of deviance.

Hawkesworth, M. (2001) 'Disabling spatialities and the regulation of a visible secret', *Urban Studies* 38, 2: 299–318. In an empirical study of facial disfigurement (specifically acne), this paper explores the problems of exclusion that arise out of human-constructed environments.

Kohn, M. (1996) *The Race Gallery*, London: Vintage. This book explores resurgent racialism in science, focusing particular on the re-emergence of hierarchies of intelligence and ability in genetics and human anthropology.

Magli, P. (1989) 'The face and the soul', in M. Feher, R. Naddaf and N. Tazi (eds) *Fragments for a History of the Human Body*, Part Two, New York: Zone. An excellent discussion of the pseudoscience of physiognomics: the interpretation of facial measurements and characteristics to reveal moral character.

Park, K. and Daston, L. J. (1981) 'Unnatural conceptions: the study of monsters', *Past and Present* 92: 20–54. A useful article to read in connection with the extract by Canguilhem included in this volume.

Straayer, C. (1996) *Deviant Eyes, Deviant Bodies: Sexual Re-orientation in Film and Video*, New York: Columbia University Press. Engaging feminist and queer theory ranging from Nancy Chodorow to Judith Butler to Valerie Solanis's SCUM Manifesto, this book considers the wealth of films made by and for non-traditional viewers, to investigate transgressions of traditional gender boundaries.

Terry, J. and Urla, J. (1995) *Deviant Bodies: Critical Perspectives on Difference in Science and Popular Culture*. Bloomington, IN: Indiana University Press. A rich collection of essays on the construction of 'embodied deviance' in scientific discourse. The collection includes discussions of deviant sexual desire and practice, eugenics and genetics, 'race', anthropometry.

Williams, L. and Nind, M. (1999) 'Insiders or outsiders: normalisation and women with learning difficulties', *Disability & Society*, 14: 659–72. Building on earlier critiques of normalisation, this paper critically reviews literature on sex education for people with learning difficulties and suggests alternatives.

Bodies in health and disease

Armstrong, D. (1983) *Political Anatomy of the Body: Medical Knowledge in Britain in the Twentieth Century*, Cambridge, England: Cambridge University Press. Documents and discusses a shift in twentieth-century medical education in English, whereby not only the patient's body but the patient's subjectivity becomes the object of medical discourse. Informed by a Foucauldian approach.

Feldman, M. D. and Ford, C. V. (1994) *Patient or Pretender: Inside the Strange World of Factitious Disorders*, New York: John Wiley & Sons. A collection of cases of factitious disorder (self-inflicted or feigned illness), presented in readable style by two psychiatrists. The collection has the merit of exploring the feelings of practitioners in relation to these patients, whilst the construct of 'factitious disorder' is taken rather at face value.

Goldstein, K. (1995 [1934]) *The Organism*, New York: Zone Books. A seminal text that had a major impact on philosophical and psychological thought in the twentieth century (particularly visible in the work of Canguilhem, Merleau-Ponty, Binswanger and Gestalt psychology), and whose implications are still relevant today. The text stems from studies of brain-damaged soldiers in the First World War and presents a 'holistic' theory of the human organism. It includes discussions of the concepts of norm, health and disease.

Good, M.-J. Delvecchio, Brodwin, P. E., Good, B. J. and Kleinmann, A. (eds) (1992) *Pain as Human Experience: An Anthropological Perspective*, Berkeley, CA: University of California Press. An important collection of essays using case studies drawn from anthropological investigations of chronic pain sufferers to explore the gulf between the culturally mediated language of suffering and the traditional language of medical and psychological theorising.

Greco, M. (1998) *Illness as a Work of Thought*, New York and London: Routledge. A study of the attempt to transcend body/mind dualism in the discourse of psychosomatic medicine in the course of the twentieth century. The text maps the discursive relations between psychoanalytic psychosomatics, the biopsychosocial model and medical sociology, and discusses the ethical and political implications of psychosomatics as a form of problematisation.

Harringon, A. (ed.) (1997) *The Placebo Effect: An Interdisciplinary Exploration*, Cambridge, MA/London: Harvard University Press. A collection of essays by authors from medicine, the humanities and the social sciences, committed to the perspective 'that the placebo effect is a "real" entity in its own right, one that has much to teach us about how symbols, settings, and human relationships literally get under our skin'.

Herzlich, C. and Pierret, J. (1987) *Illness and Self in Society*, Baltimore, MD: Johns Hopkins Press. A classic work that surveys and discusses lay conceptions of health and illness, their relation to the body and the self.

King, L. S. (1975) 'Some basic explanations of disease: a historian's viewpoint', in H. T. Engelhardt and S. Spicker (eds) *Evaluation and Explanation in the Biomedical Sciences*, Dordrecht/Boston: Reidel.

Martin, E. (2001) *The Woman in the Body: A cultural Analysis of Reproduction*, Boston: Beacon Press. An analysis of women's experience of functions linked to reproduction, based on a survey of over 150 women from diverse age, ethnic, and socio-economic backgrounds. Illustrates the acceptance or rejection of medical definitions concerning reproduction among different groups of women, and argues that traditional cultures validate women's bodily functions unlike the culture of industrial society.

Moulin, D. de (1974) 'A historical-phenomenological study of bodily pain in Western man', *Bulletin of the History of Medicine* 48: 540–70. A study illustrating the notion that fear of pain is characteristically modern.

Picone, M. (1989) 'The ghost in the machine: religious healing and representations of the body in Japan', in M. Feher, R. Naddaff and N. Tazi (eds) *Fragments for a History of the Human Body*, Part Two, New York: Zone Books. A discussion of the main religious and philosophical systems that gave rise to Japanese ideas of the body. Contains a useful summary of key principles in Buddhist and Chinese medicine, correcting the non-specialist Western understanding of East Asian 'holism'.

Porter, R. (ed.) (1985) *Patients and Practitioners: Lay Perceptions of Medicine in Pre-Industrial Societies*, Cambridge: Cambridge University Press. The essays use autobiographical sources from sixteenth- to eighteenth-century England to illustrate lay beliefs about health and illness and traditional ways of coping with pain and other bodily ailments.

Seale, C. (1998) *Constructing Death: The Sociology of Dying and Bereavement*, Cambridge, NY, England: Cambridge University Press. An accessible and yet original analysis of the problem of death as a basic motivation for social and cultural life, including an extensive review of existing literature on this relatively neglected subject. Seale examines the experience of dying and bereaved people, as well as institutional responses to death, to argue against the thesis that we live in a 'death-denying' society, and to demonstrate the importance of death for an understanding of embodiment in social life.

Shapiro, A. K. and Shapiro, E. (1997) *The Powerful Placebo: From Ancient Priest to Modern Physician*, Baltimore, MD/London: John Hopkins University Press. A critical and informative study of the placebo effect, written by two psychiatrists. Contains chapters on the placebo effect in medical history; on the semantics of placebo; on the history of clinical trials and of the double-blind procedure; on ethical controversies about the use of placebos.

Slattery, D. P. and Romanyshyn, R. D. (1999) *The Wounded Body: Remembering the Markings of Flesh*, New York: State University of New York Press. An ambitious interdisciplinary exploration of the wounded body in literature from Homer to Toni Morrison.

Starobinski, J. (1989) 'The natural and literary history of bodily sensation' with appendix by Paul Valéry, in M. Feher, R. Naddaff and N. Tazi (eds) *Fragments for a History of the Human Body*, Part Two, New York: Zone Books. Drawing on medical and psychological theory as well as literature, this essay discusses 'the way sensory experience (and, more particularly, the organic and locomotive elements) contributes to the formation – or the decomposition – of the subject or the self'.

Treichler, P. (1999) *How to Have Theory in an Epidemic: Cultural Chronicles of AIDS*, Durham and London: Duke University Press. A text that has had a long-lasting effect on conceptions of AIDS. Treichler argues that AIDS is an 'epidemic of signification'.

Williams, S. J. (2003) *Medicine and the Body*, London: Sage. This book addresses the relationship between bodies, health, disease and medicine from a broad perspective informed, among other things, by the sociology of emotions. It includes discussions of reductionism and constructionism, bodies across the lifecourse, chronic illness as biographical disruption, sleep, death and dying, hi-tech bodies, and embodied ethics.

Youngner, S. J., Fox, R. C. and O'Connell, L. (eds) (1996) *Organ Transplantation: Meanings and Realities*, Madison, WI: University of Wisconsin Press. A rich collection of essays emerging from extended discussions among a group encompassing many religious and cultural traditions and many fields of expertise: philosophy, art, religion, folklore, psychiatry, anthropology, literature, history, social psychology and surgery. The book explores the multiple meanings associated with organ donation and transplantation.

Zola, I. K. (1966) 'Culture and symptoms – an analysis of patients presenting complaints', *American Sociological Review* 31: 615–30. A classic discussion of how sociocultural background affects the perception and definition of bodily processes, as well as responses to them.

Zola, I. K. (1973) 'Pathways to the doctor – from person to patient', *Social Science and Medicine* 7: 677–89. A classic empirical study of reasons for consulting the doctor among people of different ethic origin, arguing that the perception of one's body and the resulting illness behaviour are influenced by cultural factors.

Bodies and technologies

Adam, A. (1998) *Artificial Knowing: Gender and the Thinking Machine*, London and New York: Routledge. Adam explores the gendered relations between embodiment and knowledge/ mind and between irrationality and rationality in the context of Artificial Intelligence.

Balsamo, A. (1996) *Technologies of the Gendered Body: Reading Cyborg Women*, Durham: Duke University Press. In this book, Balsamo investigates the conjunction of bodies and technologies in a most literal sense, that is, when machines assume organic functions and bodies are materially redesigned through the application of newly developed technologies. Focusing on US culture in the 1980s and 1990s, this is an account of cultural practices 'making the body gendered'.

Cartwright, L. (1995) *Screening the Body: Tracing Medicine's Visual Culture*, Minnesota: University of Minnesota Press. In this fascinating account, Cartwright traces the historical use of moving images as diagnostic tools in hospitals, clinics, and laboratories, and explores how these technologies constitute and shape knowledges of bodies.

Doane, M. A. (1982) 'Technophilia: technology, representation and the feminine', in E. Weed (ed.) *Coming to Terms*, London: Routledge. In this essay Doane argues that, in the context of science fiction, the representation of women as machine raises questions not about production, but about reproduction.

Featherstone, M. (1995) 'Post-bodies, aging and virtual reality', in M. Featherstone and A. Wernicke (eds) *Images of Aging: Cultural Representations of Later Life*, London and New York: Routledge. Featherstone explores some of the implications of an ostensibly 'disembodied' sphere (virtual reality) for the elderly, for whom the issue of embodiment is often problematic.

Featherstone, M. and Burrows, R. (eds) (1995) *Cyberspace/Cyberbodies/Cyberpunk: Cultures of Technological Embodiment*, London: Sage. On how changing relations between the body and technology offer new areas for cultural representation. This edited collection includes essays from a wide range of disciplines, with contributions from Anne Balsamo, Nick Land, Sadie Plant and Mark Poster.

Franklin, S. (1997) *Embodies Progress: A Cultural Account of Assisted Conception*, London and New York: Routledge. This ethnographic study explores the experiences of women and couples who undergo IVF.

Fraser, M. (2001) 'The nature of Prozac', *History of the Human Sciences* 20, 5: 1–26. In this article, Fraser explores some of the implications of popular scientific conceptions of the anti-depressant Prozac, and of 'Prozac people', as they challenge the conventional relations between nature, culture and artificiality.

González, J. (1999) 'The appended subject', in B. Kolko, L. Nakaumura and G. Rodman (eds) *Race in Cyberspace*, London and New York: Routledge. The essays in this book address the effects of cyberspace on racial politics and identity. González analyses the ways in which human bodies are produced in contemporary artists' representations of utopic spaces on the world wide web.

Graham, B. (1995) 'The panic button (in which our heroine goes back to the future of pornography)', in M. Lister (ed.) *The Photographic Image in Digital Culture*, London and New York: Routledge. Graham considers the similarities and differences between photographic pornography and computer-based pornography.

Kember, S. (2003) *Cyberfeminism and Artificial Life*, Routledge: London and New York. See the final chapter of this book in particular, which draws together and develops elements of feminist critiques of Artificial Life, particularly in relation to materiality and the body.

Lenoir, T. and Wei, S. X. (2002) 'Authorship and surgery: the shifting ontology of the virtual surgeon', in B. Clarke and L. D. Henderson (eds) *From Energy to Information: Representation in Science and Technology, Art, and Literature*, Stanford: Stanford University Press. This is a difficult but rewarding piece. On the basis of the claim that new inscription technologies 'real-ly' (not hyper-real-ly) write and rewrite the body, the authors argue that recent development in surgery are transforming not only what it is to be a surgeon, but what it is to be the bodily object of surgery.

Lupton, E. and Miller, J. A. (1992) 'Hygiene, cuisine and the product world of early twentieth-century America', in J. Crary and S. Kwinter (eds) *Incorporations*, New York: Zone Technology and the body in the home: this piece explores the development of the modern kitchen and bathroom and the kinds of bodies they require.

Lykke, N. and Braidotti, R. (1996) *Between Monsters, Goddesses and Cyborgs*, London and New Jersey: Zed Books. The second part of this book, 'Monsters: Biomedical Bodygames', explores human bodies and bodyparts in relation to technological modern biomedicine. Includes chapters on the maternal body, on menopausal and post-menopausal bodies, and on reproductive technologies from heterosexual contraception to lesbian mothers and assisted reproduction.

Marshall, B. and Katz, S. (2002) 'Forever functional: sexual fitness and the ageing male body', *Body and Society* 8, 4: 43–70. This article, which focuses on the 'problem' of erectile dysfunction and mid-life ageism, explores the pharmacological and scientific technologisation of male sexuality in the context of Viagra. See also Marshall, B. (2002) ' "Hard science": Gendered constructions of sexual dysfunction in the "Viagra age" ', *Sexualities* 5, 2: 131–58. In this analysis of Viagra as both biotechnological and cultural event, Marshall explores shifting and specifically gendered interpretations of sexual function and dysfunction.

Michael, M. (2000) 'These boots are made for walking ... mundane technology, the body and human–environment relations', *Body and Society* 6, 3–4: 107–26. Michael draws on Michael Serres to explore the relations between bodies and environments. He uses the example of walking boots to illustrate how these relations are mediated by technologies.

Pasveer, B. and Akrich, M. (1998) 'We deliver our children – in pain?', in B. Brenna, J. Law and I. Moser (eds) *Machines, Agency and Desire*, Oslo: Centre for Technology and Culture, University of Oslo. In this article the authors suggest that many of the emotions and sensations that occur during birth result from specific sociotechnical practices. 'Pain', in this context, is the outcome of a particular setting, rather than something that is located solely in one individual body/subject.

Shildrick, M. and Price, J. (1998) *Vital Signs: Feminist Reconfigurations of the Bio/Logical Body*, Edinburgh: Edinburgh University Press. Situated in the field of biomedicine, the chapters in this volume address a range of clinical technologies, from those deployed in dentistry, to pregnancy ultrasound and biopsychiatry.

Stanworth, M. (ed.) (1998) *Reproductive Technologies: Gender, Motherhood and Medicine*, Minnesota: University of Minnesota Press. In this classic text, a wide range of reproductive technologies, and their impact on women, are interrogated. Includes chapters on the medicalization of childbirth and representations of the foetus.

Stelarc, www.stelarc.va.com.au/ This is Stelarc's authorised website. Stelarc is an Australian-based performance artist whose work addresses the relationships between the body and technology through human–machine interfaces.

Stone, R. A. (1992) 'Will the real body please stand up?: Boundary stories about virtual cultures', in M. Benedikt (ed.) *Cyberspace: First Steps*, London: MIT Press. This oft-cited article begins from the premise that technology and culture are co-constitutive and, from there, explores 'a few boundary stories about virtual cultures'.

Webster, A. (2002) 'Innovative health technologies and the social: redefining health, medicine and the body', *Current Sociology* 50, 3: 443–57. Webster draws on the sociology of the body and science and technology studies (STS) to argue that two related innovative health technologies, genetics and informatics, are reconfiguring the relation between the 'biological' and the 'social'.

Wiess, G. (1999) *Body Images: Embodiment as Intercorporeality*, New York and London: Routledge. In chapters five and six, Wiess draws on a range of theorists, and especially Merleau-Ponty, in order to show how the interdependent relationship between bodies and technologies retemporalises (chapter five) and respatialises (chapter six) embodied existence.

Bodies in consumer culture

Back, L. and Quaade, V. (1993) 'Dream Utopias, Nightmare Realities: Imaging Race and Culture within the World of Benetton Advertising', *Third Text* 22: 65–80. Back and Quaade shows how Benetton operate within what they call a 'grammar of race'.

Boden, S. and Williams, S. J. (2002) 'Consumption and emotion: the romantic ethic revisited', *Sociology* 36, 3: 493–512. The authors return to and re-evaluate Colin Campbell's classic text, *The Romantic Ethic and the Spirit of Modern Consumerism* (1987) in the light of recent developments in the sociology of the body and of emotions.

Brickell, C. (2002) 'Through the (new) looking glass: gendered bodies, fashion and resistance in postwar New Zealand', *The Journal of Consumer Culture* 2, 2: 241–69. This article focuses on the Christian Dior's 'New Look', which was released in 1947. Although commonly cited as an example of the disciplining of women's bodies, Brickell argues for a more complex analysis of 'the Look', and for a more nuanced analysis of the relations between domination and resistance in consumer culture.

Entwhistle, J. (2000) *The Fashioned Body: Fashion, Dress and Modern Social Theory*, Cambridge: Polity Press. Entwhistle explores the relation between fashion and the body, a relation which has been neglected in literature on fashion as well as in the sociology of the body. Drawing on a wide range of social theory, she argues for an account of fashion and dress as 'situated bodily practice'.

Falk, P. (1994) *The Consuming Body*, London: Sage. In this book, Falk brings together debates on the body, the self and contemporary consumer culture. In particular, he explores the ways in which modern consumption has shaped contemporary understandings of the nature of embodiment.

Jagger, E. (2001) 'Marketing Molly and Melville: dating in a postmodern, consumer society', *Sociology* 35, 1: 39–58. Based on a content analysis of a hundred heterosexual dating advertisements, Jagger examines the different ways that men and women use (descriptions of) their bodies as a resource for 'self-fashioning'.

Katz, S. and Marshall, B. (2003) 'New sex for old: lifestyle, consumerism, and the ethics of aging well', *Journal of Aging Studies* 17, 1: 3–16. This article explores how consumer ethics associated with choice, risk management and self-care are built into new identities around the aging body. In particular, they discuss how new concepts of sexual 'function' have emerged as a pivotal concern for rehabilitating the aging body.

Kiliçbay, B. and Binark, M. (2002) 'Consumer culture, Islam and the politics of lifestyle: fashion for veiling in contemporary Turkey', *European Journal of Communication* 17, 4: 495–511. The authors consider the 'fashion for veiling' which has grown in Turkey since the 1990s, focusing on the shifting meanings of this practice for women's bodies, particularly in relation to 'political Islam'.

Kim, T. (2003) 'Neo-confucian body techniques: women's bodies in Korea's consumer society', *Body and Society* 9, 2: 97–113. Focusing on women's bodies in South Korea, Kim teases out the relations between traditional Neo-Confucian techniques of governmentality and the new principles of consumer culture.

Lury, C. (1999) 'Marking time with Nike: the illusion of the durable', *Public Culture* 11, 3: 499–527. This is a demanding but rewarding piece in which Lury shows how the brand (in this instance, Nike) produce both objects and space. The argument pays particular attention to the body in motion.

Nixon, S. (1992) 'Have you got the look? Masculinities and the Shopping Spectacle', in R. Shields (ed.) *Lifestyle Shopping: The Subject of Consumption*, London: Routledge. Drawing on a range of social theory, Nixon explores how, and with what implications, contemporary shopping 'spectacles' address and position men as physical objects to be looked at.

Sawchuk, K. A. (1995) 'From gloom to boom: age, identity and target marketing', in A. Wernicke and M. Featherstone (eds) *Images of Aging: Cultural Representations of Later Life*, London and New York: Routledge. Sawchuk explores representations of the aging body, and the body that ages, in marketing literature discourse that seek to turn 'grey to gold'.

Scheper-Hughes, N. and Wacquant, L. J. D. (eds) (2002) *Commodifying Bodies*, London: Sage. Situated in the context of recent developments in bioscience and biotechnology, the essays in this collection explore how, and with what implications, bodies and body parts are a commodify to be bought, sold and bartered for.

Sedgwick, E. K. (1992) 'Epidemics of the will', in J. Crary and S. Kwinter (eds) *Incorporations*, New York: Zone. In this extraordinary and wonderful piece, Sedgwick discusses the space between 'addictive' and 'not addictive' – the space of 'free' will or, perhaps, habit – across a range of spheres, from smoking to exercising in the context of the consumer phase of international capitalism.

Seltzer, M. (1992) *Bodies and Machines*, London and New York: Routledge. Here, Seltzer explores what he calls 'the American body-machine complex', a coupling of nature and technology, across a range of discourse from scouting manuals to rituals of consumer culture. Although this book could have been included under 'bodies and technologies', it is also a fascinating account of how 'the problem of the body' shaped the origins of, and continues to play a key role in, American mass culture.

Stacey, J. (2000) 'The global within: consuming nature, embodying health', in S. Franklin, C. Lury and J. Stacey (eds) *Global Nature, Global Culture*, London: Sage. In this chapter Stacey explores what 'the global' means in consumer markets and, in particular, extends work on the global imagination to include an analysis of subjective embodiment.

Body ethics

Bataille, G. (1987) *The Story of the Eye*, San Francisco, CA: City Lights Books. Probably Bataille's best-known work, this book is surrealistic, simultaneously fascinating and disgusting; it corresponds well to the description of Bataille as a 'metaphysician of evil' interested in profanation and blasphemy. By the same author, see also (1987) *Eroticism: Death and Sensuality*, London/NewYork: Marion Boyars, where Bataille discusses eroticism in relation to taboo and transgression (including two chapters on De Sade); and (1985) *Visions of Excess: Selected Writings 1927–1939*, Minneapolis, MN: University of Minnesota Press. A collection of essays where Bataille challenges the notion of a 'closed economy' predicated on utility, production, and rational consumption, and develops an alternative theory that takes into account the human tendency to lose, destroy, and waste.

BeDuhn, J. D. (2000) *The Manichaean Body*, John Hopkins University Press. A study of bodily ritual and discipline in the context of ancient Manichaean religion. The study discusses Manichaean dualism, asceticism, spirituality, and the pursuit of salvation, and the environment in which Christianity arose.

Butler, J. (1999) 'Revisiting bodies and pleasures', *Theory, Culture and Society* 16, 2: 11–20. In this accessible piece, Butler explores the productive nature of the sex–gender–desire relation, and argues that it would be a mistake to give this up in favour of Foucault's 'bodies and pleasures'.

Bynum, C. W. (1995) *The Resurrection of the Body in Western Christianity 200–1336*, New York: Columbia University Press. Bynum traces the evolution of lay and theological views of the soul's relationship to the body throughout early and medieval Christianity, through a synthesis of art, anthropology, history, theology and eschatology. The study includes discussions of martyrdom, the cult of relics, ideas and images of resurrection. By the same author, see also (1991) *Fragmentation and Redemption: Essays on Gender and the Human Body in Medieval Religion*, New York: Zone Books, where Bynum argues for the positive importance attributed to the body in women's appropriation of dominant social symbols, giving a new interpretation of gender in medieval texts and of the role of asceticism and mysticism in Christianity. This book is particularly interesting on account of its advocacy of a 'comic' mode of writing for historians.

Diprose, R. (1994) *The Bodies of Women: Ethics, Embodiment and Sexual Difference*, London and New York: Routledge. A philosophical study arguing that the conventional understanding of ethics and its assumptions about the individual disqualify women from ethical social exchange insofar as their bodies signify womanhood. The study examines the necessary conditions for putting sexual difference into ethics, with chapters on Foucault, Hegel and Nietzsche, and a concluding chapter on biomedical ethics.

Feher, M. with Naddaff, R. and Tazi, N. (eds) (1989a) *Fragments for a History of the Human Body*, Part One, New York: Zone. Of the three volumes that constitute this excellent collection, this one is organized around a 'vertical axis' to explore the 'distance and proximity between divinity and the human body'. Some of the essays (e.g. by Vernant, Caroline Bynum, Camporesi) focus on the threshold between humanity and divinity, to ask 'what kind of body do … [the] Greeks, Christians, Jews or Chinese endow themselves with – or attempt to acquire – given the power they attribute to the divine?' (p. 13). Others (e.g. by Oates, von Kleist, Beaune) focus on the lower end of the axis, to explore the thresholds between human and animal, living organism and machines, including discussions of ghosts and monsters.

Feher, M. with Naddaff, R. and Tazi, N. (eds) (1989b) *Fragments for a History of the Human Body*, Part Two, New York: Zone. This volume includes essays on the relationship (of containment, imprisonment, mutual expression etc.) between the body and the human soul. In particular, see essays by Loraux and by Alliez/Feher on the question of embodiment in Greek philosophy; by Schmitt on the ethics of gesture; by Vigarello on 'civility' and the ethics of posture; by Perniola on the metaphysics and erotics of undressing; by Elvin on body/person, heart/mind dualism in China; by Parry on the meanings associated with Hindu disposal of corpses; by Tazi on corporeality and resurrection.

Greco, M. (2001) 'Inconspicous anomalies: alexithymia and ethical relations to the self', *Health*, 5: 471–92. The 'alexithymia construct' refers, among other things, to a difficulty in describing or identifying feelings and a difficulty in distinguishing between psychological feelings and bodily sensations, and is hypothetically correlated to the development of somatic disease in preference to mental illness. This article discusses the construct in terms of its ethical implications.

Morris, D. B. (1991) *The Culture of Pain*, Berkeley, CA/London: University of California Press. A rich study of the meanings of pain and the politics of suffering through a wide variety of cultural sources. Contains, among others, a chapter on de Sade's radical materialism in relation to pain/pleasure and the body.

Rabinow, P. (1996) 'Severing the ties: fragmentation and dignity in late modernity', in *Severing the Ties: Essays on the Anthropology of Reason*, Princeton, NJ: Princeton University Press. Rabinow uses the case of *John Moore v. the Regents of the University of California* (in which John Moore sued doctors at UCLA for removing matter from his body to produce an immortal cell line, which they then patented) in order to explore many of the key elements in contemporary debates about the relation between the body and the person, ethics, economics and science.

Schildrick, M. (1997) *Leaky Bodies and Boundaries: Feminism, Postmodernism and (Bio-)ethics*, New York and London: Routledge. A feminist investigation into the marginalization of women in a Western discourse that denies both female moral agency and embodiment.

Weiss, G. (1999) *Body Images: Embodiment as Intercorporeality*. New York and London: Routledge. The last chapter on 'Bodily Imperatives' discusses the moral dimensions of body images and the move towards an embodied ethics. The chapter surveys moral theory in the history of philosophy in relation to the problem of embodiment and concludes with a thorough discussion of Simone de Beauvoir's embodied ethics.

Wenzel, S. (1960) *The Sin of Sloth: 'Acedia' in Medieval Thought and Literature*, Chapel Hill, NC: University of North Carolina Press. 'The bodily expression of sloth throughout the ages can be read from the iconography of sloth, depression, despondency' (Duden).

Winkler, M. G. and Cole, L. B. (eds) (1994) *The Good Body: Asceticism in Contemporary Culture*, New Haven and London: Yale University Press. A collection of essays by authors from a variety of academic and applied disciplines ranging from psychiatry to anthropology, from theology to social work, who analyse the concern with the 'good body' from a variety of contemporary and ancient cultural perspectives. Focusing on the modern epidemic of eating disorders, the authors discuss why control of our bodies through self-denial has become so important in contemporary culture.

Index